# SOCIAL STATICS

*The conditions essential to human happiness specified, and the first of them developed.*

## by HERBERT SPENCER

ROBERT SCHALKENBACH FOUNDATION
New York • 1995

Spencer, Herbert, 1820-1903.
    Social statics : the conditions essential to human happiness
  specified, and the first of them developed / by Herbert Spencer.
                    p.          cm.
    Originally published: London : J. Chapman, 1851. With new foreword
and pref.
    Includes index.
    ISBN 0-911312-33-1
    1. Social evolution.  2. Statics and dynamics (Social sciences)
  3.  Social policy.   I. title.
  HM106.S74   1995
  303.4–dc20                                        95-42083
                                                       CIP

Published by the Robert Schalkenbach Foundation
41 East 72nd Street, New York, NY 10021

Printed by United Book Press, Inc.
1807 Whitehead Road, Baltimore, MD 21207

# *Foreword*

AT THE CLOSE OF THE TWENTIETH CENTURY, IT MAY SEEM CURIOUS that there is interest in the political philosophies and disputes of the nineteenth. But there is. Herbert Spencer continues to be examined by students of social thought within and beyond the halls of *academia*.

It is perhaps unfortunate that, since the recent fall of Marxist state socialism in eastern Europe and Russia, the pursuit of political, social, and economic ideals has been discredited as "utopian." We are left with a public dialogue of the possible -- of the lowest common denominator, not of the highest common ground. One hundred years ago, being called "anarchist" excommunicated one from the public dialogue, and many of Spencer's popularizers willingly or unwilling received this label. Then "communist" was used to promote conformity and stifle dialogue. Today "liberal" has become the term of derision. Let us hope we do not return to the days of the politically manipulated "red scare" -- or shall we now say "liberal scare?"

*Social Statics* is decidedly and unashamedly a liberal document -- a *classical* liberal document. As such, it concerns the quality and equality of liberty. When first written in 1850, Herbert Spencer was a young rising star in the classical liberal tradition that included John Locke, Adam Smith, Tom Paine and Mary Wollstonecraft, and would reach its flowering with John Stuart Mill and Henry George. This tradition, in decline throughout the twentieth century, was kept alive by a coterie of Georgists and rejuvenated by latter-day libertarians.

Like the discrediting of social idealism as "utopian", liberal philosophers who base their analysis on natural law are dismissed as "old fashioned" and "nineteenth century." Let us look beyond such derisions and consider George's reminder to University of California students in 1877: "Macauley has well said, if any large pecuniary interest were concerned in denying the attraction of gravitation, that most obvious of physical facts would not lack disputers."

The book you are about to explore deals not with gravity but with *those other* natural laws that have been disputed for millenia -- because their acceptance within any society would dethrone the mighty, exalt the lowly, and "proclaim liberty throughout all the land."

June, 1995                                          MARK A. SULLIVAN

# *Preface to the 1995 Edition*

IN 1850, AT THE AGE OF THIRTY, THE YET-TO-BE-FAMOUS HERBERT Spencer wrote a book that was destined to be extremely controversial. The name of the book was *Social Statics*. It was the first of Spencer's volumes on "synthetic philosophy" (otherwise known as "natural adaptation" or evolution), and it antedated Darwin's theory by five years. The book was also a spirited presentation of individualism and anti-statism.

Witnessing the misery and poverty that existed in the world, Spencer, in *Social Statics*, traced the human distress to its cause, which he claimed to be oppressive land monopoly and despotic government (or state, words synonymously used). Discussing the various means by which the state allegedly attempted to "alleviate" the problem of social iniquity, Spencer declared that the state itself was the problem. It "created" the troublesome condition. The only function of government is to protect its citizens. By assuming other functions, government becomes aggressive and destructive. (p.238)

In keeping with the evolutionary principle of "adaptation," Spencer proclaimed the eventual coming of the "perfect society." If only the existing governments would keep their grasping hands off the evolving process, this utopian Perfect State would come about peaceably. It would be guided by the Divine Idea, and would be regulated by Moral Law. "Absolute" (eternal) ethics would prevail, and the emphasis would be on the Golden Rule and individual happiness. Once the Perfect State is realized, "the entire satisfaction of every desire, or perfect fulfillment of individual life becomes possible." (p.389)

The perfect society of the future would recognize that each person is born with certain innate "rights," one of which is the equal right of access to land, the source of all sustenance. This right was fully elaborated by Spencer.

In Chapter IX of *Social Statics,* he wrote an eloquently-phrased attack on land monopoly (and a proposal to end it). This chapter preceded by three decades Henry George's own exposé of land monopoly (and *his* proposal to end it).

The following is a pertinent passage from that chapter:

Equity... does not permit property in land. For if one portion
of the earth's surface may justly become the possession of an
individual and may be held by him for his sole use and benefit
as a thing to which he has an exclusive right, then *other*
portions of the earth's surface may be so held; and eventually
the *whole* if the earth's surface may be so held, and our planet
may thus lapse altogether into private hands.... Supposing the
entire habitable globe to be so enclosed, it follows that... all
who are not landowners have no right at all to its surface....
These landless men might equitably be expelled from the earth
altogether. (103-04)

Other innate rights are: the right of speech (132); the right to the
produce of one's own hands and brain (123); the right to be free
(slavery being a wrong and an evil) (145); the right to ignore any
government, including one's own (185); the right not be discriminated
against because of sex ("equity knows no difference in sex") (138); the
right to pursue any religion or to conform to none (192); the right to
oppose the concept of majority omnipotence ("the very existence of
majorities and minorities is indicative of an immoral state") (189); and
the right to be different (no one can judge behavior or motives from
the "outside") (205).

*Social Statics* became an international masterpiece. It was
enthusiastically praised (or violently condemned) in various books and
reviews. Its fame seemed to guarantee its immortality.

Then came the event that shocked Henry George and his followers.
In 1892, forty-two years after the initial publication of *Social Statics*,
a new edition of the book made its appearance. In this new edition,
Spencer deleted the entire Chapter IX -- as well as a number of other
passages and pages. "I had relinquished," wrote Spencer in the
Preface to the new edition, "some of the conclusions drawn from the
first principles laid down." Discarded were the topics pertaining to
God, the Divine Idea, the Perfect State, and all mention of land
monopoly. The tone of the new book was cautious, subdued -- and
dull.

Enraged by Spencer's action, George hurriedly wrote an answer to
Spencer, entitled *A Perplexed Philosopher*. In the book, he accused
Spencer of treason, and declared:

When the Justice that in the academic cloister he had so boldly invoked came forth into the streets and market- places, to raise her standard and call her lovers, Mr. Spencer, instead of hastening to greet her, did his best to get out of her way. (*A Perplexed Philosopher;* 1988, Robert Schalkenbach Foundation, New York; p. 54)

Spencer, without acknowledging George's attack on him, reluctantly defended his stand by telling other critics that in the 1850 *Social Statics* he spoke of "absolute" ethics, whereas now, in his new approach, he addressed himself "realistically" to temporary, transitory, particular conditions, and only "relative" ethics would apply to such things. This confusing "explanation" was derided by many of his detractors, and Spencer was exposed to much ridicule.

In the 1850 edition of *Social Statics*, Spencer had stated:

A system of morals which shall recognize man's present imperfections and allow for them cannot be devised, and would be useless if it could be devised. (410)

Translated: It is as ludicrous to set up a system of "relative" ethics as it is to establish a system that deals with "relative" rules of mathematics or "temporary" theorems of science. Such precepts are always expressed in permanent, "eternal" terms. Yet the 1892 Herbert Spencer evidently forgot his own words!

Henry George did not bother to hide his contempt. Sardonically, he said:

What Mr. Spencer does in the name of his convenient fiction of relative ethics, is to justify the habitual violations of the right of property... and thus to make his philosophy of things as they ought to be, conform the better with things as the ruling classes desire to maintain them. And he does this effectually,... in idle platitudes. *(A Perplexed Philosopher,* p. 56)

The dispute was never settled to anyone's satisfaction. The battle raged on, and the bitterness continued until the deaths of George and Spencer a few years later.

It is unfortunate that the Spencer of 1892 could not appreciate the revealing words of the Spencer of 1850, who, in the original *Social Statics*, had written:

> We see that the right of each man to the use of the earth, limited only by the like rights of his fellow man, is immediately deducible from the law of equal freedom. And we find... that the theory of co-heirship of all men to the soil is consistent with the highest civilization... Equity sternly commands it to be done. (113)

It is with genuine pleasure and anticipation that we welcome the 1995 republication of the original 1850 edition of *Social Statics*. Once again, we shall have a chance to meet and greet a great classic. Once again, we shall have the opportunity to hear the voice of young Herbert Spencer as he speaks to us anew. Once again, we shall have the privilege of listening to words that are often fiery, exciting, and challenging -- and *always* timely and timeless.

JACK SCHWARTZMAN

June, 1995

*Jack Schwartzman, J.S.D., Ph.D., is a professor emeritus of English at Nassau Community College, New York, and the editor-in-chief of Fragments, a literary magazine of individualist thought.*

# Preface to 1954 Edition

IT IS HIGH TIME THIS GENERATION OF ECONOMISTS AND SOCIOLO-
gists should be reminded of a book published over a hundred
years ago, which raised a great controversy. Herbert Spencer's
*Social Statics* was discussed by philosophers, statesmen, landlords
and politicians of various schools. Indeed, perhaps no work, since
Hobbes wrote the *Leviathan*, caused such an intellectual stir.
That was strange, because the principles laid down in it were
in line with English common law; in some respects as ancient as
the dooms of Aethelbert. But, seemingly, the critics, owing
to the rapacity of landlords under the Tudors, did not understand that.

Moreover, the economic principle Spencer dealt with was in
accordance with the history of every culture of which we have
record. It was Semitic, Egyptian, Greek, and Roman, for the
landmark established by these peoples was the symbol of freedom to produce from the source of their sustenance. All this I
attempted to deal with in my lectures, *In Quest of Justice*. The
principle laid down by Herbert Spencer in the first edition of
*Social Statics* differs not at all from that laid down by Socrates in
Plato's *Republic*.

Spencer, in the original version, was expounding a fundamental of economic law. He said:

> . . . It may by and by be perceived, that Equity utters
> dictates to which we have not yet listened; and men may
> then learn, that to deprive others of their rights to the use
> of the earth, is to commit a crime inferior only in wicked-
> ness to the crime of taking away their lives or personal
> liberties.

It was a mighty challenge the young philosopher tendered
to the landlords of the country. The owners of great baronial
estates learned from their solicitors and bailiffs that their lands
were in danger of confiscation. I put it this way, because Disraeli
said the nobility did not read. If that were true, they would
have to receive the information from those who did. Spencer
wrote:

After all, nobody does implicitly believe in landlordism. We hear of estates being held under the king, that is, the state; or of their being kept in trust for the public benefit; and not that they are the inalienable possessions of their nominal owners. Moreover, we daily deny landlordism by our legislation.

The ignorance prevalent at that time, even in law circles, was astonishing. Jurists were driven to make a study of English common law, not only from the times of Glanvill and Bracton, but further back, to the systems of land use under Saxon kings. Indeed, it was not until 1895 that a comprehensive work on *The History of English Law* was written by Sir Frederick Pollock and Dr. Frederic William Maitland. In this thorough inquiry into the laws of England, we learn clearly, for the first time, the difference between ownership and possession of land and movables, such as cattle and other forms of wealth. The term property is rendered in its economic sense. Spencer stood on sure economic ground when he wrote *Social Statics*, which was published in 1850.

The problem of how land was to be returned to the people for their use disturbed his mind. He might have received a hint of how it could be done by reading the suggestion made by Adam Smith in *The Wealth of Nations*. There were other authorities on this question he might have consulted, such as John Locke, Lord Bathurst, and Sir William Wyndham, who was Chancellor of the Exchequer and a large landowner.

Still, the quandary of putting an end to landlordism, ownership, was quite a secondary consideration with Spencer. He says:

No doubt great difficulties must attend the resumption, by mankind at large, of their rights to the soil. The question of compensation to existing proprietors is a complicated one—one that perhaps cannot be settled in a strictly equitable manner. Had we to deal with the parties who originally robbed the human race of its heritage, we might make short work of the matter. But, unfortunately, most of our present landowners are men who have, either mediately or immediately—either by their own acts, or by the acts of their ancestors—given for their estates equivalents of honestly earned wealth, believing that they were investing their savings in a legitimate manner. To justly estimate and liquidate the claims of such, is one of the most intricate problems society will one day have to solve. But with this perplexity and our extrication from it, abstract morality has no concern. Men having got themselves into the dilemma by disobedience to the law, must get out of it as well as they can; and with as little injury to the landed class as may be.

Meanwhile, we shall do well to recollect, that there are others besides the landed class to be considered. In our tender regard for the vested interests of the few, let us not forget that the rights of the many are in abeyance; and must remain so, as long as the earth is monopolized by individuals. . . .

Fifty years ago the book was the subject of controversy in this country. I remember distinctly several occasions when it was a matter of debate and discussion. There were academic economists who were deeply engrossed by the principles enunciated by Spencer. In recent years it seems to have disappeared as a work to be considered by professors of economics and sociology. It is time interest in it was revived.

Students will find in *Social Statics* a clean-cut contribution to our knowledge of the ethics of fundamental economics. Once the importance of the principles laid down in this work are grasped by the reader, I may safely prophesy that his interest in the subject will not wane. Indeed, he will desire to pursue the line of investigation and search for a solution of the problem. This will lead him to Henry George's great work, *Progress and Poverty*, in which he will discover the method of breaking the grip of land monopoly and bringing about a land system based upon justice. The Robert Schalkenbach Foundation deserves our gratitude for giving us a new edition of the original version of *Social Statics*.

FRANCIS NEILSON

October, 1954.

# Author's Second Preface

WHEN, IN 1864, AN AMERICAN EDITION OF THIS WORK WAS PUB-
lished, I sent over, to be prefixed, the following lines. And when,
subsequently, the American edition was imported for sale in
England, these lines were prefixed to the copies sold here.

The author desires it to be understood that the reprint of *Social Statics*,
herewith issued to the American public, must not be taken as a literal expression of his present views. During the fourteen years that have elapsed
since the original publication of the work, the general theory which it
enunciates has undergone, in his mind, considerable further development
and some accompanying modifications. So that, though he adheres to the
leading principles set forth in the following pages, he is not prepared to
abide by all the detailed applications of them.

The bases of Morality laid down in Part I., and in the preliminary chapters of Part II., must be regarded as but adumbrations of what he holds to be
the true bases. Though in the main correct as far as they go, they are in-
completely worked out, and form but a moiety of the ground work on which
a scientific system of Ethics must rest.

The deductions included in Part II. may be taken as representing, in great
measure, those which the author would still draw; but had he now to express
them, he would express some of them differently. Especially in the chapters
on "The Rights of Women," and on "The Rights of Children," he would
make qualifications which, while they left the arguments much as they
are, would alter somewhat their logical aspects.

Similarly of the deductions which make up Part III. The doctrines there
enunciated respecting Political Rights, State Functions, and the Limitations
of State Functions, are such as, in their general characters, the author continues to hold. But in re-stating them he would bring into greater promi-
nence the transitional nature of all political institutions, and the consequent
*relative* goodness of some arrangements which have no claims to *absolute*
goodness.

If it be asked why the author does not so re-model the work as to make
it accurately represent his present opinions, the reply is that he could not
do this satisfactorily without an amount of labour that would require him to
suspend the issue of the *System of Philosophy* on which he is now engaged.
When, however, he comes to the closing volumes of this System, should
he ever get so far, he proposes to set forth in them the developed conclusions of which *Social Statics* must be regarded as a rough sketch.
LONDON, *Nov.* 16, 1864.

This explanation I propose now to make in some respects
more specific. To the fundamental ethical principle, expressing
in its abstract form what we know as Justice, I still adhere. I
adhere also to the derivative principles formulated in what are

commonly called personal rights, of this or that special kind.
And I further adhere to the general conclusions deduced respecting the proper limitations of State functions. Continuing thus
to hold the cardinal doctrines set forth—continuing also to
regard them as important, I have allowed the work to remain on
sale; though in some respects it does not represent my present
views. Perhaps the above-quoted caution does not sufficiently
emphasize such divergences of belief as are indicated now in
the Study of Sociology, respecting the political status of women,
the values of ecclesiastical institutions, the useful effects wrought
by war in the earlier stages of social development, etc.—
divergences which have increased since that caution was written.
And I have not named the fact, sufficiently manifest to all who
are acquainted with my later works, that such teleological implications as are contained in the chapter on "The Divine Idea,"
I no longer abide by.

These further statements are prompted by certain recent
criticisms, which are not, I think, creditable either to the writer
or to the journal that has given them currency. In the British
Quarterly Review for January, 1876, there appeared an article
headed "Herbert Spencer's Sociology"; having prefixed to it the
titles of Social Statics, the Study of Sociology, and three numbers
of the Descriptive Sociology. Alleging that nowhere else than in
Social Statics was there to be found any statement of my sociological views in their ensemble; and alleging that the work in its
reissued form "contains no intimation" that I have modified
those views; the writer proceeded to criticise Social Statics as an
embodiment of them. Thinking this an unwarranted proceeding,
I published in the Academy for January 15, 1876, a letter pointing out the fact that Social Statics had then been published
twenty-five years; that to the current edition I had prefixed the
caution above quoted; that the reviewer had before him, in the
Study of Sociology, indications of the changes of opinion
referred to; and that he nevertheless not only ignored this
general evidence, but made special strictures on some of the
chapters named in the Preface as requiring alterations. Replies
and rejoinders followed; in the course of which the reviewer
defended himself on the ground that the cautions contained in

the Preface were inadequate; in the course of which I pointed out that the real question was whether the reviewer's statement that there was "no intimation" of change was reconciliable with the positive intimation of change in the Preface; and in the course of which I further pointed out that the reviewer had represented *Social Statics*, which simply contains an ethical doctrine with political corollaries, as embodying my sociological views—deliberately ignoring the published programme of the *Principles of Sociology*, which, besides showing that that work is to cover a different and far larger field, also describes the essential part of *Social Statics* as coinciding in subject with part of a succeeding volume on *The Principles of Morality*.

I should have let this occurrence pass without further notice had it not been for the reviewer's subsequent course. It will scarcely be believed that in the January number of the *British Quarterly Review* for the succeeding year, 1877, there appeared an article entitled "Herbert Spencer's Sociology: its Ground, Motive, and Sphere"; in which the reviewer deliberately persists in the line of criticism originally taken, as though the above-described letters had never been written. Not only does he continue to ignore the cautions in the Preface—not only does he shut his eyes to the modified views contained in the *Study of Sociology* to which I drew his attention—not only does he disregard the fact pointed out to him that the subject matter of *Social Statics* is different from, as well as far smaller than, the subject matter of the *Principles of Sociology*; but he deliberately elaborates the title of his article so as to produce more completely than before, an impression that the two works are co-extensive in their themes!

While thinking it desirable by these explanations to make still clearer the relation in which this work stands to works since written, I have also been prompted to narrate these facts by the wish to give readers one example among many which I could furnish, showing the need for accepting with great caution the representations made by critics.

*January 17, 1877.*

## Author's First Preface

BEING SOMEWHAT AT VARIANCE WITH PRECEDENT, THE TONE AND mode of treatment occasionally adopted in the following pages will, perhaps, provoke criticism. Whether, in thus innovating upon established usage, the writer has acted judiciously or otherwise, the event must determine. He has not, however, transgressed without adequate motive; having done so under the belief that, as it is the purpose of a book to influence conduct, the best way of writing a book must be the way best fitted to effect this purpose.

Should exception be taken to the manifestations of feeling now and then met with, as out of place in a treatise having so scientific a title; it is replied that, in their present phase of progress, men are but little swayed by purely intellectual considerations—that to be operative, these must be enforced by direct or implied appeals to the sentiments—and that, provided such appeals are not in place of, but merely supplementary to, the deductions of logic, no well-grounded objection can be made to them. The reader will find that the several conclusions submitted to him are primarily based on entirely impersonal reasoning, by which alone they may be judged; and if, for the sake of commending these conclusions to the many, the sympathies have been indirectly addressed, the general argument cannot have been thereby weakened, if it has not been strengthened.

Possibly the relaxations of style in some cases used, will be censured, as beneath the gravity of the subject. In defence of them it may be urged, that the measured movement which custom prescribes for philosophical works, is productive of a monotony extremely repulsive to the generality of readers. That no counterbalancing advantages are obtained, the writer does not assert. But, for his own part, he has preferred to sacrifice somewhat of conventional dignity, in the hope of rendering his theme interesting to a larger number.

LONDON, December, 1850.

# Contents

## PART III.

## PART IV.

# SOCIAL STATICS

---

## *Introduction*

# The Doctrine of Expediency

**1.** "GIVE US A GUIDE," CRY MEN TO THE PHILOSOPHER. "WE would escape from these miseries in which we are entangled. A better state is ever present to our imaginations, and we yearn after it; but all our efforts to realize it are fruitless. We are weary of perpetual failures; tell us by what rule we may attain our desire."

"Whatever is expedient is right," is one of the last of the many replies to this appeal.

"True," rejoin some of the applicants. "With the Deity right and expedient are doubtless convertible terms. For us, however, there remains the question, Which is the antecedent, and which is the consequent? Granting your assumption that right is the unknown quantity and expediency the known one, your formula may be serviceable. But we deny your premises; a painful experience has proved the two to be equally indeterminate. Nay, we begin to suspect that the right is the more easily ascertained of the two; and that your maxim would be better if transposed into—whatever is right is expedient."

"Let your rule be, the greatest happiness to the greatest number," interposes another authority.

"That, like the other, is no rule at all," it is replied, "but rather an enunciation of the problem to be solved. It is your 'greatest happiness' of which we have been so long and so fruitlessly in search, albeit we never gave it a name. You tell us nothing new; you merely give words to our want. What you call an answer is simply our own question turned the right side up. If this is your philosophy it is surely empty, for it merely echoes the interrogation."

"Have a little patience," returns the moralist, "and I will give you my opinion as to the mode of securing this greatest happiness to the greatest number."

"There again," exclaim the objectors, "you mistake our re-

3

quirement. We want something else than opinions. We have
had enough of them. Every futile scheme for the general good
has been based on opinion; and we have no guarantee that
your plan will not add one to the list of failures. Have you discovered a means of forming an infallible judgment? If not, you
are, for aught we can perceive, as much in the dark as ourselves.
True, you have obtained a clearer view of the end to be arrived
at; but concerning the route leading to it, your offer of an
opinion proves that you know nothing more certain than we
do. We demur to your maxim because it is not what we wanted
—a guide; because it dictates no sure mode of securing the
desideratum; because it puts no veto upon a mistaken policy;
because it permits all actions—bad, as readily as good—provided
only the actors *believe* them conducive to the prescribed end.
Your doctrines of 'expediency' or 'utility' or 'general good' or
'greatest happiness to the greatest number' afford not a solitary
command of a practical character. Let but rulers think, or
profess to think, that their measures will benefit the community,
and your philosophy stands mute in the presence of the most
egregious folly, or the blackest misconduct. This will not do
for us. We seek a system that can return a definite answer
when we ask, 'Is this act good?' and not, like yours, reply, 'Yes,
if it will benefit you.' If you can show us such a one—if you
can give us an axiom from which we may develop successive
propositions until we have with mathematical certainty solved
all our difficulties—we will thank you. If not, we must go elsewhere."

In his defense, our philosopher submits that such expectations are unreasonable. He doubts the possibility of a strictly
scientific morality. Moreover, he maintains that his system is
sufficient for all practical purposes. He has definitely pointed
out the goal to be attained. He has surveyed the tract lying
between us and it. He believes he has discovered the best route.
And finally he has volunteered as pioneer. Having done this, he
claims to have performed all that can be expected of him, and
deprecates the opposition of these critics as factious, and their
objections as frivolous. Let us examine this position somewhat
more closely.

**2.** ASSUMING IT TO BE IN OTHER RESPECTS SATISFACTORY, A RULE, principle, or axiom is valuable only in so far as the words in which it is expressed have a definite meaning. The terms used must be universally accepted in the same sense, otherwise the proposition will be liable to such various constructions as to lose all claim to the title—a rule. We must therefore take it for granted that when he announced "the greatest happiness to the greatest number" as the canon of social morality, its originator supposed mankind to be unanimous in their definition of "greatest happiness."

This was a most unfortunate assumption, for no fact is more palpable than that the standard of happiness is infinitely variable. In all ages—among every people—by each class—do we find different notions of it entertained. To the wandering gypsy a home is tiresome, while a Swiss is miserable without one. Progress is necessary to the well-being of the Anglo-Saxons; on the other hand, the Eskimos are content in their squalid poverty, have no latent wants, and are still what they were in the days of Tacitus. An Irishman delights in a row, a Chinese in pageantry and ceremonies, and the usually apathetic Javanese gets vociferously enthusiastic over a cockfight. The heaven of the Hebrew is "a city of gold and precious stones, with a supernatural abundance of corn and wine"; that of the Turk, a harem peopled by houris; that of the American Indian, a "happy hunting ground"; in the Norse paradise there were to be daily battles with magical healing of wounds; while the Australian hopes that after death he shall "jump up a white fellow, and have plenty of sixpences." Descending to individual instances, we find Louis XVI interpreting "greatest happiness" to mean "making locks"; instead of which his successor read "making empires." It was seemingly the opinion of Lycurgus that perfect physical development was the chief essential to human felicity; Plotinus, on the contrary, was so purely ideal in his aspirations as to be ashamed of his body. Indeed the many contradictory answers given by Grecian thinkers to the question, What constitutes happiness? have given occasion to comparisons that have now become trite. Nor has greater unanimity been shown among ourselves. To a miserly Elwes the hoarding of money was the only enjoyment of life; but Day, the philanthropic author of *Sandford and Merton*, could find no pleasurable employment save in its distribution. Rural quietude, books, and a friend are the wants of the poet; a turf hunter longs rather for a large circle of titled acquaintance, a box at the opera, and the freedom of Almack's. The ambitions of the tradesman and the artist are anything but alike; and could we compare the air castles of the plowman and the philosopher, we should find them of widely different orders of architecture.

Generalizing such facts, we see that the standard of "greatest happiness" possesses as little fixity as the other exponents of human nature. Between nations the differences of opinion are conspicuous enough. On contrasting the Hebrew patriarchs with their existing descendants, we observe that even in the same race the beau ideal of existence changes. The members of each community disagree upon the question. Neither, if we compare the wishes of the gluttonous schoolboy with those of the earth-scorning transcendentalist into whom he may afterward grow, do we find any constancy in the individual. So we may say, not only that every epoch and every people has its peculiar conceptions of happiness, but that no two men have like conceptions; and further, that in each man the conception is not the same at any two periods of life.

The rationale of this is simple enough. Happiness signifies a gratified state of all the faculties. The gratification of a faculty is produced by its exercise. To be agreeable, that exercise must be proportionate to the power of the faculty; if it is insufficient, discontent arises, and its excess produces weariness. Hence, to have complete felicity is to have all the faculties exerted in the ratio of their several developments; and an ideal arrangement of circumstances calculated to secure this constitutes the standard of "greatest happiness"; but the minds of no two individuals contain the same combination of elements. Duplicate men are not to be found. There is in each a different balance of desires. Therefore, the conditions adapted for the highest enjoyment of one would not perfectly compass the same end for any other.

And consequently the notion of happiness must vary with the disposition and character; that is, must vary indefinitely.

Whereby we are also led to the inevitable conclusion that a true conception of what human life should be is possible only to the ideal man. We may make approximate estimates, but he only in whom the component feelings exist in their normal proportions is capable of a perfect aspiration. And as the world yet contains none such, it follows that a specific idea of "greatest happiness" is for the present unattainable. It is not, then, to be wondered at if Paleys and Benthams make vain attempts at a definition. The question involves one of those mysteries which men are ever trying to penetrate and ever failing. It is the insoluble riddle which Care, Sphinx-like, puts to each newcomer, and in default of answer devours him. And as yet there is no Oedipus, nor any sign of one.

The allegation that these are hypercritical objections and that for all practical purposes we agree sufficiently well as to what "greatest happiness" means will possibly be made by some. It were easy to disprove this, but it is unnecessary, for there are plenty of questions practical enough to satisfy such cavilers, and about which men exhibit none of this pretended unanimity. For example:

What is the ratio between the mental and bodily enjoyments constituting this "greatest happiness"? There is a point up to which increase of mental activity produces increase of happiness, but beyond which it produces in the end more pain than pleasure. Where is that point? Some appear to think that intellectual culture and the gratifications derivable from it can hardly be carried too far. Others again maintain that already among the educated classes mental excitements are taken in excess, and that were more time given to a proper fulfillment of the animal functions, a larger amount of enjoyment would be obtained. If "greatest happiness" is to be the rule, it becomes needful to decide which of these opinions is correct; and further to determine the exact boundary between the use and abuse of every faculty.

Which is most truly an element in the desired felicity, content or aspiration? The generality assume, as a matter of course, that content is. They think it the chief essential to well-being. There are others, however, who hold that but for discontent we should have been still savages. It is in their eyes the greatest incentive to progress. Nay, they maintain that were content the order of the day, society would even now begin to decay. It is required to reconcile these contradictory theories.

And this synonym for "greatest happiness"—this "utility"— what shall be comprised under it? The million would confine it to the things which directly or indirectly minister to the bodily wants, and in the words of the adage, "Help to get something to put in the pot." Others there are who think mental improvement useful in itself, irrespective of so-called practical results, and would therefore teach astronomy, comparative anatomy, ethnology, and the like, together with logic and metaphysics. Unlike some of the Roman writers who held the practice of the fine arts to be absolutely vicious, there are now many who suppose utility to comprehend poetry, painting, sculpture, the decorative arts, and whatever aids the refinement of the taste. While an extreme party maintains that music, dancing, the drama, and what are commonly called amusements are equally worthy to be included. In place of all which discordance we ought to have agreement.

Whether shall we adopt—the theory of some, that felicity means the greatest possible enjoyment of this life's pleasures, or that of others, that it consists in anticipating the pleasures of a life to come? And if we compromise the matter and say it should combine both, how much of each shall go to its composition?

Or what must we think of this wealth-seeking age of ours? Shall we consider the total absorption of time and energy in business—the servitude of the mind to the needs of the body— the spending of life in the accumulation of the means to live, as constituting "greatest happiness," and act accordingly? Or shall we legislate upon the assumption that this is to be regarded as the voracity of a larva assimilating material for the development of the future psyche?

Similar unsettled questions might be indefinitely multiplied.

Not only, therefore, is an agreement as to the meaning of "greatest happiness" theoretically impossible, but it is also manifest that men are at issue upon all topics, which for their determination require defined notions of it.

So that in directing us to this "greatest happiness to the greatest number," as the object toward which we should steer, our pilot "keeps the word of promise to our ear and breaks it to our hope." What he shows us through his telescope is a *fata morgana*, and not the promised land. The real haven of our hopes dips far down below the horizon and has yet been seen by none. It is beyond the ken of seer, be he never so farsighted. Faith, not sight, must be our guide. We cannot do without a compass.

**3.** EVEN WERE THE FUNDAMENTAL PROPOSITION OF THE EXPEDI-ency system not thus vitiated by the indefiniteness of its terms, it would still be vulnerable. Granting for the sake of argument that the desideratum, "greatest happiness," is duly comprehended, its identity and nature agreed upon by all, and the direction in which it lies satisfactorily settled, there yet remains the unwarranted assumption that it is possible for the self-guided human judgment to determine, with something like precision, by what methods it may be achieved. Experience daily proves that just the same uncertainty which exists respecting the specific ends to be obtained exists likewise respecting the right mode of attaining them when supposed to be known. In their attempts to compass one after another the several items which go to make up the grand total, "greatest happiness," men have been anything but successful; their most promising measures having commonly turned out the greatest failures. Let us look at a few cases.

When it was enacted in Bavaria that no marriage should be allowed between parties without capital, unless certain authorities could "see a reasonable prospect of the parties being able to provide for their children," it was doubtless intended to advance the public weal by checking improvident unions and redundant population; a purpose most politicians will consider praiseworthy, and a provision which many will think well adapted to secure it. Nevertheless, this apparently sagacious measure has by no means answered its end; the fact being that in Munich, the capital of the kingdom, half the births are illegitimate!

Those, too, were admirable motives and very cogent reasons which led our government to establish an armed force on the coast of Africa for the suppression of the slave trade. What could be more essential to the "greatest happiness" than the annihilation of the abominable traffic? And how could forty ships of war, supported by an expenditure of £70,000 a year, fail to accomplish this, wholly or partially? The results have, however, been anything but satisfactory. When the abolitionists of England advocated it, they little thought that such a measure, instead of preventing, would only "aggravate the horrors, without sensibly mitigating the extent of the traffic"; that it would generate fast-sailing slavers with decks one foot six inches apart, suffocation from close packing, miserable diseases, and a mortality of 35 per cent. They dreamed not that when hard pressed a slaver might throw a whole cargo of 500 Negroes into the sea; nor that on a blockaded coast the disappointed chiefs would, as at Gallinas, put to death 200 men and women, and stick their heads on poles, alongshore, in sight of the squadron.[1] In short, they never anticipated having to plead as they now do for the abandonment of coercion.

Again, how great and how self-evident to the artisan mind were the promised advantages of that trades-union project whereby master manufacturers were to be dispensed with! If a body of workmen formed themselves into a joint-stock manufacturing company, with elective directors, secretary, treasurer, superintendents, foremen, etc., for managing the concern, and an organization adapted to ensure an equitable division of profits among the members, it was clear that the enormous sums previously pocketed by the employers would be shared among the employed, to the great increase of their prosperity. Yet all past attempts to act out this very plausible theory have, somehow or other, ended in miserable failures.

[1]See Anti-Slavery's Society's Report for 1847; and Evidence before Parliamentary Committee, 1848.

Another illustration is afforded by the fate which befell that kindred plan recommended by Mr. Babbage in his *Economy of Manufactures* as likely to be to the benefit of the workmen and to the interest of the master; that, namely, in which factory hands were to "unite together, and have an agent to purchase by wholesale those articles which are most in demand; as tea, sugar, bacon, etc., and to retail them at prices which will just repay the wholesale cost, together with the expenses of the agent who conducts their sale." After fourteen years' trial a concern, established in pursuance of this idea, was "abandoned with the joint consent of all parties," Mr. Babbage confessing that the opinion he had expressed "on the advantage of such societies was very much modified," and illustrating by a series of curves "the quick rise and gradual decline" of the experimental association.

The Spitalfields weavers afford us another case in point. No doubt the temptation which led them to obtain the Act of 1773, fixing a minimum of wages, was a strong one and the anticipations of greater comfort to be secured by its enforcement must have seemed reasonable enough to all. Unfortunately, however, the weavers did not consider the consequences of being interdicted from working at reduced rates, and little expected that before 1793 some four thousand looms would be brought to a stand in consequence of the trade going elsewhere.

To mitigate distress appearing needful for the production of the "greatest happiness," the English people have sanctioned upward of one hundred acts in Parliament having this end in view, each of them arising out of the failure or incompleteness of previous legislation. Men are nevertheless still discontented with the Poor Laws, and we are seemingly as far as ever from their satisfactory settlement.

But why cite individual cases? Does not the experience of all nations testify to the futility of these empirical attempts at the acquisition of happiness? What is the statute book but a record of such unhappy guesses? Or history but a narrative of their unsuccessful issues? And what forwarder are we now? Is not our government as busy still as though the work of law-making commenced but yesterday? Has it made any apparent progress toward a final settlement of social arrangements? Does it not rather each year entangle itself still further in the web of legislation, confounding the already heterogeneous mass of enactments into still greater confusion? Nearly every parliamentary proceeding is a tacit confession of incompetency. There is scarcely a bill introduced but is entitled "An Act to Amend an Act." The "Whereas" of almost every preamble heralds an account of the miscarriage of previous legislation. Alteration, explanation, and repeal form the staple employment of every session. All our great agitations are for the abolition of institutions purporting to be for the public good. Witness those for the removal of the Test and Corporation Acts, for Catholic Emancipation, for the repeal of the Corn Laws, to which may now be added that for the separation of Church and State. The history of one scheme is the history of all. First comes enactment, then probation, then failure; next an amendment and another failure; and, after many alternate tinkerings and abortive trials, arrives at length repeal, followed by the substitution of some fresh plan, doomed to run the same course and share a like fate.

The expediency philosophy, however, ignores this worldful of facts. Though men have so constantly been balked in their attempts to secure, by legislation, any desired constituent of that complex whole, "greatest happiness," it nevertheless continues to place confidence in the unaided judgment of the statesman. It asks no guide; it possesses no eclectic principle; it seeks no clue whereby the tangled web of social existence may be unraveled and its laws discovered. But, holding up to view the great desideratum, it assumes that, after an inspection of the aggregate phenomena of national life, governments are qualified to concoct such measures as shall be "expedient." It considers the philosophy of humanity so easy, the constitution of the social organism so simple, the causes of a people's conduct so obvious, that a general examination can give to "collective wisdom" the insight requisite for lawmaking. It thinks that man's intellect is competent, first to observe accurately the facts exhibited by associated human nature; to form just estimates of general and individual character, of the effects of religions, customs, superstitions, prejudices, of the mental tendencies of the age, of the probabilities of future events, etc., etc.; and then, grasping at once the multiplied phenomena of this ever-agitated, ever-changing sea of life, to derive from them that knowledge of their governing principles which shall enable him to say whether such-and-such measures will conduce to "the greatest happiness of the greatest number."

If without any previous investigation of the properties of terrestrial matter Newton had proceeded at once to study the dynamics of the universe, and after years spent with the telescope in ascertaining the distances, sizes, times of revolution, inclinations of axes, forms of orbits, perturbations, etc., of the celestial bodies had set himself to tabulate this accumulated mass of observations, and to educe from them the fundamental laws of planetary and stellar equilibrium, he might have cogitated to all eternity without arriving at a result.

But absurd as such a method of research would have been, it would have been far less absurd than is the attempt to find out the principles of public polity by a direct examination of that wonderfully intricate combination—society. It need excite no surprise when legislation, based upon the theories thus elaborated, fails. Rather would its success afford matter for extreme astonishment. Considering that men as yet so imperfectly understand man—the instrument by which and the material on which laws are to act—and that a complete knowledge of the unit, man, is but a first step to the comprehension of the mass, society, it seems obvious enough that to educe from the infinitely ramified complications of universal humanity a true philosophy of national life, and to found thereon a code of rules for the obtainment of "greatest happiness," is a task far beyond the ability of any finite mind.

**4.** YET ANOTHER FATAL OBJECTION TO THE EXPEDIENCY PHILOSophy is to be found in the fact that it implies the eternity of government. It is a mistake to assume that government must necessarily last forever. The institution marks a certain stage of civilization—is natural to a particular phase of human development. It is not essential but incidental. As among the

Bushmen we find a state antecedent to government, so may there be one in which it shall have become extinct. Already has it lost something of its importance. The time was when the history of a people was but the history of its government. It is otherwise now. The once universal despotism was but a manifestation of the extreme necessity of restraint. Feudalism, serfdom, slavery—all tyrannical institutions—are merely the most vigorous kinds of rule, springing out of, and necessary to, a bad state of man. The progress from these is in all cases the same—less government. Constitutional forms mean this. Political freedom means this. Democracy means this. In societies, associations, joint-stock companies, we have new agencies occupying fields filled in less advanced times and countries by the State. With us the legislature is dwarfed by newer and greater powers—is no longer master but slave. "Pressure from without" has come to be acknowledged as ultimate ruler. The triumph of the Anti-Corn Law League is simply the most marked instance yet of the new style of government—that of opinion overcoming the old style—that of force. It bids fair to become a trite remark that the lawmaker is but the servant of the thinker. Daily is statecraft held in less repute. Even the *Times* can see that "the social changes thickening around us establish a truth sufficiently humiliating to legislative bodies," and that "the great stages of our progress are determined rather by the spontaneous workings of society, connected as they are with the progress of art and science, the operations of nature, and other such unpolitical causes, than by the proposition of a bill, the passing of an act, or any other event of politics or of state."[2] Thus, as civilization advances, does government decay. To the bad it is essential; to the good, not. It is the check which national wickedness makes to itself, and exists only to the same degree. Its continuance is proof of still-existing barbarism. What a cage is to the wild beast, law is to the selfish man. Restraint is for the savage, the rapacious, the violent; not for the just, the gentle, the benevolent. All necessity for external force implies a morbid state. Dungeons for the felon; a strait jacket for the maniac; crutches for the lame; stays for the weak-backed;

[2] See *Times* of October 12, 1846.

for the infirm of purpose a master; for the foolish a guide; but for the sound mind, in a sound body, none of these. Were there no thieves and murderers, prisons would be unnecessary. It is only because tyranny is yet rife in the world that we have armies. Barristers, judges, juries—all the instruments of law—exist simply because knavery exists. Magisterial force is the sequence of social vice, and the policeman is but the complement of the criminal. Thus it is that we call government "a necessary evil."

What, then, must be thought of a morality which chooses this probationary institution for its basis, builds a vast fabric of conclusions upon its assumed permanence, selects acts of Parliament for its materials, and employs the statesman for its architect? The expediency philosophy does this. It takes government into partnership, assigns to it entire control of its affairs, enjoins all to defer to its judgment—makes it, in short, the vital principle, the very soul of its system. When Paley teaches that "the interest of the whole society is binding upon every part of it," he implies the existence of some supreme power by which that "interest of the whole society" is to be determined. And elsewhere he more explicitly tells us that for the attainment of a national advantage the private will of the subject is to give way, and that "the proof of this advantage lies with the legislature." Still more decisive is Bentham, when he says that "the happiness of the individuals of whom a community is composed, that is, their pleasures and their security, is the sole end which the legislator ought to have in view; the sole standard in conformity with which each individual ought, as far as depends upon the legislature, to be made to fashion his behaviour." These positions, be it remembered, are not voluntarily assumed; they are necessitated by the premises. If, as its propounder tells us, "expediency" means the benefit of the mass, not of the individual—of the future as much as of the present—it presupposes someone to judge of what will most conduce to that benefit. Upon the "utility" of this or that measure, the views are so various as to render an umpire essential. Whether protective duties, or established religions, or capital punishments, or Poor Laws do or do not minister to the "general good" are questions concerning which there is such difference of opinion that were nothing to be done till all agreed upon them we might stand still to the end of time. If each man carried out, independently of a state power, his own notions of what would best secure "the greatest happiness of the greatest number," society would quickly lapse into confusion. Clearly, therefore, a morality established upon a maxim of which the practical interpretation is questionable involves the existence of some authority whose decision respecting it shall be final—that is, a legislature. And without that authority, such a morality must ever remain inoperative.

See here, then, the predicament. A system of moral philosophy professes to be a code of correct rules for the control of human beings—fitted for the regulation of the best as well as the worst members of the race—applicable, if true, to the guidance of humanity in its highest conceivable perfection. Government, however, is an institution originating in man's imperfection; an institution confessedly begotten by necessity out of evil; one which might be dispensed with were the world peopled with the unselfish, the conscientious, the philanthropic; one, in short, inconsistent with this same "highest conceivable perfection." How, then, can that be a true system of morality which adopts government as one of its premises?

**5.** OF THE EXPEDIENCY PHILOSOPHY IT MUST THEREFORE BE SAID, in the first place, that it can make no claim to a scientific character, seeing that its fundamental proposition is not an axiom, but simply an enunciation of the problem to be solved.

Further, that even supposing its fundamental proposition were an axiom, it would still be inadmissible, because expressed in terms possessing no fixed acceptation.

Moreover, were the expediency theory otherwise satisfactory, it would still be useless, since it requires nothing less than omniscience to carry it into practice.

And, waiving all other objections, we are yet compelled to reject a system which, at the same time as it tacitly lays claim to perfection, takes imperfection for its basis.

## *The Doctrine of the Moral Sense*

**1.** THERE IS NO WAY OF COMING AT A TRUE THEORY OF SOCIETY but by inquiring into the nature of its component individuals. To understand humanity in its combinations, it is necessary to analyze that humanity in its elementary form—for the explanation of the compound, to refer back to the simple. We quickly find that every phenomenon exhibited by an aggregation of men originates in some quality of man himself. A little consideration shows us, for instance, that the very existence of society implies some natural affinity in its members for such a union. It is pretty clear, too, that without a certain fitness in mankind for ruling, and being ruled, government would be an impossibility. The infinitely complex organizations of commerce have grown up under the stimulus of certain desires existing in each of us. And it is from our possession of a sentiment to which they appeal that religious institutions have been called into existence.

In fact, on looking closely into the matter, we find that no other arrangement is conceivable. The characteristics exhibited by beings in an associated state cannot arise from the accident of combination, but must be the consequences of certain inherent properties of the beings themselves. True, the gathering together may call out these characteristics; it may make manifest what was before dormant; it may afford the opportunity for undeveloped peculiarities to appear; but it evidently does not create them. No phenomenon can be presented by a corporate body but what there is a pre-existing capacity in its individual members for producing.

This fact, that the properties of a mass are dependent upon the attributes of its component parts, we see throughout nature. In the chemical combination of one element with another, Dalton has shown us that the affinity is between atom and atom. What we call the weight of a body is the sum of the gravitative tendencies of its separate particles. The strength of a bar of metal is the total effect of an indefinite number of molecular adhesions. And the power of the magnet is a cumulative result of the polarity of its independent corpuscles. After the same manner, every social phenomenon must have its origin in some property of the individual. And just as the attractions and affinities which are latent in separate atoms become visible when those atoms are approximated, so the forces that are dormant in the isolated man are rendered active by juxtaposition with his fellows.

This consideration, though perhaps needlessly elaborated, has an important bearing on our subject. It points out the path we must pursue in our search after a true social philosophy. It suggests the idea that the *moral* law of society, like its other laws, originates in some attribute of the human being. It warns us against adopting any fundamental doctrine which, like that of "the greatest happiness to the greatest number," cannot be expressed without presupposing a state of aggregation. On the other hand, it hints that the first principle of a code for the right ruling of humanity in its state of *multitude* is to be found in humanity in its state of *unitude*; that the moral forces upon which social equilibrium depends are resident in the social atom—man, and that if we would understand the nature of those forces and the laws of that equilibrium we must look for them in the human constitution.

**2.** HAD WE NO OTHER INDUCEMENT TO EAT THAN THAT ARISING from the prospect of certain advantages to be thereby obtained, it is scarcely probable that our bodies would be so well cared for as now. One can quite imagine that were we deprived of that punctual monitor, appetite, and left to the guidance of some reasoned code of rules, such rules, were they never so philosophical and the benefits of obeying them never so obvious, would form but a very inefficient substitute. Or, instead of that powerful affection by which men are led to nourish and protect their offspring, did there exist merely an abstract opinion that it was proper or necessary to maintain the population of the globe, it is questionable whether the annoyance, anxiety, and expense of providing for a posterity would not so far exceed the anticipated good as to involve a rapid extinction of the species. And if, in addition to these needs of the body and of the race, all other requirements of our nature were similarly consigned to the sole care of the intellect—were knowledge, property, freedom, reputation, friends sought only at its dictation—then would our investigations be so perpetual, our estimates so complex, our decisions so difficult, that life would be wholly occupied in the collection of evidence and the balancing of probabilities. Under such an arrangement the utilitarian philosophy would indeed have strong argument in nature, for it would be simply applying to society that system of governance by appeal to calculated final results which already ruled the individual.

Quite different, however, is the method of nature. Answering to each of the actions which it is requisite for us to perform, we find in ourselves some prompter called a desire; and the more essential the action, the more powerful is the impulse to its performance, and the more intense the gratification derived therefrom. Thus, the longings for food, for sleep, for warmth are irresistible, and quite independent of foreseen advantages. The continuance of the race is secured by others equally strong, whose dictates are followed, not in obedience to reason, but often in defiance of it. That men are not impelled to accumulate the means of subsistence solely by a view to consequences is proved by the existence of misers, in whom the love of acquirement is gratified to the neglect of the ends meant to be subserved. We find employed a like system of regulating our conduct to our fellows. That we may behave in the public sight in the most agreeable manner, we possess a love of praise. It is desirable that there should be a segregation of those best fitted for each other's society—hence the sentiment of friendship. And in the reverence felt by men for superiority, we see a provision intended to secure the supremacy of the best.

May we not then reasonably expect to find a like instrumentality employed in impelling us to that line of conduct, in the due observance of which consists what we call morality? All must admit that we are guided to our bodily welfare by instincts; that from instincts, also, spring those domestic relationships by which other important objects are compassed; and that similar agencies are in many cases used to secure our indirect benefit by regulating social behavior. Seeing, therefore, that whenever we can readily trace our actions to their origin we find them produced after this manner, it is, to say the least of it, highly probable that the same mental mechanism is employed in all cases; that as the all-important requirements of our being are fulfilled at the solicitations of desire, so also are the less essential ones; that upright conduct in each being necessary to the happiness of all, there exists in us an impulse toward such conduct; or, in other words, that we possess a "Moral Sense," the duty of which is to dictate rectitude in our transactions with each other, which receives gratification from honest and fair dealing, and which gives birth to the sentiment of justice.

In bar of this conclusion it is indeed urged that, did there exist such an agency for controlling the behavior of man to man, we should see universal evidence of its influence. Men would exhibit a more manifest obedience to its supposed dictates than they do. There would be a greater uniformity of opinion as to the rightness or wrongness of actions. And we should not, as now, find one man or nation considering as a virtue what another regards as a vice—Malays glorying in the piracy abhorred by civilized races, a Thug regarding as a religious act that assassination at which a European shudders, a Russian piquing himself on his successful trickery, a red Indian in his undying revenge—things which with us would hardly be boasted of.

Overwhelming as this objection appears, its fallacy becomes conspicuous enough if we observe the predicament into which the general application of such a test betrays us. As thus: None deny the universal existence of that instinct already adverted to which urges us to take the food needful to support life, and none deny that such instinct is highly beneficial and in all likelihood essential to being. Nevertheless, there are not wanting infinite evils and incongruities arising out of its rule. All know that appetite does not invariably guide men aright in the choice of food, either as to quality or quantity. Neither can any maintain that its dictates are uniform, when reminded of those un-

numbered differences in the opinions called "tastes" which it
originates in each. The mere mention of "gluttony," "drunkenness," reminds us that the promptings of appetite are not
always good. Carbuncled noses, cadaverous faces, fetid breaths,
and plethoric bodies meet us at every turn; and our condolences
are perpetually asked for headaches, flatulence, nightmare,
heartburn, and endless other dyspeptic symptoms. Again:
equally great irregularities may be found in the workings of that
generally recognized feeling—parental affection. Among ourselves, its beneficial sway seems tolerably uniform. In the East,
however, infanticide is practiced now as it ever has been. During the so-called classic times it was common to expose babes
to the tender mercies of wild beasts. And it was the Spartan
practice to cast all the newly born who were not approved by
a committee of old men into a public pit provided for the purpose. If, then, it be argued that the want of uniformity in men's
moral codes, together with the weakness and partiality of their
influence, proves the nonexistence of a feeling designed for
the right regulation of our dealings with each other, it must
be inferred from analogous irregularities in men's conduct as
to food and offspring that there are no such feelings as appetite
and parental affection. As, however, we do not draw this inference in the one case, we cannot do so in the other. Hence,
notwithstanding all the incongruities, we must admit the existence of a Moral Sense to be both possible and probable.

**3.** BUT THAT WE POSSESS SUCH A SENSE MAY BE BEST PROVED BY
evidence drawn from the lips of those who assert that we have
it not. Oddly enough, Bentham unwittingly derives his initial
proposition from an oracle whose existence he denies and at
which he sneers when it is appealed to by others. "One man,"
he remarks, speaking of Shaftesbury, "says he has a thing made
on purpose to tell him what is right and what is wrong; and
that it is called *moral sense:* and then he goes to work at his
ease, and says such and such a thing is right, and such and such
a thing is wrong. Why? 'because my moral sense tells me it is.' "
Now that Bentham should have no other authority for his own
maxim than this same moral sense is somewhat unfortunate

for him. Yet, on putting that maxim into critical hands, we shall soon discover such to be the fact. Let us do this.

"And so you think," says the patrician, "that the object of our rule should be 'the greatest happiness to the greatest number.' "

"Such is our opinion," answers the petitioning plebeian.

"Well now, let us see what your principle involves. Suppose men to be, as they very commonly are, at variance in their desires on some given point; and suppose that those forming the larger party will receive a certain amount of happiness each from the adoption of one course, while those forming the smaller party will receive the same amount of happiness each from the adoption of the opposite course: then if 'greatest happiness' is to be our guide, it must follow, must it not, that the larger party ought to have their way?"

"Certainly."

"That is to say, if you—the people—are a hundred, while we are ninety-nine, your happiness must be preferred, should our wishes clash and should the individual amounts of gratification at stake on the two sides be equal."

"Exactly; our axiom involves that."

"So then it seems that as, in such a case, you decide between the two parties by numerical majority, you assume that the happiness of a member of the one party is equally important with that of a member of the other."

"Of course."

"Wherefore, if reduced to its simplest form, your doctrine turns out to be the assertion that all men have equal claims to happiness; or, applying it personally, that you have as good a right to happiness as I have."

"No doubt I have."

"And pray, sir, who told you that you have as good a right to happiness as I have?"

"Who told me? I am sure of it; I know it; I feel it; I——"

"Nay, nay, that will not do. Give me your authority. Tell me who told you this—how you got at it—whence you derived it."

Whereupon, after some shuffling, our petitioner is forced to

confess that he has no other authority but his own feeling—
that he has simply an innate perception of the fact; or, in other
words, that "his moral sense tells him so."

Whether it rightly tells him so need not now be considered.
All that demands present notice is the fact that, when cross-
examined, even the disciples of Bentham have no alternative
but to fall back upon an intuition of this much-derided moral
sense for the foundation of their own system.

**4.** IN TRUTH, NONE BUT THOSE COMMITTED TO A PRECONCEIVED
theory can fail to recognize, on every hand, the workings of
such a faculty. From early times downward there have been
constant signs of its presence—signs which happily thicken
as our own day is approached. The articles of Magna Charta
embody its protests against oppression and its demands for a
better administration of justice. Serfdom was abolished partly as
its suggestion. It encouraged Wickliffe, Huss, Luther, and Knox,
in their contests with Popery; and by it were Huguenots, Cove-
nanters, Moravians stimulated to maintain freedom of judgment in the teeth of armed Ecclesiasticism. It dictated Milton's
*Essay on the Liberty of Unlicensed Printing.* It piloted the
Pilgrim Fathers to the New World. It supported the followers
of George Fox under fines and imprisonment. And it whispered
resistance to the Presbyterian clergy of 1662. In latter days it
emitted that tide of feeling which undermined and swept away
Catholic disabilities. Through the mouths of anti-slavery orators
it poured out its fire to the scorching of the selfish, to the
melting of the good, to our national purification. It was its heat,
too, which warmed our sympathy for the Poles and made boil
our indignation against their oppressor. Pent-up accumulations
of it, let loose upon a long-standing injustice, generated the
effervescence of a reform agitation. Out of its growing flame
came those sparks by which Protectionist theories were exploded
and that light which discovered to us the truths of Free Trade.
By the passage of its subtle current is that social *electrolysis*
effected which classes men into parties, which separates the
nation into its positive and negative—its radical and conservative
—elements. At present it puts on the garb of Anti-State-Church

Associations and shows its presence in manifold societies for the extension of popular power. It builds monuments to political martyrs, agitates for the admission of Jews into Parliament, publishers books on the rights of women, petitions against class legislation, threatens to rebel against militia conscriptions, refuses to pay church rates, repeals oppressive debtor acts, laments over the distresses of Italy, and thrills with sympathy for the Hungarians. From it, as from a root, spring our aspirations after social rectitude: it blossoms in such expressions as: "Do as you would be done by," "Honesty is the best policy," "Justice before Generosity," and its fruits are Equity, Freedom, Safety.

**5.** BUT HOW, IT MAY BE ASKED, CAN A SENTIMENT HAVE A PERCEPtion? How can a desire give rise to a moral sense? Is there not here a confounding of the intellectual with the emotional? It is the office of a sense to perceive, not to induce a certain kind of action; while it is the office of an instinct to induce a certain kind of action and not to perceive. But in the foregoing arguments, motor and percipient functions are attributed to the same agent.

The objection seems a serious one and, were the term sense to be understood in its strictest acceptation, would be fatal. But the word is in this case, as in many others, used to express that feeling with which an instinct comes to regard the deeds and objects it is related to; or rather that judgment which, by a kind of reflex action, it causes the intellect to form of them. To elucidate this we must take an example, and perhaps the love of accumulation will afford us as good a one as any.

We find, then, that, conjoined with the impulse to acquire property, there is what we call a sense of the value of property; and we find the vividness of this sense to vary with the strength of the impulse. Contrast the miser and the spendthrift. Accompanying his constant desire to heap up, the miser has a quite peculiar belief in the worth of money. The most stringent economy he thinks virtuous, and anything like the most ordinary liberality vicious; while of extravagance he has an absolute horror. Whatever adds to his store seems to him good; whatever takes from it, bad. And should a passing gleam of generosity

lead him on some special occasion to open his purse, he is
pretty sure afterward to reproach himself for having done wrong.
On the other hand, while the spendthrift is deficient in the instinct of acquisition, he also fails to realize the intrinsic worth of
property; it does not come home to him; he has little sense of it.
Hence under the influence of other feelings he regards saving
habits as mean, and holds that there is something noble in pro-
fuseness. Now it is clear that these opposite perceptions of the
propriety or impropriety of certain lines of conduct do not
originate with the intellect, but with the emotional faculties.
The intellect, uninfluenced by desire, would show both miser
and spendthrift that their habits were unwise; whereas the intellect, influenced by desire, makes each think the other a
fool, but does not enable him to see his own foolishness.

Now this law is at work universally. Every feeling is accompanied by a sense of the rightness of those actions which
give it gratification; tends to generate convictions that things
are good or bad, according as they bring to it pleasure or pain;
and would always generate such convictions were it unopposed.
As, however, there is a perpetual conflict among the feelings—
some of them being in antagonism throughout life—there results
a proportionate incongruity in the beliefs, a similar conflict
among these also, a parallel antagonism. So that it is only
where a desire is very predominant, or where no adverse desire
exists, that this connection between the instincts and the
opinions they dictate becomes distinctly visible.

Applied to the elucidation of the case in hand, these
facts explain how, from an impulse to behave in the way we
call equitable, there will arise a perception that such behavior
is proper—a conviction that it is good. This instinct or sentiment, being gratified by a just action and distressed by an unjust action, produces in us an approbation of the one and a disgust toward the other; and these readily beget beliefs that the
one is virtuous and the other vicious. Or, referring again to the
illustration, we may say that as the desire to accumulate property
is accompanied by a sense of the value of property, so is the
desire to act fairly accompanied by a sense of what is fair. And
thus, limiting the word sense to the expression of this fact, there

is nothing wrong in attributing motor and percipient functions to the same agent.

It will perhaps be needful here to meet the objection, that whereas according to the foregoing statement each feeling tends to generate notions of the rightness or wrongness of the actions toward which it is related; and whereas morality should determine what is correct in all departments of conduct, it is improper to confine the term "moral sense" to that which can afford directions in only one department. This is quite true. Nevertheless, seeing that our behavior toward each other is the most important part of our behavior, and that in which we are most prone to err; seeing also that this same faculty is so purely and immediately moral in its purpose; and seeing further, as we shall shortly do, that its dictates are the only ones capable of reduction to an exact form, we may with some show of reason continue to employ that term, with this restricted meaning.

**6.** ASSUMING THE EXISTENCE IN MAN OF SUCH A FACULTY AS THIS for prompting him to right dealings with his fellows, and assuming that it generates certain intuitions[1] respecting those dealings, it seems reasonable enough to seek in such intuitions the elements of a moral code. Attempts to construct a code so founded have from time to time been made. They have resulted in systems based by Shaftesbury and Hutchinson on "Moral Sense," by Reid and Beattie on "Common Sense," by Price on "Understanding," by Clarke on "Fitness of Things," by Granville Sharpe on "Natural Equity," by others on "Rule of Right," "Natural Justice," "Law of Nature," "Law of Reason," "Right Reason," etc. Unsuccessful as these writers have been in the endeavor to develop a philosophical morality, all of them, if the foregoing reasoning be correct, have consulted a true oracle. Though they have failed to systematize its utterances, they have acted wisely in trying to do this. An analysis of right and wrong so made is not indeed the profoundest and ultimate one; but, as we shall by and by see, it is perfectly in

---

[1]As here used, this word is of course to be understood in a popular and not in a metaphysical sense.

harmony with that in its initial principle, and coincident with it in its results.

Against codes thus derived, it is indeed alleged, that they are necessarily worthless because unstable in their premises. "If," say the objectors, "this 'moral sense,' to which all these writers directly or indirectly appeal, possesses no fixity, gives no uniform response, says one thing in Europe and another in Asia—originates different notions of duty in each age, each race, each individual—how can it afford a safe foundation for a systematic morality? What can be more absurd than to seek a definite rule of right in the answers of so uncertain an authority?"

Even granting that there is no escape from this difficulty—even supposing no method to exist by which from this source a moral philosophy can be drawn free from so fatal an imperfection—there still results merely that same dilemma, in which every other proposed scheme is involved. If such a guide is unfit because its dictates are variable, then must Expediency also be rejected for the same reason. If Bentham is right in condemning Moral Sense as an "anarchical and capricious principle, founded solely upon internal and peculiar feelings," then is his own maxim doubly fallacious. Is not the idea, "greatest happiness," a capricious one? Is not that also "founded solely upon internal and peculiar feelings"? (See p. 5.) And even were the idea "greatest happiness" alike in all, would not his principle be still "anarchical," in virtue of the infinite disagreement as to the means of realizing this "greatest happiness"? All utilitarian philosophies are in fact liable to this charge of indefiniteness, for there ever recurs the same unsettled question—what is utility?—a question which, as every newspaper shows us, gives rise to endless disputes, both as to the goodness of each desired end and the efficiency of every proposed means. At the worst, therefore, in so far as want of scientific precision is concerned, a philosophy founded on Moral Sense, simply stands in the same category with all other known systems.

**7.** BUT HAPPILY THERE IS AN ALTERNATIVE. THE FORCE OF THE objection above set forth may be fully admitted without in any degree invalidating the theory. Notwithstanding appearances to the contrary, it is still possible to construct upon this basis a purely synthetic morality proof against all such criticism.

The error pointed out is not one of doctrine but of application. Those who committed it did not start from a wrong principle but rather missed the right way from that principle to the sought-for conclusions. It was not in the oracle to which they appealed, but in their method of interpretation, that the writers of the Shaftesbury school erred. Confounding the functions of feeling and reason, they required a sentiment to do that which should have been left to the intellect. They were right in believing that there exists some governing instinct generating in us an approval of certain actions we call good and a repugnance to certain others we call bad. But they were not right in assuming such instinct to be capable of intuitively solving every ethical problem submitted to it. To suppose this was to suppose that moral sense could supply the place of logic.

For the better explanation of this point, let us take an analogy from mathematics, or rather some branch of it, as geometry. The human mind possesses a faculty that takes cognizance of measurable quantity, which faculty, to carry out the analogy, let us term a geometric sense. By the help of this we estimate the linear dimensions, surfaces, and bulks of surrounding objects and form ideas of their relationship to each other. But in the endeavor to reduce the knowledge thus obtained to a scientific form, we find that no reliance can be placed on the unaided decisions of this geometric sense, in consequence of the conflicting judgments it makes in different persons. On comparing notes, however, we discover that there are certain simple propositions upon which we all think alike, such as: "Things which are equal to the same thing are equal to one another"; "The whole is greater than its part"; and agreeing upon these axioms, as we call them—these fundamental truths recognized by our geometric sense—we find it becomes possible by successive deductions to settle all disputed points and to solve with certainty problems of the most complicated nature.[2] Now

[2]Whether we adopt the views of Locke or of Kant as to the ultimate nature of what is here, for analogy's sake, called geometric sense does not affect the

if instead of adopting this method geometricians had persisted in determining all questions concerning lines, angles, squares, circles, and the like, by the geometric sense—if they had tried to discover whether the three angles of a triangle were or were not equal to two right angles, and whether the areas of similar polygons were or were not in the duplicate ratio of their homologous sides—by an effort of simple perception they would have made the same mistake that moralists make who try to solve all the problems of morality by the moral sense.

The reader will at once perceive the conclusion toward which this analogy points; namely, that the perception of the primary laws of quantity bears the same relationship to mathematics; that this instinct of right bears to a moral system; and that as it is the office of the geometric sense to originate a geometric axiom from which reason may deduce a scientific geometry, so it is the office of the moral sense to originate a moral axiom from which reason may develop a systematic morality.

And, varying the illustration, it may be further remarked that just as erroneous notions in mechanics—for instance, that large bodies fall faster than small ones;[3] that water rises in a pump by suction; that perpetual motion is possible, together with the many other mistaken opinions formed by unaided mechanical sense—are set aside by the conclusions synthetically deduced from those primary laws of matter which the mechanical sense recognizes, so may we expect the multitudes of conflicting beliefs about human duty dictated by unaided moral sense to disappear before the deductions scientifically drawn from some primary law of man which the moral sense recognizes.

**8.** ON REVIEWING THE CLAIMS OF THE MORAL SENSE DOCTRINE, IT appears that there is a priori reason for expecting the first principle of social morality to originate in some feeling, power, or faculty of the individual. Quite in harmony with this belief is the inference that as desire is found to be the incentive to action

---

question. However originated, the fundamental perceptions attaching to it form the undecomposable basis of exact science. And this is all that is now assumed.

[3]A doctrine held by Aristotle and his followers.

where motives are readily analyzable, it is probably the universal incentive; and that the conduct we call moral is determined by it as well as other conduct. Moreover, we find that even the great maxim of the expediency philosophy presupposes some tendency in man toward right relationship with his fellow and some correlative perception of what that right relationship consists in. There are sundry phenomena of social life, both past and present, that well illustrate the influence of this supposed moral sense, and which are not readily explicable upon any other hypothesis. Assuming the existence of such a faculty, there appears reason to think that its monitions afford a proper basis for a systematic morality; and to the demurrer that their variability unfits them for this purpose, it is replied that, to say the least, the foundations of all other systems are equally open to the same objection. Finally, however, we discover that this difficulty is apparent only, and not real: for that while the decisions of this moral sense upon the complex cases referred to it are inaccurate and often contradictory, it may still be capable of generating a true fundamental intuition, which can be logically unfolded into a scientific morality.

## Lemma I

**1.** IT SEEMS AT FIRST SIGHT A VERY RATIONAL WAY OF TESTING any proposed rule of conduct to ask, How will it work? Taking men as we know them and institutions as they are, what will result from carrying such a theory into practice? This very common-sense style of inquiry is that by which most opinions on morals and politics are formed. People consider of any system whether it seems feasible, whether it will square with this or the other social arrangement, whether it fits what they see of human nature. They have got certain notions of what man *is* and what society must be, and their verdict on any ethical doctrine depends upon its accordance or discordance with these.

Such a mode of settling moral questions in clearly open to

all the criticisms so fatal to the expediency philosophy. Incapacity for guiding ourselves in detail by making estimates of consequences implies incapacity for judging of first principles by that method. But passing over this, there is yet another reason for rejecting an inquiry so pursued as worthless; namely, that it assumes the character of mankind to be constant. If moral systems are adopted or condemned because of their consistency or inconsistency with what we know of men and things, then it is taken for granted that men and things will ever be as they are. It would be absurd to measure with a variable standard. If existing humanity is the gauge by which truth must be determined, then must that gauge—existing humanity—be fixed.

Now that it is not fixed might have been thought sufficiently obvious without any proving—so obvious indeed as to make proof look ridiculous. But, unfortunately, those whose prejudices make them think otherwise are too numerous to be passed by. Their skepticism needs to be met by facts; and, wearisome though it may be to the philosophic reader, there is no alternative but to go into these.

**2.** AND FIRST LET US PAUSE A MOMENT TO CONSIDER THE ANTECEDent improbability of this alleged constancy in human nature. It is a trite enough remark that change is the law of all things: true equally of a single object and of the universe. Nature in its infinite complexity is ever growing to a new development. Each successive result becomes the parent of an additional influence, destined in some degree to modify all future results. No fresh thread enters into the texture of that endless web, woven in "the roaring loom of Time," but what more or less alters the pattern. It has been so from the beginning. As we turn over the leaves of the earth's primeval history, as we interpret the hieroglyphics in which are recorded the events of the unknown past, we find this same ever-beginning, never-ceasing change. We see it alike in the organic and the inorganic, in the decompositions and recombinations of matter, and in the constantly varying forms of animal and vegetable life. Old formations are worn down; new ones are deposited. Forests and bogs become coal basins, and the now igneous rock was once sedimentary.

With an altering atmosphere and a decreasing temperature, land and sea perpetually bring forth fresh races of insects, plants, and animals. All things are metamorphosed; infusorial shells into chalk and flint, sand into stone, stone into gravel. Strata get contorted; seas fill up; lands are alternately upheaved and sunk. Where once rolled a fathomless ocean now tower the snow-covered peaks of a widespread, richly clothed country teeming with existance; and where a vast continent once stretched, there remain but a few lonely coral islets to mark the graves of its submerged mountains. Thus also is it with systems, as well as with worlds. Orbits vary in their forms, axes in their inclinations, suns in their brightness. Fixed only in name, the stars are incessantly changing their relationships to each other. New ones from time to time suddenly appear, increase, and wane, while the members of each nebula—suns, planets, and their satellites—sweep forever onward into unexplored infinity.

Strange indeed would it be if, in the midst of this universal mutation, man alone were constant, unchangeable. But it is not so. He also obeys the law of indefinite variation. His circumstances are ever altering, and he is ever adapting himself to them. Between the naked houseless savage and the Shakespeares and Newtons of a civilized state lie unnumbered degrees of difference. The contrasts of races in form, color, and feature are not greater than the contrasts in their moral and intellectual qualities. That superiority of sight which enables a Bushman to see farther with the naked eye than a European with a telescope is fully paralleled by the European's more perfect intellectual vision. The Calmuck in delicacy of smell and the red Indian in acuteness of hearing do not excel the white man more than the white man excels them in moral susceptibility. Every age, every nation, every climate exhibits a modified form of humanity; and in all times and among all peoples a greater or less amount of change is going on.

There cannot indeed be a more astounding instance of the tenacity with which men will cling to an opinion in spite of an overwhelming mass of adverse evidence than is shown in this prevalent belief that human nature is uniform. One would have thought it impossible to use eyes or ears without learning that mankind varies indefinitely, in instincts, in morals, in opinions, in tastes, in rationality, in everything. Even a stroll through the nearest museum would show that some law of modification was at work. Mark the grotesque frescoes of the Egyptians or the shadowless drawings of the Chinese. Does the contrast between these and the works of European artists indicate no difference in the perceptive powers of the races? Compare the sculptures of Athens with those of Hindustan or Mexico. Is not a greater sense of beauty implied by the one than the others? But, passing to the more significant facts supplied by historians and travelers, what are we to think on reading that the Greeks and Romans had a deity to sanction and patronize every conceivable iniquity? Or when we hear of Polynesian tribes who believe that their gods feed upon the souls of the departed? Surely the characters indicated by such conceptions of Divinity differ somewhat from ours! Surely, too, we may claim some essential superiority over those Tartars who leave infirm parents to die of hunger in the desert, and over those Fiji Islanders, among whom members of the same family have to keep watch against each other's treachery. It is not the custom of an Englishman to dine, like a Carib, upon a roasted captive; or even as the Abyssinian, on a quivering slice from the haunch of a live ox. Neither does he, like a red Indian, delight in the writhing of a victim at the stake; nor, like a Hindu, burn his wife that her spirit may haunt his enemy.

What one respect is there in which it can be asserted that human nature is always the same? Is it in rationality? Why, Anaxagoras had to fly his country for having blasphemously asserted that the sun was not the chariot of the deity Helios; while among ourselves a child often puzzles its seniors by the question, Who made God? Is it in justice? No; badly as the moderns have treated slaves, they have never, like the Spartans, encouraged their young warriors to waylay and assassinate helots for practice. Is it in honesty? If so, how come we to read that "piracy was the exercise, the trade, the glory, and the virtue of the Scandinavian youth"; while among ourselves privateering, even in time of war, is disapproved? Is it in want of mercy? Not so; for much as Austrian butcheries have lately disgraced Europe, they have not paralleled the doings of Genghis Khan, who signalized his first victory by casting seventy prisoners into cauldrons of boiling water; or of Timour, who massacred 100,000 Indian prisoners and erected a pyramid of 90,000 human heads on the smoking ruins of Bagdad; or of Attila, who totally extirpated and erased seventy cities. Is it in vindictiveness? Why no; for while we are told of the Begum Sumroo, who, having ordered one of her dancing girls to be bricked up in a vault, had her bed placed over it that she might listen to her victim's dying moans, we find our own Queen requesting, much to her credit, that the man who fired at her should not be flogged. Where now is the sameness? It is not in actions as we see. Is it then in manners and opinions? Certainly not. Society in our day would hardly receive a lady or gentleman known to have poisoned an enemy; in Italy, however, there was a time when disgrace did not attach to such. No family would now follow the example of the Visconti and choose the viper for an armorial bearing. Nor could we in the nineteenth century find a match to that German captain of mercenaries who in silver letters labeled himself "Duke Werner, Lord of the great Company; the enemy of mercy, of pity, and of God."

But why go abroad for illustrations of human variability? Have we not plenty at home? In those early days when it was thought "quite sufficient for noblemen to winde their horn, and carry their hawke fair, and leave study and learning to the children of mean people"—in those days when men secured themselves inside thick walls and behind deep moats, and when women wore daggers—character was not just what we now find it. While all nominally held the creed professed by ourselves, the Borderer was most zealous at his prayers when going on a foray; saints' names were battle cries; bishops led on their retainers to fight; and the highest piety was in the slaying of Saracens. Must not our natures have changed somewhat, when we translate this same religion into peace, into philanthropic effort of all kinds, into missionary enterprise, into advocacy of temperance, into inquiries about "labor and the poor"? Does the agitation for the abolition of death punishment indicate no revolution in men's feelings since the days when Cromwell's body was exhumed and his head stuck on Temple Bar—the days when criminals were drawn and quartered as well as hung—the days when there were murmurs "because Stafford was suffered to die without seeing his bowels burned before his face"—the days when creaking gibbets were scattered over the country—the days when church doors were covered with the skins of men who had committed sacrilege? And when we read that Sir John Hawkins, in honor of his having been the first to commence the slave trade, received the addition to his coat of arms of "a demi-moor proper bound with a cord," does it not seem that the national character has improved between his times and ours, when, out of sympathy for the Negroes, 300,000 persons pledged themselves to abstain from all West India produce?

But really it is absurd to argue the matter. The very assertors of this fixedness of human nature tacitly disown their belief in it. They constantly stultify themselves by remarks on differences of national character, on peculiarities in their friends' dispositions, and on their own special tastes and feelings. Admissions thus accidentally made quite invalidate their dogma. Nay, not even these are needed. No comparison between the habits of separate races, between man as he is and as he was, between the tempers and talents of individuals, is necessary for this. To the man of any insight, the mere fact that he himself changes with circumstances, from day to day and from year to year, in sentiments, capacities, and desires, is sufficient to show that humanity is indefinitely variable.

**3.** AND IF HUMANITY IS INDEFINITELY VARIABLE, IT CANNOT BE used as a gauge for testing moral truth. When we see that institutions impracticable in one age have flourished in a subsequent one, and that what were once salutary laws and customs have become repugnant, we may shrewdly suspect that the like changes will take place in future. That incongruity with the state of men and things which at present gives to certain proposed principles an appearance of impracticability may, in a coming age, no longer exist; and those principles that now seem

so well adapted to our social condition may then no longer
harmonize with it. Unless, therefore, we assume that human
nature, although hitherto variable, will henceforth remain fixed
—a somewhat unwarrantable assumption—we must not allow
the disagreement between any system of ethics and the present
state of mankind to be taken as evidence against that system.

Nay, more: not only ought we to regard such disagreement,
when it appears, without prejudice; but we ought to expect it,
and to consider it, if anything, rather an indication of truth
than of error. It is preposterous to look for consistency between
absolute moral truth and the defective characters and usages
of our existing state! As already said, Morality professes to be a
code of rules proper for "the guidance of humanity in its
highest conceivable perfection." A universal obedience to its
precepts implies an ideal society. How, then, can it be expected
to harmonize with the ideas and actions and institutions of
man as he now is? When we say that mankind are sinful, weak,
frail, we simply mean that they do not habitually fulfill the
appointed law. Imperfection is merely another word for disobedience. So that congruity between a true theory of duty and
an untrue state of humanity is an impossibility, a contradiction
in the nature of things. Whoever, by way of recommending his
scheme of ethics, sets forth its immediate and entire practicability
thereby inevitably proves its falsehood. Right principles of
action become practicable only as man becomes perfect; or
rather, to put the expressions in proper sequence, man becomes
perfect just in so far as he is able to obey them.

A total disagreement may therefore be looked for between
the doctrines promulgated in the following pages and the institutions amid which we live. And the reader will be prepared
to view such disagreement not only as consistent with their
truth, but as adding to its probability.

## *Lemma* II

**1.** AND YET, UNABLE AS THE IMPERFECT MAN MAY BE TO FULFILL the perfect law, there is no other law for him. One right course only is open; and he must either follow that or take the consequences. The conditions of existence will not bend before his perversity, nor relax in consideration of his weakness. Neither, when they are broken, may any exception from penalties be hoped for. "Obey or suffer" are the ever-repeated alternatives. Disobedience is sure to be convicted. And there are no reprieves.

It is indeed the favorite maxim of a certain popular philosophy that "there is no rule without an exception"—a maxim about as respectable as the proverbs along with which it commonly passes current. Applied to conventional usages—to the tenets of state policy; to social regulations; to the precepts of pocket prudence; to the laws of grammar, of art, of etiquette; or to those common aphorisms which roughly classify the experiences of everyday life—it may be true enough; but if affirmed of the essential principles of things, of society, of man, it is utterly false.

Nature's rules, on the contrary, have no exceptions. The apparent ones are only apparent, not real. They are indications either that we have not found the true law or that we have got an imperfect expression of it. Thus, if terrestrial gravitation be defined as "a tendency possessed by all free bodies to descend toward the center of the earth," you may triumphantly add—"all free bodies *except* the balloon." But your balloon is no exception. Its ascent is just as much a result of gravitation as the falling of a stone. You have merely proved that the definition does not adequately express the law. Again, to the assertion that exercise increases strength, you may answer that, although generally true, it is not true of invalids, to whom exercise is often detrimental, and that it is only true of the healthy within certain limits. Just so. But such qualifications would have been needless if the law had been completely stated. Had it been said that so long as the power of assimilation is sufficient to make good the waste consequent upon exercise, exercise increases strength, no limitations could have been discovered. The so-called exceptions are in ourselves, not in nature. They show either that the law eludes our perception or baffles our power of expression.

Rightly understood, the progress from deepest ignorance to highest enlightenment is a progress from entire unconsciousness of law to the conviction that law is universal and inevitable. Accumulating knowledge and continual induction are ever restricting the old ideas of special causation within narrower limits. Each new discovery in science—every anomaly solved—strengthens men in the belief that phenomena result from general uniform forces. And at length, by dint of constantly repeated evidence, they begin to perceive that there are no suspensions of these forces even for the avoidance of the most terrific catastrophes. They see that, although fleets be sent to the bottom by the resulting storm, yet must atmospheric equilibrium be restored. They see that the earth does not cease its attraction, even to save a village from the impending avalanche. They see that, regardless of the consequent destruction of a church or blowing up of a vessel, the electric fluid will still follow "the line of least resistance." They see that chemical affinity must act, notwithstanding it ends in the burning of a city to ashes, in the submergence of half a country by volcanic disturbance, or in the loss of a hundred thousand lives by an epidemic. Every increment of knowledge goes to show that constancy is an essential attribute of the Divine rule: an unvaryingness which renders the eclipse of a hundred years hence predicable to a moment! And for the end of these unbending ordinances of nature, we find it to be the universal good. To render the world habitable; that is the great object. The minor evils owing to this persistency of action are as nothing compared with the infinite benefits secured. Whether those evils might or might not have been avoided, we need not now consider. It is enough for us to know that constancy is the law, and we have no alternative but to assume that law to be the best possible one.

**2.** AS WITH THE PHYSICAL, SO WITH THE ETHICAL. A BELIEF, AS yet fitful and partial, is beginning to spread among men that here also there is an indissoluble bond between cause and consequence, an inexorable destiny, a "law which altereth not." Confounded by the multiplied and ever-new aspects of human affairs, it is not perhaps surprising that men should fail duly to recognize the systematic character of the Divine rule. Yet in the moral as in the material world, accumulated evidence is gradually generating the conviction that events are not at bottom fortuitous, but that they are wrought out in a certain inevitable way by unchanging forces. In all ages there has been some glimmering perception of this truth, and experience is ever giving to that perception increased distinctness. Indeed even now all men do, in one mode or other, testify of such a faith. Every known creed is an assertion of it. What are the moral codes of the Mohammedan, the Brahman, the Buddhist, but so many acknowledgments of the inseparable connection between conduct and its results? Do they not all say you shall not do this, and this, because they *will* produce evil; and you shall do that, and that, because they *will* produce good? No matter that their founders erred in the attempt to refer each effect to its special cause and so botched their systems of morality; notwithstanding this, they evinced the belief that there *is* an inevitable law of causation in human affairs, which it is for man to learn and conform to. And is not this the doctrine of the highest known religion? Does not Christianity also teach that such-and-such deeds shall *surely* end in such-and-such issues —evil-doing in punishment, well-doing in reward—and that these things are *necessarily* and *indissolubly* connected? We imply such a faith, too, in our everyday conversations; in our maxims and precepts, in our education of children, in our advice to friends. In judging men and things we instinctively refer them to some standard of ascertained principles. We predict good or evil of this or the other scheme because of its accordance or discordance with certain perceived laws of life. Nay, even the pettifogging red-tapist, with his hand-to-mouth expediency and professed contempt for "abstract principles," has really a secret consciousness of some such invariable sequence of events—does really believe in the sway of that "beneficent necessity" which to a given act attaches a fixed result. For what is the true meaning of his "measures"—his "projects of law"? He does not think it a toss-up whether this or that effect will be produced by them. If he did, he would be as ready to adopt one plan as another. Evidently he sees that there are constant influences at work which, from each circumstance or set of circumstances, educe an unavoidable consequence, and that under like conditions like events will again follow.

Surely, then, if all believe in the persistency of these secondary laws, much more should they believe in the persistency of those primary ones which underlie human existence and out of which our everyday truths grow. We cannot deny the root if we recognize the branches. And if such is the constitution of things, we are compelled to admit this same "beneficent necessity." There is no alternative. Either society has laws or it has not. If it has not, there can be no order, no certainty, no system in its phenomena. If it has, then are they like the other laws of the universe—sure, inflexible, ever active, and having no exceptions.

**3.** HOW INFINITELY IMPORTANT IS IT THAT WE SHOULD ASCERTAIN what these laws are; and, having ascertained, implicitly obey them! If they really exist, then only by submission to them can anything permanently succeed. Just in so far as it complies with the principles of moral equilibrium can it stand. Our social edifice may be constructed with all possible labor and ingenuity and be strongly cramped together with cunningly devised enactments, but if there be no rectitude in its component parts—if it is not built on upright principles—it will assuredly tumble to pieces. As well might we seek to light a fire with ice, feed cattle on stones, hang our hats on cobwebs, or otherwise disregard the physical laws of the world, as go contrary to its equally imperative ethical laws.

Yes, but there are exceptions, say you. We cannot always be strictly guided by abstract principles. Prudential considerations must have some weight. It is necessary to use a little policy.

Very specious, no doubt, are your reasons for advocating this or the other exception. But if there be any truth in the foregoing argument, no infraction of the law can be made with impunity. Those cherished schemes by which you propose to attain some desired good by a little politic disobedience are all delusive. Were anyone to tell you that he had invented a mechanical combination which doubled power without diminishing velocity, or that he had discovered the quadrature of the circle, or that he knew the receipt for the philosopher's stone, or that he could sell you a child's caul which would save you from drowning, you would reply that while there were laws of matter such things could not be—that they were proved impossiblities. Exactly so. But rest satisfied that they are not more complete impossibilities than are your proposed achievements which similarly conflict with the essential laws of life.

It may indeed be difficult for those who have but little faith in the invisible to follow out a principle unflinchingly, in spite of every threatening evil—to give up their own power judging what seems best, from the belief that that only is best which is abstractedly right—to say, "Although appearances are against it, yet will I obey the law." Nevertheless, this is the true attitude to assume: the conduct which it has been the object of all moral teaching to inculcate; the only conduct which can eventually answer.[1]

**4.** EVEN SUPPOSING FOR A MOMENT THAT A SOLITARY ACT OF disobedience may pass without evil results—nay, may bring beneficial ones—even supposing this, the wisdom of the act is not thereby proved. For consider the probable effects of a wrong precedent. As Paley truly says, "The bad consequences of actions are twofold, particular and general." And admitting

---

[1]Coleridge clearly expresses such a belief. He says, "This is indeed the main characteristic of the moral system taught by the Friend throughout; that the distinct foresight of consequences belongs exclusively to the Infinite Wisdom which is one with the Almighty Will, on which all consequences depend; but that for man—to obey the simple unconditional commandment of eschewing every act that implies a self-contradiction, or, in other words, to produce and maintain the greatest possible harmony in the component impulses and faculties of his nature, involves the effects of prudence."—The Friend.

even that a *particular* good has been secured, a far greater *general* evil has been entailed by opening the way to future disobedience. There is no security in this lax creed. One breach of the law leaves a gap for numberless subsequent trespasses. If the first false step has been taken with seeming impunity, it will inevitably be followed by others. Schoolboy promises of "only this once" are not to be believed. Make a hole through a principle to admit a solitary exception, and, on one pretense or other, exceptions will by and by be thrust through after it, as to render the principle utterly good for nothing. In fact, if its consequences are closely traced, this same plea for license in special cases turns out to be the source of nearly all the evils that afflict us. Almost every wrongdoing is excused by the doer on this ground. He confesses his act is at variance with the moral law, which he admits to be, and in some sort believes to be, the best guide. He thinks, however, that his interest requires him now and then to make exceptions. All men do this—and see the result.

**5.** BUT CAN WE EVER BE SURE THAT AN EXCEPTIONAL DISOBEDIENCE *will* bring the anticipated benefits? Whoso would forsake for a time a confessedly legitimate guide should remember that he is falling back upon that expediency hypothesis of which we have already seen the falsity. He is laying claim to a perfect knowledge of man, of society, of institutions, of events, of all the complex, ever-varying phenomena of human existence; and to a grasp of mind that can infer from these how things will go in future. In short, he is assuming that same omniscience which, as we saw, is requisite for the successful carrying out of such a system. Does he shrink from arrogating as much? Then observe his dilemma. He deserts what he admits to be on the whole a safe rule of conduct, to follow one which is difficult to understand, unsettled in its directions, doubtful in its consequences.

If the foolishness of such conduct needs illustrating by facts, there are plenty at hand. The constant failure of schemes devised without consulting ethical principles has been already exemplified (see pp. 9, 10). Let us now, however, take a few cases specially applying to the present point—cases in which benefit has been sought by going in palpable opposition to those principles—cases in which men, dissatisfied with the road whose finger-post declares that "honesty is the best policy," have diverged into the byways of injustice, in the hope of more readily attaining their ends.

The enslavement of the Negroes serves for a good example. Nothing could have seemed more conclusive than the reasoning of unscrupulous colonists on this matter. Here were rich soils, a splendid climate, and a large market for the sale of produce. Now, could but a sufficiency of laborers be imported and reduced to servitude, what profit they would bring to their possessors! Maintained at a cheap rate, made to work hard and to keep long at it, what a surplus would they not create! Here was a mine of wealth! Well, the planters acted out their thought —did that which, although it might not be just, was apparently "the best policy," so far as they were concerned. Their golden visions have been far from realized, however. Slave countries are comparatively poverty-stricken all over the world. Though Jamaica at one time sent up a few overgrown nabobs, yet West Indian history has been a history of distress and complainings, in spite of continual assistance and artificial advantages. The Southern states of America are far behind their Northern neighbors in prosperity—are in process of abandoning slavery one after another, in consequence of its ruinous results. Somehow the scheme has not answered as was expected. Though worked in some cases sixteen hours out of the twenty-four; though supported on "a pint of flour and one salt herring per day"; though kept to his work by whips, yet did not the slave bring to his owner the large profit calculated upon. Indeed it has turned out that, under like circumstances, free labor is much cheaper. And then, besides the disappointment, there came results that were never looked for. Slavery brought in its train the multiplied curses of a diseased social state; a reign of mutual hatred and terror, of universal demoralization, of sin-begotten recklessness, of extravagant expenditure, of bad cultivation, exhausted soils, mortgaged estates, bankruptcy, beggary. After all, the moral law would have been the safest guide.

When Philip of Valois swore the officers of his mint to

conceal the debasement of the coinage and to endeavor to make
the merchants believe that the gold and silver pieces were of
full value, he thought that, although perhaps unprincipled,
such a measure would be vastly profitable. And so no doubt
believed the other kings, who, in the "good old times," almost
universally did the like. They overreached themselves, however,
as all such schemers do. It is true that their debts were diminished "in proportion to the reduction in the value of the currency; but their revenues were at the same time reduced in the
like ratio. Moreover, the loss of their reputation for honesty
made them afterward unable to borrow money, except at proportionately high rates of interest, to cover the risk ran by the
lender." So that they not only lost on the creditor side of their
accounts what they gained on the debtor side, but put themselves at a great disadvantage for the future. After centuries of
dearly bought experience, the practice was reluctantly abandoned
and is now universally exploded as essentially suicidal—just as
suicidal, in fact, as all other infringements of the rule of right.

Let us remember also the failure of those attempts to profit
at the expense of our American colonies, and the disastrous results to which they led. Our governors thought it would be
highly beneficial to the mother country if the colonies were
constrained to become her customers, and in pursuance of this
conclusion not only prohibited the settlers from purchasing
certain goods from any other country than England but actually
denied them the right to make those goods for themselves! As
usual, the maneuver proved worse than abortive. The outlay
required to keep open this national truck-shop was greater than
the receipts. Nay, indeed, that outlay was wholly thrown away,
and worse than thrown away, for it turns out that artificial trades
so obtained entail loss upon both parties. Then, too, came
the punishment, the resistance of the settlers, the War of Independence, and the hundred and odd millions added to our
national burdens!

What an astounding illustration of the defeat of dishonesty
by the eternal laws of things we have in the history of the
East India Company! Selfish, unscrupulous, worldly-wise in

policy, and with unlimited force to back it, this oligarchy, year by year, perseveringly carried out its schemes of aggrandizement. It subjugated province upon province; it laid one prince after another under tribute; it made exorbitant demands upon adjacent rulers and construed refusal into a pretext for aggression; it became sole proprietor of the land, claiming nearly one half the produce as rent; and it entirely monopolized commerce: thus uniting in itself the character of conqueror, ruler, landowner, and merchant. With all these resources, what could it be but prosperous? From the spoils of victorious war, the rent of millions of acres, the tribute of dependent monarchs, the profits of an exclusive trade, what untold wealth must have poured in upon it! What revenues? What a bursting exchequer! Alas! The Company is some £50,000,000 in debt.

Protected trades, too, have afforded many proofs of the impolicy of injustice. The history of the wool business some centuries ago might be quoted as one, but let us take the more recent case of silk. Under the now happily exploded plea of protection to native industry, the silk manufacturers were freed from all foreign competition. Their prices were thus artificially raised, and all the nation was compelled to buy of them. And so, having a large market and profits, they thought their prosperity ensured. They were doomed to disappointment, however. Instead of a brisk and extensive trade, they obtained a languishing and confined one; and that branch of manufacture which was to have been a pattern of commercial greatness became a by-word for whining poverty. How utterly absurd, under such a lamentable state of things, must have appeared the proposal to return toward equitable dealing by lowering the duties! What "impracticables" must those men have been thought who, because monopoly was unjust, wished to expose the almost ruined manufacturers to the additional difficulty of foreign competition! Could anything be more contrary to common sense? Here, surely, was a case in which "abstract principles" must give way to "policy." No; even here, too, obedience to the moral law proved to be the best. Rebellion against it had been punished by accumulated distresses; a partial submission was rewarded by an increase of prosperity. Within fourteen years from the date at which the duties were lowered the trade had more than doubled itself—had increased more within that period than during the preceding century. And those who, but a short time before, were unable to meet their French compeers in the home markets not only began to compete with them in the marts of other nations but to send large quantities of goods to France itself.

These are but a few samples from a universal experience. If diligently traced, the results of abandoning the *right* to pursue the *politic* will uniformly be found to end thus. Men who are insane enough to think that they may safely violate the fundamental laws of right conduct may read in such defeats and disasters their own fate. Let them but inquire, and they will find that each petty evil, each great catastrophe, is in some way or other a sequence of injustice. Monetary panics, South Sea bubbles, railway manias, Irish rebellions, French revolutions—these and the miseries flowing from them are but the cumulative effects of dishonesty. A bitter experience teaches all men when it is too late that, alike in national and individual affairs, entire submission is the wisest course. Even Napoleon, after his seeming success, his triumphs, his profound statesmanship, his far-seeing "policy," ended in the belief that "there is no power without justice."

Yet this commentary on the moral code—this History, as we call it—men forever read in vain! Poring with microscopic eye over the symbols in which it is written, they are heedless of the great facts expressed by them. Instead of collecting evidence bearing upon the all-important question—What are the laws that determine national success or failure, stability or revolution?—they gossip about state intrigues, sieges and battles, court scandal, the crimes of nobles, the quarrels of parties, the births, deaths, and marriages of kings, and other like trifles. Minutiae, pettifogging details, the vanity and frippery of bygone times, the mere decorations of the web of existence, they examine, analyze, and learnedly descant upon, yet are blind to those stern realties which each age shrouds in its superficial tissue of events—those terrible truths which glare out upon us from the gloom of the past. From the successive strata of our historical deposits, they diligently gather all the highly colored fragments, pounce upon everything that is curious and sparkling, and chuckle like children over their glittering acquisitions; meanwhile the rich veins of wisdom that ramify amid this worthless debris lie utterly neglected. Cumbrous volumes of rubbish are greedily accumulated, while those masses of rich ore that should have been dug out and from which golden truths might have been smelted are left unthought of and unsought.

**6.** BUT WHY ALL THIS LABORED EXAMINATION INTO THE PROPRIETY, or impropriety, of making exceptions to an ascertained ethical law? The very question is absurd. For what does a man really mean by saying of a thing that it is "theoretically just," or "true in principle," or "abstractedly right"? Simply that it accords with what he, in some way or other, perceives to be the established arrangements of Divine rule. When he admits that an act is "theoretically just," he admits it to be that which, in strict duty, should be done. By "true in principle," he means in harmony with the conduct decreed for us. The course which he calls "abstractedly right" he believes to be the appointed way to human happiness. There is no escape. The expressions mean this, or they mean nothing. Practically, therefore, when he proposes to disobey, he does so in the hope of improving on this guidance! Though told that such-and-such are the true roads to happiness, he opines that he knows shorter ones! To the Creator's silent command, "Do this," he replies that, all things considered, he thinks he can do better! This is the real Infidelity; the true Atheism: to doubt the foresight and efficiency of the Divine arrangements, and with infinite presumption to suppose a human judgment less fallible! When will man "cease his frantic pretension of scanning this great God's World in his small fraction of a brain, and know that it has verily, though deep beyond his soundings, a Just Law; that the soul of it is good; that his part in it is to conform to the Law of the Whole, and in devout silence follow that, not questioning it, obeying it as unquestionable."[2]

---

[2] Advice, by the way, which in these latter days the giver might properly enough take home to himself.

**7.** BRIEFLY REVIEWING THE ARGUMENT, WE MARK FIRST THAT physical laws are characterized by constancy and universality and that there is every reason to believe the like true of ethical ones. It is inferred that, if so, there is no safety but in entire obedience, even in spite of threatening appearances. This inference is enforced by the consideration that any departure from principle to escape some anticipated evil is a return to the proved errors of expediency. It is again enforced by the fact that the innumerable attempts of a stiff-necked worldly wisdom to benefit by disobedience have failed. And it is yet further enforced by the reflection that to think we can better ourselves by deserting the road marked out for us is an impious assumption of more than Divine omniscience.

The reasons for thus specially insisting on implicit obedience will become apparent as the reader proceeds. Among the conclusions inevitably following from an admitted principle, he will most likely find several for which he is hardly prepared. Some of these will seem strange; others impracticable; and, it may be, one or two wholly at variance with his ideas of duty. Nevertheless, should he find them logically derived from a fundamental truth, he will have no alternative but to adopt them as rules of conduct which ought to be followed without exception. If there be any weight in the considerations above set forth, then, no matter how seemingly inexpedient, dangerous, injurious even, may be the course which morality points out as "abstractedly right," the highest wisdom is in perfect and fearless submission.

# SOCIAL STATICS

---

*Part I*

□

## CHAPTER I

## *Definition of Morality*

**1.** THERE DOES NOT SEEM TO EXIST ANY SETTLED IDEA AS TO WHAT a Moral Philosophy properly embraces. Moralists have either omitted to prelude their inquiries by any strict definition of the work to be done, or a definition of a very loose and indiscriminating character has been framed. Instead of confining themselves to the discovery and application of certain essential principles of right conduct, they have attempted to give rules for all possible actions, under all possible circumstances. Properly understood, the subject matter for investigation lies within comparatively narrow limits; but, overlooking these, they have entered upon a multitude of questions which we shall shortly find to be quite beyond their province.

**2.** AS ALREADY SAID (P. 16), THE MORAL LAW MUST BE THE LAW OF the perfect man—the law in obedience to which perfection consists. There are but two propositions for us to choose between. It may either be asserted that morality is a code of rules for the behavior of man as he *is*—a code which recognizes existing defects of character and allows for them; or otherwise that it is a code of rules for the regulation of conduct among men as they *should* be. Of the first alternative we must say that any proposed system of morals which recognizes existing defects and countenances acts made needful by them stands self-condemned; seeing that, by the hypothesis, acts thus excused are not the best conceivable —that is, are not perfectly *right*, not perfectly *moral*—and therefore a morality which permits them is, in so far as it does this, not a morality at all. To escape from this contradiction is impossible, save by adopting the other alternative; namely, that the moral law ignoring all vicious conditions, defects, and incapacities prescribes the conduct of an ideal humanity. Pure and absolute rectitude can alone be its subject matter. Its object must be to determine the relationships in which men ought to stand to each other—to point out the principles of action in a normal society. By successive propositions it must aim to give a systematic statement of those conditions under which human beings may harmoniously combine; and to this end it requires as its postulate that those human beings be perfect. Or we may term it the science of social life; a science that, in common with all other sciences, assumes perfection in the elements with which it deals.

**3.** TREATING, THEREFORE, AS IT DOES ON THE ABSTRACT PRINCIPLES of right conduct and the deductions to be made from these, a system of pure ethics cannot recognize evil or any of those conditions which evil generates. It entirely ignores wrong, injustice, or crime, and gives no information as to what must be done when they have been committed. It knows no such thing as an infraction of the laws, for it is merely a statement of what the laws are. It simply says such-and-such are the principles on which men should act, and when these are broken it can do nothing but say that they are broken. If asked what anyone ought to do when another has knocked him down, it will not tell; it can only answer that an assault is a trespass against the law and gives rise to a wrong relationship. It is silent as to the manner in which we should behave to a thief; all the information it affords is that theft is a disturbance of social equilibrium. We may learn from it that debt implies an infraction of the moral code; but whether the debtor should or should not be imprisoned cannot be decided by it. To all questions which presuppose some antecedent unlawful action, such as—Should a barrister defend anyone whom he believes to be guilty? Ought a man to break an oath which he has taken to do something wrong? Is it proper to publish the misconduct of our fellows?— the perfect law can give no reply, because it does not recognize the premises. In seeking to settle such points on purely ethical principles, moralists have attempted impossibilities. As well might they have tried to solve mathematically a series of problems respecting crooked lines and broken-backed curves or to deduce from the theorems of mechanics the proper method of setting to work a dislocated machine. No conclusions can lay claim to absolute truth, but such as depend upon truths that are themselves absolute. Before there can be exactness in an inference, there must be exactness in the antecedent propositions. A geometrician requires that the straight lines with which he deals shall be veritably straight and that his circles and ellipses and parabolas shall agree with precise definitions—shall perfectly and invariably answer to specified equations. If you put to him a question in which these conditions are not complied with, he tells you that it cannot be answered. So likewise is it with the philosophical moralist. He treats solely of the *straight* man. He determines the properties of the straight man; describes how the straight man comports himself; shows in what relationship he stands to other straight men; shows how a community of straight men is constituted. Any deviation from strict rectitude he is obliged wholly to ignore. It cannot be admitted into his premises without vitiating all his conclusions. A problem in which a crooked man forms one of the elements is insoluble by him. He may state what he thinks about it—may give an approximate solution; but anything more is impossible. His decision is no longer scientific and authoritative but is now merely an opinion.

Or perhaps the point may be most conveniently enforced by using the science of the animal man to illustrate that of the moral man. Physiology is defined as a classified statement of the phenomena of bodily life. It treats of the functions of our several organs in their normal states. It explains the relationships in which the members stand to each other—what are their respective duties, how such duties are performed, and why they are necessary. It exhibits the mutual dependence of the vital actions, points out how these are maintained in due balance, and describes the condition of things constituting perfect health. Disease it does not even recognize and can therefore solve no questions concerning it. To the inquiry—What is the cause of fever? or What is the best remedy for a cold?—it gives no answer. Such matters are out of its sphere. Could it reply, it would be no longer Physiology, but Pathology, or Therapeutics. Just so it is with a true morality, which might properly enough be called Moral Physiology. Its office is simply to expound the principles of moral health. Like its analogue, it has nothing to do with morbid actions and deranged functions. It deals only with the laws of a normal humanity and cannot recognize a wrong, a depraved, or a disordered condition.

Hence it appears that in treating of two such matters as the right of property and the impropriety of dueling as parts of the same science moralists have confounded together subjects that are essentially distinct. The question, What are the right principles of human conduct? is one thing; the question, What must be done when those principles have been broken through? is another and widely different thing. Whether this last admits of any solution—whether it is possible to develop scientifically a Moral Pathology and a Moral Therapeutics—seems very doubtful. Be this as it may, however, it is very clear that a system of pure Ethics is independent of these. And it will be considered so throughout the ensuing investigations.

CHAPTER II

_____

## The Evanescence of Evil

**1.** ALL EVIL RESULTS FROM THE NON-ADAPTATION OF CONSTITUtion to conditions. This is true of everything that lives. Does a shrub dwindle in poor soil, or become sickly when deprived of light, or die outright if removed to a cold climate? It is because the harmony between its organization and its circumstances has been destroyed. Those experiences of the farmyard and the menageries which show that pain, disease, and death are entailed upon animals by certain kinds of treatment may all be generalized under the same law. Every suffering incident to the human body, from a headache up to a fatal illness—from a burn or a sprain to accidental loss of life—is similarly traceable to the having placed that body in a situation for which its powers did not fit it. Nor is the expression confined in its application to physical evil; it comprehends moral evil also. Is the kindhearted man distressed by the sight of misery? Is the bachelor unhappy because his means will not permit him to marry? Does the mother mourn over her lost child? Does the emigrant lament leaving his fatherland? Are some made uncomfortable by having to pass their lives in distasteful occupations, and others from having no occupation at all? The explanation is still the same. No matter what the special nature of the evil, it is invariably referable to the one generic cause—want of congruity between the faculties and their spheres of action.

**2.** EQUALLY TRUE IS IT THAT EVIL PERPETUALLY TENDS TO DISAPpear. In virtue of an essential principle of life, this non-adaptation of an organism to its conditions is ever being rectified; and modification of one or both continues until the adaptation is complete. Whatever possesses vitality, from the elementary cell up to man himself, inclusive, obeys this law. We see it illustrated in the acclimatization of plants, in the altered habits of domesticated animals, in the varying characteristics of our own race. Accustomed to the brief arctic summer, the Siberian herbs and shrubs spring up, flower, and ripen their seeds in the space of a few weeks. If exposed to the rigor of northern winters, animals of the Temperate Zone get thicker coats and become white. The greyhound, which, when first transported to the high plateaus of the Andes, fails in the chase from want of breath, acquires, in the course of generations, a more efficient pair of lungs. Cattle, which in their wild state gave milk but for short periods, now give it almost continuously. Ambling is a pace not natural to the horse, yet there are American breeds that now take to it without training.

Man exhibits just the same adaptability. He alters in color according to temperature—lives here upon rice and there upon whale oil—gets larger digestive organs if he habitually eats innutritious food—acquires the power of long fasting if his mode of life is irregular, and loses it when the supply of food is certain—becomes fleet and agile in the wilderness and inert in the city

—attains acute vision, hearing, and scent when his habits of life call for them, and gets these senses blunted when they are less needful. That such changes are toward fitness for surrounding circumstances no one can question. When he sees that the dweller in marshes lives in an atmosphere which is certain death to a stranger—when he sees that the Hindu can lie down and sleep under a tropical sun while his white master, with closed blinds and water sprinklings and punkah, can hardly get a doze —when he sees that the Greenlander and the Neapolitan subsist comfortably on their respective foods, blubber and macaroni, but would be made miserable by an interchange of them—when he sees that in other cases there is still this fitness to diet, to climate, and to modes of life, even the most skeptical must admit that some law of adaptation is at work. Nay, indeed, if he interprets facts aright, he will find that the action of such a law is traceable down to the minutest ramifications of individual experience. In the drunkard who needs an increasing quantity of spirits to intoxicate him, and in the opium eater who has to keep taking a larger dose to produce the usual effect, he may mark how the system gradually acquires power to resist what is noxious. Those who smoke, who take snuff, or who habitually use medicines can furnish like illustrations. Nor, in fact, is there any permanent change of bodily state or capability which is not to be accounted for on the same principle.

This universal law of physical modification is the law of mental modification also. The multitudinous differences of capacity and disposition that have in course of time grown up among the Indian, African, Mongolian, and Caucasian races and among the various subdivisions of them must all be ascribed to the acquirement in each case of fitness for surrounding circumstances. Those strong contrasts between the characters of nations and of times awhile since exemplified (p. 33) admit of no other conceivable explanation. Why all this divergence from the one common original type? If adaptation of constitution to conditions is not the cause, what is the cause?

There are none, however, who can with anything like consistency combat this doctrine, for all use arguments that presuppose its truth. Even those to whose prejudices the theory of man's indefinite adaptability is most opposed are continually betraying their involuntary belief in it. They do this when they attribute differences of national character to differences in social customs and arrangements; and again when they comment on the force of habit; and again when they discuss the probable influence of a proposed measure upon public morality; and again when they recommend practice as a means of acquiring increased aptitude; and again when they describe certain pursuits as elevating and others as degrading; and again when they talk of getting used to anything; and again when they advocate certain systems of mental discipline—when they teach that virtuous conduct eventually becomes pleasurable, and when they warn against the power of a long-encouraged vice.

In fact, if we consider the question closely, no other arrangement of things can be imagined. For we must adopt one of three propositions. We must either affirm that the human being is wholly unaltered by the influences that are brought to bear upon him—his circumstances, as we call them; or that he perpetually tends to become more and more unfitted to those circumstances; or that he tends to become fitted to them. If the first is true, then all schemes of education, of government, of social reform—all instrumentalities by which it is proposed to act upon man—are utterly useless, seeing that he cannot be acted upon at all. If the second is true, then the way to make a man virtuous is to accustom him to vicious practices, and vice versa. Both of which propositions being absurd, we are compelled to admit the remaining one.

**3.** KEEPING IN MIND, THEN, THE TWO FACTS, THAT ALL EVIL RESULTS from the non-adaptation of constitution to conditions, and that where this non-adaptation exists it is continually being diminished by the changing of constitution to suit conditions, we shall be prepared for comprehending the present position of the human race.

By the increase of population the state of existence we call social has been necessitated. Men living in this state suffer under numerous evils. By the hypothesis it follows that their characters are not completely adapted to such a state.

In what respect are they not so adapted? What is the special qualification which the social state requires?

It requires that each individual shall have such desires only as may be fully satisfied without trenching upon the ability of other individuals to obtain like satisfaction. If the desires of each are not thus limited, then either all must have certain of their desires ungratified, or some must get gratification for them at the corresponding expense of others. Both of which alternatives, necessitating pain, imply non-adaptation.

But why is not man adapted to the social state?

Simply because he yet partially retains the characteristics that adapted him for an antecedent state. The respects in which he is not fitted to society are the respects in which he is fitted for his original predatory life. His primitive circumstances required that he should sacrifice the welfare of other beings to his own; his present circumstances require that he should not do so; and in so far as his old attribute still clings to him, in so far is he unfit for the social state. All sins of men against each other, from the cannibalism of the Carib to the crimes and venalities that we see around us—the felonies that fill our prisons, the trickeries of trade, the quarrelings of nation with nation and of class with class, the corruptness of institutions, the jealousies of caste, and the scandal of drawing rooms—have their causes comprehended under this generalization.

Concerning the present position of the human race, we must therefore say that man needed one moral constitution to fit him for his original state; that he needs another to fit him for his present state; and that he has been, is, and will long continue to be in process of adaptation. By the term *civilization* we signify the adaptation that has already taken place. The changes that constitute progress are the successive steps of the transition. And the belief in human perfectibility merely amounts to the belief that in virtue of this process man will eventually become completely suited to his mode of life.

**4.** IF THERE BE ANY CONCLUSIVENESS IN THE FOREGOING ARGU-ments, such a faith is well founded. As commonly supported by evidence drawn from history, it cannot be considered indisputable. The inference that as advancement has been hitherto the rule it will be the rule henceforth, may be called a plausible speculation. But when it is shown that this advancement is due to the working of a universal law, and that in virtue of that law it must continue until the state we call perfection is reached, then the advent of such a state is removed out of the region of probability into that of certainty. If anyone demurs to this, let him point out the error. Here are the several steps of the argument.

All imperfection is unfitness to the conditions of existence.

This unfitness must consist either in having a faculty or faculties in excess, or in having a faculty or faculties deficient, or in both.

A faculty in excess is one to which the conditions of existence do not afford full exercise; and a faculty that is deficient is one from which the conditions of existence demand more than it can perform.

But it is an essential principle of life that a faculty to which circumstances do not allow full exercise diminishes, and that a faculty on which circumstances make excessive demands increases.

And so long as this excess and this deficiency continue, there must continue decrease on the one hand and growth on the other.

Finally, all excess and all deficiency must disappear; that is, all unfitness must disappear; that is, all imperfection must disappear.

Thus the ultimate development of the ideal man is logically certain—as certain as any conclusion in which we place the most implicit faith; for instance, that all men will die. For why do we infer that all men will die? Simply because, in an immense number of past experiences, death has uniformly occurred. Similarly, then, as the experiences of all people in all times—experiences that are embodied in maxims, proverbs, and moral precepts, and that are illustrated in biographies and histories—go to prove that organs, faculties, powers, capacities, or whatever else we call them grow by use and diminish from disuse, it is inferred that they will continue to do so. And if this inference is unquestionable, then is the one above deduced from it—that humanity must in the end become completely adapted to its conditions—unquestionable also.

Progress, therefore, is not an accident, but a necessity. Instead of civilization being artificial, it is a part of nature; all of a piece with the development of the embryo or the unfolding of a flower. The modifications mankind have undergone and are still undergoing result from a law underlying the whole organic creation; and provided the human race continues and the constitution of things remains the same, those modifications must end in completeness. As surely as the tree becomes bulky when it stands alone, and slender if one of a group; as surely as the same creature assumes the different forms of cart horse and race horse, according as its habits demand strength or speed; as surely as a blacksmith's arm grows large and the skin of a laborer's hand thick; as surely as the eye tends to become long-sighted in the sailor and short-sighted in the student; as surely as the blind attain a more delicate sense of touch; as surely as a clerk acquires rapidity in writing and calculation; as surely as the musician learns to detect an error of a semitone amid what seems to others a very babel of sounds; as surely as a passion grows by indulgence and diminishes when restrained; as surely as a disregarded conscience becomes inert and one that is obeyed active; as surely as there is any efficacy in educational culture or any meaning in such terms as *habit, custom, practice;* so surely must the human faculties be molded into complete fitness for the social state; so surely must the things we call evil and immorality disappear; so surely must man become perfect.

CHAPTER III

## The Divine Idea, and the Conditions of Its Realization

**1.** IF, INSTEAD OF PROPOSING IT AS THE RULE OF HUMAN CONDUCT, Bentham had simply assumed "greatest happiness" to be the creative purpose, his position would have been tenable enough. Almost all men do in one way or other assert the same. There have indeed been times when such a faith was far from universal. Had the proposition been made before Simeon Stylites on the top of his column, he would very likely have demurred to it. Probably the Flagellants of the thirteenth century may have thought otherwise. And even now it is possible that the Fakirs of India hold a contrary opinion. But while it may be true that a savage asceticism attributes to the Deity a barbarity equal to its own and conceives Him as delighting in human sacrifices; while it may be true that among ourselves the same notion yet lingers under the form of occasional fasts and penances; still there are few if any among civilized people who do not agree that human well-being is in accordance with the Divine will. The doctrine is taught by all our religious teachers; it is assumed by every writer on morality: we may therefore safely consider it as an admitted truth.

It is one thing, however, to hold that greatest happiness is the creative purpose, and a quite different thing to hold that greatest happiness should be the *immediate* aim of man. It has been the fatal error of the expediency philosophers to confound these positions. They have not observed that the truth has two sides, a Divine side and a human side, and that it matters much to us which we look at. Greatest Happiness and Morality are the face and obverse of the same fact: what is written on the one surface is beyond our interpretation; what is written on the other we may read easily enough.

Or dropping metaphor and speaking in philosophical language, we may say that it is for us to ascertain the *conditions* by conforming to which this greatest happiness may be attained. Not to put trust in guesses; not to do this or that because we *think* it will be beneficial, but to find out what really *is* the line of conduct that leads to the desired end. For unquestionably there must be in the nature of things some definite and fixed prerequisites to success. Man is a visible, tangible entity, having properties. In the circumstances that surround him there are certain unchanging necessities. Life is dependent upon the fulfillment of specific functions, and happiness is a particular kind

of life. Surely, then, if we would know how, in the midst of
these appointed circumstances, the being Man must live so as to
achieve the result—greatest happiness—we ought first to determine what the essential conditions are. If we solve the problem,
it can only be by consulting these and submitting ourselves to
them. To suppose that we may, in ignorance or disregard of
them, succeed by some haphazard speculation is sheer folly.
Only in one way can the desideratum be reached. What that
one way is must depend upon the fundamental necessities of
our position. And if we would discover it, our first step must be
to ascertain those necessities.

**2.** AT THE HEAD OF THEM STANDS THIS UNALTERABLE FACT—THE
social state. In the preordained course of things, men have multiplied until they are constrained to live more or less in presence
of each other. That, as being needful for the support of the
greatest sum of life, such a condition is preliminary to the production of the greatest sum of happiness seems highly probable.
Be that as it may, however, we find this state established, are
henceforth to continue in it, and must therefore set it down as
one of those necessities which our rules for the achievement of
the greatest happiness must recognize and conform to.

In this social state, the sphere of activity of each individual
being limited by the spheres of activity of other individuals, it
follows that the men who are to realize this greatest sum of
happiness must be men of whom each can obtain complete
happiness within his own sphere of activity without diminishing
the spheres of activity required for the acquisition of happiness
by others. For manifestly, if each or any of them cannot receive
complete happiness without lessening the spheres of activity of
one or more of the rest, he must either himself come short of
complete happiness or must make one or more do so; and hence,
under such circumstances, the sum total of happiness cannot be
as great as is conceivable, or cannot be greatest happiness. Here,
then, is the first of those fixed conditions to the obtainment of
greatest happiness necessitated by the social state. It is the
fulfillment of this condition which we express by the word
justice.

To this all-essential prerequisite there is a supplementary one of kindred nature. We find that without trenching upon each other's spheres of activity men may yet behave to one another in such a way as to produce painful emotions. And if any have feelings that lead them to do this, it is clear that the total amount of happiness is not so great as it would be were they devoid of those feelings. Hence, to compass greatest happiness, the human constitution must be such as that each man may perfectly fulfill his own nature, not only without diminishing other men's spheres of activity, but without giving unhappiness to other men in any direct or indirect way. This condition, as we shall by and by see, needs to be kept quite distinct from the foregoing one. The observance of it may be called *negative beneficence.*

Yet another requirement is there by fulfillment of which the happiness flowing from compliance with the foregoing ones is indefinitely multiplied. Let a race of beings be so constituted as that each individual may be able to obtain full satisfaction for all his desires without deducting from the satisfaction obtainable by other individuals, and we have a state of things in which the amount of *isolated* happiness is the greatest conceivable. But let these beings be so constituted as that each, in addition to the pleasurable emotions personally received by him, can sympathetically participate in the pleasurable emotions of all others, and the sum total of happiness becomes largely increased. Hence, to the primary requisite that each shall be able to get complete happiness without diminishing the happiness of the rest, we must now add the secondary one that each shall be capable of receiving happiness from the happiness of the rest. Compliance with this requisite implies *positive beneficence.*

Lastly, there must go to the production of the greatest happiness the further condition that, while duly regardful of the preceding limitations, each individual shall perform all those acts required to fill up the measure of his own private happiness.

These, then, are necessities. They are not matters of opinion, but matters of unalterable fact. Denial of them is impossible, for nothing else can be stated but what is self-contradictory. Without any alternative, beings who are to realize the Divine

Idea must be thus constituted. Before greatest happiness can be brought about, every man must answer to these definitions; and all approach to greatest happiness presupposes an approach toward conformity with them. Schemes of government and culture which ignore them cannot but be essentially absurd. Everything must be good or bad, right or wrong, in virtue of its accordance or discordance with them. We have no need to perplex ourselves with investigations into the expediency of every measure, by trying to trace out its ultimate results in all their infinite ramifications—a task which it is folly to attempt. Our course is to inquire concerning such measure whether or not it fully recognizes these fundamental necessities, and to be sure that it must be proper or improper accordingly. Our whole code of duty is comprehended in the endeavor to live up to these necessities. If we find pleasure in doing this, it is well; if not, our aim must be to acquire that pleasure. Greatest happiness is obtained only when conformity to them is spontaneous, seeing that the restraint of desires inciting to trespass implies pain or deduction from greatest happiness. Hence it is for us to habituate ourselves to fulfill these requirements as fast as we can. The social state is a necessity. The conditions of greatest happiness under that state are fixed. Our characters are the only things not fixed. They, then, must be molded into fitness for the conditions. And all moral teaching and discipline must have for its object to hasten this process.

**3.** OBJECTION MAY BE TAKEN TO THE FOREGOING CLASSIFICATION of the conditions needful to greatest happiness as being in some degree artificial. It will perhaps be said that the distinction between justice and beneficence cannot be maintained, for that the two graduate into each other imperceptibly. Some may argue that it is not allowable to assume any essential difference between right conduct toward others and right conduct toward self, seeing that what are generally considered purely private actions do eventually affect others to such a degree as to render them public actions, as witness the collateral effects of drunkenness or suicide. Others again may contend that all morality should be classed as private, because with the righty constituted or moral man correct conduct to others is merely incidental upon the fulfillment of his own nature.

In each of these allegations there is much truth, and it is not to be denied that under a final analysis all such distinctions as those above made must disappear. But it should be borne in mind that similar criticisms may be passed upon all classifications whatever. It might, after the same fashion, be argued that we ought not to separate the laws of heat from those of mechanics, because fire when applied to water generates mechanical force. On like grounds, Optics ought to be identified with Chemistry, seeing that in the photographic process light becomes a chemical agent. Considering that muscles contract when stimulated by a galvanic current, we ought to treat of Physiology and Electricity as forming one science. Nor should we even distinguish between vegetable and animal life, for these are found to have a common root, and it is hardly possible to say of the lowest organisms which division they belong to. So that unless such objectors are prepared to say that Botany and Zoology should be regarded as one and that all lines of demarcation between the physical sciences should be abolished, they must in consistency tolerate an analogous classification in moral science and must admit that while this is in a certain sense artificial it may be an essential preliminary to anything like systematic investigation. The same finite power of comprehension which compels us to deal with natural phenomena by separating them into groups and studying each group by itself may also compel us to separate those actions which place a man in direct relationship with his fellows from others which do not so place him, although it may be true that such a separation cannot be strictly maintained. And even in dealing with one of these sections, in developing the principles of right conduct to others, it may be further necessary to distinguish, as above, the primary and most imperative principle from the secondary and less imperative one, notwithstanding that these have a common root.

**4.** THE REALIZATION OF THE DIVINE IDEA BEING REDUCED TO THE fulfillment of certain conditions, it becomes the office of a scientific morality to make a detailed statement of the mode in

which life must be regulated so as to conform to them. On each
of these axiomatic truths it must be possible to build a series of
theorems immediately bearing upon our daily conduct; or, in-
verting the thought, every act stands in a certain relationships to
these truths, and it must be possible in some way or other to
solve the problem, whether that relationship is one of accordance or discordance. When such a series of theorems has been
elaborated and solutions have been given to such a series of
problems, the task of the moralist is accomplished.

Each of these axioms, however, may have its own set of consequences separately deduced, or indeed, as already hinted, must
have them so deduced. Their respective developments constitute independent departments of moral science, requiring to be
dealt with in the order of their natural sequence. For the present,
therefore, our attention will be confined to the first and most
essential of them. Individual or private morality, as distinguished from social or public morality, is not to be entered upon
in the following pages. Neither will there be found in them any
statement of that class of moral obligations above comprehended under the terms *positive* and *negative beneficence*.[1] It
is with the several inferences to be drawn from that primary
condition to greatest happiness, the observance of which is
vaguely signified by the word *justice*, that we have now to deal.
Our work will be to unfold that condition into a system of
equity; to mark out those limits put to each man's proper sphere
of activity by the like spheres of other men; to delineate the
relationships that are necessitated by a recognition of those
limits; or, in other words, to develop the principles of Social
Statics.

[1] These other divisions of the subject may be taken up on a future occasion,
should circumstances favor.

# SOCIAL STATICS

---

## Part II

## CHAPTER IV

## *Derivation of a First Principle*

**1.** THERE WILL POSSIBLY BE SOME FOR WHOM THE A PRIORI CON-siderations set forth in the foregoing chapter are too abstract for distinct comprehension. It is easy, however, to reason our way to that first principle of ethical science which we are about to fol-low out to its consequences, without any appeal to these. And it will be desirable now to do this. Starting afresh, then, from the admitted truth, that human happiness is the Divine will, let us look at the means appointed for the obtainment of that happi-ness and observe what conditions they presuppose.

Happiness is a certain state of consciousness. That state must be produced by the action upon consciousness of certain modi-fying influences—by certain affections of it. All affections of consciousness we term sensations. Among the rest, those affections of it which constitute happiness must be sensations.

But how do we receive sensations? Through what are called faculties. It is certain that a man cannot see without eyes. Equally certain is it that he can experience no impression of any kind unless he is endowed with some power fitted to take in that impression; that is, a faculty. All the mental states which he calls feelings and ideas are affections of his consciousness re-ceived through the faculties—sensations given to it by them.

There next comes the question: Under what circumstances do the faculties yield those sensations of which happiness con-sists? The reply is: When they are exercised. It is from the ac-tivity of one or more of them that all gratification arises. To the healthful performance of each function of mind or body at-taches a pleasurable feeling. And this pleasurable feeling is obtainable only by the performance of the function; that is, by the exercise of the correlative faculty. Every faculty in turn affords its special emotion, and the sum of these constitutes happiness.

Or the matter may be briefly put thus: A desire is the need for some species of sensation. A sensation is producible only by the exercise of a faculty. Hence no desire can be satisfied except through the exercise of a faculty. But happiness consists in the due satisfaction of all the desires; that is, happiness consists in the due exercise of all the faculties.

**2.** NOW IF GOD WILLS MAN'S HAPPINESS, AND MAN'S HAPPINESS can be obtained only by the exercise of his faculties, then God wills that man should exercise his faculties; that is, it is man's duty to exercise his faculties, for duty means fulfillment of the Divine will. That it is man's duty to exercise his faculties is further proved by the fact that what we call *punishment* attaches to the neglect of that exercise. Not only is the normal activity of each faculty productive of pleasure, but the continued suspension of that activity is productive of pain. As the stomach hungers to digest food, so does every bodily and mental agent hunger to perform its appointed action. And as the refusal to satisfy the cravings of the digestive faculty is productive of suffering, so is the refusal to satisfy the cravings of any other faculty also productive of suffering, to an extent proportionate to the importance of that faculty. But as God wills man's happiness, that line of conduct which produces unhappiness is contrary to his will. Therefore, the non-exercise of the faculties is contrary to his will. Either way, then, we find that the exercise of the faculties is God's will and man's duty.

But the fulfillment of this duty necessarily presupposes freedom of action. Man cannot exercise his faculties without certain scope. He must have liberty to go and to come, to see, to feel, to speak, to work; to get food, raiment, shelter, and to provide for each and all of the needs of his nature. He must be free to do everything which is directly or indirectly requisite for the due satisfaction of every mental and bodily want. Without this he cannot fulfill his duty or God's will. But if he cannot fulfill God's will without it, then God commands him to take it. He has Divine authority, therefore, for claiming this freedom of action. God intended him to have it; that is, he has a *right* to it.

From this conclusion there seems no possibility of escape. Let us repeat the steps by which we arrive at it. God wills man's happiness. Man's happiness can be produced only by the exercise of his faculties. Then God wills that he should exercise his faculties. But to exercise his faculties he must have liberty to do all that his faculties naturally impel him to do. Then God intends he should have that liberty. Therefore, he has a *right* to that liberty.

**3.** THIS, HOWEVER, IS NOT THE RIGHT OF ONE BUT OF ALL. ALL ARE endowed with faculties. All are bound to fulfill the Divine will by exercising them. All, therefore, must be free to do those things in which the exercise of them consists. That is, all must have rights to liberty of action.

And hence there necessarily arises a limitation. For if men have like claims to that freedom which is needful for the exercise of their faculties, then must the freedom of each be bounded by the similar freedom of all. When, in the pursuit of their respective ends, two individuals clash, the movements of the one remain free only in so far as they do not interfere with the like movements of the other. This sphere of existence into which we are thrown not affording room for the unrestrained activity of all, and yet all possessing in virtue of their constitutions similar claims to such unrestrained activity, there is no course but to apportion out the unavoidable restraint equally. Wherefore we arrive at the general proposition that every man may claim the fullest liberty to exercise his faculties compatible with the possession of like liberty by every other man.

**4.** UPON A PARTIAL CONSIDERATION THIS STATEMENT OF THE LAW will perhaps seem open to criticism. It may be thought better to limit the right of each to exercise his faculties by the proviso that he shall not *hurt* anyone else—shall not inflict *pain* on anyone else. But although at first sight satisfactory, this expression of the law allows of erroneous deductions. It is true that men, answering to those conditions of greatest happiness set forth in

the foregoing chapter, cannot exercise their faculties to the
aggrieving of one another. It is not, however, that each avoids
giving pain by refraining from the full exercise of his faculties;
but it is that the faculties of each are such that the full exercise
of them offends no one. And herein lies the difference. The
giving of any pain may have two causes. Either the abnormally
constituted man may do something displeasing to the normal
feelings of his neighbors, in which case he acts wrongly; or the
behavior of the normally constituted man may irritate the abnormal feelings of his neighbors, in which case it is not his behavior that is wrong but their characters that are so. Under such
circumstances the due exercise of his faculties is right, although
it gives pain; and the remedy for the evil lies in the modification
of those abnormal feelings to which pain is given.

To elucidate this distinction let us take a few illustrations. An
honest man discovers some friend, of whom he had previously
thought well, to be a rogue. He has certain high instincts to
which roguery is repugnant; and allowing free play to these, he
drops the acquaintanceship of this unworthy one. Now, though
in doing so he gives pain, it does not follow that he transgresses
the law. The evil must be ascribed, not to an undue exercise of
faculties by him, but to the immorality of the man who suffers.
Again, a Protestant in a Roman Catholic country refuses to uncover his head on the passing of the host. In so obeying the
promptings of certain sentiments, he annoys the spectators and,
were the above modified expression of the law correct, would be
blamable. The fault, however, is not with him but with those
who are offended. It is not that he is culpable in thus testifying
to his belief, but it is that they ought not to have so tyrannical
an intolerance of other opinions than their own. Or again, a
son, to the great displeasure of his father and family, marries
one who, though in all respects admirable, is dowerless. In thus
obeying the dictates of his nature he may entail considerable
distress of mind upon his relatives, but it does not follow that
his conduct is bad; it follows rather that the feelings which his
conduct has wounded are bad.

Hence we see that, in hourly occurring cases like these, to
limit the exercise of faculties by the necessity of not giving pain

to others would be to stop the proper exercise of faculties in some persons for the purpose of allowing the improper exercise of faculties in the rest. Moreover, the observance of such a rule does not, as at first sight appears, prevent pain. For though he who is restrained by it avoids inflicting suffering on his fellows, he does so at the expense of suffering to himself. The evil must be borne by someone, and the question is by whom? Shall the Protestant, by showing reverence for what he does not revere, tell a virtual lie, and thus do violence to his conscientious feeling that he may avoid vexing the intolerant spirit of his Catholic neighbors? Or shall he give the rein to his own healthy sincerity and independence, and offend their unhealthy bigotry? Shall the honest man repress those sentiments that make him honest, lest the exhibition of them should give pain to a rogue? Or shall he respect his own nobler feelings and hurt the other's baser ones? Between these alternatives no one can well pause. And here indeed we get down to the root of the matter. For be it remembered, the universal law of life is that the exercise or gratification of faculties strengthens them; while, on the contrary, the curbing or inflicting pain upon them entails a diminution of their power. And hence it follows that, when the action of a normal faculty is checked to prevent pain being given to the abnormal faculties of others, those abnormal faculties remain as active as they were, and the normal one becomes weaker or abnormal. Whereas under converse circumstances the normal one remains strong, and the abnormal ones are weakened or made more normal. In the one case the pain is detrimental, because it retards the approximation to that form of human nature under which the faculties of each may be fully exercised without displeasure to the like faculties of all. In the other case the pain is beneficial, because it aids the approximation to that form. Thus, that first expression of the law which arises immediately from the conditions of social existence turns out to be the true one: any such modification of it as the above necessitating conduct that is in many cases absolutely mischievous.

And yet, on the other hand, when we seek to express the law by saying that every man has full liberty to exercise his

faculties, provided always he does not trench upon the similar
liberty of any other, we commit ourselves to an imperfection
of an opposite character; and we find that there are many cases
in which the above modified expression answers better. Various
ways exist in which the faculties may be exercised to the aggrieving of other persons without the law of equal freedom being
overstepped. A man may behave unamiably, may use harsh
language or annoy by disgusting habits; and whoso thus offends
the normal feelings of his fellows manifestly diminishes happiness. If we say that everyone is free to exercise his faculties so
long only as he does not inflict pain upon anyone else, we forbid
all such conduct. Whereas if we simply limit the liberty of each
by the like liberty of all, we do not forbid it, seeing that he
who exercises his faculties in this way does not hinder others
from exercising theirs in the same way and to the same extent.
How, then, are we to escape from this difficulty? Neither statement of the law quite fulfills our requirement, and yet we must
choose one of them. Which must it be, and why?

It must be the original one, and for a very good reason.
Limiting the liberty of each by the like liberty of all excludes a
wide range of improper actions but does not exclude certain
other improper ones. Limiting the liberty of each by the necessity of not giving pain to the rest excludes the whole of these
improper actions but excludes along with them many others
that are proper. The one does not cut off enough; the other
cuts off too much. The one is negatively erroneous; the other
is positively so. Evidently, then, we must adopt the negatively erroneous one, seeing that its shortcomings may be made
good by a supplementary law. And here we find the need for
that distinction lately drawn between *justice* and *negative
beneficence*—a distinction which we habitually make in the
affairs of life. Justice imposes upon the exercise of faculties a
primary series of limitations, which is strictly true as far as it
goes. Negative beneficence imposes a secondary series. It is no
defect in the first of these that it does not include the last. The
two are, in the main, distinct; and, as we have just seen, the
attempt to unite them under one expression leads us into fatal
errors.

**5.** YET ANOTHER OBJECTION WILL PROBABLY BE STARTED. BY FULL liberty to exercise the faculties is meant full liberty to do all that the faculties prompt, or, in other words, to do all that the individual wills; and it may be said that if the individual is free to do all that he wills, provided he does not trespass upon certain specified claims of others, then he is free to do things that are injurious to himself—is free to get drunk or to commit suicide. To this it must be in the first place replied, as above, that while the law now laid down forbids a certain class of actions as immoral it does not recognize all kinds of immorality—that the restriction it puts on the free exercise of faculties, though the chief, is not the sole restriction and must be received without prejudice to further ones. Of the need for such further ones, the difficulty here raised furnishes a second instance.

Mark now, however, that these supplementary restrictions are of quite inferior authority to the original law. Instead of being, like it, capable of strictly scientific development, they (under existing circumstances) can be unfolded only into superior forms of expediency. The limit put to each man's freedom, by the like freedom of every other man, is a limit almost always possible of exact ascertainment; for let the condition of things be what it may, the respective amounts of freedom men assume can be compared and the equality or inequality of those amounts recognized. But when we set about drawing practical deductions from the propositions that a man is not at liberty to do things injurious to himself and that he is not at liberty (except in cases like those lately cited) to do what may give unhappiness to his neighbors, we find ourselves involved in complicated estimates of pleasures and pains, to the obvious peril of our conclusions. It is very true that to trace out the consequences a given act will entail upon oneself or another is incomparably less difficult than to determine the ultimate effects of some public measure upon a whole nation; and hence the being guided by expediency in private life is proportionably less dangerous. Yet it is also true that even here trustworthy inferences are attainable in but a minority of cases. In the first place, we frequently cannot say whether the bad results will exceed the good ones; and in the second place, we frequently cannot say whether the faculties on which suffering will be inflicted are in normal or abnormal states. For example, though it is very manifest that drunkenness is an injurious exercise of faculties, as being clearly productive of more pain than pleasure, it is by no means manifest how much work is proper for us and when work becomes detrimental; it is by no means manifest where lies the line between due and undue intellectual activity; it is by no means manifest what amount of advantage will justify a man in submitting to unsuitable climate and mode of life; and yet in each of these cases happiness is at stake, and the wrong course is wrong for the same reason that drunkenness is so. Even were it possible to say of each private action whether the resulting gratification did or did not preponderate over the resulting suffering, there would still present itself this second difficulty, that we cannot with certainty distinguish suffering that is detrimental from suffering that is beneficial. While we are as yet imperfectly adapted to our conditions, pain must inevitably arise from the repression of faculties that are too active and from the overtasking of those that are not equal to their duties; and, as being needful to the development of the ultimate man, such pain cannot be held damnatory of the actions causing it. Thus, referring again to the instances just cited, it is self-evident that the ability to work is needful for the production of the greatest happiness; yet is the acquirement of this ability by the uncivilized man so distressing that only the severest discipline will force him to it? That degree of intelligence which our existing mode of life necessitates cannot be arrived at without ages of wearisome application, and perhaps cannot get organized in the race without a partial and temporary sacrifice of bodily health. The realization of the Divine Idea implies the peopling of every habitable region; and this implies the adaptation of mankind to a variety of climates—an adaptation which cannot be undergone without great suffering. Here, then, are cases in which men's liberty must not be limited by the necessity of not injuring themselves, seeing that it cannot be so limited without a suspension of our approach to greatest happiness. Similarly we saw a while since (p. 70) that there are cases in which for the same reason men's liberty must not be limited by the necessity of not inflicting pain upon others. And the fact now to be noticed is that we possess no certain way of distinguishing the two groups of cases thus exemplified from those cases in which the doing what diminishes happiness, either in ourselves or others, is both immediately and ultimately detrimental, and therefore wrong. Not being able to define specifically the constitution of the ideal man, but being able to define it generically only—not being able to determine the ratios of the several faculties composing that constitution, but being able simply to lay down certain laws which their action must conform to—we are quite incompetent to say of every particular deed whether it is or is not accordant with that constitution. Or, putting the difficulty in its simplest form, we may say that as both of these supplementary limitations involve the term happiness, and as happiness is for the present capable only of a generic and not of a specific definition (p. 6), they do not admit of scientific development. Though abstractedly correct limitations, and limitations which the ideal man will strictly observe, they cannot be reduced to concrete forms until the ideal man exists.

**6.** AND NOW WE HAVE ARRIVED AT THE THRESHOLD OF AN IMportant truth touching this matter; the truth, namely, that only by a universal exercise of this alleged liberty of each, limited alone by the like liberty of all, can there ever arise a separation of those acts which, though incidentally and temporarily injurious to ourselves or others, are indirectly beneficial, from those acts which are necessarily and eternally injurious. For manifestly, that non-adaptation of faculties to their functions, from which springs every species of evil, must consist either in excess or defect. And manifestly, in the wide range of cases we are now treating of, there exists no mode but a tentative one of distinguishing that exercise of faculties which produces suffering because it oversteps the conditions of normal existence, from that other exercise of faculties which produces suffering because it falls short of those conditions. And manifestly, the due employment of this tentative mode requires that each man

shall have the greatest freedom compatible with the like freedom of all others. Or, turning the proposition the other
side up, we may say that while these secondary conditions of
greatest happiness are really fixed, yet the practical interpretation of them requiring a detailed knowledge of the ultimate
human constitution, bodily and mental, and such detailed
knowledge being unattainable, our course is to regard the law of
equal freedom as setting up the only recognizable limit to the
exercise of faculties, knowing that the other limits will inevitably make themselves felt and that in virtue of the law of
adaptation there must eventually arise a complete conformity to
them.

That, on this course being pursued, there will happen a
gradual cessation of the detrimentally painful actions, while
the beneficially painful ones will be continued until they have
ceased to be painful, may be made clear by a few illustrations.
Thus, the change from the impulsive nature of the savage to
that nature which enables the civilized man to sacrifice a
present gratification for a future greater one involves much
suffering; but the necessities of social life demanding such a
change, and continually visiting the lack of a self-restraining
power with severe punishment, ensure a constant though irksome endeavor on the part of all to acquire this power—an
endeavor that must surely though slowly succeed. Conversely,
the prevalence among men of a somewhat undue desire for food,
entailing as it perpetually does much bodily, and some mental,
affliction, is sure to be therefore accompanied by such attempts
at abstemiousness as must, by constantly curbing it, finally reduce this desire to a normal intensity.[1] And what so manifestly
happens in these simple cases with equal certainty happens in
those complex ones above exemplified, where the good and bad

---

[1]Why the appetite for food should now be greater than is proper seems at
first difficult to understand. On calling to mind, however, the conditions of
the aboriginal man, we shall find an explanation of this apparent anomaly
in the fact that the irregularity in his supplies of food necessitated an ability
to eat largely when food was attainable, and necessitated, therefore, a corresponding desire. Now that the supplies of food have become regular and no
contingent periods of long fasting have to be provided against, the desire is
in excess and has to be abated.

results are more nearly balanced: for although it may be impossible in such cases for the intellect to estimate the respective amounts of pleasure and pain consequent upon each alternative, yet will experience enable *the constitution itself* to do this, and will further cause it instinctively to shun that course which produces on the whole most suffering, or, in other words, most sins against the necessities of existence, and to choose that which least sins against them. Turning to those actions which put us in direct relationship to other men, it must in the same manner happen that such of them as give no necessary displeasure to anyone will be persevered in, and the faculties answering to them developed; while, on the contrary, actions necessarily displeasing to our neighbors must, by virtue of the disagreeable reaction which they commonly entail upon ourselves, be, in the average of cases, subject to a certain degree of repression—a repression that must ultimately tell upon the desires they spring from. And now observe what it is the special purpose of the present argument to show; namely, that in the course of this process there must be continually produced a different effect upon conduct which is necessarily painful to others from that produced upon conduct that is incidentally painful only. Conduct which hurts *necessary* feelings in others will, as just explained, inevitably undergo restraint and consequent diminution; conduct which hurts only their *incidental* feelings, as those of caste or prejudice, will not inevitably do so; but, if it springs from necessary feelings, will, on the contrary, be continued at the expense of these incidental feelings and to the final suppression of them. When men mutually behave in a way that offends some essential element in the nature of each, and all in turn have to bear the consequent suffering, there will arise a tendency to curb the desire that makes them so behave. When, instead of this, they keep hurting in each other those nonessential elements of character peculiar to a passing phase of things and are impelled to do this by impulses that are permanently requisite, then will these nonessential elements be extirpated. Thus, the existing confusion of necessary and conventional feelings, necessary and conventional circumstances, and feelings and circumstances that are partly necessary and partly conventional will eventually work itself clear. Conventional feelings will give way before necessary circumstances, and conventional circumstances before necessary feelings. And when, as a result of this process, complete adaptation between constitution and conditions has been arrived at, a complete classification of actions into essentially injurious and essentially beneficial will have been arrived at also.

If, then, we find that the one thing needful to produce ultimate subordination to these secondary limits of right conduct is that we should have the opportunity of freely coming in contact with them—should be allowed freely to expand our natures in all directions until the available space has been filled and the true bounds have made themselves felt—if a development of these secondary limits into practical codes of duty can only thus be accomplished, then does the supreme authority of our first law—the liberty of each limited alone by the like liberty of all—become still more manifest, seeing that that right to exercise the faculties which it asserts must precede the unfolding of this supplementary morality. Indeed, regarding it from this point of view, we may almost say that the first law is the sole law, for we find that of the several conditions to greatest happiness it is the only one at present capable of a systematic development, and we further find that conformity to it ensures ultimate conformity to the others.

**7.** NEVERTHELESS, IT MUST STILL BE ADMITTED THAT IN CASES where these secondary limitations to the exercise of faculties are undoubtedly transgressed, the full assertion of this law of equal freedom betrays us into an apparent dilemma. By drunkenness or by brutality of manner, our own happiness or the happiness of others is diminished, and that not in an incidental but in a necessary way. And if by affirming a man's liberty to do all that he wills so long as he respects the like liberty of every other we imply that he is at liberty to get drunk or to behave brutally, then we fall into the inconsistency of affirming that he is at liberty to do something essentially destructive of happiness.

Of this difficulty nothing can be said save that it seems in part due to the impossibility of making the perfect law recognize an imperfect state, and in part to that defect in our powers of expression elsewhere exemplified (p. 37). As matters stand, however, we must deal with it as best we may. There is clearly no alternative but to declare man's freedom to exercise his faculties, for without this freedom fulfillment of the Divine will is impossible. There is clearly no alternative but to declare the several limitations of that freedom needful for the achievement of greatest happiness. And there is clearly no alternative but to develop the first and chief of these limitations separately; seeing as we have done that a development of the others is at present impossible. Against the consequence of neglecting these secondary limitations, we must therefore guard ourselves as well as we can, supplying the place of scientific deductions from them by such inferences as observation and experience enable us to make.

**8.** FINALLY, HOWEVER, THERE IS SATISFACTION IN THE THOUGHT that no such imperfection as this can in the least vitiate any of the conclusions we are now about to draw. Liberty of action being the first essential to exercise of faculties, and therefore the first essential to happiness; and the liberty of each limited by the like liberty of all being the form which this first essential assumes when applied to many instead of to one, it follows that this liberty of each, limited by the like liberty of all, is the rule in conformity with which society must be organized. Freedom being the prerequisite to normal life in the individual, equal freedom becomes the prerequisite to normal life in society. And if this law of equal freedom is the primary law of right relationship between man and man, then no desire to get fulfilled a secondary law can warrant us in breaking it.

Now we shall find that in the unfolding of this primary limitation to the exercise of faculties into a series of practical regulations it is impossible to recognize any secondary limitations without committing a breach of the primary one. For in what must recognition of any secondary limitations consist? It must consist in the establishment in our social organization of certain further restrictions on the exercise of faculties besides those imposed by the law of equal freedom. And how are these further restrictions to be enforced? Manifestly, by men. Now the men who enforce them must necessarily assume in so doing a greater amount of freedom than those on whom they are enforced; that is to say, they must transgress the primary law to prevent others transgressing secondary ones.

Hence, in drawing from it deductions respecting the equitable constitution of society, we may safely assert in full this liberty of each limited alone by the like liberty of all—must so assert it. The neglect of other limitations will in no way affect the accuracy of our conclusions, so long as we confine ourselves to deducing from this fundamental law the just relationships of men to each other; whereas we cannot include these other limitations in our premises without vitiating those conclusions. We have no alternative therefore but, for the time being, to ignore such other limitations, leaving that partial interpretation of them which is at present possible to us for subsequent statement.

### NOTE TO CHAPTER IV

Does the reader understand the argument of the foregoing chapter to constitute "a negation of the natural supremacy of Reason over impulse"? Does any part of it imply that "in short, Reason is to abdicate in favor of Instinct"? He will perhaps be startled at so strange a question; but he will be more startled on learning that the outcome of the argument has been described in the words above quoted; and that, too, by a writer of repute— Mr. Sidgwick. See his *Methods of Ethics*, pp. 166–67.

In Mr. Sidgwick's statement are involved two grave misrepresentations. For one of them I can see but little excuse, and for the other I can find none. I will take first that which is least serious.

The title of the chapter is "Derivation of a First Principle." Both the positive and negative elements of this first principle are deduced from the laws of sentient life as carried on under social conditions. Primarily affirming the claims of the desires to satisfaction, the chapter secondarily affirms a fundamental limit to be recognized in the pursuit of satisfaction—a restraint upon impulse that is, on no plea whatever, public or private, to be relaxed.

In the argument defending this first principle, I have admitted "that the restriction it puts on the free exercise of faculties, though the chief, is not the sole restriction and must be received without prejudice to further ones." But I have asserted that "these supplementary restrictions are of quite inferior authority to the original law" (again *restrictions*, be it observed, and not, as anyone would suppose from the above description, relaxations). I have gone on to show that within the limits of equal freedom, which the original law formulates, the settling of these supplementary restrictions involves us in "complicated estimates of pleasures and pains." I have pointed out that while in certain cases (as drunkenness) calculation of results is easy, in other cases (as in amount of mental labor) ascertainment by reason of the line between due and undue is difficult. But I have contended that, kept within the rigid bounds set by the law of equal freedom, the individual may advantageously be left to restrain himself as best he can; because even where the guidance by conscious observation of results fails, it will be supplemented by the guidance of accumulated experiences not consciously reasoned about but unconsciously registered. I have argued that

> although it may be impossible in such cases for the intellect to estimate the respective amounts of pleasure and pain consequent upon each alternative, yet will experience enable *the constitution itself* to do this, and will further cause it instinctively to shun that course which produces on the whole most suffering.

The clear meaning of this statement is that the reason of the individual, where it fails to estimate rightly, will have its judgments supplemented by the intuitive judgments which perpetually repeated experiences generate. My assertion that the free play of the whole nature within the assigned limits may safely be left to mold the character by adaptation does not in the least imply that "reason is to abdicate in favor of instinct." The manifest aim of the chapter is to show what claims of the individual to act as he pleases are to be held valid against the claims of other individuals to control him; and to show that, subject to the fundamental limitation necessitated by their equal claims, other individuals may most advantageously leave him to self-guidance, rational and instinctive. The conclusion is that, left free within these bounds which are never to be violated, each citizen, suffering and benefiting by his own conduct, and checking himself by his own judgments (wise or foolish as the case may be), will become adapted to the requirements of social life more rapidly than when subject to additional restraints by the reason of Society, as embodied in law; since the reason of Society is inevitably vitiated by the ignorance and defective sentiment of the time, and its decisions, when legislatively established, are far less modifiable than are such decisions when left unestablished and subject to correction by individual experiences.

Thus much for the first of these misrepresentations. Strange as it is, it is less strange than the further one embodied with it. Mr. Sidgwick says:

> In short, it is so paradoxical to put forward, as the *dernier mot* of ethical philosophy, a negation of the natural supremacy of Reason over impulse; that I am perhaps wrong in understanding Mr. Spencer to take up so extreme a position. But I have examined the paradox carefully, because it only expresses, in an extreme form . . .

I do not doubt that Mr. Sidgwick's argument gains clearness by presenting this paradox, even in a hypothetically qualified way; but I question the propriety of gaining clearness by representing me as holding, or apparently holding, so foolish a doctrine. I have shown that his statement is unwarranted, even when considered in connection only with the subordinate argument above described. I have still to point out that it is diametrically opposed to the larger argument of which that forms a part. For the most conspicuous trait of the chapter quoted from is the endeavor to establish by reason a definite and absolute principle of restraint. And the aim of the work as a whole is to deduce by reason, from this fundamental principle reached by reason, a set of derivative restraints. Instead of being true that "the dernier mot of ethical philosophy" as uttered by me is "a negation of the natural supremacy of Reason over impulse," it is, contrariwise, true that Reason, asserting the law of equal freedom and drawing inferences from it, is placed as supreme over all impulse, egoistic or altruistic, prompting breach of that law. The entire motive of the work is that of establishing judgments rationally formed in place of unenlightened moral intuitions and vague estimations of results. For guidance by mere unaided sentiment it would substitute guidance by a definitely formulated fundamental principle to which that sentiment emphatically responds; and for guidance by the unscientific non-quantitative reasoning of mere empirical utilitarianism it would substitute guidance by scientific or quantitative reasoning—reasoning pervaded by that cardinal idea of equalness, which alone makes possible exact conclusions.

I feel it needful to rebut these misrepresentations because they are more injurious than they would be did they come from a critic of no weight. Mr. Sidgwick's work has throughout an appearance of care and candor and discrimination, such as will lead his readers to assume that his description of my view is correct; or, at any rate, that it cannot be so wide of the truth as I have shown it to be.

April, 1875.

P.S.—It seems well to say that were I now to rewrite this chapter the theological implications of the argument would be avoided. But exclusion of these would leave the ethical doctrine unshaken.

CHAPTER V

## Secondary Derivation of a First Principle

1. HAVING INQUIRED HOW THE DIVINE IDEA, GREATEST HAPPINESS, is to be realized—having found that it is to be realized through the exercise of faculties—and having found that, to fulfill its end, such exercise of faculties must be confined within certain limits, let us now pursue the investigation a step further and see whether there does not exist in man himself an impulse to claim that exercise and an impulse to respect those limits. Some such provisions are clearly needful for the completion of the creative scheme. It would be quite at variance with the general law of our structure that there should be nothing to restrain us from the undue exercise of faculties but abstract considerations like those set forth in the last chapter. As elsewhere pointed out

(p. 19), man is ruled by quite other instrumentalities than intellectual ones. The regulation of his conduct is not left to the accident of a philosophical inquiry. We may therefore expect to find some special agent by which the distinction between right and wrong exercise of faculties is recognized and responded to.

**2.** FROM WHAT HE HAS ALREADY GATHERED, THE READER WILL OF course infer that this agent is that Moral Sense, in whose existence we elsewhere saw good reason to believe. And possibly he will anticipate the further inference that this first and all-essential law, declaratory of the liberty of each limited only by the like liberty of all, is that fundamental truth of which the moral sense is to give an intuition and which the intellect is to develop into a scientific morality.

Of the correctness of this inference there are various proofs, upon an examination of which we must now enter. And first on the list stands the fact that, out of some source or other in men's minds, there keep continually coming utterances more or less completely expressive of this truth. Quite independently of any such analytical examinations as that just concluded, men perpetually exhibit a tendency to assert the equality of human rights. In all ages, but more especially in later ones, has this tendency been visible. In our own history we may detect signs of its presence as early as the time of Edward I, in whose writs of summons it was said to be "a most equitable rule, that what concerns all should be approved of by all." How our institutions have been influenced by it may be seen in the judicial principle that "all men are equal before the law." The doctrine that "all men are naturally equal" (of course only in so far as their claims are concerned), has not only been asserted by philanthropists like Granville Sharpe, but as Sir Robert Filmer, a once renowned champion of absolute monarchy, tells us, "Heyward, Blackwood, Barclay, and others that have bravely vindicated the rights of kings . . . with one consent admitted the natural liberty and equality of mankind." Again, we find the declaration of American Independence affirming that "all men have equal rights to life, liberty, and the pursuit of happiness"; and the similar assertion that "every man has an equal right with every other man to a voice in the making of the laws which all are required to obey" was the maxim of the Complete Suffrage movement. In his essay on Civil Government, Locke, too, expresses the opinion that there is "nothing more evident than that creatures of the same species and rank, promiscuously born to the same advantages of nature, and the use of the same faculties, should also be equal one among another without subordination or subjection." And those who wish for more authorities who have expressed the same conviction may add the names of Judge Blackstone and "the judicious Hooker."

The sayings and doings of daily life continually imply some intuitive belief of this kind. We take for granted its universality when we appeal to men's sense of justice. In moments of irritation it shows itself in such expressions as: "How would you like it?" "What is that to you?" "I've as good a right as you," etc. Our praises of liberty are prevaded by it, and it gives bitterness to the invectives with which we assail the oppressors of mankind. Nay, indeed, so spontaneous is this faith in the equality of human rights that our very language embodies it. Equity and equal are from the same root; and equity literally means equalness.

It is manifest, moreover, that some such faith is continually increasing in strength. Rightly understood, the advance from a savage to a cultivated state is the advance of its dominion. It is by their greater harmony with it that the laws, opinions, and usages of a civilized society are chiefly distinguished from those of a barbarous one. How instrumental it has been in modifying the events of the past was elsewhere hinted (p. 23). If we call to mind the political agitations that have run a successful course within these few years, and consider likewise those that are going on around us, we shall find them nearly all strongly tinctured by it. Nor can we contemplate the late European revolutions and read the preambles to the new constitutions that have sprung out of them without perceiving that a conviction of the equality of human rights is now stronger and more general than ever.

Not without meaning is the continued life and growth of this conviction. He must indeed have a strange way of interpreting social phenomena who can believe that the reappearance of it, with ever-increasing frequency, in laws, books, agitations, revolutions, means nothing. If we analyze them, we shall find all beliefs to be in some way dependent upon mental conformation—temporary ones upon temporary characteristics of our nature, permanent ones upon its permanent characteristics. And when we find that a belief like this in the equal freedom of all men is not only permanent, but daily gaining ground, we have good reason to conclude that it corresponds to some essential element of our moral constitution: more especially since we find that its existence is in harmony with that chief prerequisite to greatest happiness lately dwelt upon, and that its growth is in harmony with that law of adaptation by which this greatest happiness is being wrought out.

Such, at least, is the hypothesis here adopted. From the above accumulation of evidence it is inferred that there exists in man what may be termed an *instinct of personal rights*—a feeling that leads him to claim as great a share of natural privilege as is claimed by others—a feeling that leads him to repel anything like an encroachment upon what he thinks his sphere of original freedom. By virtue of this impulse, individuals, as units of the social mass, tend to assume like relationships with the atoms of matter, surrounded as these are by their respective atmospheres of repulsion as well as of attraction. And perhaps social stability may ultimately be seen to depend upon the due balance of these forces.

**3.** THERE EXISTS, HOWEVER, A DOMINANT SECT OF SO-CALLED philosophical politicians who treat with contempt this belief that men have any claims antecedent to those endorsed by governments. As disciples of Bentham, consistency requires them to do this. Accordingly, although it does violence to their secret perceptions, they boldly deny the existence of "rights" entirely. They nevertheless perpetually betray a belief in the doctrines which they professedly reject. They inadvertently talk about justice, especially when it concerns themselves, in much the same style as their opponents. They draw the same distinction between law and equity that other people do. They applaud fairness and honor, quite as if they thought them something more than mere words. And when robbed, or assaulted, or wrongly imprisoned, they exhibit the same indignation, the same determination to oppose the aggressor, utter the same denunciations of tyranny and the same loud demands for redress as the sternest assertors of the rights of man. By way of explaining such inconsistencies, it is indeed alleged that the feeling thus manifested is nothing but the result of a gradually acquired conviction that benefits flow from some kinds of actions and evils from other kinds; and it is said that the sympathies and antipathies respectively contracted toward these exhibit themselves as a love of justice and a hatred of injustice. To which supposition it was by implication elsewhere replied that it would be equally wise to conclude that hunger springs from a conviction of the benefit of eating, or that love of offspring is the result of a wish to maintain the species!

But it is amusing when, after all, it turns out that the ground on which these philosophers have taken their stand, and from which with such self-complacency they shower their sarcasms, is nothing but an adversary's mine, destined to blow the vast fabric of conclusions they have based on it into nonentity. This so solid-looking principle of "the greatest happiness to the greatest number" needs but to have a light brought near it, and lo! it explodes into the astounding assertion that all men have equal rights to happiness (p. 22)—an assertion far more sweeping and revolutionary than any of those which are assailed with so much scorn.[1]

When we see, then, that an instinct of personal rights manifests itself unceasingly in opinions and institutions; when further we find that the attempt to trace the monitions of this instinct to experience betrays us into an absurdity; and when, lastly, the dogma of those who most sturdily deny that there is such an instinct proves to be only another emanation from it, we find ourselves in possession of the strongest possible evidence

[1] We do not here debate the claims of this maxim. It is sufficient for present purposes to remark that were it true it would be utterly useless as a first principle; both from the impossibility of determining specifically what happiness is, and from the want of a measure by which equitably to mete it out, could we define it.

of its existence—the testimony of all parties. We are therefore justified in considering that existence as sufficiently proved.

**4.** BUT WHY, IT MAY BE ASKED, SHOULD THERE NEED BE ANY SENTI-ment leading men to claim the liberty of action requisite for the due exercise of faculties, and prompting them to resist encroachments upon that liberty? Will not the several faculties themselves do this, by virtue of their desires for activity, which cannot otherwise be gratified? Surely there is no necessity for a special impulse to make a man do that which all his impulses conjointly tend to make him do.

This is not so serious an objection as it appears to be. For although were there no such sentiment as this supposed one each faculty in turn might impel its possessor to oppose a diminution of its own sphere of action, yet during the dormancy of that faculty there would be nothing to prevent the freedom requisite for its future exercise from being infringed upon. It may, perhaps, be rejoined that the mere consciousness that there must again occur occasions for the use of such freedom will constitute a sufficient incentive to defend it. But plausible as this supposition looks, it does not tally with facts. We do not find on inquiry that each faculty has a special foresight—takes thought for its gratifications to come; we find, on the contrary, that to provide for the future gratification of the faculties at large is the office of faculties appointed solely for that purpose. Thus, referring once more by way of illustration to the acquisitive instinct, we see that when this is wanting, the desires for food, for clothing, for shelter, together with those many other desires which property ministers to, do not of themselves prompt that accumulation of property on which the continuance of their satisfaction depends. Each of them, when active, impels the individual to take means for its present fulfillment, but does not prompt him to lay by the means for its future fulfillment. To so prompt him there needs a certain amount of this acquisitive instinct, which, in pursuing its own gratification, incidentally secures to other instincts the means of their gratification. Similarly, then, with liberty of action. It is argued that as each faculty does not look after its own particular fund of necessaries, so neither does it look after its own particular sphere of activity, and that as there is a special faculty to which the providing of a general fund of necessaries is consigned, so likewise is there a special faculty to which the maintenance of a general sphere of activity is consigned. Or perhaps we may most clearly express the relationship in which these two faculties stand to the rest by saying that, while it is the function of the one to accumulate the matter on which the faculties at large are to be exercised, it is the function of the other to preserve the freedom of motion by which that matter is both obtained and made use of.

**5.** SEEING, HOWEVER, THAT THIS INSTINCT OF PERSONAL RIGHTS IS a purely selfish instinct, leading each man to assert and defend his own liberty of action, there remains the question, Whence comes our perception of the rights of others?

The way to a solution of this difficulty has been opened by Adam Smith in his *Theory of Moral Sentiments*. It is the aim of that work to show that the proper regulation of our conduct to one another is secured by means of a faculty whose function it is to excite in each being the emotions displayed by surrounding ones—a faculty which awakens a like state of sentiment, or, as he terms it, "a fellow feeling with the passions of others"—the faculty, in short, which we commonly call Sympathy. As illustrations of the mode in which this agent acts, he quotes cases like these:

"Persons of delicate fibres, and weak constitution of body, complain that in looking on the sores and ulcers which are exposed by beggars in the streets, they are apt to feel an itching or uneasy sensation in the corresponding part of their own bodies." "Men of most robust make observe, that in looking upon sore eyes they often feel a very sensible soreness in their own." "Our joy for the deliverance of those heroes of tragedy or romance who interest us, is as sincere as our grief for their distress, and our fellow-feeling for their misery, is not more real than that for their happiness." "We blush for the impudence and rudeness of another, though he himself appears to have no sense of the impropriety of his behaviour."

To these facts cited by Adam Smith may be added many

others of like import; such as that people—women especially—
start or shriek on seeing an accident occur to others; that un-
practiced assistants at surgical operations often faint; that out of
the soldiers drawn up to witness a flogging, usually several drop
down in the ranks; that a boy has been known to die on witnessing an execution. We have all experienced the uncomfortable
feeling of shame produced in us by the blunders and confusion
of a nervous speaker; and most likely everyone has sometime or
other been put into a horrible tremor on seeing another at the
edge of a precipice. The converse action of the faculty is equally
observable. Thus, we find ourselves unable to avoid joining in
the merriment of our friends, while unaware of its cause; and
children, much to their annoyance, are often forced to laugh in
the midst of their tears by witnessing the laughter of those
around them. These and many like evidences prove that, as
Burke says, "sympathy must be considered as a sort of substitution by which we are put into the place of another man, and
affected in many respects as he is affected."

In tracing our benevolent actions to the influence of such a
faculty, in concluding that we are led to relieve the miseries of
others from a desire to rid ourselves of the pain given by the
sight of misery, and to make others happy because we participate in their happiness, Adam Smith puts forth what seems to
be a quite satisfactory theory. But he has overlooked one of its
most important applications. Not recognizing any such impulse
as that which urges men to maintain their claims, he did not see
that their respect for the claims of others may be explained in the
same way. He did not perceive that the sentiment of justice is
nothing but a sympathetic affection of the instinct of personal
rights—a sort of reflex function of it. Such, however, must be
the case, if that instinct exists, and if this hypothesis of Adam
Smith's be true. Here lies the explanation of those qualms of
conscience, as we call them, felt by men who have committed
dishonest actions. It is through this instrumentality that we
receive satisfaction on paying another what is due to him. And
with these two faculties, also, originate that indignation which
narratives of political oppression excite in us and that gnashing
of the teeth with which we read of the slave dealer's barbarities.

It was elsewhere hinted (p. 64) that though we must keep up the distinction between them it is nevertheless true that *justice* and *beneficence* have a common root, and the reader will now at once perceive that the common root is—Sympathy. All the actions properly classified under the one, and which we describe as fair, equitable, upright, spring from the sympathetic excitement of the instinct of personal rights; while those usually grouped under the other, as mercy, charity, good nature, generosity, amiability, considerateness, are due to the action of Sympathy upon one or more of the other feelings.

**6.** IN SUPPORT OF THE FOREGOING THEORY MUCH DETAILED EVIdence can be adduced. If it be true that men's perceptions of justice are generated in the way alleged, it will follow that, other things equal, those who have the strongest sense of their own rights will have the strongest sense of the rights of their neighbors. And, by observing whether this is the case or not, we may put the theory to the proof. Let us do this.

The first illustration that suggests itself is afforded by the Society of Friends. Ever since they appeared in the days of Charles I, the members of that body have been remarkable for their determined assertion of personal liberty. They have shown it in their continued resistance to ecclesiastical power; in the obstinacy with which they successfully defied persecution; in their still-continued refusal to pay church rates; and even in their creed, which does not permit a priesthood. Observe, now, how the sentiment which these peculiarities imply has manifested itself sympathetically. Penn and his followers were the only emigrants of their age who made any acknowledgment to the aborigines for the land they colonized. Of this same sect were the philanthropists who commenced the agitation for abolishing the slave trade, and who were most energetic in carrying it on. Among lunatic asylums, the York Retreat was one of the first, if not the first, in which a non-coercive treatment of the insane was adopted. They were Quakers, too, who years ago began publicly to exclaim against the injustice as well as the cruelty of war. And, while it may be true that in business they are firm in the assertion of their claims, it is not less true that on the whole they are remarkable for honest dealing.

The English national character, as contrasted with that of other races, will supply a further illustration. We are universally distinguished for our jealous love of freedom—for the firm maintenance of our rights. At the same time we are not less distinguished for the greater equity of our general conduct. Although our behavior to the natives of lands on which we have settled has been anything but praiseworthy, it has never been so abominable as that of the Spaniards and others. According to all accounts, English merchants are noted everywhere for good faith and straightforwardness. Even among the most brutal of our population, even in the prize ring itself, there is shown in that maxim which forbids the striking of a man when down a greater sense of what is fair than the people of other countries show. And during these latter times, in which the popular demand for equal political rights has been so loud and so increasing, we have, as a nation, proved our greater regard for the rights of others by an attempt to put down slavery all over the world.

Conversely, we find that those who have not a strong sense of what is just to themselves are likewise deficient in a sense of what is just to their fellow men. This has long been a common remark. As one of our living writers puts it, the tyrant is nothing but a slave turned inside out. In earlier days, when feudal lords were vassals to the king, they were also despots to their retainers. In our own time, the Russian noble is alike a serf to his autocrat, and an autocrat to his serf. It is remarked even by schoolboys that the bully is the most ready of all to knock under to a bigger bully. We constantly observe that those who fawn upon the great are overbearing to their inferiors. That "emancipated slaves exceed all other owners (of slaves) in cruelty and oppression"[2] is a truth established on numerous authorities. And that where opportunity offers the submissive nature becomes a tyrannical one is further illustrated by the fact that the Negroes are frequently caught and sold by their own kings.

Thus we find the proposed theory to be supported both by direct and converse evidence. One qualification must be made, however. There is no necessary connection between a sense of

[2]*Four Years in the Pacific*, by Lt. Walpole.

what is due to self and a sense of what is due to others. Sympathy and instinct of rights do not always coexist in equal strength any more than other faculties do. Either of them may be present in normal amount, while the other is almost wanting. And, if devoid of sympathy, it is possible for a man who has a sufficient impulse to assert his own claims, to show no corresponding respect for the claims of his fellows. The instinct of rights, being of itself entirely selfish, merely impels its possessor to maintain his own privileges. Only by the sympathetic excitement of it is a desire to behave equitably to others awakened; and when sympathy is absent such a desire is impossible. Nevertheless, this does not affect the general proposition that, where there exists the usual amount of sympathy, respect for the rights of others will be great or small, according as the amount of the instinct of personal rights is great or small. And thus in the average of cases we may safely conclude that a man's sense of justice to himself and his sense of justice to his neighbors bear a constant ratio to each other.

**7.** FURTHER PROOF THAT THERE EXISTS THE MENTAL ARRANGEMENT here described may be found in the fact that some of the peculiar moral notions traceable to it are perfectly in harmony with certain of the abstract conclusions arrived at in the preceding chapter. We find in ourselves a conviction, for which we can give no satisfactory reason, that we are free, if we please, to do particular things which it is yet blamable to do. Though it may greatly diminish his happiness, a man feels that he has a *right*, if he likes, to cut off a limb or to destroy his property. While we condemn the want of consideration he shows toward some miserable debtor, we yet admit that the hard creditor is, in *strict justice*, entitled to the uttermost farthing. Notwithstanding our disgust at the selfishness of one who refuses to afford some friendly accommodation, we cannot deny that he is quite at *liberty* so to refuse. Now these perceptions, which, if the hypothesis be true, are referable to the instinct of personal rights acting in the one case directly and in the other cases sympathetically, quite accord with foregoing inferences. We found that the law of equal freedom was the fundamental law. We found (p. 75) that no other limitations of activity could be as authoritative as that which it sets up. And we found further (p. 79) that in this, our state of adaptation, it would be wrong to establish any fixed boundary to the liberty of each, save the similar liberty of others. Such a correspondence between our instinctive beliefs and the conclusions previously arrived at lends additional probability to the hypothesis here advanced.

**8.** THAT THERE EXISTS IN US A MENTAL MECHANISM BY WHICH the essential prerequisite to greatest happiness is recognized and enforced seems therefore abundantly manifest. We find the general principles of our structure to imply some such provision. In that Moral Sense, of whose existence we elsewhere saw the probability, we have an agent apparently answering to the requirement; and in this first condition to greatest happiness, we discover the axiom which the Moral Sense was to respond to. That man does possess a feeling which responds to this axiom is evidenced by the more or less complete expression spontaneously given to it in political dogmas, in laws, and in the sayings of daily life; further proof of its existence being found in the fact that those who nominally repudiate the belief it gives utterance to themselves profess that belief in a disguised and incorrect form. By an analogy drawn from the impulse to accumulate, we are shown that an impulse to maintain liberty of action is most likely essential to the completeness of the human constitution. How this impulse to maintain liberty of action can generate regard for the liberty of action of others is explicable by an extension of Adam Smith's doctrine of Sympathy; and that our sentiment of justice is really due to a sympathetic excitement of such impulse numerous facts conspire to prove. Lastly, we find that the convictions originated in us after the manner here supposed correspond with the results of abstract reasoning, not only as to the possession by each of a right to exercise his faculties, and as to a consequent limit of that right, but as to the peculiar sacredness of that right and this limit.

## CHAPTER VI

## First Principle

**1.** THUS ARE WE BROUGHT BY SEVERAL ROUTES TO THE SAME CON-
clusion. Whether we reason our way from those fixed conditions
under which only the Divine Idea—greatest happiness—can be
realized; whether we draw our inferences from man's constitution, considering him as a congeries of faculties; or whether we
listen to the monitions of a certain mental agency which seems
to have the function of guiding us in this matter, we are alike
taught as the law of right social relationships that—*Every man
has freedom to do all that he wills, provided he infringes not the
equal freedom of any other man.* Though further qualifications
of the liberty of action thus asserted may be necessary, yet we
have seen (p. 79) that in the just regulation of a community
no further qualifications of it can be recognized. Such further
qualifications must ever remain for private and individual application. We must therefore adopt this law of equal freedom in its
entirety as the law on which a correct system of equity is to be
based.

**2.** SOME WILL PERHAPS OBJECT TO THIS FIRST PRINCIPLE, THAT,
being in the nature of an axiomatic truth, standing toward the
inferences to be drawn from it in the position of one, it ought to
be recognizable by all; which it is not.

Respecting the fact thus alleged, that there have been, and
are, men impervious to this first principle, there can be no question. Probably it would have been dissented from by Aristotle,
who considered it a "self-evident maxim that nature intended
barbarians to be slaves." Cardinal Julian, who "abhorred the
impiety of keeping faith with infidels," might possibly have disputed it. It is a doctrine which would scarcely have suited the
abbot Guilbert, who, in his sermons, called the free cities of
France "those execrable communities, where serfs, against law

and justice, withdraw themselves from the power of their lords."
And perhaps the Highlanders, who in 1748 were reluctant to
receive their freedom on the abolition of the heritable jurisdic-
tions, would not have admitted it. But the confession that the
truth of this first principle is not self-evident to all by no means
invalidates it. The Bushman can count as high as only three; yet
arithmetic is a fact: and we have got a Calculus of Functions by
the aid of which we find new planets. As, then, the disability of
the savage to perceive the elementary truths of number is no
argument against their existence, and no obstacle to their discovery and development, so the circumstance that some do not
see the law of equal freedom to be an elementary truth of ethics
does not prevent its being one.

So far indeed is this difference in men's moral perceptions
from being a difficulty in our way that it serves to illustrate a
doctrine already set forth. As explained in Chapter II, man's
original circumstances "required that he should sacrifice the welfare of other beings to his own"; whereas his present circumstances require that "each individual shall have such desires only
as may be fully satisfied without trenching upon the ability of
other individuals to obtain like satisfaction." And it was pointed
out that, in virtue of the law of adaptation, the human constitution is changing from the form that fitted it to the first set of
conditions to a form fitting it for the last. Now it is by the
growth of those two faculties which together originate what we
term a Moral Sense that fitness for these last conditions is
secured. In proportion to the strengths of sympathy and the
instinct of personal rights will be the impulse to conform to the
law of equal freedom. And in the mode elsewhere shown (p.
25), the impulse to conform to this law will generate a correlative belief in it. Only, therefore, after the process of adaptation
has made considerable advance can there arise either subordination to this law or a perception of its truth. And hence any
general recognition of it during the earlier stages of social development must not be looked for.

**3.** TO THE DIRECT EVIDENCE THAT HAS BEEN ACCUMULATED IN
proof of our first principle may now, however, be added abun-

dant indirect evidence furnished by the absurdities into which a denial of it betrays us. He who asserts that the law of equal freedom is not true—that is, he who asserts that men have not equal rights—has two alternatives. He may either say that men have no rights at all, or that they have unequal rights. Let us examine these positions.

Foremost of those who deny rights altogether stands that same Sir Robert Filmer already named, with his dogma that "men are not naturally free." Starting thus, he readily finds his way to the conclusion that the only proper form of government is an absolute monarchy. For if men are not naturally free—that is, if men have naturally no rights—then he only has rights to whom they are specially given by God. From which inference to "the divine right of kings" is an easy step. It has become very manifest in later times, however, that this divine right of kings means the divine right of anyone who can get uppermost. For since, according to its assertors, no man can be supposed to occupy the position of supreme ruler in opposition to the will of the Deity, it follows that whoever attains to that position, whether by fair means or by foul, be he legitimate or be he usurper, has Divine authority on his side. So that to say "men are not naturally free" is to say that though men have no rights, yet whoever can get power to coerce the rest has a right to do so!

**4.** BUT THIS DOCTRINE BETRAYS ITS SUPPORTERS INTO A STILL more serious dilemma. On referring back to Chapter IV, we shall find that the denial of rights amounts to a libel on the Deity. For, as we there saw, that which a man has a right to is that which God intended for him. And to say that man has no right to freedom of action is to say that God did not mean him to have it. Without freedom of action, however, man cannot fulfill his desires. Then God willed that he should not fulfill them. But the non-fulfillment of the desires produces misery. Therefore, God intended that he should be miserable. By which absurdity we may safely consider the position disproved.

**5.** FOR ESPOUSING THE OTHER ALTERNATIVE—NAMELY, THAT men's rights are unequal—no conceivable motive can be assigned but a desire to ensure the supremacy of the best. There are not a few good sort of people who commonly reply to strictures upon social inequalities by quoting that couplet, which, beginning with the postulate, "Order is heaven's first law," ends with the inference, "Some are, and must be, greater than the rest." And on this maxim, with ludicrous inconsistency, they found a defense of conventional distinctions. Not daring to trust "heaven's first law" to itself, they wish to help it by artificial classification. They fear that the desired "order" will not be maintained unless it is looked after; and so these "greater than the rest" are picked out by official divination, ranged in tiers, and ticketed with their respective values.

These people, and others akin to them, who hold that rights are unequal, belong to that large class who believe in nothing but externals, who can recognize no forces but those of prescription —votes, authority, rank, and the like—who "adore an institution, and do not see that it is founded on a thought." A modicum of penetration, however, would show them that the great need none of this patronage at their hands. Real superiority will assert itself without factitious aid. Do away with disturbing arrangements, and just in proportion to the force resident in each will be the influence each exercises upon the rest. Allow things to take their natural course, and if a man have in him that which transcends the common, it must eventually draw to itself respect and obedience.

**6.** BUT EVEN WERE IT ADMITTED THAT, TO ENSURE SUPREMACY OF the best, liberty of action should be apportioned out to men in the ratio of their merits, the maintainers of unequal rights would be none the forwarder; for there remains the question, How are relative merits to be determined? Where are the standards by which we may test the respective values of different kinds and degrees of ability? We cannot appeal to public opinion, for it is not uniform. And were it uniform, there is no reason to think that it would be correct. On the contrary, if anything is to gathered from surrounding facts, very erroneous estimates would be formed of it. Can confidence be placed in the judgments of men who subscribe Hudson testimonials and yet leave the original projector of railways to die in poverty? Are those fit to decide upon comparative greatness who ornament their drawing-room tables with a copy of Burke's Peerage; who read though the lists of court presentations and gossip about the movements of the *haut ton*—people who would trace back their lineage to some bandit baron, some Front-de-boeuf, rather than to a Watt or an Arkwright? Is any dependence to be placed on the decision of an authority which has erected half a dozen public monuments to its Wellington and none to its Shakespeare, its Newton, or its Bacon—an authority that awards to the door-keeper of its House of Commons £74 a year more than to its astronomer royal? According to Johnson, "the chief glory of every people arises from its authors," yet our literary men are less honored than people of title; the writers of our leading journals are unknown; and we see much more respect shown to a Rothschild or a Baring than to our Faradays and our Owens.

If, then, public opinion is so fallible a test of relative merits, where shall a trustworthy test be found? Manifestly, if the freedom to which each is entitled varies with his worth, some satisfactory mode of estimating worth must be discovered before any settlement of men's right relationships can become possible. Who now will point out such a mode?

**7.** EVEN WERE A STILL FURTHER ADMISSION MADE—EVEN WERE we to assume that men's respective claims could be fairly rated —it would still be impossible to reduce the theory of unequal rights to practice. We should yet have to find a rule by which to allot these different shares of privilege. Where is the scale that would enable us to mark off the portion proper for each individual? What unit of measure must be used for this kind of division? Supposing a shopkeeper's rights to be symbolized by ten and a fraction, what number will represent those of a doctor? What multiple are the liberties of a banker, of those of a seamstress? Given two artists, one half as clever again as the other, it is required to find the limits within which each may exercise his faculties. As the greatness of a prime minister is to that of a plowboy, so is full freedom of action to the desired answer. Here are a few out of numberless like questions. When a method for

their solution has been found, it will be time enough to reconsider the theory of unequal rights.

**8.** THUS TO THE SEVERAL POSITIVE REASONS FOR AFFIRMING THAT
every man has freedom to do all that he wills, provided he infringes not the equal freedom of any other man, we must now
add the foregoing negative ones. Neither of the alternatives, to
which the rejection of this first principle leaves us, is acceptable.
The doctrine that men have naturally no rights leads to the
awkward inferences that might makes right and that the Deity is
a malevolent being. While to say that men have unequal rights
is to assume two impossibilities; namely, that we are able to
determine the ratios of men's merits; and, having done this, to
assign to each his due proportion of privilege.

CHAPTER VII

_____

## *Application of this First Principle*

**1.** THE PROCESS BY WHICH WE MAY DEVELOP THIS FIRST PRINCIPLE
into a system of equity is sufficiently obvious. We have just to
distinguish the actions that are included under its permit from
those which are excluded by it—to find what lies inside the
sphere appointed for each individual and what outside. Our aim
must be to discover how far the territory of may extends and
where it borders upon that of may not. We shall have to consider of every deed, whether, in committing it, a man does or
does not trespass upon the ordained freedom of his neighbor—
whether, when placed side by side, the shares of liberty the two
parties respectively assume are equal. And by thus separating
that which can be done by each without trenching on the privileges of others from that which cannot be so done, we may classify actions into lawful and unlawful.

**2.** DIFFICULTIES MAY NOW AND THEN OCCUR IN THE PERFORM-
ance of this process. We shall perhaps occasionally find our-

selves unable to decide whether a given action does or does not trespass against the law of equal freedom. But such an admission by no means implies any defect in that law. It merely implies human incapacity—an incapacity which puts a limit to our discovery of physical as well as of moral truth. It is, for instance, quite beyond the power of any mathematician to state in degrees and minutes the angle at which a man may lean without falling. Not being able to find accurately the center of gravity of a man's body, he cannot say with certainty whether, at a given inclination, the *line of direction* will or will not fall outside the base. But we do not, therefore, take exception to the first principles of mechanics. We know that, in spite of our inability to follow out those first principles to all their consequences, the stability or instability of a man's attitude might still be accurately determined by them, were our perceptions competent to take in all the conditions of such a problem. Similarly, it is argued that, although there may possibly arise out of the more complex social relationships questions that are apparently not soluble by comparing the respective amounts of freedom the concerned parties assume, it must nevertheless be granted that, whether we see it or not, their claims are either equal or unequal, and the dependent actions right or wrong accordingly.

**3.** FOR THOSE WHO HAVE FAITH IN THE ABSTRACT AND WHO DARE to follow wherever an acknowledged doctrine may lead, it will be sufficient to point out the several conclusions which may be drawn from this first principle, and to leave those conclusions to stand or fall by the logicalness of their deduction. It is to be feared, however, that results arrived at by so purely philosophical a process will weigh but little with the majority. People who "cannot understand a principle until its light falls upon a fact" are not to be swayed by inferences so deduced. Wedded as they are to the guidance of a superficial experience, they are deaf to the enunciation of those laws of which the complex phenomena they draw their experience from are the workings out. We have, nevertheless, to deal with such as best we may; and, to meet their case, evidence of a so-called "practical" nature must be adduced. Whenever, therefore, we arrive at inferences conflicting with the general opinion, it is intended to follow up the argument by showing that "experience," rightly interpreted, enforces these inferences.

CHAPTER VIII

## *The Rights of Life and Personal Liberty*

**1.** THESE ARE SELF-EVIDENT COROLLARIES FROM OUR FIRST PRINciple as scarcely to need a separate statement. If every man has freedom to do all that he wills, provided he infringes not the equal freedom of any other man, it is manifest that he has a claim to his life, for without it he can do nothing that he has willed; and to his personal liberty, for the withdrawal of it partially, if not wholly, restrains him from the fulfillment of his will. It is just as clear, too, that each man is forbidden to deprive his fellow of life or liberty, inasmuch as he cannot do this without breaking the law, which, in asserting his freedom, declares that he shall not infringe "the equal freedom of any other." For he who is killed or enslaved is obviously no longer equally free with his killer or enslaver.

**2.** IT IS UNNECESSARY TO COMMEND THESE CONCLUSIONS BY ANY exposition of advantages. All spontaneously assent to them. There are a few simple truths of which the moral sense gives a sufficiently clear perception without the aid of logic; and these are of the number. The time was, indeed, when the law of adaptation having as yet produced but little effect, the feelings that respond to these truths were comparatively undeveloped and consequently produced no spontaneous recognition of them. And did we live in the old Assyrian days when a subject was the property of his king; were it our custom to chain a porter to his cell on one side of the door, opposite to the kennel of the house dog on the other, as in Athens and Rome; did we sacrifice men to the gods or send our prisoners of war to be torn to pieces in an amphitheater, it might be needful to enforce the doctrines here enunciated, by showing the expediency of acting upon them. But happily we live in better times and may congratulate ourselves on having reached a phase of civilization in which the rights of life and personal liberty no longer require inculcating.

**3.** INTO SUCH QUESTIONS AS THE PUNISHMENT OF DEATH, THE PERpetual imprisonment of criminals, and the like, we cannot here enter. These, implying, as they do, antecedent infractions of the law, and being, as they are, remedial measures for a diseased moral state, belong to what has been elsewhere termed Therapeutical Ethics, with which we have now nothing to do.

CHAPTER IX

## The Right to the Use of the Earth

**1.** GIVEN A RACE OF BEINGS HAVING LIKE CLAIMS TO PURSUE THE objects of their desires; given a world adapted to the gratification of those desires—a world into which such beings are similarly born—and it unavoidably follows that they have equal rights to the use of this world. For if each of them "has freedom to do all that he wills, provided he infringes not the equal freedom of any other," then each of them is free to use the earth for the satisfaction of his wants, provided he allows all others the same liberty. And conversely, it is manifest that no one, or part of them, may use the earth in such a way as to prevent the rest from similarly using it; seeing that to do this is to assume greater freedom than the rest, and consequently to break the law.

**2.** EQUITY, THEREFORE, DOES NOT PERMIT PROPERTY IN LAND. FOR if one portion of the earth's surface may justly become the possession of an individual and may be held by him for his sole use and benefit as a thing to which he has an exclusive right, then *other* portions of the earth's surface may be so held; and eventually the *whole* of the earth's surface may be so held, and our planet may thus lapse altogether into private hands. Observe now the dilemma to which this leads. Supposing the entire habitable globe to be so enclosed, it follows that if the landowners have a valid right to its surface, all who are not landowners have no right at all to its surface. Hence, such can exist on the earth by sufferance only. They are all trespassers. Save by the permission of the lords of the soil, they can have no room for the soles of their feet. Nay, should the others think fit to deny them a resting place, these landless men might equitably be expelled from the earth altogether. If, then, the assumption that land can be held as property involves that the whole globe may become the private domain of a part of its inhabitants; and if, by consequence, the rest of its inhabitants can then exercise their faculties—can then exist even—only by consent of the landowners, it is manifest that an exclusive possession of the soil necessitates an infringement of the law of equal freedom. For men who cannot "live and move and have their being" without the leave of others cannot be equally free with those others.

**3.** PASSING FROM THE CONSIDERATION OF THE POSSIBLE TO THAT of the actual, we find yet further reason to deny the rectitude of property in land. It can never be pretended that the existing titles to such property are legitimate. Should anyone think so, let him look in the chronicles. Violence, fraud, the prerogative of force, the claims of superior cunning—these are the sources to which those titles may be traced. The original deeds were written with the sword rather than with the pen: not lawyers, but soldiers, were the conveyancers; blows were the current coin given in payment; and for seals, blood was used in preference to wax. Could valid claims be thus constituted? Hardly. And if not, what becomes of the pretensions of all subsequent holders of estates so obtained? Does sale or bequest generate a right where it did not previously exist? Would the original claimants be nonsuited at the bar of reason because the thing stolen from them had changed hands? Certainly not. And if one act of transfer can give no title, can many? No; though *nothing* be multiplied forever, it will not produce *one*. Even the law recognizes this principle. An existing holder must, if called upon, substantiate the claims of those from whom he purchased or inherited his property; and any flaw in the original parchment, even though the property should have had a score of intermediate owners, quashes his right.

"But Time," say some, "is a great legalizer. Immemorial possession must be taken to constitute a legitimate claim. That which has been held from age to age as private property, and has been bought and sold as such, must now be considered as irrevocably belonging to individuals." To which proposition a willing assent shall be given when its propounders can assign it a definite meaning. To do this, however, they must find satisfactory answers to such questions as: How long does it take for what was originally a *wrong* to grow into a *right*? At what rate per annum do invalid claims become valid? If a title gets perfect in a thousand years, how much more than perfect will it be in two thousand years?—and so forth. For the solution of which they will require a new calculus. Whether it may be expedient to admit claims of a certain standing is not the point. We have here nothing to do with considerations of conventional privilege or legislative convenience. We have simply to inquire what is the verdict given by pure equity in the matter. And this verdict enjoins a protest against every existing pretension to the individual possession of the soil, and dictates the assertion that the right of mankind at large to the earth's surface is still valid, all deeds, customs, and laws notwithstanding.

**4.** NOT ONLY HAVE PRESENT LAND TENURES AN INDEFENSIBLE origin, but it is impossible to discover any mode in which land can become private property. Cultivation is commonly considered to give a legitimate title. He who has reclaimed a tract of ground from its primitive wildness is supposed to have thereby made it his own. But if his right is disputed, by what system of logic can he vindicate it? Let us listen a moment to his pleadings.

"Hallo, you, sir," cries the cosmopolite to some backwoodsman smoking at the door of his shanty, "by what authority do you take possession of these acres that you have cleared, round which you have put up a snake fence and on which you have built this log house?"

"By what authority? I squatted here because there was no one to say nay—because I was as much at liberty to do so as any other man. Besides, now that I have cut down the wood and plowed and cropped the ground, this farm is more mine than yours or anybody's, and I mean to keep it."

"Ay, so you all say. But I do not yet see how you have substantiated your claim. When you came here you found the land producing trees—sugar maples, perhaps; or maybe it was covered with prairie grass and wild strawberries. Well, instead of these you made it yield wheat, or maize, or tobacco. Now I want to understand how, by exterminating one set of plants and making the soil bear another set in their place, you have constituted yourself lord of this soil for all succeeding time."

"Oh, those natural products which I destroyed were of little or no use; whereas I caused the earth to bring forth things good for food—things that help to give life and happiness."

"Still you have not shown why such a process makes the portion of earth you have so modified yours. What is it that you have done? You have turned over the soil to a few inches in depth with a spade or a plow; you have scattered over this prepared surface a few seeds; and you have gathered the fruits which the sun, rain, and air helped the soil to produce. Just tell me, if you please, by what magic have these acts made you sole owner of that vast mass of matter, having for its base the surface of your estate and for its apex the center of the globe? All of which it appears you would monopolize to yourself and your descendants forever."

"Well, if it isn't mine, whose is it? I have dispossessed nobody. When I crossed the Mississippi yonder I found nothing but the silent woods. If someone else had settled here and made this clearing, he would have had as good a right to the location as I have. I have done nothing but what any other person was at liberty to do had he come before me. While they were unreclaimed, these lands belonged to all men—as much to one as to another—and they are now mine simply because I was the first to discover and improve them."

"You say truly when you say that 'while they were unreclaimed these lands belonged to all men.' And it is my duty to tell you that they belong to all men still, and that your 'improvements,' as you call them, cannot vitiate the claim of all men. You may plow and harrow, and sow and reap; you may turn over the soil as often as you like; but all your manipulations will fail to make that soil yours, which was not yours to begin with. Let me put a case. Suppose now that in the course of your wanderings you come upon an empty house, which in spite of its dilapidated state takes your fancy; suppose that with the intention of making it your abode you expend much time and trouble in repairing it—that you paint and paper and whitewash, and at considerable cost bring it into a habitable state. Suppose further that on some fatal day a stranger is announced who turns out to be the heir to whom this house has been bequeathed, and that this professed heir is prepared with all the necessary proofs of his identity; what becomes of your improvements? Do they give you a valid title to the house? Do they quash the title of the original claimant?"

"No."

"Neither, then, do your pioneering operations give you a valid title to this land. Neither do they quash the title of its original claimants—the human race. The world is God's bequest to mankind. All men are joint heirs to it; you among the number. And because you have taken up your residence on a certain part of it and have subdued, cultivated, beautified that part—improved it, as you say—you are not therefore warranted in appropriating it as entirely private property. At least if you do so, you may at any moment be justly expelled by the lawful owner—Society."

"Well, but surely you would not eject me without making some recompense for the great additional value I have given to this tract, by reducing what was a wilderness into fertile fields. You would not turn me adrift and deprive me of all the benefit of those years of toil it has cost me to bring this spot into its present state."

"Of course not; just as in the case of the house, you would have an equitable title to compensation from the proprietor for repairs and new fittings, so the community cannot justly take possession of this estate without paying for all that you have done to it. This extra worth which your labor has imparted to it is fairly yours; and although you have, without leave, busied yourself in bettering what belongs to the community, yet no doubt the community will duly discharge your claim. But admitting this is quite a different thing from recognizing your right to the land itself. It may be true that you are entitled to compensation for the improvements this enclosure has received at your hands; and at the same time it may be equally true that no act, form, proceeding, or ceremony can make this enclosure your private property."

**5.** IT DOES INDEED AT FIRST SIGHT SEEM POSSIBLE FOR THE EARTH to become the exclusive possession of individuals by some process of equitable distribution. "Why," it may be asked, "should not men agree to a fair subdivision? If all are co-heirs, why may not the estate be equally apportioned and each be afterward perfect master of his own share?"

To this question it may in the first place be replied that such a division is vetoed by the difficulty of fixing the values of respective tracts of land. Variations in productiveness, different degrees of accessibility, advantages of climate, proximity to the centers of civilization—these and other such considerations remove the problem out of the sphere of mere mensuration into the region of impossibility.

But, waiving this, let us inquire who are to be the allottees. Shall adult males and all who have reached twenty-one on a specified day be the fortunate individuals? If so, what is to be done with those who come of age on the morrow? Is it proposed that each man, woman, and child shall have a section? If so, what becomes of all who are to be born next year? And what will be the fate of those whose fathers sell their estates and squander the proceeds? These portionless ones must constitute a class already described as having no right to a resting place on earth—as living by the sufferance of their fellow men—as being practically serfs. And the existence of such a class is wholly at variance with the law of equal freedom.

Until, therefore, we can produce a valid commission authorizing us to make this distribution, until it can be proved that God has given one charter of privileges to one generation and another to the next, until we can demonstrate that men born after a certain date are doomed to slavery, we must consider that no such allotment is permissible.

**6.** PROBABLY SOME WILL REGARD THE DIFFICULTIES INSEPARABLE from individual ownership of the soil as caused by pushing to excess a doctrine applicable only within rational limits. This is a very favorite style of thinking with some. There are people who hate anything in the shape of exact conclusions, and these are of them. According to such, the right is never in either extreme, but always halfway between the extremes. They are continually trying to reconcile Yes and No. Its and buts and excepts are their delight. They have so great a faith in "the judicious mean" that they would scarcely believe an oracle if it uttered a full-length principle. Were you to inquire of them whether the earth turns on its axis from east to west or from west to east, you might almost expect the reply, "A little of both," or "Not exactly either." It is doubtful whether they would assent to the axiom that the whole is greater than its part, without making some qualification. They have a passion for compromises. To meet their taste, Truth must always be spiced with a little Error. They cannot conceive of a pure, definite, entire, and unlimited law. And hence, in discussions like the present, they are constantly petitioning for limitations—always wishing to abate and modify and moderate—ever protesting against doctrines being pursued to their ultimate consequences.

But it behooves such to recollect that ethical truth is as exact and as peremptory as physical truth; and that in this matter of land tenure the verdict of morality must be distinctly yea or nay. Either men *have* a right to make the soil private property or they *have not*. There is no medium. We must choose one of the two positions. There can be no half-and-half opinion. In the nature of things the fact must be either one way or the other.

If men *have not* such a right, we are at once delivered from the several predicaments already pointed out. If they *have* such a right, then is that right absolute, sacred, not on any pretense to be violated. If they *have* such a right, then is his Grace of Leeds justified in warning off tourists from Ben Mac Dhui, the Duke of Atholl in closing Glen Tilt, the Duke of Buccleugh in denying sites to the Free Church, and the Duke of Sutherland in banishing the Highlanders to make room for sheep walks. If they *have* such a right, then it would be proper for the sole proprietor of any kingdom—a Jersey or Guernsey, for example—to impose just what regulations he might choose on its inhabitants—to tell them that they should not live on his property unless they professed a certain religion, spoke a particular language, paid him a specified reverence, adopted an authorized dress, and conformed to all other conditions he might see fit to make. If they *have* such a right, then is there truth in that tenet of the ultra-Tory school, that the landowners are the only legitimate rulers of a country—that the people at large remain in it only by the landowner's permission and ought consequently to submit to the landowners' rule and respect whatever institutions the landowners set up. There is no escape from these inferences. They are necessary corollaries to the theory that the earth can become individual property. And they can be repudiated only by denying that theory.

7. AFTER ALL, NOBODY DOES IMPLICITLY BELIEVE IN LANDLORDism. We hear of estates being held under the king—that is, the State—or of their being kept in trust for the public benefit; and not that they are the inalienable possessions of their nominal owners. Moreover, we daily deny landlordism by our legislation. Is a canal, a railway, or a turnpike road to be made, we do not scruple to seize just as many acres as may be requisite, allowing the holders compensation for the capital invested. We do not wait for consent. An act of Parliament supersedes the authority of title deeds and serves proprietors with notices to quit,

whether they will or not. Either this is equitable or it is not. Either the public are free to resume as much of the earth's surface as they think fit, or the titles of the landowners must be considered absolute, and all national works must be postponed until lords and squires please to part with the requisite slices of their estates. If we decide that the claims of individual ownership must give way, then we imply that the right of the nation at large to the soil is supreme; that the right of private possession exists only by general consent; that general consent being withdrawn, it ceases—or, in other words, that it is no right at all.

**8.** "BUT TO WHAT DOES THIS DOCTRINE, THAT MEN ARE EQUALLY entitled to the use of the earth, lead? Must we return to the times of unenclosed wilds and subsist on roots, berries, and game? Or are we to be left to the management of Messrs. Fourier, Owen, Louis Blanc, and Co.?"

Neither. Such a doctrine is consistent with the highest state of civilization; may be carried out without involving a community of goods; and need cause no very serious revolution in existing arrangements. The change required would simply be a change of landlords. Separate ownerships would merge into the joint-stock ownership of the public. Instead of being in the possession of individuals, the country would be held by the great corporate body—Society. Instead of leasing his acres from an isolated proprietor, the farmer would lease them from the nation. Instead of paying his rent to the agent of Sir John or His Grace, he would pay it to an agent or deputy agent of the community. Stewards would be public officials instead of private ones, and tenancy the only land tenure.

A state of things so ordered would be in perfect harmony with the moral law. Under it all men would be equally landlords; all men would be alike free to become tenants. A, B, C, and the rest might compete for a vacant farm as now, and one of them might take that farm, without in any way violating the principles of pure equity. All would be equally free to bid; all would be equally free to refrain. And when the farm had been let to A, B, or C, all parties would have done that which they willed—the one in choosing to pay a given sum to his fellow men for the use of certain lands—the others in refusing to pay that sum. Clearly, therefore, on such a system, the earth might be enclosed, occupied, and cultivated in entire subordination to the law of equal freedom.

**9.** NO DOUBT GREAT DIFFICULTIES MUST ATTEND THE RESUMPTION, by mankind at large, of their rights to the soil. The question of compensation to existing proprietors is a complicated one— one that perhaps cannot be settled in a strictly equitable man- ner. Had we to deal with the parties who originally robbed the human race of its heritage, we might make short work of the matter. But, unfortunately, most of our present landowners are men who have, either mediately or immediately—either by their own acts or by the acts of their ancestors—given for their estates equivalents of honestly earned wealth, believing that they were investing their savings in a legitimate manner. To estimate justly and liquidate the claims of such is one of the most intricate problems society will one day have to solve. But with this perplexity and our extrication from it, abstract morality has no concern. Men, having got themselves into the dilemma by disobedience to the law, must get out of it as well as they can, and with as little injury to the landed class as may be.

Meanwhile, we shall do well to recollect that there are others besides the landed class to be considered. In our tender regard for the vested interests of the few, let us not forget that the rights of the many are in abeyance, and must remain so, as long as the earth is monopolized by individuals. Let us remember, too, that the injustice thus inflicted on the mass of mankind is an injustice of the gravest nature. The fact that it is not so regarded proves nothing. In early phases of civilization even homicide is thought lightly of. The suttees of India, together with the practice elsewhere followed of sacrificing a hecatomb of human victims at the burial of a chief, shows this; and prob- ably cannibals consider the slaughter of those whom "the for- tune of war" has made their prisoners perfectly justifiable. It was once also universally supposed that slavery was a natural and quite legitimate institution—a condition into which some were born and to which they ought to submit as to a Divine ordination; nay, indeed, a great proportion of mankind hold this opinion still. A higher social development, however, has generated in us a better faith, and we now to a considerable extent recognize the claims of humanity. But our civilization is only partial. It may by and by be perceived that Equity utters dictates to which we have not yet listened; and men may then learn that to deprive others of their rights to the use of the earth is to commit a crime inferior only in wickedness to the crime of taking away their lives or personal liberties.

**10.** BRIEFLY REVIEWING THE ARGUMENT, WE SEE THAT THE RIGHT of each man to the use of the earth, limited only by the like rights of his fellow men, is immediately deducible from the law of equal freedom. We see that the maintenance of this right necessarily forbids private property in land. On examination, all existing titles to such property turn out to be invalid; those founded on reclamation, inclusive. It appears that not even an equal apportionment of the earth among its inhabitants could generate a legitimate proprietorship. We find that if pushed to its ultimate consequences a claim to exclusive possession of the soil involves a landowning despotism. We further find that such a claim is constantly denied by the enactments of our legislature. And we find lastly that the theory of the co-heirship of all men to the soil is consistent with the highest civilization, and that, however difficult it may be to embody that theory in fact, Equity sternly commands it to be done.

CHAPTER X

# The Right of Property

**1.** THE MORAL LAW, BEING THE LAW OF THE SOCIAL STATE, is obliged wholly to ignore the ante-social state. Constituting, as the principles of pure morality do, a code of conduct for the perfect man, they cannot be made to adapt themselves to the actions of the uncivilized man, even under the most ingenious hypothetical conditions—cannot be made even to recognize those actions so as to pass any definite sentence upon them. Overlooking this fact, thinkers, in their attempts to prove some of the first theorems of ethics, have commonly fallen into the error of referring back to an imaginary state of savage wildness, instead of referring forward to an ideal civilization, as they should have done, and have, in consequence, entangled themselves in difficulties arising out of the discordance between ethical principles and the assumed premises. To this circumstance is attributable that vagueness by which the arguments used to establish the right of property in a logical manner are characterized. While possessed of a certain plausibility, they yet cannot be considered conclusive, inasmuch as they suggest questions and objections that admit of no satisfactory answers. Let us take a sample of these arguments and examine its defects.

"Though the earth and all inferior creatures," says Locke, "be common to all men, yet every man has a property in his own person: this nobody has a right to but himself. The labour of his body, and the work of his hands, we may say are properly his. Whatever, then, he removes out of the state that nature hath provided and left it in, he hath mixed his labour with, and joined to it something that is his own, and thereby makes it his property. It being by him removed from the common state nature hath placed it in, it hath by this labour something annexed to it that excludes the common right of other men. For this labour being the unquestionable property of the labourer, no man but he can have a right to what that is once joined to, at least when there is enough and as good left in common for others.'

If inclined to cavil, one might in reply to this observe that as, according to the premises, "the earth and all inferior creatures"—all things, in fact, that the earth produces—are "common to all men," the consent of all men must be obtained before any article can be equitably "removed from the common state nature hath placed it in." It might be argued that the real question is overlooked, when it is said that, by gathering any natural product, a man "hath mixed his labour with it, and joined to it something that is his own, and thereby made it his property"; for that the point to be debated is whether he had any right to gather, or mix his labor with that which, by the hypothesis, previously belonged to mankind at large. The reasoning used in the last chapter to prove that no amount of labor, bestowed by an individual upon a part of the earth's surface, can nullify the title of society to that part might be similarly employed to show that no one can, by the mere act of appropriating to himself any wild unclaimed animal or fruit, supersede the joint claims of other men to it. It may be quite true that the labor a man expends in catching or gathering gives him a better right to the thing caught or gathered than any one other man; but the question at issue is whether by labor so expended he has made his right to the thing caught or gathered greater than the pre-existing rights of all other men put together. And unless he can prove that he has done this, his title to possession cannot be admitted as a matter of right, but can be conceded only on the ground of convenience.

Further difficulties are suggested by the qualification that the claim to any article of property thus obtained is valid only "when there is enough and as good left in common for others." A condition like this gives birth to such a host of queries, doubts, and limitations as practically to neutralize the general proposition entirely. It may be asked, for example: How is it to be known that enough is "left in common for others"? Who can determine whether what remains is "as good" as what is taken? How if the remnant is less accessible? If there is not enough "left in common for others," how must the right of appropriation be exercised? Why, in such case, does the mixing of labor with the acquired object cease to "exclude the common right of other men"? Supposing enough to be attainable, but not all equally good, by what rule must each man choose? Out of which inquisition it seems impossible to liberate the alleged right, without such mutilations as to render it, in an ethical point of view, entirely valueless.

Thus, as already hinted, we find that the circumstances of

savage life render the principles of abstract morality inapplicable; for it is impossible, under ante-social conditions, to determine the rightness or wrongness of certain actions by an exact measurement of the amount of freedom assumed by the parties concerned. We must not expect, therefore, that the right of property can be satisfactorily based upon the premises afforded by such a state of existence.

**2.** BUT UNDER THE SYSTEM OF LAND TENURE POINTED OUT IN THE last chapter as the only one that is consistent with the equal claims of all men to the use of the earth, these difficulties disappear, and the right of property obtains a legitimate foundation. We have seen that, without any infraction of the law of equal freedom, an individual may lease from society a given surface of soil, by agreeing to pay in return a stated amount of the produce he obtains from that soil. We found that, in doing this, he does no more than what every other man is equally free with himself to do; that each has the same power with himself to become the tenant; and that the rent he pays accrues alike to all. Having thus hired a tract of land from his fellow men, for a given period, for understood purposes, and on specified terms—having thus obtained, for a time, the exclusive use of that land by a definite agreement with its owners, it is manifest that an individual may, without any infringement of the rights of others, appropriate to himself that portion of produce which remains after he has paid to mankind the promised rent. He has now, to use Locke's expression, "mixed his labour with" certain products of the earth; and his claim to them is in this case valid, because he obtained the consent of society before so expending his labor; and having fulfilled the condition which society imposed in giving that consent—the payment of rent— society, to fulfill its part of the agreement, must acknowledge his title to that surplus which remains after the rent has been paid. "Provided you deliver to us a stated share of the produce which by cultivation you can obtain from this piece of land, we give you the exclusive use of the remainder of that produce": these are the words of the contract; and in virtue of this contract, the tenant may equitably claim the supplementary share as his private property; may so claim it without any disobedience to the law of equal freedom; and has therefore a right so to claim it.

Any doubt that may be felt as to the fact that this is a logical deduction from our first principle, that every man has freedom to do all that he wills, provided he infringes not the equal freedom of any other man, may be readily cleared up by comparing the respective degrees of freedom assumed in such a case by the occupier and the members of society with whom he bargains. As was shown in the preceding chapter, if the public altogether deprive any individual of the use of the earth, they allow him less liberty than they themselves claim; and by so breaking the law of equal freedom commit a wrong. If, conversely, an individual usurps a given portion of the earth, to which, as we have seen, all other men have as good a title as himself, he breaks the law by assuming more liberty than the rest. But when an individual holds land as a tenant of society, a balance is maintained between these extremes, and the claims of both parties are respected. A price is paid by the one for a certain privilege granted by the other. By the fact of the agreement being made, it is shown that such price and privilege are considered to be equivalents. The lessor and the lessee have both, within the prescribed limits, done that which they willed: the one in letting a certain holding for a specified sum, the other in agreeing to give that sum. And so long as this contract remains intact, the law of equal freedom is duly observed. If, however, any of the prescribed conditions be not fulfilled, the law is necessarily broken, and the parties are involved in one of the predicaments above named. If the tenant refuses to pay the rent, then he tacitly lays claim to the exclusive use and benefit of the land he occupies—practically asserts that he is the sole owner of its produce, and consequently violates the law by assuming a greater share of freedom than the rest of mankind. If, on the other hand, society take from the tenant that portion of the fruits obtained by the culture of his farm, which remains with him after the payment of rent, they virtually deny him the use of the earth entirely (for by the use of the earth we mean the use of its products), and in so doing claim for themselves

a greater share of liberty than they allow him. Clearly, therefore, this surplus produce equitably remains with the tenant;
society cannot take it without trespassing upon his freedom;
he can take it without trespassing on the freedom of society.
And as, according to the law, he is free to do all that he wills,
provided he infringes not the equal freedom of any other, he
is free to take possession of such surplus as his property.

**3.** THE DOCTRINE THAT ALL MEN HAVE EQUAL RIGHTS TO THE USE
of the earth does indeed, at first sight, seem to countenance a
species of social organization at variance with that from which
the right of property has just been deduced; an organization,
namely, in which the public, instead of letting out the land to
individual members of their body, shall retain it in their own
hands, cultivate it by joint-stock agency, and share the produce:
in fact, what is usually termed Socialism or Communism.

Plausible though it may be, such a scheme is not capable of
realization in strict conformity with the moral law. Of the two
forms under which it may be presented, the one is ethically
imperfect; and the other, although correct in theory, is impracticable.

Thus, if an equal portion of the earth's produce is awarded to
every man, irrespective of the amount or quality of the labor he
has contributed toward the obtainment of that produce, a
breach of equity is committed. Our first principle requires,
not that all shall have like shares of the things which minister
to the gratification of the faculties, but that all shall have like
freedom to pursue those things—shall have like scope. It is one
thing to give to each an opportunity of acquiring the objects
he desires; it is another, and quite a different thing, to give the
objects themselves, no matter whether due endeavor has or has
not been made to obtain them. The one we have seen to be the
primary law of the Divine scheme; the other, by interfering
with the ordained connection between desire and gratification,
shows its disagreement with that scheme. Nay, more, it necessitates an absolute violation of the principle of equal freedom.
For when we assert the entire liberty of each, bounded only
by the like liberty of all, we assert that each is free to do what-

ever his desires dictate, within the prescribed limits; that each
is free, therefore, to claim for himself all those gratifications
and sources of gratification attainable by him within those limits
—all those gratifications and sources of gratification which he
can procure without trespassing upon the spheres of action of
his neighbors. If, therefore, out of many starting with like
fields of activity, one obtains by his greater strength, greater
ingenuity, or greater application more gratifications and sources
of gratification than the rest, and does this without in any way
trenching upon the equal freedom of the rest, the moral law
assigns him an exclusive right to all those extra gratifications
and sources of gratification; nor can the rest take from him without claiming for themselves greater liberty of action than he
claims, and thereby violating that law. Whence it follows that
an equal apportionment of the fruits of the earth among all is
not consistent with pure justice.

If, on the other hand, each is to have allotted to him a
share of produce proportionate to the degree in which he has
aided production, the proposal, while it is abstractedly just,
is no longer practicable. Were all men cultivators of the soil,
it would perhaps be possible to form an approximate estimate
of their several claims. But to ascertain the respective amounts
of help given by different kinds of mental and bodily laborers
toward procuring the general stock of the necessaries of life is
an utter impossibility. We have no means of making such a
division save that afforded by the law of supply and demand,
and this means the hypothesis excludes.[1]

**4.** AN ARGUMENT FATAL TO THE COMMUNIST THEORY IS SUGGESTED
by the fact that a desire for property is one of the elements
of our nature. Repeated allusion has been made to the admitted truth, that acquisitiveness is an unreasoning impulse
quite distinct from the desires whose gratifications property
secures—an impulse that is often obeyed at the expense of those
desires. And if a propensity to personal acquisition be really a
component of man's constitution, then that cannot be a right

[1] These inferences do not at all militate against joint-stock systems of production and living, which are in all probability what Socialism prophesies.

form of society which affords it no scope. Socialists do indeed allege that private appropriation is an abuse of this propensity, whose normal function, they say, is to impel us to accumulate for the benefit of the public at large. But in thus attempting to escape from one difficulty, they do but entangle themselves in another. Such an explanation overlooks the fact that the use and abuse of a faculty (whatever the etymology of the words may imply) differ only in degree; whereas their assumption is that they differ in kind. Gluttony is an abuse of the desire for food; timidity, an abuse of the feeling which in moderation produces prudence; servility, an abuse of the sentiment that generates respect; obstinacy, of that from which firmness springs: in all of which cases we find that the legitimate manifestations differ from the illegitimate ones merely in quantity and not in quality. So also with the instinct of accumulation. It may be quite true that its dictates have been and still are followed to an absurd excess, but it is also true that no change in the state of society will alter its nature and its office. To whatever extent moderated, it must still be a desire for personal acquisition. Whence it follows that a system affording opportunity for its exercise must ever be retained; which means that the system of private property must be retained, and this presupposes a right of private property, for by right we mean that which harmonizes with the human constitution as divinely ordained.

**5.** THERE IS, HOWEVER, A STILL MORE AWKWARD DILEMMA INTO which M. Proudhon and his party betray themselves. For if, as they assert, "all property is robbery"—if no one can equitably become the exclusive possessor of any article, or, as we say, obtain a right to it—then, among other consequences, it follows that a man can have no right to the things he consumes for food. And if these are not his before eating them, how can they become his at all? As Locke asks, "When do they begin to be his? When he digests? Or when he eats? Or when he boils? Or when he brings them home?" If no previous acts can make them his property, neither can any process of assimilation do it: not even their absorption into the tissues. Wherefore, pursuing the idea, we arrive at the curious conclusion that as the whole of his bones, muscles, skin, etc., have been thus built up from nutriment not belonging to him, a man has no property in his own flesh and blood, can have no valid title to himself, has no more claim to his own limbs than he has to the limbs of another, and has as good a right to his neighbor's body as to his own! Did we exist after the same fashion as those compound polyps, in which a number of individuals are based upon a living trunk common to them all, such a theory would be rational enough. But until Communism can be carried to that extent, it will be best to stand by the old doctrine.

**6.** FURTHER ARGUMENT APPEARS TO BE UNNECESSARY. WE HAVE seen that the right of property is deducible from the law of equal freedom, that it is presupposed by the human constitution, and that its denial involves absurdities.

Were it not that we shall frequently have to refer to the fact hereafter, it would be scarcely needful to show that the taking away another's property is an infringement of the law of equal freedom and is therefore wrong. If A appropriates to himself something belonging to B, one of two things must take place: either B does the like to A, or he does not. If A has no property, or if his property is inaccessible to B, B has evidently no opportunity of exercising equal freedom with A by claiming from him something of like value, and A has therefore assumed a greater share of freedom than he allows B and has broken the law. If, again, A's property is open to B, and A permits B to use like freedom with himself by taking an equivalent, there is no violation of the law, and the affair practically becomes one of barter. But such a transaction will never take place save in theory, for A has no motive to appropriate B's property with the intention of letting B take an equivalent; seeing that if he really means to let B have what B thinks an equivalent, he will prefer to make the exchange by consent in the ordinary way. The only case simulating this is one in which A takes from B a thing that B does not wish to part with—that is, a thing for which A can give B nothing that B thinks an equivalent—and as

the amount of gratification which B has in the possession of
this thing is the measure of its value to him, it follows that if
A cannot give B a thing which affords B equal gratification, or
in other words what he thinks an equivalent, then A has taken
from B what affords A satisfaction, but does not return to B
what affords B satisfaction, and has therefore broken the law
by assuming the greater share of freedom. Wherefore we find it
to be a logical deduction from the law of equal freedom that no
man can rightfully take property from another against his will.

CHAPTER XI

---

## The Right of Property in Ideas

**1.** IT IS TOLERABLY SELF-EVIDENT THAT NO VIOLATION OF THE LAW
of equal freedom is committed in the acquisition of knowledge—
that knowledge, at least, which is open to all. A man may
read, hear, and observe to as great an extent as he pleases, without in the least diminishing the liberty of others to do the like
—in fact, without affecting the condition of others in any way.
It is clear, too, that the knowledge thus obtained may be
digested, reorganized, or combined afresh, and new knowledge
educed from it by its possessor, without the rights of his fellows
being thereby trespassed upon. And it is further manifest that
the moral law permits a man who has by his intellectual labor
obtained such new knowledge to keep it for his own exclusive
use, or claim it as his private property. He who does this in no
degree exceeds the prescribed limits of individual freedom. He
abridges no one's liberty of action. Every other person retains
as much scope for thought and deed as before. And each is free
to acquire the same facts—to elaborate from them, if he can,
the same new ideas—and in a similar manner employ those
new ideas for his private advantage. Seeing, therefore, that a
man may claim the exclusive use of his original ideas without
overstepping the boundaries of equal freedom, it follows that he
has a right so to claim them; or, in other words, such ideas are
his property.

Of course the argument used in the last chapter to show that material property cannot be taken from its possessor without a breach of the law is applicable to property of this kind also.

**2.** THAT A MAN'S RIGHT TO THE PRODUCE OF HIS BRAIN IS EQUALLY valid with his right to the produce of his hands is a fact which has yet obtained but a very imperfect recognition. It is true that we have patent laws, a law of copyright, and acts for the registration of designs; but these, or at any rate two of them, have been enacted not so much in obedience to the dictates of justice as in deference to the suggestions of trade policy. "A patent is not a thing which can be claimed as a right," we are told by legal authorities, but is intended to "act as a stimulus to industry and talent." It is not because the piracy of patterns would be wrong that legislators forbid it, but because they wish to afford "encouragement to manufactures." Similar also are the current opinions. Measures of this nature are commonly considered by the public as giving to inventors a certain "privilege," a "reward," a sort of modified "monopoly." It is on the ground of commercial statesmanship that they are approved, and not as being necessary for the administration of justice.

The prevalence of such a belief is by no means creditable to the national conscience and indicates a sad bluntness of moral feeling. To think that the profits which a speculator makes by a rise in the share market should be recognized as legally and equitably his property, and yet that some new combination of ideas, which it may have cost an ingenious man years of application to complete, cannot be "claimed as a right" by that man! To think that a sinecurist should be held to have a "vested interest" in his office and a just title to compensation if it is abolished, and yet that an invention over which no end of mental toil has been spent, and on which the poor mechanic has laid out perhaps his last sixpence—an invention which he has completed entirely by his own labor and with his own materials—has wrought, as it were, out of the very substance of his own mind—should not be acknowledged as his property! To think that his title to it should be admitted merely as a

matter of convenience—admitted even then only on payment
of some £400—and, after all, quashed on the most trifling
pretenses! What a thick-skinned perception of justice does this
show! What a want of ability to appreciate matters at all removed beyond the sphere of the external senses! One would
think that equity afforded no guidance beyond transactions in
material things—weights, measures, and money. Let a shop boy
take from his master's till a visible, tangible, ponderable sovereign, and all can see that the rights of ownership have been
violated. Yet those who exclaim with such indignant virtue
against theft will purchase a pirated edition of a book without
any qualms of conscience concerning the receipt of stolen
goods. Dishonesty, when shown in house-breaking or sheep-
stealing, is held up to eternal infamy, and those convicted of
it are forever excluded from society; but the manufacturer who
steals his foreman's improved plan for the spinning of cotton
or the building of steam engines continues to be held in high
respect. The law is active enough in apprehending the urchin
who may have deprived some comfortable citizen of his pocket
handkerchief, and will deal with the young scapegrace at the
public expense; but there is no redress for the poverty-stricken
schemer who is robbed by some wealthy scamp of that which
formed the sole hope of his life. Strong illustrations these of
the fact that the moral sense, when unguided by systematic
deduction, fails to find its way through the labyrinth of confused opinion to a correct code of duty.

**3.** AS ALREADY REMARKED, IT IS A COMMON NOTION, AND ONE
more especially pervading the operative classes, that the exclusive
use by its discoverer of any new or improved mode of production
is a species of monopoly, in the sense in which that word is
conventionally used. To let a man have the entire benefit accruing from the employment of some more efficient machine or
better process invented by him, and to allow no other person
to adopt and apply for his own advantage the same plan, they
hold to be an injustice. Nor are there wanting philanthropic
and even thinking men who consider that the valuable ideas
originated by individuals—ideas which may be of great national

advantage—should be taken out of private hands and thrown open to the public at large.

"And pray, gentlemen," an inventor might fairly reply, "why may not I make the same proposal respecting your goods and chattels, your clothing, your houses, your railway shares, and your money in the funds? If you are right in the interpretation you give to the term 'monopoly,' I do not see why that term should not be applied to the coats upon your backs and the provisions on your dinner tables. With equal reason I might argue that you unjustly 'monopolize' your furniture and that you ought not in equity to have the 'exclusive use' of so many apartments. If 'national advantage' is to be the supreme rule, why should we not appropriate your wealth, and the wealth of others like you, to the liquidation of the state debt? True, as you say, you came honestly by all this property; but so did I by my invention. True, as you say, this capital, on the interest of which you subsist, was acquired by years of toil—is the reward of persevering industry; well, I may say the like of this machine. While you were gathering profits, I was collecting ideas; the time you spent in conning the prices current was employed by me in studying mechanics; your speculations in new articles of merchandise answer to my experiments, many of which were costly and fruitless; when you were writing out your accounts, I was making drawings; and the same perseverance, patience, thought, and toil which enabled you to make a fortune have enabled me to complete my invention. Like your wealth, it represents so much accumulated labor; and I am living upon the profits it produces me, just as you are living upon the interest of your invested savings. Beware, then, how you question my claim. I am a monopolist, so also are you; so also is every man. If I have no right to these products of my brain, neither have you to those of your hands; no one can become the sole owner of any article whatever, and 'all property is robbery.' "

**4.** THEY FALL INTO A SERIOUS ERROR WHO SUPPOSE THAT THE EX-clusive right assumed by a discoverer is something taken from the public. He who in any way increases the powers of production

is seen by all, save a few insane Luddites, to be a general benefactor who gives rather than takes. The successful inventor
makes a further conquest over nature. By him the laws of
matter are rendered still more subservient to the wants of mankind. He economizes labor, helps to emancipate men from their
slavery to the needs of the body, harnesses a new power to the
car of human happiness. He cannot, if he would, prevent society
from largely participating in his good fortune. Before he can
realize any benefit from his new process or apparatus, he must
first confer a benefit on his fellow men—must either offer them
a better article at the price usually charged, or the same article
at a less price. If he fails to do this, his invention is a dead letter;
if he does it, he makes society a partner in the new mine of
wealth he has opened. For all the exertion he has had in subjugating a previously unknown region of nature, he simply
asks an extra proportion of the fruits. The rest of mankind
unavoidably come in for the main advantage—will in a short
time have the whole. Meanwhile, they cannot without injustice
disregard his claims.

Let us remember, too, that in this, as in other cases, disobedience to the moral law is ultimately detrimental to all
parties—to those who infringe the rights of the individual as well
as to the individual himself. It is a well-proved fact that that
insecurity of material property which results from general dishonesty inevitably reacts to the punishment of all. The rationale
of this is obvious. Industrial energy diminishes just in proportion to the uncertainty of its reward. Those who do not
know that they shall reap will not sow. Instead of employing it
in business, capitalists hoard what they possess, because productive investments are dangerous. Hence arises a universal
straitness of means. Every enterprise is crippled by want of
confidence. And from general distrust spring general discourage-
ment, apathy, idleness, poverty, and their attendant miseries,
involving alike all grades of men. Similar in kind, and less only
in degree, is the curse attendant upon insecurity of property in
ideas. Just in so far as the benefits likely to accrue to the inventor are precarious will he be deterred from carrying out his
plans. "If," thinks he to himself, "others are to enjoy the fruits

of these wearisome studies and these numberless experiments, why should I continue them? If, in addition to all the possibilities of failure in the scheme itself, all the time, trouble, and expense of my investigations, all the chances of destruction to my claim by disclosure of the plan, all the heavy costs attendant upon obtaining legal protection, I am liable to be deprived of my right by any scoundrel who may infringe it in the expectation that I shall not have money or madness enough to institute a chancery suit against him, I had better abandon the project at once." And although such reflections may often fail to extinguish the sanguine hopes of an inventor; although he may still prosecute his scheme to the end, regardless of all risks, yet after having once suffered the losses which ten to one society will inflict upon him, he will take good care never again to enter upon a similar undertaking. Whatever other ideas he may then or subsequently entertain—some of them most likely valuable ones—will remain undeveloped and probably die with him. Did mankind know the many important discoveries which the ingenious are prevented from giving to the world by the cost of obtaining legal protection, or by the distrust of that protection if obtained; were people duly to appreciate the consequent check put upon the development of the means of production; and could they properly estimate the loss thereby entailed upon themselves, they would begin to see that the recognition of the right of property in ideas is only less important than the recognition of the right of property in goods.

**5.** IN CONSEQUENCE OF THE PROBABILITY, OR PERHAPS WE MAY SAY the certainty, that the causes leading to the evolution of a new idea in our mind will eventually produce a like result in some other mind, the claim above set forth must not be admitted without limitation. Many have remarked the tendency that exists for an important invention or discovery to be made by independent investigators nearly at the same time. There is nothing really mysterious in this. A certain state of knowledge, a recent advancement in science, the occurrence of some new social want—these form the conditions under which minds of similar characters are stimulated to like trains of thought, ending as they are prone to do in the same result. Such being the fact, there arises a qualification to the right of property in ideas, which it seems difficult and even impossible to specify definitely. The laws of patent and copyright express this qualification by confining the inventor's or author's privilege within a certain term of years. But in what way the length of that term may be found with correctness there is no saying. In the meantime, as already pointed out (p. 100), such a difficulty does not in the least militate against the right itself.

CHAPTER XII

# The Right of Property in Character

**1.** COULD WE ACCURATELY ANALYZE THE STIMULUS BY WHICH men are usually impelled to action, could we determine the proportions of the several motives which go to make up that stimulus, we should probably find that, among those classes removed from the absolute pressure of bodily wants, its chief component is a desire for the good opinion, regard, or admiration of others. Whether we observe this feeling as shown by the tattooed savage in his willingness to undergo torture that he may obtain a character for fortitude, and to risk any amount of danger that he may be called brave; or whether, turning to civilized life, we contemplate that ambition so universally exhibited by poets, orators, statesmen, artists, soldiers, and others known to fame; or whether, by taking off its disguises, we discover the true nature of that insane eagerness with which people pursue wealth, we are alike instructed in the fact that, after those instincts immediately connected with the preservation of life, love of approbation exercises the greatest influence over human conduct.

Reputation, therefore, as a thing which men strive so incessantly to acquire and preserve, may be regarded as property. Earned like other property by labor, care, and perseverance, similarly surrounding its owner with facilities for securing his ends, and affording him as it does a constant supply of food for divers of his desires, the esteem of others is a possession, having many analogies with possessions of a more palpable nature. An estate in the general good will appears to many of more worth than one in land. By some great action to have bought golden opinions may be a richer source of gratification than to have obtained bank stock or railway shares. There are those to whom a crown of bay leaves would be a greater treasure than a fat legacy. Titles had once a definite pounds, shillings, and pence price; and if they are now becoming depreciated in value when compared with the honors spontaneously awarded by the public voice, it is that they do not represent so large an amount of genuine approbation. Men, therefore, who cultivate character and live on the harvests of praise they reap—men who have invested their labor in noble deeds and receive by way of interest the best wishes and cordial greetings of society—may be considered as having claims to these rewards of good conduct, resembling the claims of others to the rewards of their industry. Of course this is true not only of such as are distinguished by unusual worth; it is true of all. To the degree in which each has shown probity, kindness, truth, or other virtue, and has gained among his fellows a reputation for it, we must hold him entitled to the character he has thus fairly won, as to a species of property; a species of property, too, which, without quoting the hackneyed saying of Iago, may be described as of greater value than property of any other kind.

Those who hesitate to admit that a good name is property should remember that it has really a money value. To be accounted honest is to be preferred as one with whom commercial dealings may be most safely carried on. Whoso is said to be particularly industrious is likely, other things being equal, to get better pay than his competitors. The celebrity attending great intellectual capacity introduces those possessing it to responsible and remunerative situations. It is quite allowable, therefore, to classify reputation under this head, seeing that, like capital, it may bring its owner an actual revenue in hard cash.

**2.** THE POSITION THAT A GOOD CHARACTER IS PROPERTY BEING granted, a right to the possession of it when fairly earned, is demonstrable by arguments similar to those used in the two preceding chapters. Such character is attainable without any infringement of the freedom of others; is indeed a concrete result of habitual regard for that freedom; and being thus a source of gratification which its owner legitimately obtains—a species of property, as we say—it can no more be taken away from him without a breach of equity than property of other kinds can. This conclusion manifestly serves as the foundation for a law of libel.

**3.** POSSIBLY THIS REASONING WILL BE THOUGHT INCONCLUSIVE. THE position that character is property may be considered open to dispute; and it must be confessed that the propriety of so classifying it is not provable with logical precision. Should any urge that this admission is fatal to the argument, they have the alternative of regarding slander as a breach, not of that primary law which forbids us to trench upon each other's spheres of activity, but of that secondary one which forbids us to inflict pain on each other. If the destruction of a fellow man's deserved reputation does not amount to a trespass against the law of equal freedom, then the flagitiousness of such an act remains to be treated of in that supplementary department of morals elsewhere generalized under the term negative beneficence. Of these alternatives each must make his own choice, for there seems to be no way of deciding between them with certainty. And here indeed we meet with an illustration of a remark previously made (p. 64); namely, that the division of morality into separate sections, though needful for our due comprehension of it, is yet artificial; and that the lines of demarcation are not always capable of being maintained.

## CHAPTER XIII

## *The Right of Exchange*

**1.** FREEDOM TO EXCHANGE HIS PROPERTY FOR THE PROPERTY OF others is manifestly included in a man's general freedom. In claiming this as his right, he in no way transgresses the proper limit put to his sphere of action by the like spheres of action of others. The two parties in a trade transaction, while doing all that they will to do, are not assuming more liberty than they leave to others. Indeed their act ends with themselves, does not affect the condition of the bystanders at all, leaves these as much power to pursue the objects of their desires as before. Hence, exchanges may be made in complete conformity with the law of equal freedom.

Possibly it will be said that in cases where several men are wishing to deal with the same man, and a bargain is ultimately made between him and one of them, the rest are by this event excluded from a certain prospective field for the fulfillment of their wants, which was previously open to them; and that consequently they have had the liberty to exercise their faculties diminished by the success of their competitor. This, however, is a distorted view of the matter. Let us for a moment turn back to first principles. What is it that we have to do? We have to divide out equally among all men the whole of that freedom which the conditions of social existence afford. Observe, then, in respect of trade relationships, how much falls to the share of each. Evidently each is free to offer; each is free to accept; each is free to refuse; for each may do these to any extent without preventing his neighbors from doing the like to the same extent and at the same time. But no one may do more; no one may force another to part with his goods; no one may force another to take a specified price; for no one can do so without assuming more liberty of action than the man whom he thus treats. If, therefore, everyone is entitled to offer, to accept, and to refuse, but to do nothing more, it is clear that, under the circumstances above put, the closing of an agreement between two of the parties implies no infringement of the claims of the disappointed ones; seeing that each of them remains as free as ever, to offer, accept, and refuse.

**2.** TO SAY THAT, AS A COROLLARY FROM THIS, ALL INTERFERENCE between those who would traffic with each other amounts to a breach of equity is hardly needful. Nor is there any occasion here to assign reasons why the recognition of liberty of trade is expedient. Harmonizing as it does with the settled convictions of thinking people, the foregoing conclusion may safely be left to stand unsupported. Some remarks upon the limits it puts to legislation are indeed called for. But these will come in more appropriately elsewhere.

CHAPTER XIV

---

## The Right of Free Speech

**1.** THE UTTERANCE OF THOUGHT BEING ONE SPECIES OF ACTION, there arises from the proposition that every man is free within specified bounds to do what he wills the self-evident corollary that, with the like qualification, he is free to say what he wills; or, in other words, as the rights of his fellow men form the only legitimate restraint upon his deeds, so likewise do they form the only legitimate restraint upon his words.

There are two modes in which speech may exceed the ordained limits. It may be used for the propagation of slander, which, as we have seen in a foregoing chapter, involves a disregard of moral obligation; or it may be used in inciting and directing another to injure a third party. In this last case, the instigator, although not personally concerned in the trespass proposed by him, must be considered as having virtually com-

mitted it. We should not exonerate an assassin who pretended
that his dagger was guilty of the murder laid to his charge
rather than himself. We should reply that having moved a
dagger with the intention of taking away life constituted his
crime. Following up the idea, we must also assert that he who,
by bribes or persuasion, moved the man who moved the dagger
is equally guilty with his agent. He had just the same intention
and similarly used means for its fulfillment, the only difference
being that he produced death through a more complicated
mechanism. As, however, no one will argue that the interposing
of an additional lever between a motive force and its ultimate
effect alters the relationship between the two, so neither can
it be said that he who gets a wrong done by proxy is less guilty
than if he had done it himself. Hence, whoso suggests or urges
the infraction of another's rights must be held to have transgressed the law of equal freedom.

Liberty of speech, then, like liberty of action, may be claimed
by each to the fullest extent compatible with the equal rights
of all. Exceeding the limits thus arising, it becomes immoral.
Within them, no restraint of it is permissible.

**2.** A NEW "AREOPAGITICA," WERE IT POSSIBLE TO WRITE ONE,
would surely be needless in our age of the world and in this
country. And yet there still prevails, and that too among men
who plume themselves on their liberality, no small amount of
the feeling which Milton combated in his celebrated essay. Notwithstanding the abatement of intolerance and the growth of
free institutions, the repressive policy of the past has occasional
advocates even now. Were it put to the vote, probably not a
few would say ay to the proposition that the public safety requires some restriction to be placed on the freedom of speech.
The imprisonment of a socialist for blasphemy some few years
since called forth no indignant protest against the violation of
"the liberty of unlicensed" speaking but was even approved
by staunch maintainers of religious freedom. Many would like
to make it a penal offense to preach discontent to the people;
and there are not wanting others who would hang up a few
demagogues by way of scarecrows. Let us look at what may be

said by the advocates of a mild censorship on behalf of their opinions.

**3.** IT IS AN ASSERTION OFTEN MADE, AS OF INDISPUTABLE TRUTH, that government ought to guarantee to its subjects "security and a sense of security." From which maxim to the inference that it is the duty of the magistrate to keep an ear open to the sayings of popular orators and to stop violent declamation as being calculated to create alarm is an obvious step. Were the premises good, the deduction might pass; but the premises are more than questionable. That it is the special function of the legislator to guard every man in the peaceable possession of his person and property, all admit; but that the legislator is called upon to quiet the fears aroused by every trifling excitement is a notion almost too ridiculous for serious argument. Consider a moment to what it leads. Coupled as are the ideas "security and a sense of security," we must suppose that as governors are required to carry home "security" to every individual, so also may every individual claim the "sense of security" at their hands. Here is a pretty prospect for overburdened premiers! If such a doctrine be true, where shall the cares of the statesman end? Must he listen to the apprehensions of every hypochondriac in whose morbid imagination Reform is pictured as a grim ogre of anthropophagous propensities, with pikes for claws and guillotines for teeth? If not, why not? "Sense of security" in such a one has been destroyed by the violent denunciations of some hot patriot; he wishes his trepidations allayed by the suppression of what he thinks dangerous speaking; and, according to the hypothesis, his wishes ought to be obeyed. On the same grounds, all agitation should be extinguished, for there are invariably some—and not a small number either—who regard the discussion of every public question that comes uppermost with dread and predict all kinds of disasters from its continuance. Old women of both sexes working themselves into a state of great tribulation over the terrible vaticinations of a *Standard* or the melancholy wailings of a *Herald* would fain have put down the Free Trade propaganda; and if their "sense of security" had been duly consulted, they should have had their way.

Religious disabilities, too, ought, for the like reason, to have been still maintained, for the proposal to repeal them was productive of extreme consternation to multitudes of weak-minded people. Prophecies were rife of the return of papal persecutions; every horror narrated in the Book of Martyrs was expected to be acted over afresh; and an epidemic fright invalided its thousands. Credulous individuals listened with raised eyebrows and pendant jaws to the dismal tales of some incipient Titus Oates, and straightway had visions of fire and faggots; each saw himself in Smithfield with a stake at his back and a torch at his feet, or dreamed he was in the torture chamber of an inquisition, and awoke in a cold perspiration to find that he had mistaken the squeak of a mouse for the creak of a thumbscrew. Well, here was a woeful loss of the "sense of security," and therefore the authorities ought to have stopped the movement for Catholic emancipation by gagging all its advocates, fettering its press, and preventing its meetings.

It is useless to say that these are exaggerations and that the alarms of nervous valetudinarians or foolish bigots are to be disregarded. If the fears of a hundred are not to be attended to, why those of a thousand? If not those of a thousand, why those of ten thousand? How shall the line be drawn? Where is the requisite standard? Who shall tell when the sense of insecurity has become general enough to merit respect? Is it to be when the majority participate in it? If so, who shall decide when they do this? Perhaps it will be said that the apprehensions must be reasonable ones. Good; but who is to determine whether they are so or not? Where is the pope who shall give an infallible judgment on such a matter? To all which questions those who would make the preservation of a "sense of security" the limit to liberty of speech must first find answers.

**4.** OF THOSE ANIMADVERSIONS UPON STATE AFFAIRS WHICH CONstitute the legal offense of bringing government into contempt, and of which offense, by the way, all parties might be accused, from a chartist orator to the leader of the opposition—from the Times, with its burlesques upon the pitiful results of an annual "great talk," to its facetious contemporary who quizzes

the eccentricities of a versatile ex-chancellor—of such animadversions the only needful question to be asked is: Are they
deserved? Are the allegations contained in them true? If it can
be shown that they are not—that is, if it can be shown that
the parties referred to have been unjustly aspersed—that is, if
it can be shown that a violation of the law has been committed
—there is an end of the matter, so far as the moralist is concerned. But, on the other hand, should they prove to be sub-
stantially correct, on what grounds shall the suppression of them
be defended? That which is really contemptible ought to be exposed to contempt; and, if so, derogatory charges ought to have
full publicity. To argue otherwise is to take up the Machiavellian
position that it is right for the legislature to be an imposture, an
"organized hypocrisy"; that it is necessary for a nation to be
cheated by the semblance of virtue when there is no reality; that
public opinion ought to be in error rather than in truth; or
that it is well for the people to believe a lie!

**5.** THERE MAY BE MUCH DANGER IN PLACING AN INVALID UNDER
the regimen proper to people in robust health. For a dyspeptic,
chicken broth may be in all respects better suited than more
substantial fare. And whoso is suffering under an attack of in-
fluenza will do wisely to avoid a blustering northwester, or even
a gentle breeze from the south. But he would be thought
more than silly who inferred from such facts that solid food
and fresh air are bad things. To ascribe any evil results to these,
rather than to the unhealthy condition of the patients, would
imply extremely crude ideas of causation.

Similarly crude, however, are the ideas of those who infer
that unlimited liberty of speech is improper because productive
in certain states of society of disastrous results. It is to the abnormal condition of the body politic that all evils arising from
an unrestrained expression of opinion must be attributed, and
not to the unrestrained expression itself. Under a sound social
regime and its accompanying contentment, nothing is to be
feared from the most uncontrolled utterance of thought and
feeling. On the other hand, it may happen that where disease
exists, exposure of the sore places of the state to the cold

breath of criticism will superinduce alarming symptoms. But what then? A Louis Philippe, a General Cavaignac, or a Louis Napoleon may find excuse in a corrupted and disorganized state of things for espionage, censorships, and the suppression of public meetings. But what then? If a nation cannot be governed on principles of pure equity, so much the worse for the nation. Those principles remain true notwithstanding. As elsewhere pointed out (p. 35), there must necessarily exist incongruity between the perfect law and the imperfect man. And if evils are entailed upon a people by immediate and entire recognition of the law of equal freedom, in the matter of speech as well as in that of action, such evils are merely significant of the incomplete adaptation of that people to the social state, and not of any defect in the law.

CHAPTER XV

## Further Rights

DID CIRCUMSTANCES DEMAND IT, SUNDRY OTHER CHAPTERS OF THE same nature as the preceding ones could be added. Were this France, it might be needful formally to deduce from the law of equal freedom the right to move from place to place without leave of a governmental official. In addressing the Chinese, some proof that a man is at liberty to cut his clothes after whatever fashion may best suit him would perhaps be called for. And, similarly, there might be found in different times and places many other directions in which the law of equal freedom required asserting. But it is unnecessary now to repeat over again the reasoning so many times used. These that we call *rights* are nothing but artificial divisions of the general claim to exercise the faculties—applications of that general claim to particular cases; and each of them is proved in the same way, by showing that the particular exercise of faculties referred to is possible without preventing the like exercise of faculties by other persons. The reader has already seen the most important rights thus established; and the establishment of such minor ones as have not been touched upon may safely be left with himself.

**CHAPTER XVI**

---

## *The Rights of Women*

**1.** EQUITY KNOWS NO DIFFERENCE OF SEX. IN ITS VOCABULARY the word man must be understood in a generic and not in a specific sense. The law of equal freedom manifestly applies to the whole race—female as well as male. The same a priori reasoning which establishes that law for men (Chapters III and IV) may be used with equal cogency on behalf of women. The Moral Sense, by virtue of which the masculine mind responds to that law, exists in the feminine mind as well. Hence the several rights deducible from that law must appertain equally to both sexes.

This might have been thought a self-evident truth, needing only to be stated to meet with universal acceptation. There are many, however, who either tacitly, or in so many words, express their dissent from it. For what reasons they do so does not appear. They admit the axiom that human happiness is the Divine will, from which axiom what we call rights are primarily derived. And why the differences of bodily organization and those trifling mental variations which distinguish female from male should exclude one half of the race from the benefits of this ordination remains to be shown. The onus of proof lies on those who affirm that such is the fact; and it would be perfectly in order to assume that the law of equal freedom comprehends both sexes, until the contrary has been demonstrated. But without taking advantage of this, suppose we go at once into the controversy.

Three positions only are open to us. It may be said that women have no rights at all, that their rights are, not so great as those of men, or that they are equal to those of men.

Whoever maintains the first of these dogmas, that women have no rights at all, must show that the Creator intended women to be wholly at the mercy of men—their happiness, their liberties, their lives at men's disposal; or, in other words, that they were meant to be treated as creatures of an inferior order. Few will have hardihood to assert this.

From the second proposition, that the rights of women are not so great as those of men, there immediately arise such queries as: If they are not so great, by how much are they less? What is the exact ratio between the legitimate claims of the two sexes? How shall we tell which rights are common to both, and where those of the male exceed those of the female? Who can show us a scale that will serve for the apportionment? Or, putting the question practically, is it required to determine by some logical method whether the Turk is justified in plunging an offending Circassian into the Bosphorus? Whether the rights of women were violated by that Athenian law which allowed a citizen under certain circumstances to sell his daughter or sister? Whether our own statute, which permits a man to beat his wife in moderation and to imprison her in any room in his house, is morally defensible? Whether it is equitable that a married woman should be incapable of holding property? Whether a husband may justly take possession of his wife's earnings against her will, as our law allows him to do?—and so forth. These and a multitude of similar problems present themselves for solution. Some principle rooted in the nature of things has to be found by which they may be scientifically decided —decided, not on grounds of expediency, but in some definite, philosophical way. Does anyone holding the doctrine that women's rights are not so great as men's think he can find such a principle?

If not, there remains no alternative but to take up the third position—that the rights of women are equal with those of men.

**2.** WHOSO URGES THE MENTAL INFERIORITY OF WOMEN IN BAR of their claim to equal rights with men may be met in various ways.

In the first place, the alleged fact may be disputed. A defender of her sex might name many whose achievements in government, in science, in literature, and in art have obtained no small share of renown. Powerful and sagacious queens the world has seen in plenty, from Zenobia, down to the empresses Catherine and Maria Theresa. In the exact sciences, Mrs. Somerville, Miss Herschel, and Miss Zornlin have gained applause; in political economy, Miss Martineau; in general philosophy, Madame de Staël; in politics, Madame Roland. Poetry has its Tighes, its Hemanses, its Landons, its Brownings; the drama its Joanna Baillie; and fiction its Austens, Bremers, Gores, Dudevants, etc., without end. In sculpture, fame has been acquired by a princess; a picture like "The Momentous Question" is tolerable proof of female capacity for painting; and on the stage it is certain that women are on a level with men, if they do not even bear away the palm. Joining to such facts the important consideration that women have always been, and are still, placed at a disadvantage in every department of learning, thought, or skill—seeing that they are not admissible to the academies and universities in which men get their training; that the kind of life they have to look forward to does not present so great a range of ambitions; that they are rarely exposed to that most powerful of all stimuli—necessity; that the education custom dictates for them is one that leaves uncultivated many of the higher faculties; and that the prejudice against bluestockings, hitherto so prevalent among men, has greatly tended to deter women from the pursuit of literary honors—adding these considerations to the above facts, we shall see good reason for thinking that the alleged inferiority of the feminine mind is by no means self-evident.

But, waiving this point, let us contend with the proposition on its own premises. Let it be granted that the intellect of woman is less profound than that of man—that she is more uniformly ruled by feeling, more impulsive, and less reflective than man is—let all this be granted; and let us now see what basis such an admission affords to the doctrine that the rights of women are not coextensive with those of men.

1. If rights are to be meted out to the two sexes in the ratio

of their respective amounts of intelligence, then must the same system be acted upon in the apportionment of rights between man and man. Whence must proceed all those multiplied perplexities already pointed out. (See pp. 98 and 99.)

2. In like manner, it will follow that, as there are here and there women of unquestionably greater ability than the average of men, some women ought to have greater rights than some men.

3. Wherefore, instead of a certain fixed allotment of rights to all males and another to all females, the hypothesis itself involves an infinite gradation of rights, irrespective of sex entirely, and sends us once more in search of those unattainable desiderata—a standard by which to measure capacity and another by which to measure rights.

Not only, however, does the theory thus fall to pieces under the mere process of inspection; it is absurd on the very face of it, when freed from the disguise of hackneyed phraseology. For what is it that we mean by rights? Nothing else than freedom to exercise the faculties. And what is the meaning of the assertion that women is mentally inferior to man? Simply that her faculties are less powerful. What then does the dogma that because woman is mentally inferior to man she has less extensive rights amount to? Just this—that because woman has weaker faculties than man she ought not to have like liberty with him, to exercise the faculties she *has!*

**3.** BELIEF ALWAYS BEARS THE IMPRESS OF CHARACTER—IS, IN fact, its product. Anthropomorphism sufficiently proves this. Men's wishes eventually get expressed in their faiths—their real faiths, that is; not their normal ones. Pull to pieces a man's Theory of Things, and you will find it based upon facts collected at the suggestion of his desires. A fiery passion consumes all evidences opposed to its gratification and, fusing together those that serve its purpose, casts them into weapons by which to achieve its end. There is no deed so vicious but what the actor makes for himself an excuse to justify; and if the deed is often repeated, such excuse becomes a creed. The vilest transactions on record—Bartholomew massacre and the like—have had defenders; nay, have been inculcated as fulfillments of the Divine will. There is wisdom in the fable which represents the wolf as raising accusations against the lamb before devouring it. It is always thus among men. No invader ever raised standard but persuaded himself that he had a just cause. Sacrifices and prayers have preceded every military expedition, from one of Caesar's campaigns down to a border foray. "God is on our side," is the universal cry. Each of two conflicting nations consecrates its flags; and whichever conquers sings a *Te Deum*. Attila conceived himself to have a "divine claim to the dominion of the earth"; the Spaniards subdued the Indians under plea of converting them to Christianity, hanging thirteen refractory ones in honor of Jesus Christ and his apostles; and we English justify our colonial aggressions by saying that the Creator intends the Anglo-Saxon race to people the world! An insatiate lust of conquest transmutes manslaying into a virtue; and, among more races than one, implacable revenge has made assassination a duty. A clever theft was praiseworthy among the Spartans; and it is equally so among Christians, provided it be on a sufficiently large scale. Piracy was heroism with Jason and his followers; was so also with the Norsemen; is so still with the Malays; and there is never wanting some golden fleece for a pretext. Among money-hunting people a man is commended in proportion to the number of hours he spends in business; in our day the rage for accumulation has apotheosized work; and even the miser is not without a code of morals by which to defend his parsimony. The ruling classes argue themselves into the belief that property should be represented rather than person—that the landed interest should preponderate. The pauper is thoroughly persuaded that he has a *right* to relief. The monks held printing to be an invention of the devil, and some of our modern sectaries regard their refractory breathren as under demoniacal possession.[1] To the clergy nothing is more obvious than that a state-church is just and essential to the maintenance of religion. The sinecurist thinks himself rightly indignant at any disregard of his vested interests. And so on throughout society.

[1] Speech of Mr. Garland, one of the Conference Methodists.

Perhaps the slaveowner's assertion that Negroes are not human beings and the kindred dogma of the Mohammedans that women have no souls[2] are the strangest samples of convictions so formed. In these, as in the foregoing cases, selfishness finds out a satisfactory reason why it may do what it wills— collects and distorts, exaggerates and suppresses, so as ultimately to cheat itself into the desired conclusion. Does anyone doubt that men can really believe things thus palpably opposed to the plainest facts? Does anyone assert that those who profess opinions so manifestly absurd must be hypocrites? Let him beware. Let him consider whether selfishness has not deluded him into absurdities almost as gross. The laws of England and the public opinion of England contenance doctrines nearly as preposterous as these that look to us inconceivable; nay, the very same doctrines somewhat softened down. For what, when closely examined, is this notion that the rights of women are not equal with those of men? Simply an evanescent form of the theory that women have no souls.

**4.** THAT A PEOPLE'S CONDITION MAY BE JUDGED BY THE TREATment which women receive under it is a remark that has become almost trite. The facts, of which this remark is a generalization, are abundant enough. Look where we will, we find that just as far as the law of the strongest regulates the relationships between man and man does it regulate the relationships between man and woman. To the same extent that the triumph of might over right is seen in a nation's political institutions it is seen in its domestic ones. Despotism in the state is necessarily associated with despotism in the family. The two, being alike moral in their origin, cannot fail to coexist. Turkey, Egypt, India, China, Russia, the feudal states of Europe—it needs but to name these to suggest hosts of facts illustrative of such an accordance.

Yet, strangely enough, almost all of us who let fall this

[2]Though Washington Irving has pointed out that the Koran does not teach this, he has not shown that Mohammed's followers do not hold it. Most likely the Mohammedan faith has undergone corruptions similar to those suffered by Christianity

observation overlook its application to ourselves. Here we sit over our tea tables and pass criticisms upon national character or philosophize upon the development of civilized institutions, quietly taking it for granted that we are civilized—that the state of things we live under is the right one, or thereabouts. Although the people of every past age have thought the like and have been uniformly mistaken, there are still many to whom it never occurs that we may be mistaken too. Amid their strictures upon the ill treatment of women in the East and the unhealthy social arrangements implied by it, most persons do not see that the same connection between political and domestic oppression exists in this England of ours at the present hour, and that in as far as our laws and customs violate the rights of humanity by giving the richer classes power over the poorer, in so far do they similarly violate those rights by giving the stronger sex power over the weaker. Yet, looking at the matter apart from prejudice, and considering all institutions to be, as they are, products of the popular character, we cannot avoid confessing that such must be the case. To the same extent that the old leaven of tyranny shows itself in the transactions of the senate, it will creep out in the doings of the household. If injustice sways men's public acts, it will inevitably sway their private ones also. The mere fact, therefore, that oppression marks the relationships of outdoor life is ample proof that it exists in the relationships of the fireside.

**5.** THE DESIRE TO COMMAND IS ESSENTIALLY A BARBAROUS DESIRE. Whether seen in the ukase of a czar or in the order of an Eton bully to his fag, it is alike significant of brutality. Command cannot be otherwise than savage, for it implies an appeal to force, should force be needful. Behind its "You shall" there lies the scarcely hidden "If you won't, I'll make you." Command is the growl of coercion crouching in ambush. Or we might aptly term it—violence in a latent state. All its accessories—its frown, its voice, its gestures—prove it akin to the ferocity of the uncivilized man. Command is the foe of peace, for it breeds war of words and feelings—sometimes of deeds. It

is inconsistent with the first law of morality. It is radically
wrong.

All the barbarisms of the past have their types in the present.
All the barbarisms of the past grew out of certain dispositions:
those dispositions may be weakened, but they are not extinct;
and so long as they exist there must be manifestations of them.
What we commonly understand by command and obedience
are the modern forms of bygone despotism and slavery. Philosophically considered, they are identical with these. Despotism
may be defined as the making of another's will bend to the fulfillment of our own; and its counterpart, slavery, as the having
our own will subordinated to the will of another. True, we
apply the terms only when the rule of one will over another is
extreme—when the one wholly, or almost wholly, extinguishes
the other. But if the subjection of man to man is bad when
carried to its full extent, it is bad in any degree. If every man has
freedom to exercise his faculties within specified limits; and if,
as we have see (Chapter VIII), slavery is wrong because it
transgresses that freedom and makes one man use his powers to
satisfy not his own wants but the wants of another, then whatsoever involves command or whatsoever implies obedience is
wrong also; seeing that it, too, necessitates the subserviency of
one man's actions to the gratifications of another. "You must
not do as you will, but as I will," is the basis of every mandate,
whether used by a planter to his Negro, or by a husband to his
wife. Not satisfied with being sole ruler over his own doings,
the petty autocrat oversteps the boundary dividing his sphere
of action from his neighbor's and takes upon himself to direct
his or her doings also. It matters not, in point of principle,
whether such domination is entire or partial. To whatever
extent the will of the one is overborne by the will of the other,
to that extent the parties are tyrant and slave.

There are, without doubt, many who will rebel against this
doctrine. There are many who hold that the obedience of one
human being to another is proper, virtuous, praiseworthy. There
are many to whose moral sense command is not repugnant.
There are many who think the subjection of the weaker sex to

the stronger legitimate and beneficial. Let them not be deceived. Let them remember that a nation's institutions and beliefs are determined by its character. Let them remember that men's perceptions are warped by their passions. Let them remember that our social state proves our superior feelings to be very imperfectly developed. And let them remember that, as many customs deemed right by our ancestors appear detestable to us, so many customs which we think proper our more civilized descendants may regard with aversion—even as we loathe those barbarian manners which forbid a woman to sit at table with her lord and master, so may mankind one day loathe that subserviency of wife to husband, which existing laws enjoin.

As elsewhere shown (p. 28), moral sense becomes a trustworthy guide only when it has logic for an interpreter. Nothing but its primary institution is authoritative. From the fundamental law to which it gives utterance, reason has to deduce the consequences; and from these, when corectly drawn, there is no appeal. It proves nothing, therefore, that there are some who do not feel command to be improper. It is for such to inquire whether command is or is not consistent with that first principle expressive of the Divine will—that axiom to which the Moral Sense responds. And they will find that, thus judged by the law of equal freedom, command is at once pronounced wrong; for whoso commands manifestly claims more freedom than whoso is commanded.

**6.** A FUTURE BELIEF THAT SUBORDINATION OF SEX IS INEQUITABLE is clearly prohesied by the change civilization is working in men's sentiments. The arbitrary rule of one human being over another, no matter in what form it may appear, is fast getting recognized as essentially rude and brutal. In our day, the man of refined feeling does not like to play the despot over his fellow. He is disgusted if one in humble circumstances cringes to him. So far from wishing to elevate himself by depressing his poor and ignorant neighbors, he strives to put them at their ease in his presence—encourages them to behave in a less submissive and more self-respecting manner. He feels that a fellow man may be enslaved by imperious words and manners as well as by tyrannical deeds, and hence he avoids a dictatorial style of speech to those below him. Even paid domestics, to whose services he has obtained a right by contract, he does not like to address in a tone of authority. He seeks rather to disguise his character of master: to this end wraps up his commands in the shape of requests, and continually employs the phrases, "If you please," and "Thank you."

In the conduct of the modern gentleman to his friend, we have additional signs of this growing respect for another's dignity. Everyone must have observed the carefulness with which those who are on terms of affectionate intimacy shun anything in the form of supremacy on either side or endeavor to banish from rememberance, by their behavior to each other, whatever of supremacy there may exist. Who is there that has not witnessed the dilemma in which the wealthier of two such is sometimes placed, between the wish to confer a benefit on the other and the fear that is so doing he may offend by assuming the attitude of a patron? And who is there that does not feel how destructive it would be of the sentiment subsisting between himself and his friend were he to play the master over his friend, or his friend to play the master over him?

A further increase of this same refinement will show men that there is a fatal incongruity between the matrimonial servitude which our law recognizes and the relationship that *ought* to exist between husband and wife. Surely if he who possesses any generosity of nature dislikes speaking to a hired domestic in a tone of authority—if he cannot bear assuming toward his friend the behavior of a superior—how utterly repugnant to him should it be to make himself ruler over one on whose behalf all his kindly sentiments are specially enlisted; one to whom he is bound by the strongest attachment that his nature is capable of, and for whose rights and dignity he ought to have the most active sympathy!

**7.** COMMAND IS A BLIGHT TO THE AFFECTIONS. WHATSOEVER OF refinement, whatsoever of beauty, whatsoever of poetry there is in the passion that unites the sexes withers up and dies in the cold atmosphere of authority. Native as they are to such widely

separated regions of our nature, Love and Coercion cannot
possibly flourish together. The one grows out of our best feelings; the other has its root in our worst. Love is sympathetic;
Coercion is callous. Love is gentle; Coercion is harsh. Love is
self-sacrificing; Coercion is selfish. How, then, can they coexist?
It is the property of the first to attract, while it is that of the
last to repel: and, conflicting as they thus do, it is the constant
tendency of each to destroy the other. Let whoever thinks
the two compatible imagine himself acting the master over his
bethrothed. Does he believe that he could do this without any
injury to the subsisting relationship? Does he not know rather
that a bad effect would be produced upon the feelings of both
parties by the assumption of such an attitude? And confessing
this, as he must, is he superstitious enough to suppose that the
going through a form of words will render harmless that use of
command which was previously hurtful?

Of all the causes which conspire to produce the disappointment of those glowing hopes with which married life is usually
entered upon, none is so potent as this supremacy of sex—this
degradation of what should be a free and equal relationship into
one of ruler and subject—this supplanting of the sway of affection by the sway of authority. Only as that condition of slavery
to which women are condemned among barbarous nations is
ameliorated does ideal love become possible; and only when that
condition of slavery shall have been *wholly* abolished will ideal
love attain fullness and permanence. The facts around us plainly
indicate this. Wherever anything worth calling connubial happiness at present exists, we shall find that the subjugation of
wife to husband is not enforced; though perhaps still held in
theory, it is practically repudiated.

**8.** THERE ARE MANY WHO THINK THAT AUTHORITY AND ITS ALLY,
compulsion, are the sole agencies by which human beings can be
controlled. Anarchy or government are, with them, the only
conceivable alternatives. Believing in nothing but what they see,
they cannot realize the possibility of a condition of things in
which peace and order shall be maintained without force or the
fear of force. By such as these, the doctrine that the reign of

man over woman is wrong will no doubt be combated on the ground that the domestic relationship can exist only by the help of such supremacy. The impracticability of an equality of rights between the sexes will be urged by them in disproof of its rectitude. It will be argued that were they put upon a level husband and wife would be forever in antagonism; that, as when their wishes clashed each would possess a like claim to have his or her way, the matrimonial bond would daily be endangered by the jar of opposing wills; and that, involving as it would a perpetual conflict, such an arrangement of married life must necessarily be an erroneous one.

A very superficial conclusion this. It has been already pointed out (p. 35) that there *must* be an inconsistency between the perfect law and an imperfect state. The worse the condition of society, the more visionary must a true code of morality appear. The fact that any proposed principle of conduct is at once fully practicable—requires no reformation of human nature for its complete realization—is not a proof of its truth; is proof, rather, of its error. And, conversely, a certain degree of incongruity between such a principle and humanity as we know it, though no proof of the correctness of that principle, is at any rate a fact in its favor. Hence the allegation that mankind are not good enough to admit of the sexes living together harmoniously under the law of equal freedom in no way militates against the validity or sacredness of that law.

But the never-ceasing process of adaptation will gradually remove this obstacle to domestic rectitude. Recognition of the moral law and an impulse to act up to it going hand in hand, as we have seen that they must do (p. 25), equality of rights in the married state will become possible as fast as there arises a perception of its justness. That selfish conflict of claims which, according to the foregoing objection, would reduce a union, founded on the law of equal freedom, to a condition of anarchy presupposes a deficiency in those feelings with which a belief in the law of equal freedom originates and would decrease with the growth of those feelings. As elsewhere shown (p. 89), the same sentiment which leads us to maintain our own rights leads us, by its sympathetic excitement, to respect the rights of our neighbors. Other things equal, the sense of justice to ourselves and the sense of justice to our fellow creatures bear a constant ratio to each other. A state in which everyone is jealous of his natural claims is not therefore a litigious state, because it is one in which there is of necessity a diminished tendency to aggression. Experience proves this. For as it cannot be denied that there is now a greater disposition among men toward the assertion of individual liberty than existed during the feudal ages, so neither can it be denied that there is now a less disposition among men to trespass against each other than was then exhibited. The two changes are co-ordinate and must continue to be so. Hence, whenever society shall have become civilized enough to recognize the equality of rights between the sexes—when women shall have attained to a clear perception of what is due to them, and men to a nobility of feeling which shall make them concede to women the freedom which they themselves claim—humanity will have undergone such a modification as to render an equality of rights practicable.

Married life under this ultimate state of things will not be characterized by perpetual squabbles, but by mutual concessions. Instead of a desire on the part of the husband to assert his claims to the uttermost, regardless of those of his wife, or on the part of the wife to do the like, there will be a watchful desire on both sides not to transgress. Neither will have to stand on the defensive, because each will be solicitous for the rights of the other. Not encroachment, but self-sacrifice will be the ruling principle. The struggle will not be which shall gain the mastery, but which shall give way. Committing a trespass will be the thing feared, and not the being trespassed against. And thus, instead of domestic discord, will come a higher harmony than any we yet know.

There is nothing Utopian in this. We may already trace the beginnings of it. An attitude like that described is not uncommonly maintained in the dealings of honorable men with each other; and if so, why should it not exist between the sexes? Here and there, indeed, may be found, even now, a wedded pair who preserve such a relationship. And what is at present the exception may one day be the rule.

**9.** THE EXTENSION OF THE LAW OF EQUAL FREEDOM TO BOTH sexes will doubtless be objected to on the ground that the political privileges exercised by men must thereby be ceded to women also. Of course they must; and why not? Is it that women are ignorant of state affairs? Why, then their opinions would be those of their husbands and brothers; and the practical effect would be merely that of giving each male elector two votes instead of one. Is it that they might by and by become better informed and might then begin to act independently? Why, in such case, they would be pretty much as competent to use their power with intelligence as the members of our present constituencies.

We are told, however, that "woman's mission" is a domestic one; that her character and position do not admit of her taking a part in the decision of public questions; that politics are beyond her sphere. But this raises the question: Who shall say what her sphere is? Among the Pawnees and Sioux it is that of a beast of burden; she has to carry the baggage, to drag home fuel from the woods, and to do everything that is menial and laborious. In slave countries it is within woman's sphere to work side by side with men, under the lash of the taskmaster. Clerkships, cashierships, and other responsible business situations are comprised in her sphere in modern France. While, on the other hand, the sphere of a Turkish or Egyptian lady extends scarcely an inch beyond the walls of the harem. Who now will tell us what woman's sphere really is? As the usages of mankind vary so much, let us hear how it is to be shown that the sphere we assign her is the true one—that the limits we have set to female activity are just the proper limits. Let us hear why on this one point of our social polity we are exactly right, while we are wrong on so many others.

It is indeed said that the exercise of political power by women is repugnant to our sense of propriety—conflicts with our ideas of the feminine character—is altogether condemned by our feelings. Granted; but what then? The same plea has been urged in defense of a thousand absurdities, and if valid in one case is equally so in all others. Should a traveler in the East inquire of a

Turk why women in his country conceal their faces, he would be told that for them to go unveiled would be considered indecent; would offend the *feelings* of the spectators. In Russia female voices are never heard in church, women not being thought worthy "to sing the praises of God in the presence of men"; and the disregard of this regulation would be censured as an outrage upon public *feeling*. There was a time in France when men were so enamored of ignorance that a lady who pronounced any but the commonest words correctly was blushed for by her companions; a tolerable proof that people's *feelings* then blamed in a woman that literateness which it is now thought a disgrace for her to be without. In China cramped feet are essential to female refinement; and so strong is the *feeling* in this matter that a Chinese will not believe that an Englishwoman who walks naturally can be one of a superior class. It was once held unfeminine for a lady to write a book; and no doubt those who thought it so would have quoted *feelings* in support of their opinion. Yet, with facts like these on every hand, people assume that the enfranchisement of women cannot be right because it is repugnant to their feelings!

We have some feelings that are necessary and eternal; we have others that, being the results of custom, are changeable and evanescent. And there is no way of distinguishing those feelings which are natural from those which are conventional, except by an appeal to first principles. If a sentiment responds to some necessity of our condition, its dictates must be respected. If otherwise—if opposed to a necessity, instead of in harmony with one—we must regard that sentiment as the product of circumstances, of education, of habit, and consequently without weight. However much, therefore, the giving of political power to women may disagree with our notions of propriety, we must conclude that, being required by that first prerequisite to greatest happiness—the law of equal freedom—such a concession is unquestionably right and good.

**10.** THUS IT HAS BEEN SHOWN THAT THE RIGHTS OF WOMEN MUST stand or fall with those of men, derived as they are from the same authority, involved in the same axiom, demonstrated by the same argument. That the law of equal freedom applies alike to both sexes has been further proved by the fact that any other hypothesis involves us in inextricable difficulties. The idea that the rights of women are not equal to those of men has been condemned as akin to the Eastern dogma that women have no souls. It has been argued that the position at present held by the weaker sex is of necessity a wrong one, seeing that the same selfishness which vitiates our political institutions must inevitably vitiate our domestic ones also. Subordination of females to males has been also repudiated, because it implies the use of command, and thereby reveals its descent from barbarism. Proof has been given that the attitudes of mastery on the one side and submission on the other are essentially at variance with that refined sentiment which should subsist between husband and wife. The argument that married life would be impracticable under any other arrangement has been met by pointing out how the relationship of equality must become possible as fast as its justness is recognized. And lastly, it has been shown that the objections commonly raised against giving political power to women are founded on notions and prejudices that will not bear examination.

CHAPTER XVII

## The Rights of Children

**1.** IF WE ARE ONCE SURE OF OUR LAW—SURE THAT IT IS A DIVINE ordination—sure that it is rooted in the nature of things, then whithersoever it leads we may safely follow. As elsewhere pointed out (Lemma II), a true rule has no exceptions. When therefore that first principle from which the rights of adults are derived turns out to be a source from which we may derive the rights of children, and when the two processes of deduction prove to be identical, we have no choice but to abide by the

result, and to assume that the one inference is equally authoritative with the other.

That the law—every man has freedom to do all that he wills,
provided he infringes not the equal freedom of any other man—
applies as much to the young as to the mature becomes manifest
on referring back to its origin. God wills human happiness; that
happiness is attainable only through the medium of faculties;
for the production of happiness those faculties must be exercised; the exercise of them presupposes liberty of action; these
are the steps by which we find our way from the Divine will to
the law of equal freedom. But the demonstration is fully as complete when used on behalf of the child as when used on behalf
of the man. The child's happiness, too, is willed by the Deity;
the child, too, has faculties to be exercised; the child, too, needs
scope for the exercise of those faculties; the child therefore has
claims to freedom—rights, as we call them—coextensive with
those of the adult. We cannot avoid this conclusion if we
would. Either we must reject the law altogether, or we must
include under it both sexes and all ages.

The candid thinker will find himself obliged to concede this
when he considers the many perplexities which follow in the
train of any other theory. For, if it be asserted that the law of
equal freedom applies only to adults—that is, if it be asserted
that men have rights but that children have none—we are immediately met by the question: When does the child become a
man? At what period does the human being pass out of the condition of having no rights into the condition of having rights?
None will have the folly to quote the arbitrary dictum of the
statute book as an answer. The appeal is to an authority above
that of legislative enactments—demands on what these are to be
founded—on what attribute of manhood recognition by the law
of equal freedom depends. Shall the youth be entitled to the
rights of humanity when the pitch of his voice sinks an octave?
Or when he begins to shave? Or when he ceases growing? Or
when he can lift a hundredweight? Are we to adopt the test of
age, of stature, of weight, of strength, of virility, or of intelligence? Much may no doubt be said in favor of each of these,
but who can select the true one? And who can answer the objec-

tion that whichever qualification is chosen will class many as
men who are not at present considered such, while it will reject
from the list others who are now by universal consent included
in it?

Nor is this all. For even supposing that, by some undiscovered
species of logic, it has been determined on what particular day
of his life the human being may equitably claim his freedom, it
still remains to define the position he holds previously to this
period. Has the minor absolutely no rights at all? If so, there is
nothing wrong in infanticide. If so, robbery is justifiable, provided the party robbed be under age. If so, a child may equitably
be enslaved. For, as already shown (pp. 102, 121), murder,
theft, and the holding of others in bondage are wrong, simply
because they are violations of human rights; and if children have
no rights, they cannot become the subjects of these crimes. But
if, on the other hand, it be held, as it is held, that children have
some rights; if it be held that the youth has an equal claim to
life with the adult; if it be held that he has something like the
same title to liberty; and if it be held (though not by law, yet by
public opinion) that he is similarly capable of owning property,
then it becomes needful to show why these primary rights must
be conceded, but no others. They who assert that children are
wholly without rights, and that, like the inferior animals, they
exist only by permission of grown men, take up a precise, unmistakable position. But they who suppose children to occupy a
place morally above that of brutes, and yet maintain that while
children have certain rights their rights are not equal with those
of men, are called upon to draw the line, to explain, to define.
They must say what rights are common to children and adults,
and why. They must say where the rights of adults exceed those
of children, and why. And their answers to these queries must
be drawn, not from considerations of expediency, but from the
original constitution of things.

Should it be argued that the relationship in which a parent
stands to his child, as supplying it with the necessaries of life, is
a different one from that subsisting between man and man, and
that consequently the law of equal freedom does not apply, the
answer is that though by so maintaining it a parent establishes a

certain claim upon his child—a claim which he may fairly expect
to have discharged by a like kindness toward himself should he
ever need it—yet he establishes no title to dominion. For if the
conferring an obligation establishes a title to dominion in this
case, then must it do so in others; whence it will follow that if
one man becomes a benefactor to another he thereby obtains
the right to play the master over that other, a conclusion which
we do not admit. Moreover, if in virtue of his position a parent
may trench upon the liberties of his child, there necessarily
arises the question: To what extent may he do this; may he destroy them entirely, as by committing murder? If not, it is required to ascertain the limit up to which he may go but which
he must not exceed; a problem equally insoluble with the similar one just noticed.

Unless, therefore, the reader can show that the train of reasoning by which the law of equal freedom is deduced from the
Divine will does not recognize children, which he cannot; unless
he can show exactly at what time the child becomes a man,
which he cannot; unless he can show why a certain share of
liberty naturally attaches to both childhood and manhood, and
another share to only one, which he cannot, he must admit that
the rights of the youth and the adult are coextensive.

There is indeed one plausible-looking way of meeting these
arguments. It may be urged that in the child many of the faculties of the future man are undeveloped, and that as rights are
primarily dependent on faculties, the rights of children cannot
be coextensive with those of adults, because their faculties are
not so. A fatal objection this, did it touch the question; but it
happens to be wholly beside it. The fullest endowment of rights
that any being can posses is *perfect* freedom to exercise *all* his
faculties. And if each of two beings possesses *perfect* freedom to
exercise *all* his faculties, each possesses *complete* rights; that is,
the rights of the two are equal; no matter whether their faculties
are equal or not. For, to say that the rights of the one are less
than those of the other, because his faculties are fewer, is to say
that he has no right to exercise the faculties he has not got!—a
curious compound of truism and absurdity.

**2.** DUE WARNING WAS GIVEN (P. 48) THAT OUR FIRST PRINCIPLE carried in it the germs of sundry unlooked-for conclusions. We have now met with one of these. We have just found ourselves committed to a proposition at war with the convictions of almost all. Truth, however, must of necessity be consistent. We have therefore no alternative but to re-examine our preconceived opinions, in the expectation of finding them erroneous.

That we may enter upon this task in a philosophical spirit, it will be well, at the risk even of something like repetition, to glance at the influences by which our beliefs are in danger of being warped. We need constant reminding of these. As an abstract truth, we all admit that passion distorts judgment, yet never inquire whether our passions are influencing us. We all decry prejudice, yet are all prejudiced. We see how habits and interests and likings mold the theories of those around us, yet forget that our own theories are similarly molded. Nevertheless, the instances in which our feelings bias us in spite of ourselves are of hourly recurrence. That proprietary passion which a man has for his ideas veils their defects to him as effectually as maternal fondness blinds a mother to the imperfections of her offspring. An author cannot, for the life, of him, judge correctly of what he has just written; he has to wait until lapse of time enables him to read it as though it were a stranger's, and he then discerns flaws where all had seemed perfect. It is only when his enthusiasm on its behalf has grown cold that the artist is able to see the faults of his picture. While they are transpiring, we do not perceive the ultimate bearing of our own acts or the acts of others toward us; only in after years are we able to philosophize upon them. Just so, too, is it with successive generations. Men of the past quite misunderstood the institutions they lived under; they pertinaciously adhered to the most vicious principles and were bitter in their opposition to right ones, at the dictates of their attachments and antipathies. So difficult is it for man to emancipate himself from the invisible fetters which habit and education cast over his intellect, and so palpable is the consequent incompetency of a people to judge rightly of itself and its deeds or opinions, that the fact has been embodied in the current aphorism—"No age can write its own history"; an aphorism sufficiently expressive of the universality of prejudice.

If we act wisely, we shall assume that the reasonings of modern society are subject to the like disturbing influences. We shall conclude that, even now, as in times gone by, opinion is but the counterpart of condition—merely expresses the degree of civilization to which we have attained. We shall suspect that many of those convictions which seem the results of dispassionate thinking have been nurtured in us by circumstances. We shall confess that as heretofore fanatical opposition to this doctrine and bigoted adhesion to that have been no tests of the truth or falsity of the said doctrines, so neither is the strength of attachment or dislike which a nation now exhibits toward certain principles any proof of their correctness or their fallacy. Nay, more —we shall not only admit that public opinion may be wrong, but that it must be so. Without a general equilibrium between institutions and ideas society cannot subsist; and hence, if error pervades our institutions, it must similarly pervade our ideas. Just as much as a people falls short of perfection in its state will it lack of truth in its beliefs.

Thus much by way of bespeaking a calm hearing. As lately said, the proposition about to be maintained conflicts with the habits, associations, and most cherished convictions of the great majority. That the law of equal freedom applies to children as much as to adults; that consequently the rights of children are coextensive with those of adults; that, as violating those rights, the use of coercion is wrong; and that the relationship now commonly existing between parents and children is therefore a vicious one—these are assertions which perhaps few will listen to with equanimity. Nevertheless, if there be any weight in the foregoing considerations, we shall do well to disregard all protests of feeling, and place implicit faith in the conclusions of abstract equity.

**3.** WE SAY THAT A MAN'S CHARACTER MAY BE TOLD BY THE COMpany he keeps. We might similarly say that the truth of a belief may be judged by the morality with which it is associated. Given a theory universally current among the most degraded sections of our race, a theory received only with considerable

abatements by civilized nations, a theory in which men's confidence diminishes as fast as society advances, and we may safely
pronounce that theory to be a false one. On such, along with
other evidence, the subordination of sex was lately condemned.
Those commonly observed facts that the enslavement of woman
is invariably associated with a low type of social life and that,
conversely, her elevation toward an equality with man uniformly accompanies progress were cited in part proof that the
subjection of female to male is essentially wrong. If now, instead
of *women* we read *children*, similar facts may be cited, and a
similar deduction may be drawn. If it be true that the dominion
of man over woman has been oppressive in proportion to the
badness of the age or the people, it is also true that parental
authority has been stringent and unlimited in a like proportion.
If it be a fact that the emancipation of women has kept pace
with the emancipation of society, it is likewise a fact that the
once despotic rule of the old over the young has been ameliorated at the same rate. And if, in our own day, we find the fast-
spreading recognition of popular rights accompanied by a
silently growing perception of the rights of women, we also find
it accompanied by a tendency toward systems of non-coercive
education—that is, toward a practical admission of the rights of
children.

Whoever wants illustrations of this alleged harmony between
the political, connubial, and filial relationships may discover
them anywhere and everywhere. Scanning that aboriginal state
of existence during which the aggressive conduct of man to man
renders society scarcely possible, he will see not only that wives
are slaves and exist by sufferance, but that children hold their
lives by the same tenure and are sacrificed to the gods when
fathers so will. He may observe how during the classic times the
thralldom of five sixths of the population was accompanied both
by a theory that the child is the property and slave of its male
parent and by a legal fiction which regarded wives as children
similarly owned. That political degradation of the present East
Indian races for whom absolute monarchy seems still the only
possible form of rule, he will find accompanied alike by suttees
and by infanticide. The same connection of facts will be seen by

him in China, where under a government purely autocratic
there exists a public opinion which deems it an unpardonable
offense for a wife to accuse her husband to the magistrate, and
which ranks filial disobedience as a crime next in atrocity to
murder. Nor is our own history barren of illustrations. On reviewing those times when constitutional liberty was but a name,
when men were denied freedom of speech and belief, when the
people's representatives were openly bribed and justice was
bought—the times, too, with which the laws enacting the servitude of women were in complete harmony—the observer cannot
fail to be struck with the harshness of parental behavior and the
attitude of humble subjection which sons and daughters had to
assume. Between the close of the last century, when our domestic condition was marked by the use of *Sir* and *Madam* in
addressing parents and by the doctrine that a child ought un-
hesitatingly to marry whomsoever a father appointed; and when
our political condition was marked by aristocratic supremacy, by
the occurrence of church-and-king riots, and by the persecution
of reformers—between that day and ours, the decline in the
rigor of paternal authority and in the severity of political oppression has been simultaneous. And, as already remarked, the like
companionship of facts is seen in the present rapid growth of
democratic feeling and the equally rapid spread of a milder
system of juvenile training.

Thus, the biography of the race affords ample illustration of
the alleged law. That uniformity of moral tone which it was
asserted must necessarily pervade a nation's arrangements—
social, marital, and parental—we see exemplified alike under all
phases of civilization. Indeed this position hardly needed proof,
being, as it is, a direct corollary from self-evident truths. As
surely as a man's character shines through all his deeds, so surely
does the character of a people shine through all its laws and
customs. Having a common root in human nature, contemporary
institutions cannot fail to be equally affected by the imperfection of that nature. They must all be right or wrong together.
The evil which taints one must taint all. The change which
reforms one must at the same time reform all. The progress
which perfects one must eventually perfect all.

Consequently, whoever admits that injustice is still visible in the dealings of class with class, whoever admits that it similarly exhibits itself in the behavior of one sex to the other, cannot but admit that it necessarily exists in the conduct of the old to the young. And he must further admit that, being most implicitly received among the most barbarous nations, and waning as its influence does with the advance of civilization, the doctrine of filial subjection is entirely condemned by its associations.

**4.** IF COERCIVE EDUCATION BE RIGHT, IT MUST BE PRODUCTIVE OF good; and if wrong, of evil. By an analysis of its results, therefore, we shall obtain so much evidence for or against the doctrine that the liberties of children are coextensive with those of adults.

That coercive education is impolitic may be strongly suspected from the fact lately adverted to—the evident disposition toward the abandonment of it which modern systems of training evince. Considering what universal attention the culture of the young has lately received—the books written about it, the lectures delivered on it, the experiments made to elucidate it— there is reason for concluding that as the use of brute force for educational purposes has greatly declined, something radically wrong must be involved in it. But without dwelling upon this, which, like all inferences drawn from expediency, is liable to have its premises called in question, let us judge of coercive education, not by the effects it is *believed* to produce, but by those it *must* produce.

Education has for its object the formation of character. To curb restive propensities, to awaken dormant sentiments, to strengthen the perceptions and cultivate the tastes, to encourage this feeling and repress that, so as finally to develop the child into a man of well-proportioned and harmonious nature—this is alike the aim of parent and teacher. Those, therefore, who advocate the use of authority—and, if need be, force—in the management of children must do so because they think these the best means of compassing the desired object—formation of character. Paternity has to devise some kind of rule for the nursery. Impelled partly by the creed, partly by custom, partly by inclination, paternity decides in favor of a pure despotism, proclaims its word the supreme law, anathematizes disobedience, and exhibits the rod as the final arbiter in all disputes. And of course this system of discipline is defended as the one best calculated to curb restive propensities, awaken dormant sentiments, etc., etc., as aforesaid. Suppose, now, we inquire how the plan works. An unamiable little urchin, in pursuing his own gratification regardless of the comfort of others, is perhaps annoyingly vociferous in his play, or is amusing himself by teasing a companion, or is trying to monopolize the toys intended for others in common with himself. Well, some kind of interposition is manifestly called for. Paternity, with knit brows and in a severe tone, commands desistance; visits anything like reluctant submission with a sharp "Do as I bid you"; if need be, hints at a whipping or the black hole—in short, carries coercion or the threat of coercion far enough to produce obedience. After sundry exhibitions of perverse feeling, the child gives in; showing, however, by its sullenness the animosity it entertains. Meanwhile paternity pokes the fire and complacently resumes the newspaper under the impression that all is as it should be: most unfortunate mistake!

If the thing wanted had been the mere repression of noise or the mechanical transfer of a plaything, perhaps no better course could have been pursued. Had it been of no consequence under what impulse the child acted, so long as it fulfilled a given mandate, nothing would remain to be said. But something else was needed. Character was the thing to be changed rather than conduct. It was not the deeds but the feeling from which the deeds sprang that required dealing with. Here were palpable manifestations of selfishness—an indifference to the wishes of others, a marked desire to tyrannize, an endeavor to engross benefits intended for all—in short, here were exhibitions on a small scale of that unsympathetic nature to which our social evils are mainly attributable. What, then, was the thing wanted? Evidently an alteration in the child's disposition. What was the problem to be solved? Clearly to generate a state of mind which, had it previously existed, would have prevented the offending actions. What was the final end to be achieved? Unquestionably the formation of a character which should spontaneously produce greater generosity of conduct. Or, speaking definitely, it was necessary to strengthen that sympathy to the weakness of which this ill behavior was traceable.

But sympathy can be strengthened only by exercise. No faculty whatever will grow, save by the performance of its special function—a muscle by contraction; the intellect by perceiving and thinking; a moral sentiment by feeling. Sympathy, therefore, can be increased only by exciting sympathetic emotions. A selfish child is to be rendered less selfish only by arousing in it a fellow feeling with the desires of others. If this is not done, nothing is done.

Observe, then, how the case stands. A grasping, hard-natured boy is to be humanized—is to have whatever germ of better spirit may be in him developed; and to this end it is proposed to use frowns, threats, and the stick! To stimulate that faculty which originates our regard for the happiness of others, we are told to inflict pain or the fear of pain! The problem is—to generate in a child's mind a sympathetic feeling; and the answer is—beat it or send it supperless to bed!

Thus we have but to reduce the subjection theory to a definite form to render its absurdity self-evident. Contrasting the means to be employed with the work to be done, we are at once struck with their utter unfitness. Instead of creating a new internal state which shall exhibit itself in better deeds, coercion can manifestly do nothing but forcibly mold externals into a coarse semblance of such a state. In the family, as in society, it can simply restrain; it cannot educate. Just as the recollection of Bridewell and the dread of a policeman, while they serve to check the thief's depredations, effect no change in his morals, so, although a father's threats may produce in a child a certain outside conformity with rectitude, they cannot generate any real attachment to it. As someone has well said, the utmost that severity can do is to make hypocrites; it can never make converts.

**5.** LET THOSE WHO HAVE NO FAITH IN ANY INSTRUMENTALITIES for the rule of human beings save the stern will and the strong hand, visit the Hanwell Asylum for the insane. Let all self-styled practical men who, in the pride of their semi-savage theories, shower sarcasms upon the movements for peace, for the abolition of capital punishments and the like, go and witness to their confusion how a thousand lunatics can be managed without the use of force. Let these sneerers at "sentimentalisms" reflect on the horrors of madhouses as they used to be, where were more weeping and wailing and gnashing of teeth, where chains clanked dismally, and where the silence of the night was rent by shrieks that made the belated passer-by hurry on shudderingly; let them contrast with these horrors the calmness, the contentment, the tractability, the improved health of mind and body, and the not unfrequent recoveries that have followed the abandonment of the strait-jacket regime:[1] and then let them blush for their creed.

And shall the poor maniac, with diseased feelings and a warped intellect, persecuted as he constantly is by the suggestions of a morbid imagination, shall a being with a mind so hopelessly chaotic that even the most earnest pleader for human rights would make his case an exception, shall he be amenable to a non-coercive treatment, and shall a child not be amenable to it? Will anyone maintain that madmen can be managed by suasion, but not children? That moral-force methods are best for those deprived of reason, but physical-force methods for those possessing it? Hardly. The boldest defender of domestic despotism will not assert so much. If by judicious conduct the confidence even of the insane may be obtained; if even to the beclouded intelligence of a lunatic kind attentions and a sympathetic manner will carry the conviction that he is surrounded by friends and not by demons; and if, under that conviction, even he, though a slave to every disordered impulse, becomes comparatively docile, how much more under the same influence will a child become so. Do but gain a boy's trust; convince him by your behavior that you have his happiness at heart; let him discover that you are the wiser of the two; let him experience the benefits of following your advice, and the evils that arise from disregarding it; and fear not, you will readily enough guide him.

[1]See Dr. Gonnolly on Lunatic Asylums.

Not by authority is your sway to be obtained; neither by reasoning, but by inducement. Show in all your conduct that you are thoroughly your child's friend, and there is nothing that you may not lead him to. The faintest sign of your approval or dissent will be his law. You have won from him the key of all his feelings; and, instead of the vindicative passions that severe treatment would have aroused, you may by a word call forth tears, or blushes, or the thrill of sympathy—may excite any emotion you please—may, in short, effect something worth calling education.

**6.** IF WE WISH A BOY TO BECOME A GOOD MECHANIC, WE INSURE his expertness by an early apprenticeship. The young musician that is to be passes several hours a day at his instrument. Initiatory courses of outline drawing and shading are gone through by the intended artist. For the future accountant, a thorough drilling in arithmetic is prescribed. The reflective powers are sought to be developed by the study of mathematics. Thus, all training is founded on the principle that culture must precede proficiency. In such proverbs as "Habit is second nature" and "Practice makes perfect," men have expressed those net products of universal observation on which every educational system is ostensibly based. The maxims of a village schoolmistress and the speculations of a Pestalozzi are alike pervaded by the theory that the child should be accustomed to those exertions of body and mind which will in future life be required of it. Education means this or nothing.

What now is the most important attribute of man as a moral being? What faculty above all others should we be solicitous to cultivate? May we not answer—the faculty of self-control? This it is which forms a chief distinction between the human being and the brute. It is in virtue of this that man is defined as a creature "looking before and after." It is in their larger endowment of this that the civilized races are superior to the savage. In supremacy of this consists one of the perfections of the ideal man. Not to be impulsive—not to be spurred hither and thither by each desire that in turn comes uppermost; but to be self-restrained, self-balanced, governed by the joint decision of the feelings in council assembled, before whom every action shall have been fully debated and calmly determined—this it is which education—moral education at least—strives to produce.

But the power of self-government, like all other powers, can be developed only by exercise. Whoso is to rule over his passions in maturity must be practiced in ruling over his passions during youth. Observe, then, the absurdity of the coercive system. Instead of habituating a boy to be a law to himself as he is required in afterlife to be, it administers the law for him. Instead of preparing him against the day when he shall leave the paternal roof, by inducing him to fix the boundaries of his actions and voluntarily confine himself within them, it marks out these boundaries for him and says, "Cross them at your peril." Here we have a being who, in a few years, is to become his own master, and, by way of fitting him for such a condition, he is allowed to be his own master as little as possible. While in every other particular it is thought desirable that what the man will have to do the child should be well drilled in doing, in this most important of all particulars—the controlling of himself—it is thought that the less practice he has, the better. No wonder that those who have been brought up under the severest discipline should so frequently turn out the wildest of the wild. Such a result is just what might have been looked for.

Indeed, not only does the physical-force system fail to fit the youth for his future position; it absolutely tends to unfit him. Were slavery to be his lot—if his afterlife had to be passed under the rule of a Russian autocrat or of an American cotton planter—no better method of training could be devised than one which accustomed him to that attitude of complete subordination he would subsequently have to assume. But just to the degree in which such treatment would fit him for servitude must it unfit him for being a free man among free men.

**7.** BUT WHY IS EDUCATION NEEDED AT ALL? WHY DOES NOT THE child grow spontaneously into a normal human being? Why should it be requisite to curb this propensity, to stimulate the other sentiment, and thus by artificial aids to mold the mind into something different from what it would of itself become? Is not there here an anomaly in nature? Throughout the rest of creation we find the seed and the embryo attaining to perfect maturity without external aid. Drop an acorn into the ground and it will in due time become a healthy oak without either pruning or training. The insect passes through its several transformations unhelped, and arrives at its final form possessed of every needful capacity and instinct. No coercion is needed to make the young bird or quadruped adopt the habits proper to its future life. Its character, like its body, spontaneously assumes complete fitness for the part it has to play in the world. How happens it, then, that the human mind alone tends to develop itself wrongly? Must there not be some exceptional cause for this? Manifestly; and if so a true theory of education must recognize this cause.

It is an indisputable fact that the moral constitution which fitted man for his original predatory state differs from the one needed to fit him for this social state to which multiplication of the race has led. In a foregoing part of our inquiry (Chapter II), it was shown that the law of adaptation is effecting a transition from the one constitution to the other. Living, then, as we do, in the midst of this transition, we must expect to find sundry phenomena which are explicable only upon the hypothesis that humanity is at present partially adapted to both these states and not completely to either, has only in a degree lost the dispositions needed for savage life, and has but imperfectly acquired those needed for social life. The anomaly just specified is one of these. The tendency of each new generation to develop itself wrongly, indicates the degree of modification that has yet to take place. Those respects in which a child requires restraint are just the respects in which he is taking after the aboriginal man. The selfish squabbles of the nursery, the persecution of the playground, the lyings and petty thefts, the rough treatment of inferior creatures, the propensity to destroy—all these imply that tendency to pursue gratification at the expense of other beings, which qualified man for the wilderness and which disqualifies him for civilized life.

We have seen, however, that this incongruity between man's attributes and his conditions is in course of being remedied. We have seen that the instincts of the savage must die of inanition, that the sentiments called forth by the social state must grow by exercise, and that if the laws of life remain constant, this modification will continue until our desires are brought into perfect conformity with our circumstances. When now the ultimate state in which morality shall have become organic is arrived at, this anomaly in the development of the child's character will have disappeared. The young human being will no longer be an exception in nature, will not as now tend to grow into unfitness for the requirements of afterlife, but will spontaneously unfold itself into that ideal manhood whose every impulse coincides with the dictates of the moral law.

Education, therefore, in so far as it seeks to form character, serves only a temporary purpose, and, like other institutions resulting from the non-adaptation of man to the social state, must in the end die out. Hence we see how doubly incongruous with the moral law in the system of training by coercion. Not only does it necessitate direct violations of that law, but the very work which it so futilely attempts to perform will not need performing when that law has attained to its final supremacy. Force in the domestic circle, like magisterial force, is merely the complement of immorality; immorality we have found to be resolvable into non-adaptation: non-adaptation must in time cease: and thus the postulate with which this old theory of education starts will eventually become false. Rods and ferules, equally with the staffs and handcuffs of the constable, the jailer's keys, the swords, bayonets, and cannon with which nations restrain each other, are the offspring of iniquity—can exist only while supported by it, and necessarily share in the badness of their parentage. Born, therefore, as it is of man's imperfections, governing as it does by means of those imperfections, and abdicating as it must when Equity begins to reign, Coercion in all its forms—educational or other—is essentially vicious.

**8.** AND HERE WE ARE NATURALLY LED TO REMARK ONCE MORE THE necessary incongruity between the perfect law and the imperfect man. Whatsoever of Utopianism there may seem to be in the foregoing doctrines is due not to any error in them but to faults in ourselves. A partial impracticability must not perplex us; must, on the contrary, be expected. Just in proportion to our distance below the purely moral state must be our difficulty in acting up to the moral law, either in the treatment of children or in anything else. It is not for us, however, to magnify and ponder over this difficulty. Our course is simple. We have just to fulfill the law as far as in us lies, resting satisfied that the limitations necessitated by our present condition will quite soon enough assert themselves.

Meanwhile let it be remarked that the main obstacle to the right conduct of education lies rather in the parent than in the child. It is not that the child is insensible to influences higher than that of force, but that the parent is not virtuous enough to use them. Fathers and mothers who enlarge upon the trouble which filial misbehavior entails upon them strangely assume that all the blame is due to the evil propensities of their offspring and none to their own. Though on their knees they confess to being miserable sinners, yet to hear their complaints of undutiful sons and daughters you might suppose that they were themselves immaculate. They forget that the depravity of their children is a reproduction of their own depravity. They do not recognize in these much-scolded, often-beaten little ones so many looking glasses wherein they may see reflected their own selfishness. It would astonish them to assert that they behave as improperly to their children as their children do to them. Yet a little candid self-analysis would show them that half their commands are issued more for their own convenience or gratification than for corrective purposes. "I won't have that noise!" exclaims a disturbed father to some group of vociferous juveniles; and, the noise ceasing, he claims to have done something toward making his family orderly. Perhaps he has; but how? By exhibiting that same evil disposition which he seeks to check in his children—a determination to sacrifice to his own happiness the happiness of others. Observe, too, the impulse under which a refractory child is punished. Instead of anxiety for the delinquent's welfare, that severe eye and compressed lip denote rather the ire of an offended ruler—express some such inward thought as "You little wretch, we'll soon see who is to be master." Uncover its roots, and the theory of parental authority will be found to grow not out of man's love for his offspring, but out of his love of dominion. Let anyone who doubts this listen to that common reprimand, "How dare you disobey me?" and then consider what the emphasis means. No, no, moral-force education is widely practicable even now, if parents were civilized enough to use it.

But of course the obstacle is in a measure reciprocal. Even the best samples of childhood as we now know it will be occasionally unmanageable by suasion; and when inferior natures have to be dealt with, the difficulty of doing without coercion must be proportionably great. Nevertheless, patience, self-denial, a sufficient insight into youthful emotions, and a due sympathy with them, added to a little ingenuity in the choice of means, will usually accomplish all that can be wished. Only let a parent's actions and words and manner show that his own feeling is a thoroughly right one, and he will rarely fail to awaken a responsive feeling in the breast of his child.

**9.** ONE FURTHER OBJECTION REMAINS TO BE NOTICED. IT WILL probably be said that if the rights of children are coextensive with those of adults, it must follow that children are equally entitled with adults to citizenship and ought to be similarly endowed with political power. This inference looks somewhat alarming; and it is easy to imagine the triumphant air of those who draw it and the smiles with which they meditate upon the absurdities it suggests. Nevertheless, the answer is simple and decisive. There must go two things to originate an incongruity; and, before passing censure, it is needful to say which of the two incongruous things is in fault. In the present case the incongruity is between the institution of government on the one side and a certain consequence of the law of equal freedom on the other. Which of the two is to be condemned for this? In the above objection it is tacitly assumed that the blame lies with this consequence of the law of equal freedom; whereas the fact is just the other way. It is with the institution of government that the blame lies. Were the institution of government an essentially right one, there would be reason to suppose that our conclusion was fallacious; but being as it is the offspring of immorality, it must be condemned for conflicting with the moral law, and not the moral law for conflicting with it. Were the moral law universally obeyed, government would not exist; and did government not exist, the moral law could not dictate the political enfranchisement of children. Hence the alleged absurdity is traceable to the present evil constitution of society, and not to some defect in our conclusion.

**10.** CONCERNING THE EXTENSION OF THE LAW OF EQUAL FREEDOM to children, we must therefore say that equity commands it and that expediency recommends it. We find the rights of children to be deducible from the same axiom and by the same argument as the rights of adults, while denial of them involves us in perplexities out of which there seems to be no escape. The association between filial subservience and barbarism—the evident kinship of filial subservience to social and marital slavery—and the fact that filial subservience declines with the advance of civilization suggest that such subservience is bad. The viciousness of a coercive treatment of children is further proved by its utter failure to accomplish the chief end of moral education—the culture of the sympathies—by its tendency to excite feelings of antagonism and hate, and by the check which it necessarily puts upon the development of the all-important faculty of self-control. While, on the other hand, a non-coercive treatment being favorable to, and almost necessitating, constant appeals to the higher feelings must, by exercising those feelings, improve the character; and must, at the same time, accustom the child to that condition of freedom in which its afterlife is to be passed. It turns out, too, that the very need for a moral training of children is but temporary, and that, consequently, a true theory of the filial relationship must not presuppose, like the command-and-obedience theory, that such a need is permanent. Lastly, we find reason to attribute whatever of incompatibility there may be between these conclusions and our daily experience, not to any error in them, but to the necessary incongruity between the perfect law and an imperfect humanity.

# SOCIAL STATICS

---

## Part III

## CHAPTER XVIII

## *Political Rights*

**1.** OUR PRINCIPLE IS THE PRIMORDIAL ONE. IT IS THE FIRST PRE-requisite to the realization of the Divine will. Every mode of interpreting that will points to this as the all-essential condition of its fulfillment. If we start with an a priori view of creative design, we are immediately led to the law of equal freedom (Chapter III). Do we appeal to the general character of the human constitution, the law of equal freedom is its corollary (Chapter IV). And when, pursuing the examination further, we observe the detailed arrangements of that constitution, we discover a faculty by which the law of equal freedom is recognized and responded to (Chapter V). Otherwise viewed, this law is seen to be a direct deduction from the necessities of existence, as thus: Life depends upon the performance of certain actions. Abrogate entirely the liberty to exercise the faculties, and we have death; abrogate it partially, and we have pain or partial death. This remains true of man, whether he be savage or civilized—isolated or social. And as there must be life before there can be society, this first principle of life must take precedence of the first principle of society—must fix or govern it. Or, speaking definitely, as liberty to exercise the faculties is the first condition of individual life, the liberty of each, limited only by the like liberty of all, must be the first condition of social life.

Derived, therefore, as it is, directly from the Divine will, and underlying as it does the right organization of society, the law of equal freedom is of higher authority than all other laws. The creative purpose demands that everything shall be subordinated to it. Institutions and social forms must just marshal themselves as it commands. It dates from the creation; they are of yester-

day. It is constant; they are changeable. It appertains to the perfect; they to the imperfect. It is coenduring with humanity; they
may die tomorrow. As surely, then, as the incidental must bow
before the necessary, so surely must all conventional arrangements be subject to the absolute moral law.

**2.** ALLUSION HAS FROM TIME TO TIME BEEN MADE TO A SCHOOL OF
politicians, especially claiming for themselves the title of philosophical, who demur to this. They do not recognize any such
supreme authority to which all human regulations must bend.
Practically, if not professedly, they hold, with Archelaus, that
nothing is intrinsically right or wrong, but that it becomes
either by the dictum of the state. If we are to credit them, government determines what shall be morality, and not morality
what shall be government. They believe in no oracular principle
by whose yea or nay we may be guided: their Delphi is the
House of Commons. By their account man lives and moves and
has his being by legislative permit. His freedom to do this or
that is not natural, but conferred. The question, Has the citizen
any claim to the work of his hands? can be decided only by a
parliamentary division. If "the ayes have it," he has; if "the
noes," he has not.

The reader who has arrived thus far needs not to have the
fallacy of this doctrine pointed out. The expediency system, of
which it forms an essential part, has been repeatedly proved untenable, and with it must fall its dependent propositions. And
having, moreover, been collaterally refused in the foregoing
chapters, the notion that man has no rights save those of government manufacture might safely be left where it lies. There
are, however, additional evidences of its untruth, which it may
be as well to state. And first let us inquire how it has originated.

**3.** CONSIDERING SOCIETY AS A CORPORATE BODY, WE MAY SAY THAT
man, when he first enters into it, has the repulsive force in
excess, while in the cohesive force he is deficient. His passions
are strong, his sympathies weak. Those propensities which fitted
him for savage life necessarily tend to breed war between himself and his neighbors. His condition has been that of perpetual

antagonism, and his antagonistic habits must of course accompany him into the social state. Aggression, dispute, anger, hatred, revenge—these are the several stages of the process by which the members of a primitive community are continually being sundered. Hence the smallness of the first communities. Populations burst as fast as they increase. Races split into tribes, tribes into factions. Only as civilization advances do larger unions become possible. And even these have to pass through some such stage as that of feudalism, with its small chieftainships and right of private war, showing that the tendency to repel is still active.

Now, in proportion to the repulsive force subsisting between atoms of matter must be the restraint required to keep them from exploding. And in proportion to the repulsive force subsisting between the units of a society must be the strength of the bonds requisite to prevent that society from flying to pieces. Some powerful concentrative influence there must be to produce even these smallest unions, and this influence must be strong in proportion to the savageness of the people; otherwise the unions cannot be maintained. Such an influence we have in the sentiment of veneration, reverence for power, loyalty, or, as Carlyle terms it, hero worship. By this feeling it is that society begins to be organized; and where the barbarism is greatest, there is this feeling strongest. Hence the fact that all traditions abound in superhuman beings, in giants and demigods. The mythical accounts of Bacchus and Hercules, of Thor and Odin, and of the various divine and half-divine personages who figure in the early histories of all races merely prove the intensity of the awe with which superiority was once regarded. In that belief of some of the Polynesian islanders that only their chiefs have souls, we find a still extant example of the almost incredible influence which this sentiment of reverence has over savage men. Through it only does all authority, whether that of ruler, teacher, or priest, become possible. It was alike the parent of beliefs in the miraculous conception of Genghis Khan, in the prophetic characters of Zoroaster, Confucius, and Mohammed, and in the infallibility of the Pope. Where it no longer deifies power, it associates it with divine attributes. Thus it was death for the Assyrian to enter unbidden into the presence of his monarch. The still stationary Orientals ascribe to their emperors celestial relationships. Shamyl, the prophet-chief of the Circassians, is believed to have entire union with the Divine essence. And the Russian soldiers pray for their Czar as "our God upon earth." The fealty of vassal to feudal lord, the devotion of Highland Celt to chief were exhibitions of the same feeling. Loyalty it made the brightest virtue and treason the blackest crime.

With the advance of civilization this awe of power diminishes. Instead of looking up to the monarch as a god, it begins to view him as a man reigning by Divine authority—as "the Lord's anointed." Submission becomes less abject. Subjects no longer prostrate themselves before their rulers, nor do serfs kiss their master's feet. Obedience ceases to be unlimited; men will choose their own faiths. Gradually, as there grow up those sentiments which lead each to maintain his own rights and sympathetically to respect the rights of others—gradually as each, thus, by the acquirement of self-restraining power becomes fitted to live in harmony with his fellow—so gradually do men cease to need external restraint, and so gradually does this feeling which makes them submit to that external restraint decrease. The law of adaptation necessitates this. The feeling must lose power just as fast as it ceases to be needful. As the new regulator grows, the old one must dwindle. The first amelioration of a pure despotism is a partial supplanting of the one by the other. Mixed constitutions exhibit the two acting conjointly. And while the one advances to supremacy, the other sinks into decreptitude: divine right of kings is exploded, and monarchical power becomes but a name.

Although the adaptation of man to the social state has already made considerable progress, although the need for external restraint is less, and although consequently that reverence for authority which makes restraint possible has greatly diminished—diminished to such an extent that the holders of power are daily caricatured and men begin to listen to the National Anthem with their hats on—still the change is far from complete. The attributes of the aboriginal man have not yet died out. We still trench upon each other's claims—still pursue happiness at each other's expense. Our savage selfishness is seen in commerce, in legislation, in social arrangements, in amusements. The shopkeeper imposes on his lady customer; his lady customer beats down the shopkeeper. Classes quarrel about their respective "interests," and corruption is defended by those who profit from it. The spirit of caste morally tortures its victims with as much coolness as the Indian tortures his enemy. Gamblers pocket their gains with unconcern, and your share speculator cares not who loses, so that he gets his premium. No matter what their rank, no matter in what they are engaged—whether in enacting a Corn Law or in struggling with each other at the doors of a theater—men show themselves as yet little else than barbarians in broadcloth.

Hence we still require shackles, rulers to impose them, and power worship to make those rulers obeyed. Just as much as the love of God's law is deficient must the fear of man's law be called in to supply its place. And to the extent that man's law is needful there must be reverence for it to ensure the necessary allegiance. Hence, as men are still under the influence of this sentiment, we must expect their customs, creeds, and philosophies to testify of its presence.

Here, then, we have a rationale of the expediency idea of government. It is the latest and most refined form assumed by this disposition to exalt the state at the expense of the individual. There have been books written to prove that the monarch's will should be the subject's absolute law; and if instead of monarch we read legislature, we have the expediency theory. It merely modifies "divine right of kings" into divine right of government. It is despotism democratized. Between that old Eastern regime under which the citizen was the private property of his ruler, having no rights at all, and that final state under which his rights will be entire and inviolable, there comes this intermediate state in which he is allowed to possess rights, but only by sufferance of Parliament. Thus the expediency philosophy falls naturally into its place as a phenomena attending our progress from past slavery to future freedom. It is one of a series of creeds through which mankind have to pass. Like each of its predecessors, it is natural to a certain phase of human development. And it is fated to lose its hold as fast as our adaptation to the social state increases.

**4.** IT IS ONLY BY BEARING IN MIND THAT A THEORY OF SOME KIND being needful for men they will espouse any absurdity in default of something better, that we can understand how Rousseau's doctrine of Social Contract ever came to be so widely received. This fact remembered, however, the belief in such a doctrine becomes comprehensible. Here were men combined together under government and law. It seemed clear that the arrangement was on the whole a beneficial one. Hence the very natural, though erroneous, conclusion that state authority was a moral institute. And state authority being taken for a moral institute, it became needful to account for it, to defend it, to reconcile it with justice and truth. Under which stimulus there suggested itself this theory of a covenant originally entered into between individuals on the one hand and the community, or agents acting for it, on the other, by which allegiance was agreed to be exchanged for protection, and in virtue of which supposed covenant governments continue to exercise power and demand obedience.

That such an explanation should have satisfied the unthinking is not to be wondered at, but it is passing strange that it should have gained credence among educated men. Observe the battery of fatal objections which may be opened upon it.

In the first place, the assumption is a purely gratuitous one. Before submitting to legislative control on the strength of an agreement alleged to have been made by our forefathers, we ought surely to have some proof that such agreement was made. But no proof is given. On the contrary, the facts, so far as we can ascertain them, rather imply that under the earliest social forms, whether savage, patriarchal, or feudal, obedience to authority was given *unconditionally*; and that when the ruler afforded protection it was because he resented the attempt to exercise over one of his subjects a power similar to his own— a conclusion quite in harmony with what we know of oaths of allegiance taken in later times.

Again, even supposing the contract to have been made, we are no forwarder, for it has been repeatedly invalidated by the violation of its terms. There is no people but what has from time to time rebelled; and there is no government but what has, in an infinity of cases, failed to give the promised protection. How, then, can this hypothetical contract be considered binding, when, if ever made, it has been broken by both parties?

But, granting the agreement, and granting that nothing positive has occurred to vitiate it, we have still to be shown on what principle that agreement—made, no one knows when; by, no one knows whom—can be held to tie people now living. Dynasties have changed, and different forms of government have supplanted each other, since the alleged transaction could have taken place; while between the people who are supposed to have been parties to it and their existing descendants unnumbered generations have lived and died. So we must assume that this covenant has over and over again survived the deaths of all parties concerned! Truly a strange power, this, which our forefathers wielded—to be able to fix the behavior of their descendants for all futurity! What would anyone think of being required to kiss the Pope's toe because his great-great-great-grandfather promised that he should do so?

However, there never was such a contract. If there had been, constant breaches must have destroyed it. And even if undestroyed it could not bind us, but only those who made it.

**5.** THE SELF-IMPORTANCE OF A MALVOLIO IS SUFFICIENTLY LUDIcrous, but we must go far beyond it to parallel the presumption of legislatures. Some steward who, deluded by an intense craving after dominion and an impudence equal to his craving, should construe his stewardship into proprietorship would more fitly illustrate it. Were such a one to argue that the estate he was appointed to manage had been virtually resigned into his possession, that to secure the advantages of his administration its owner had given up all title to it, that he now lived on it only by his (the steward's) sufferance, and that he was in future to receive no emoluments from it except at his (the steward's) good pleasure, then should we have an appropriate travesty upon the behavior of governments to nations; then should we have a doctrine perfectly analogous to this fashionable one, which teaches how men on becoming members of a community give up, for the sake of certain social advantages, their natural rights. Adherents of this fashionable doctrine will doubtless protest against such an interpretation of it. They have no reasonable cause for doing so, however, as will appear on submitting them to a cross-examination. Suppose we begin it thus:

"Your hypothesis that men, when they entered into the social state, surrendered their original freedom implies that they entered into such state voluntarily, does it not?"

"It does."

"Then they must have considered the social state preferable to that under which they had previously lived?"

"Necessarily."

"Why did it appear preferable?"

"Because it offered greater security."

"Greater security for what?"

"Greater security for life, for property, for the things that minister to happiness."

"Exactly. To get more happiness: that must have been the object. If they had expected to get more unhappiness, they would not have willingly made the change, would they?"

"No."

"Does not happiness consist in the due satisfaction of all the desires? In the due exercise of all the faculties?"

"Yes."

"And this exercise of the faculties is impossible without freedom of action. The desires cannot be satisfied without liberty to pursue and use the objects of them."

"True."

"Now it is this freedom to exercise the faculties within specific limits which we signify by the term 'rights,' is it not?" (P. 68.)

"It is."

"Well, then, summing up your answers, it seems that, by your hypothesis, man entered the social state voluntarily; which means that he entered it for the sake of obtaining greater happiness; which means that he entered it to obtain fuller exercise of his faculties; which means that he entered it to obtain security for such exercise; which means that he entered it for the guaranteeing of his 'rights.' "

"Put your proposition in a more tangible form."

"Very good. If this is too abstract a statement for you, let us attempt a simpler one. You say that a state of political combination was preferred mainly because it afforded greater security for life and property than the isolated state, do you not?"

"Certainly."

"Are not a man's claims to his life and his property among what we term his rights, and moreover, the most important of them?"

"They are."

"Then to say that men formed themselves into communities to prevent the constant violation of their claims to life and property is to say that they did it for the preservation of their rights?"

"It is."

"Wherefore, either way we find that the preservation of rights was the object sought."

"So it would seem."

"But your hypothesis is that men give up their rights on entering the social state?"

"Yes."

"See now how you contradict yourself. You assert that on becoming members of a society men give up what by your own showing they joined it the better to obtain!"

"Well, perhaps I ought not to have said that they 'give up' their rights, but that they place them in trust."

"In whose trust?"

"In that of a government."

"A government, then, is a kind of agent employed by the members of a community to take care of, and administer for their benefit, something given into its charge?"

"Exactly."

"And of course, like all other agents, exercises authority only at the will of those who appoint it—performs all that it is commissioned to do subject to their approval?"

"Just so."

"And the things committed to its charge still belong to the original owners? The title of the people to the rights they have placed in trust continues valid; the people may demand from this agent the full benefit accruing from these rights and may, if they please, resume possession of them?"

"Not so."

"Not so! What, can they not reclaim their own?"

"No. Having once consigned their rights to the keeping of a legislature, they must be content with such use of them as that legislature permits."

And thus we arrive at the curious doctrine above referred to, that the members of a community, having entrusted an estate (their rights) to the care of a steward (their government), thereby lose all proprietorship in such estate and can have no benefit from it, except what their steward pleases to vouchsafe!

**6.** BUT IT IS NEEDLESS TO ASSAULT THIS THEORY OF GOVERNMENT omnipotence from without, for it is betrayed from within. It is self-destructive. It is disproved by its own innermost principle. The very witness called to testify of its truth lets out its falsity. For to what end is this attempted denial of rights? It is to the end of establishing the law of the greatest happiness to the greatest number—a law to carry out which government is said to exist—a law by whose dictates alone government ought to be guided—a law, therefore, of higher authority than government; antecedent to it—a law to which government must be subservient, subordinate. But what, when scrutinized, does this law of the greatest happiness to the greatest number resolve itself into? Why, into the ultra-democratic dogma—all men have equal rights to happiness (p. 22). Wherefore, it is to carry out the law—all men have equal rights to happiness—that government exists. And thus, even according to the opposition hypothesis, rights are the be-all and end-all of government; and rank above it, as the end above the means.

## CHAPTER XIX

# The Right to Ignore the State

**1.** AS A COROLLARY TO THE PROPOSITION THAT ALL INSTITUTIONS must be subordinated to the law of equal freedom, we cannot choose but admit the right of the citizen to adopt a condition of voluntary outlawry. If every man has freedom to do all that he wills, provided he infringes not the equal freedom of any other man, then he is free to drop connection with the state—to relinquish its protection and to refuse paying toward its support. It is self-evident that in so behaving he in no way trenches upon the liberty of others, for his position is a passive one, and while passive he cannot become an aggressor. It is equally self-evident that he cannot be compelled to continue one of a political corporation without a breach of the moral law, seeing that citizenship involves payment of taxes; and the taking away of a man's property against his will is an infringement of his rights (p. 121). Government being simply an agent employed in common by a number of individuals to secure to them certain advantages, the very nature of the connection implies that it is for each to say whether he will employ such an agent or not. If any one of them determines to ignore this mutual-safety confederation, nothing can be said except that he loses all claim to its good offices and exposes himself to the danger of maltreatment—a thing he is quite at liberty to do if he likes. He cannot be coerced into political combination without a breach of the law of equal freedom; he can withdraw from it without committing any such breach, and he has therefore a right so to withdraw.

**2.** "NO HUMAN LAWS ARE OF ANY VALIDITY IF CONTRARY TO THE law of nature; and such of them as are valid derive all their force and all their authority mediately or immediately from this original." Thus writes Blackstone, to whom let all honor be given for having so far outseen the ideas of his time and, indeed, we may say of our time. A good antidote, this, for those political superstitions which so widely prevail. A good check upon that sentiment of power worship which still misleads us by magnifying the prerogatives of constitutional governments as it once did those of monarchs. Let men learn that a legislature is not "our God upon earth," though, by the authority they ascribe to it and the things they expect from it, they would seem to think it is. Let them learn rather that it is an institution serving a purely temporary purpose, whose power, when not stolen, is at the best borrowed.

Nay, indeed, have we not seen (p. 14) that government is essentially immoral? Is it not the offspring of evil, bearing about it all the marks of its parentage? Does it not exist because crime exists? Is it not strong—or, as we say, despotic—when crime is great? Is there not more liberty—that is, less government—as crime diminishes? And must not government cease when crime ceases, for very lack of objects on which to perform its function? Not only does magisterial power exist because of evil, but it exists by evil. Violence is employed to maintain it, and all violence involves criminality. Soldiers, policemen, and jailers; swords, batons, and fetters are instruments for inflicting pain; and all inflection of pain is in the abstract wrong. The state employs evil weapons to subjugate evil and is alike contaminated by the objects with which it deals and the means by which it works. Morality cannot recognize it, for morality, being simply a statement of the perfect law, can give no countenance to anything growing out of, and living by, breaches of that law (Chapter I). Wherefore, legislative authority can never be ethical—must always be conventional merely.

Hence, there is a certain inconsistency in the attempt to determine the right position, structure, and conduct of a government by appeal to the first principles of rectitude. For, as just pointed out, the acts of an institution which is in both nature and origin imperfect cannot be made to square with the perfect law. All that we can do is to ascertain, firstly, in what attitude a legislature must stand to the community to avoid being by its mere existence an embodied wrong; secondly, in what manner it must be constituted so as to exhibit the least incongruity with the moral law; and thirdly, to what sphere its actions must be limited to prevent it from multiplying those breaches of equity it is set up to prevent.

The first condition to be conformed to before a legislature can be established without violating the law of equal freedom is the acknowledgment of the right now under discussion—the right to ignore the state.[1]

**3.** UPHOLDERS OF PURE DESPOTISM MAY FITLY BELIEVE STATE control to be unlimited and unconditional. They who assert that men are made for governments and not governments for men may consistently hold that no one can remove himself beyond the pale of political organization. But they who maintain that the people are the only legitimate source of power—that legislative authority is not original, but deputed—cannot deny the right to ignore the state without entangling themselves in an absurdity.

For, if legislative authority is deputed, it follows that those from whom it proceeds are the masters of those on whom it is conferred; it follows further that as masters they confer the said authority voluntarily; and this implies that they may give or withhold it as they please. To call that deputed which is wrenched from men, whether they will or not, is nonsense. But what is here true of all collectively is equally true of each separately. As a government can rightly act for the people only when empowered by them, so also can it rightly act for the individual only when empowered by him. If A, B, and C debate whether they shall employ an agent to perform for them a certain service, and if while A and B agree to do so C dissents, C cannot equitably be made a party to the agreement in spite of himself. And this must be equally true of thirty as of three; and if of thirty, why not of three hundred, or three thousand, or three million?

[1] Hence may be drawn an argument for direct taxation, seeing that only when taxation is direct does repudiation of state burdens become possible.

**4.** OF THE POLITICAL SUPERSTITIONS LATELY ALLUDED TO, NONE is so universally diffused as the notion that majorities are omnipotent. Under the impression that the preservation of order will ever require power to be wielded by some party, the moral sense of our time feels that such power cannot rightly be conferred on any but the largest moiety of society. It interprets literally the saying that "the voice of the people is the voice of God," and, transferring to the one the sacredness attached to the other, it concludes that from the will of the people—that is, of the majority—there can be no appeal. Yet is this belief entirely erroneous.

Suppose, for the sake of argument, that, struck by some Malthusian panic, a legislature duly representing public opinion were to enact that all children born during the next ten years should be drowned. Does anyone think such an enactment would be warrantable? If not, there is evidently a limit to the power of a majority. Suppose, again, that of two races living together—Celts and Saxons, for example—the most numerous determined to make the others their slaves. Would the authority of the greatest number be in such case valid? If not, there is something to which its authority must be subordinate. Suppose, once more, that all men having incomes under £50 a year were to resolve upon reducing every income above that amount to their own standard, and appropriating the excess for public purposes. Could their resolution be justified? If not, it must be a third time confessed that there is a law to which the popular voice must defer. What, then, is that law, if not the law of pure equity—the law of equal freedom? These restraints, which all would put to the will of the majority, are exactly the restraints set up by that law. We deny the right of a majority to murder, to enslave, or to rob, simply because murder, enslaving, and robbery are violations of that law—violations too gross to be overlooked. But if great violations of it are wrong, so also are smaller ones. If the will of the many cannot supersede the first principle of morality in these cases, neither can it in any. So that, however insignificant the minority, and however trifling the proposed trespass against their rights, no such trespass is permissible.

When we have made our constitution purely democratic, thinks to himself the earnest reformer, we shall have brought government into harmony with absolute justice. Such a faith, though perhaps needful for the age, is a very erroneous one. By no process can coercion be made equitable. The freest form of government is only the least objectional form. The rule of the many by the few we call tyranny; the rule of the few by the many is tyranny also, only of a less intense kind. "You shall do as we will, and not as you will," is in either case the declaration; and if the hundred make it to the ninety-nine, instead of the ninety-nine to the hundred, it is only a fraction less immoral. Of two such parties, whichever fulfills this declaration necessarily breaks the law of equal freedom: the only difference being that by the one it is broken in the persons of ninety-nine, while by the other it is broken in the persons of a hundred. And the merit of the democratic form of government consists solely in this, that it trespasses against the smallest number.

The very existence of majorities and minorities is indicative of an immoral state. The man whose character harmonizes with the moral law, we found to be one who can obtain complete happiness without diminishing the happiness of his fellows (Chapter III). But the enactment of public arrangements by vote implies a society consisting of men otherwise constituted —implies that the desires of some cannot be satisfied without sacrificing the desires of others—implies that in the pursuit of their happiness the majority inflict a certain amount of unhappiness on the minority—implies, therefore, organic immorality. Thus, from another point of view, we again perceive that even in its most equitable form it is impossible for government to dissociate itself from evil; and further, that unless the right to ignore the state is recognized, its acts must be essentially criminal.

**5.** THAT A MAN IS FREE TO ABANDON THE BENEFITS AND THROW off the burdens of citizenship may indeed be inferred from the admissions of existing authorities and of current opinion. Unprepared as they probably are for so extreme a doctrine as the one here maintained, the radicals of our day yet unwittingly profess their belief in a maxim which obviously embodies this doctrine. Do we not continually hear them quote Blackstone's assertion that "no subject of England can be constrained to pay any aids or taxes even for the defence of the realm or the support of government, but such as are imposed by his own consent, or that of his representative in parliament?" And what does this mean? It means, say they, that every man should have a vote. True, but it means much more. If there is any sense in words it is a distinct enunciation of the very right now contended for. In affirming that a man may not be taxed unless he has directly or indirectly given his consent, it affirms that he may refuse to be so taxed; and to refuse to be taxed is to cut all connection with the state. Perhaps it will be said that this consent is not a specific, but a general one, and that the citizen is understood to have assented to everything his representative may do when he voted for him. But suppose he did not vote for him, and on the contrary did all in his power to get elected someone holding opposite views—what then? The reply will probably be that, by taking part in such an election, he tacitly agreed to abide by the decision of the majority. And how if he did not vote at all? Why, then he cannot justly complain of any tax, seeing that he made no protest against its imposition. So, curiously enough, it seems that he gave his consent in whatever way he acted—whether he said yes, whether he said no, or whether he remained neuter! A rather awkward doctrine, this. Here stands an unfortunate citizen who is asked if he will pay money for a certain proffered advantage; and whether he employs the only means of expressing his refusal or does not employ it, we are told that he practically agrees, if only the number of others who agree is greater than the number of those who dissent. And thus we are introduced to the novel principle that A's consent to a thing is not determined by what A says, but by what B may happen to say!

It is for those who quote Blackstone to choose between this absurdity and the doctrine above set forth. Either his maxim implies the right to ignore the state, or it is sheer nonsense.

**6.** THERE IS A STRANGE HETEROGENEITY IN OUR POLITICAL FAITHS. Systems that have had their day and are beginning here and there to let the daylight through are patched with modern notions utterly unlike in quality and color; and men gravely display these systems, wear them, and walk about in them, quite unconscious of their grotesqueness. This transition state of ours, partaking as it does equally of the past and the future, breeds hybrid theories exhibiting the oddest union of bygone despotism and coming freedom. Here are types of the old organization curiously disguised by germs of the new, peculiarities showing adaptation to a preceding state modified by rudiments that prophesy of something to come, making altogether so chaotic a mixture of relationships that there is no saying to what class these births of the age should be referred.

As ideas must of necessity bear the stamp of the time, it is useless to lament the contentment with which these incongruous beliefs are held. Otherwise it would seem unfortunate that men do not pursue to the end the trains of reasoning which have led to these partial modifications. In the present case, for example, consistency would force them to admit that, on other points besides the one just noticed, they hold opinions and use arguments in which the right to ignore the state is involved.

For what is the meaning of Dissent? The time was when a man's faith and his mode of worship were as much determinable by law as his secular acts; and, according to provisions extant in our statute book, are so still. Thanks to the growth of a Protestant spirit, however, we have ignored the state in this matter—wholly in theory, and partly in practice. But how have we done so? By assuming an attitude which, if consistently maintained, implies a right to ignore the state entirely. Observe the positions of the two parties. "This is your creed," says the legislator; "you must believe and openly profess what is here set down for you." "I shall not do anything of the kind," answers the nonconformist; "I will go to prison rather." "Your religious ordinances," pursues the legislator, "shall be such as we have prescribed. You shall attend the churches we have endowed and adopt the cer-

emonies used in them." "Nothing shall induce me to do so,"
is the reply; "I altogether deny your power to dictate to me in
such matters, and mean to resist to the uttermost." "Lastly,"
adds the legislator, "we shall require you to pay such sums of
money toward the support of these religious institutions as we
may see fit to ask." "Not a farthing will you have from me,"
exclaims our sturdy Independent; "even did I believe in the
doctrines of your church (which I do not), I should still rebel
against your interference; and if you take my property, it shall
be by force and under protest."

What now does this proceeding amount to when regarded
in the abstract? It amounts to an assertion by the individual
of the right to exercise one of his faculties—the religious sentiment—without let or hindrance, and with no limit save that set
up by the equal claims of others. And what is meant by ignoring
the state? Simply an assertion of the right similarly to exercise
all the faculties. The one is just an expansion of the other—rests
on the same footing with the other—must stand or fall with the
other. Men do indeed speak of civil and religious liberty as
different things: but the distinction is quite arbitrary. They are
parts of the same whole and cannot philosophically be separated.

"Yes, they can," interposes an objector; "assertion of the one
is imperative as being a religious duty. The liberty to worship
God in the way that seems to him right is a liberty without
which a man cannot fulfill what he believes to be Divine commands, and therefore conscience requires him to maintain it."
True enough; but how if the same can be asserted of all other
liberty? How if maintenance of this also turns out to be a
matter of conscience? Have we not seen that human happiness
is the Divine will—that only by exercising our faculties is this
happiness obtainable—and that it is impossible to exercise them
without freedom? (Chapter IV.) And if this freedom for the
exercise of faculties is a condition without which the Divine
will cannot be fulfilled, the preservation of it is, by our objector's own showing, a duty. Or, in other words, it appears not
only that the maintenance of liberty of action may be a point
of conscience, but that it ought to be one. And thus we are

clearly shown that the claims to ignore the state in religious and in secular matters are in essence identical.

The other reason commonly assigned for nonconformity admits of similar treatment. Besides resisting state dictation in the abstract, the dissenter resists it from disapprobation of the doctrines taught. No legislative injunction will make him adopt what he considers an erroneous belief; and, bearing in mind his duty toward his fellow men, he refuses to help through the medium of his purse in disseminating this erroneous belief. The position is perfectly intelligible. But it is one which either commits its adherents to civil nonconformity also, or leaves them in a dilemma. For why do they refuse to be instrumental in spreading error? Because error is adverse to human happiness. And on what ground is any piece of secular legislation disapproved? For the same reason—because thought adverse to human happiness. How, then, can it be shown that the state ought to be resisted in the one case and not in the other? Will anyone deliberately assert that if a government demands money from us to aid in *teaching* what we think will produce evil we ought to refuse it, but that if the money is for the purpose of *doing* what we think will produce evil we ought not to refuse it? Yet such is the hopeful proposition which those have to maintain who recognize the right to ignore the state in religious matters but deny it in civil matters.

**7.** THE SUBSTANCE OF THIS CHAPTER ONCE MORE REMINDS US OF the incongruity between a perfect law and an imperfect state. The practicability of the principle here laid down varies directly as social morality. In a thoroughly vicious community its admission would be productive of anarchy. In a completely virtuous one its admission will be both innocuous and inevitable. Progress toward a condition of social health—a condition, that is, in which the remedial measures of legislation will no longer be needed—is progress toward a condition in which those remedial measures will be cast aside and the authority prescribing them disregarded. The two changes are of necessity co-ordinate. That moral sense whose supremacy will make society harmonious and government unnecessary is the same moral sense which will then make each man assert his freedom even to the extent of ignoring the state—is the same moral sense which, by deterring the majority from coercing the minority, will eventually render government impossible. And as what are merely different manifestations of the same sentiment must bear a constant ratio to each other, the tendency to repudiate governments will increase only at the same rate that governments become needless.

Let not any be alarmed, therefore, at the promulgation of the foregoing doctrine. There are many changes yet to be passed through before it can begin to exercise much influence. Probably a long time will elapse before the right to ignore the state will be generally admitted, even in theory. It will be still longer before it receives legislative recognition. And even then there will be plenty of checks upon the premature exercise of it. A sharp experience will sufficiently instruct those who may too soon abandon legal protection. While, in the majority of men, there is such a love of tried arrangements and so great a dread of experiments that they will probably not act upon this right until long after it is safe to do so.

CHAPTER XX

---

## *The Constitution of the State*[1]

**1.** OF THE SEVERAL CONCLUSIONS DEDUCIBLE FROM THE LAW OF equal freedom there are few more manifest or more generally agreed to than this, that all members of a community have like claims to political power. If every man has freedom to do all that he wills, provided he infringes not the equal freedom of any other man, then each is free to exercise the same authority in legislation as his fellows; and no individual or class can exercise greater authority than the rest without violating the law.

[1]The immediate interest of the subject will sufficiently explain the length to which this chapter is extended; and if the style of argument used in it is somewhat too popular for a work like the present, the same consideration must serve as an excuse. Two of the sections have already appeared in print.

Evidently, therefore, a purely democratic government is the only one which is morally admissible—is the only one that is not intrinsically criminal. As lately shown, no government can have any ethical authority. The highest form it can assume is that in which the moral law remains passive with regard to it— tolerates it—no longer protests against it. The first condition of that form is that citizenship shall be voluntary; the second, that it shall confer equal privileges.

**2.** IT IS A TOLERABLY WELL-ASCERTAINED FACT THAT MEN ARE still selfish. And that beings answering to this epithet will employ the power placed in their hands for their own advantage is self-evident. Directly or indirectly, either by hook or by crook, if not openly, then in secret, their private ends will be served. Granting the proposition that men are selfish, we cannot avoid the corollary that those who possess authority will, if permitted, use it for selfish purposes.

Should anyone need facts in proof of this, he may find them at every page in the nearest volume of history. Under the head, Monarchy, he will read of insatiable cravings after more territory; of confiscations of the subjects' property; of justice sold to the highest bidder; of continued debasements of coinage; and of a greediness which could even descend to share the gains of prostitutes.

He will find Feudalism exemplifying the same spirit by the cruelties inflicted upon serfs; by the right of private war; by the predatory incursions of borderers; by robberies practised on Jews; and by the extortionate tribute wrung from burghers— all of them illustrations of ·that motto, so characteristic of the system, "Thou shalt want ere I want."

Does he seek like evidence in the conduct of later aristocracies? He may discover it in every state in Europe: in Spain, where the lands of nobles and clergy were long exempted from direct taxation; in Hungary, where, until lately, men of rank were free of all turnpikes and only the mercantile and working classes paid; in France, before the first revolution, where the tiers-état had to bear all the state burdens; in Scotland, where less than two centuries ago it was the custom of lairds to kidnap the common people and export them as slaves; in Ireland, where at the rebellion a band of usurping landowners hunted and shot the Catholics as they would game, for daring to claim their own.

If more proofs are wanted that power will be made to serve the purposes of its possessors, English legislation can furnish many such. Take, for example, the significantly named "Black Act" (9th of George I), which declares that anyone disguised and in possession of an offensive weapon "appearing in any warren, or place where hares or conies have been, or shall be usually kept, and being thereof duly convicted, shall be adjudged guilty of felony, and shall suffer death, as in cases of felony, without benefit of clergy." Instance again the Inclosure Laws, by which commons were divided among the neighboring landowners in the ratios of their holdings, regardless of the claims of the poor cottagers. Notice also the maneuver by which the land tax has been kept stationary, or has even decreased, while other taxes have so enormously increased. Add to these the private monopolies (obtained from the King for "a consideration"), the perversion of the funds of public schools, the manufacture of places, and pensions.

Nor is the disposition to use power for private ends less manifest in our own day. It shows itself in the assertion that an electoral system should give a preponderance to the landed interest. We see it in the legislation which relieves farmers from sundry assessed taxes, that they may be enabled to pay more rent. It is palpably indicated in the Game Laws. The conduct of the squire, who gets his mansion rated at one third of its value, bears witness to it. It appears in the law enabling a landlord to anticipate other creditors and to obtain his rent by immediate seizure of his tenant's property. We are reminded of it by the often-mentioned legacy and probate duties. It is implied by the fact that, while no one dreams of compensating the discharged workman, gentlemen sinecurists must have their "vested interests" bought up if their offices are abolished. In the tracts of the Anti-Corn Law League it received abundant illustration. It is seen in the votes of the hundred and fifty military and naval members of Parliament. And lastly, we find this self-seeking of those in authority creeps out, even in the doings of the "Right Reverend Fathers in God" forming the Ecclesiastical Commission, who have appropriated, for the embellishment of their own palaces, funds entrusted to them for the benefit of the Church.

But it is needless to accumulate illustrations. Though every historian the world has seen should be subpoenaed as a witness, the fact could not be rendered one whit more certain than it is already. Why ask whether those in power *have* sought their own advantage in preference to that of others? With human nature as we know it, they must have done so. It is this same tendency in men to pursue gratification at the expense of their neighbors that renders government needful. Were we not selfish, legislative restraint would be unnecessary. Evidently, then, the very existence of a state authority proves that irresponsible rulers will sacrifice the public good to their personal benefit; all solemn promises, specious professions, and carefully arranged checks and safeguards notwithstanding.

If, therefore, class legislation is the *inevitable* consequence of class power, there is no escape from the conclusion that the interest of the *whole* society can be secured only by giving power into the hands of the *whole* people.

**3.** AGAINST THE POSITION THAT TO ENSURE JUSTICE TO THE NATION at large all its members must be endowed with like powers, it is indeed urged that, as the working classes constitute the majority, to endow all with like powers is practically to make the working classes supreme. And it will probably be added that by virtue of this same self-seeking tendency just insisted upon, legislation in their hands would inevitably be twisted to serve the ends of labor regardless of the claims of property.

Of course those who raise this objection do not wish to insinuate that the people would use their power after the fashion of brigands. Although in the old Norman day, when the sacking and burning of towns by neighboring nobles was not unfrequent, a change to popular rule involved retaliatory attacks upon the strongholds of these feudal buccaneers, yet we may fairly conclude that the increased social morality which deters modern aristocracies from *direct* robbery of the people would also prevent the people from inflicting any *direct* injury upon them. The danger this objection points to—the only danger to be rationally feared—is that the same insensible bias by which our present rulers are swayed would lead the working classes to sacrifice the rights of the rich on the altar of their own desires—would give rise to a code of laws favoring poverty at the expense of wealth.

Even were there no answer to this, the evidence would still preponderate in favor of popular enfranchisement. For what at the utmost does the argument amount to? Just this: that the few must continue to trespass against the many, lest the many should trespass against the few. The well fed, the luxuriously housed and clothed, the placemen and pensioners may perhaps think it better that the masses should suffer for their benefit (as they do) than that they should suffer for the benefit of the masses (as they might). But would a just arbitrator say this? Would he not say, on the contrary, that even if their respective members were blessed with equal advantages, the minority ought to be sacrificed rather than the majority; but that as the most numerous are at the same time the least favored, their claim becomes still more imperative? Surely, if one of the two parties must submit to injustice, it ought to be the rich hundreds and not the poor thousands.

The foregoing objection, however, is not so sound as it looks. It is one thing for a comparatively small class to unite in the pursuit of a common advantage, and it is another thing for a dispersed multitude to do so. Some thousands of individuals having identical interests, moving together in the same circle, brought up with like prejudices, educated in one creed, bound together by family ties, and meeting annually in the same city may easily enough combine for the obtainment of a desired object. But for half a dozen millions of workingmen, distributed over a vast area, engaged in various occupations, belonging to different religious sects, and divided into two totally distinct bodies, the one imbued with the feelings and theories of town life, the other retaining all those prejudices of the past which yet linger in the country—for these to act with unanimity is scarcely possible. Their mass is too great, too incongruous, too scattered, for effective combination. We have current proof of this. The Chartist agitation shows us men who, during the last twenty years, have gradually imbibed ideas of political freedom —men who have been irritated by a sense of injustice—men who have been slighted by their fellow citizens—men who have been suffering daily privations—men, therefore, who have had an accumulated stimulus to unite in obtaining what they feel themselves entitled to and what they see reason to believe would greatly benefit them. And how have they prospered in the attempt to carry their point? Disputes, divisions, apathy, adverse influences of every kind have joined to produce repeated failures. Now if, with the aid of that enthusiasm which a righteous cause always inspires, the masses have not attained to that unity of action needful for the accomplishment of their object, much less would they be able successfully to unite were that object a dishonest one.

**4.** WHOEVER DEMURS TO THE ENFRANCHISEMENT OF THE WORKingmen on the ground that they are immoral is bound to point out a constituency which is not immoral. When it is alleged that the venality of the people renders them unfit for the possession of votes, it is assumed that some class not chargeable with venality may be found. But no such class exists. Bring them all to trial, and not a single section of the community would obtain a verdict of "not guilty."

Were the shopkeepers put upon their examination, how would they excuse their trade practices? Is it moral to put potatoes and alum in bread; to add salt, tobacco, and colchicum to beer; to mix lard with butter; to manufacture milk in various known and unknown ways; to adulterate oils, chemicals, colors, wines—in short, every thing capable of adulteration? Does the existence of inspectors of weights and measures indicate morality? Or is it honest to sell over the counter goods whose quality is inferior to that of the samples ticketed in the window?

Did the manufacturers make any pretension to purity, they might have to encounter some awkward hints as to the practice of tearing up old rags into *shoddy* to be worked into cloth along with new wool. Disagreeable questions might be asked concerning the proportion of cotton woven into some fabrics pretended to be wholly of silk. The piracy of patterns, too, would be a delicate subject. And the practice of using gypsum to increase the weight and substance of paper could hardly be defended on the principles of the Decalogue.

Not less discreditable would be the sentence deserved by the agriculturists. In spite of the refining effects which poets ascribe to intercourse with nature, it is nevertheless an undoubted fact that the farmers—in Dorsetshire, at least—have been convicted of paying their laborers in damaged wheat, charged at the full price—a habit not altogether conscientious. It is matter of history, too, that before the enactment of the New Poor Law it was in many districts the custom to give farm servants but half wages, the remainder being made up to them out of the poor-rates, over which their masters exercised the chief control. And to these samples of morality the transactions of the cattle market and the horse fair would probably furnish fit companions.

Neither in such a scrutiny would the professions escape unscathed. Who can hear the word "venality" without straightway thinking of the law? Attorneys already stand in too bad repute to need their sins hinting at; and even the gentlemen of the bar are not without reproach. The attempt to make a known felon appear innocent denotes rather confused ideas of right and wrong. Then their habit of taking fees to plead in a cause, which other engagements will not permit them to attend, and keeping the pay, although they do not perform the work, scarcely implies that honesty deemed so requisite for the proper use of political power.

Our members of Parliament, too, were the gauntlet taken up on their behalf, would come off but indifferently. That arrangement which places them beyond the reach of their creditors is hardly consistent with the moral law; nor does it imply the nicest sense of honor. And then that disease of the representative system—bribery; ought the rich to escape all the odium attaching to it—should all the disgrace fall upon the poor electors?

Nor can those who move in titled circles boast of superior integrity. In the trickeries of the turf and in the midnight scenes at gaming houses, the denizens of Mayfair and Belgravia play a sufficiently conspicuous part. The Huntingtower bankruptcy was not to the credit of the caste, any more than are those acts of outlawry to which, from time to time, members of it are subjected. And did the aristocracy possess strict notions of equity, it is probable that a little more respect would be shown by them to the claims of their tradesmen than is indicated by their proverbially bad character as paymasters.

Nay, even our highest officers of state participate in the general contamination. Did not the Mazzini affair show some laxity of principle? Was it nothing, as the *Westminster Review* put it, to teach that *theft* is permissible when officials wish to *steal* information from a letter—that *lying* is permissible if they desire to conceal the theft by resealing that letter—that *forgery* is permissible for the purpose of counterfeiting seals? And then our present ministers—are they any better than their predecessors? If so, how shall we explain away the garbling of some of the West Indian despatches and the suppression of others?

No, no; let not anyone oppose the enfranchisement of the people on the score of their immorality, lest he be put to the blush by the exposure of his own offenses or the offenses of his class. Let him that is guiltless cast the first stone. Vice, dishonesty, venality pervade all ranks; and if political power must be denied to workingmen because they are corrupt, it must be denied to all classes whatever for the same reason.

**5.** SOME, INDEED, ALLEGE THAT THE MASSES ARE more VICIOUS than the rest of the community. But those who express this opinion arrive at it very illogically. They glance at assize proceedings, read through the names and occupations in the calendar of prisoners, skim over statistics of crime, and because they meet with an immense preponderance of vagrants, farm servants, bricklayers, drovers, bargemen, porters, factory hands, and the like, they forthwith set down the peasant and artisan class as greatly inferior in moral character to every other class. They take no account of the fact that, in number, the laboring population

is at least six times all the rest put together. They do not inquire whether, if the cases that appear in the police sheets of
swindling advertisers, of false-ticketing tradesmen, of embez-
zling clerks, of young gentlemen concerned in drunken sprees,
attacks on the police, insults to women, and so on, were multiplied by six, they would not approach in number the other cases
daily reported. Were this done, however—were the crimes committed by each class reduced to a percentage upon the size of
that class—there would be found much less inequality than is
commonly thought to exist.

Moreover, it should be remembered that the immorality of
the middle and upper ranks assumes a different guise from that
worn by the vices of the poor. Men comparatively well off are
not likely to be guilty of those grosser offenses seen among the
lower orders, for their circumstances remove them almost beyond temptation to these. But the bad propensities may and do
exist in full force notwithstanding, and enough of their workings may any day be seen in courts of law. Fraudulent bankrupt-
cies, actions for debt, suits for the restitution of usurped rights,
quarrels about wills—all these show the activity of passions
which, under other conditions, might have produced acts tech-
nically called crimes. Men who, by legal chicanery, cheat others
out of their property, or who refuse to discharge the claims
justly made upon them until forced by law, are men who, in a
lower walk of life, would have picked pockets or robbed hen
roosts. We must measure morality by motives, not by deeds.
And if we thus estimate the characters of the trading and richer
grades, taking into account also the consideration above adverted to—number—we shall find that the data on the strength
of which we attribute especial immorality to the labouring
classes are by no means sufficient.

**6.** IT IS A PITY THAT THOSE WHO SPEAK DISPARAGINGLY OF THE
masses have not wisdom enough, or candor enough, to make
due allowance for the unfavorable circumstances in which the
masses are placed. Suppose that after carefully weighing the
evidence it should turn out that the workingmen do exhibit
greater vices than those more comfortably off; does it therefore

follow that they are morally worse? Are the additional temptations under which they labor to be left out of the estimate? Shall as much be expected at their hands as from those born into a more fortunate position? Ought the same demands to be made upon the possessors of five talents as upon the possessors of ten? Surely the lot of the hard-handed laborer is pitiable enough without having harsh judgments passed upon him. To be wholly sacrificed to other men's happiness; to be made a mere human tool; to have every faculty subordinated to the sole function of work—this, one would say, is alone a misfortune, needing all sympathy for its mitigation. Consider well these endowments of his—these capacities, affections, tastes, and the vague yearnings to which they give birth. Think of him now, with his caged-up desires, doomed to a daily, weekly, yearly round of painful toil, with scarcely any remission but for food and sleep. Observe how he is tantalized by the pleasures he sees his richer brethren partaking of but from which he must be forever debarred. Note the humiliation he suffers from being looked down upon as of no account among men. And then remember that he has nothing to look forward to but a monotonous continuance of this till death. Is this a salutary state of things to live under?

It is very easy for you, O respectable citizen, seated in your easy chair, with your feet on the fender, to hold forth on the misconduct of the people—very easy for you to censure their extravagant and vicious habits—very easy for you to be a pattern of frugality, of rectitude, of sobriety. What else should you be? Here are you surrounded by comforts, possessing multiplied sources of lawful happiness, with a reputation to maintain, an ambition to fulfill, and the prospect of a competency for your old age. A shame indeed would it be if with these advantages you were not well regulated in your behavior. You have a cheerful home, are warmly and cleanly clad, and fare, if not sumptuously every day, at any rate abundantly. For your hours of relaxation there are amusements. A newspaper arrives regularly to satisfy your curiosity; if your tastes are literary, books may be had in plenty; and there is a piano if you like music. You can afford to entertain your friends and are entertained in return.

There are lectures and concerts and exhibitions accessible if you incline to them. You may have a holiday when you choose to take one, and can spare money for an annual trip to the seaside. And enjoying all these privileges, you take credit to yourself for being a well-conducted man! Small praise to you for it! If you do not contract dissipated habits, where is the merit? You have few incentives to do so. It is no honor to you that you do not spend your savings in sensual gratification; you have pleasures enough without. But what would you do if placed in the position of the laborer? How would these virtues of yours stand the wear and tear of poverty? Where would your prudence and self-denial be if you were deprived of all the hopes that now stimulate you; if you had no better prospect than that of the Dorsetshire farm servant with his 7s. a week, or that of the perpetually straitened stocking weaver, or that of the mill hand with his periodical suspensions of work? Let us see you tied to an irksome employment from dawn till dusk; fed on meager food, and scarcely enough of that; married to a factory girl ignorant of domestic management; deprived of the enjoyments which education opens up; with no place of recreation but the pothouse; and then let us see whether you would be as steady as you are. Suppose your savings had to be made, not, as now, out of surplus income, but out of wages already insufficient for necessaries; and then consider whether to be provident would be as easy as you at present find it. Conceive yourself one of a despised class contemptuously termed "the great unwashed"; stigmatized as brutish, stolid, vicious; suspected of harboring wicked designs; excluded from the dignity of citizenship; and then say whether the desire to be respectable would be as practically operative on you as now. Lastly, imagine that seeing your capacities were but ordinary, your education next to nothing, and your competitors innumerable, you despaired of ever attaining to a higher station; and then think whether the incentives to perseverance and forethought would be as strong as your existing ones. Realize these circumstances, O comfortable citizen, and then answer whether the reckless, disorderly habits of the people are so inexcusable.

How offensive is it to hear some pert, self-approving personage, who thanks God that he is not as other men are, passing harsh sentence on his poor, hard-worked, heavily burdened fellow countrymen; including them all in one sweeping condemnation, because in their struggles for existence they do not maintain the same prim respectability as himself. Of all stupidities, there are few greater, and yet few in which we more doggedly persist, than this of estimating other men's conduct by the standard of our own feelings. There is no more mischievous absurdity than this judging of actions from the *outside* as they look to us, instead of from the *inside* as they look to the actors; nothing more irrational than to criticize deeds as though the doers of them had the same desires, hopes, fears, and restraints as ourselves. We cannot understand another's character except by abandoning our own identity, and realizing to ourselves his frame of mind, his want of knowledge, his hardships, temptations, and discouragements. And if the wealthier classes would do this before forming their opinions of the workingman, their verdicts would savor somewhat more of that charity which covereth a multitude of sins.

**7.** AFTER ALL, IT IS A PITIFUL CONTROVERSY, THIS ABOUT THE relative vices of rich and poor. Two schoolboys taunting each other with faults of which they were equally guilty would best parody it. While indignant Radicalism denounces "the vile aristocrats," these in their turn enlarge with horror on the brutality of the mob. Neither party sees its own sins. Neither party recognizes in the other itself in a different dress. Neither party can believe that it would do all the other does if placed in like circumstances. Yet a cool bystander finds nothing to choose between them; knows that these class recriminations are but the inflammatory symptoms of a uniformly diffused immorality. Label men how you please with titles of "upper" and "middle" and "lower," you cannot prevent them from being units of the same society, acted upon by the same spirit of the age, molded after the same type of character. The mechanical law that action and reaction are equal has its moral analogue. The deed of one man to another tends ultimately to produce a like effect upon both, be the deed good or bad. Do but put them in relationship,

and no division into castes, no differences of wealth, can prevent
men from assimilating. Whoso is placed among the savage will
in process of time get savage too; let his companions be treacherous, and he will become treacherous in self-defense; surround
him with the kindhearted, and he will soften; amid the refined
he will acquire polish; and the same influences which thus
rapidly adapt the individual to his society ensure, though by a
slower process, the general uniformity of a national character.
This is no unsupported theory. Look when or where we please,
thickly strewn proofs may be gathered. The cruelties of the old
Roman rulers were fully paralleled by those over which the
populace gloated in their arenas. During the servile wars of the
Middle Ages, barons tortured rebels, and rebels tortured barons,
with equally diabolical ferocity. Those massacres which took
place a few years since in Galicia covered with infamy both the
people who committed them and the government who paid for
them at per head. The Assam chiefs, to whom the East India
Company have allowed compensation for abandoning their established right of plunder, are neither better nor worse than the
mass of the people, among whom joint-stock robbing companies
are common. A similar sameness is exhibited in Russia, where
all are alike swindlers, from the Prince Marshal who cheats the
troops out of their rations, the officers who rob the Emperor of
his stores, the magistrates who require bribing before they will
act, the police who have secret treaties with the thieves, the
shopkeepers who boast of their successful trickeries, down to the
postmasters and droshky drivers with their endless impositions.
In Ireland, during the last century, while the people had their
faction fights and secret revenge societies, dueling formed the
amusement of the gentry and was carried to such a pitch that
the barrister was bound to give satisfaction to the witness he had
bullied, or to the client who was dissatisfied with him.[2] And let
us not forget how completely this unity of character is exhibited
by the Irish of today, among whom Orangemen and Catholics
display the same truculent bigotry; among whom magistrates

---

[2]"It is time," said a veteran of this school, "to retire from the bar since this
new-fangled special pleading has superseded the use of gunpowder."
—*Sketches of Ireland Sixty Years Ago.*

and people join in party riots; and among whom the improvidence of the peasantry is only to be paralleled by that of the landlords. Our own history furnishes like illustrations in plenty. The time when England swarmed with highwaymen and outlaws, and when the populace had that sneaking kindness for a bold robber still shown in some parts of the Continent, was the time when kings also played the bandit; when they cheated their creditors by debasing the coinage; when they impressed laborers to build their palaces (Windsor Castle, for instance), obliging them under pain of imprisonment to take the wages offered; and when they seized and sold men's goods, paying the owners less than a third of what the goods realized. During the age of religious persecution, Papists martyred Protestants, and Protestants martyred Papists with equal cruelty; and Cavaliers and Roundheads treated each other with the same rancor. In the present day dishonesty shows itself not less in the falsification of dockyard accounts or the "cooking" of railway reports than in burglary or sheep stealing; while those who see heartlessness in the dealings of slop tailors and their sweaters may also find it in the conduct of rich landlords, who get double rent from poor allotment holders,[3] and in that of respectable ladies who underpay half-starved seamstresses.[4] Changes in tastes and amusements are similarly common to all. The contrast between the Squire Westerns and their descendants has its analogy among the

[3]"Allotments are generally given on poor and useless pieces of land, but the thorough cultivation they receive soon raises them to a high pitch of fertility. The more fertile they become, the more the rent of each portion is increased, and we were informed that there are at present allotments on the Duke's property, which, under the influence of the same competition which exists with reference to farms, bring his Grace a rent of 2l., 3l., and even 4l. an acre."—*Times Agricultural Commissioner on the Blenheim Estates.*

[4]See Letters on "Labour and the Poor." An officer's widow says: "Generally, the ladies are much harder as to their terms than the tradespeople; oh, yes, the tradespeople usually show more lenity towards the needlewomen than the ladies. I know the mistress of an institution who refused some chemises of a lady who wanted to have them made at 9d. She said she would not impose upon the poor workpeople so much as to get them made at that price."—*Morning Chronicle,* November 16, 1849. A vender of groundsel and turfs for singing birds says: "The ladies are very hard with a body. They tries to beat me down, and particular in the matter of turfs. They tell me they can buy half-a-dozen for 1d., so I'm obligated to let 'em have three or four."—*Morning Chronicle,* November 20, 1849.

people. As in Spain a bullfight is still the favorite pastime of both the Queen and her subjects, so in England fifty years ago the cock pit and the prize ring were patronized alike by peer and pauper; and a reference to the sporting papers will show that the lingering instincts of the savage are at this moment exhibited by about an equal percentage of all classes.

Thus the alleged homogeneity of national character is abundantly exemplified. And so long as the assimilating influences productive of it continue at work, it is folly to suppose any one grade of a community can be morally different from the rest. In whichever rank you see corruption, be assured it equally pervades all ranks—be assured it is the symptom of a bad social diathesis. While the virus of depravity exists in one part of the body politic, no other part can remain healthy.

**8.** WHEN IT IS URGED THAT THE WORKING CLASSES OUGHT NOT TO be admitted within the pale of the constitution because they are ignorant, it is tacitly assumed that the existing electors are enlightened. And, quietly making this assumption, the opponents of popular enfranchisement argue, at their ease, that it would be extremely impolitic to swamp intelligent ten-pound householders, freeholders, and tenants at will by letting in upon them the masses lying in outer darkness.

Painful as it may be, the pleasing illusion that our present constituency is thus honorably distinguished must be dispelled. If by ignorance is meant want of information on matters which, for the due performance of his function, the citizen should understand (and no other definition is to the point), then it is a great error to suppose that ignorance is peculiar to the unenfranchised. Were there no other illustrations, sufficient proof that this ignorance is shared by those on the register might be gathered from their conduct at elections. Much might be inferred from the tuft-hunting spirit exhibited in the choice of aristocratic representatives. It might be asked whether those are intelligent voters whose ears are tickled by the euphony of a title, whose eyes are attracted by heraldric emblazonry, or whose votes are determined by the acreage of a candidate's estates. Some doubts might be cast on the penetration of men who, while they complain of the pressure of taxation, send to Parliament hordes of military and naval officers who have an interest in making that taxation still greater. Or the pretensions of the present monopolists of political power might be tested by quotations from the debates of a farmer's market ordinary, and from those of the assembly into which electoral wisdom is distilled. But without dilating upon these general considerations, let us examine a few of the opinions entertained by the mercantile classes upon state questions and see how far these opinions entitle them to a reputation for enlightenment.

"Money is wealth" was the dogma universally held by legislators and economists before the days of Adam Smith, as a self-evident truth; and in conformity with it acts of Parliament were, by general consent, framed to attract and retain in the country as much coin as possible. Mr. Mill, in the introduction to his recent elaborate work, assumes that this belief is now extinct. It may be so among philosophers, but it is still prevalent in the trading world. We continue to hear acts praised as tending to "circulate money"; and on analyzing the alarm periodically raised that "the money is going out of the country," we find such an occurrence regarded as a disaster in itself, and not simply as indicating that the country is poor in some essential commodity. Is there not occasion for a little "enlightenment" here?

Again, no small number of respectable people, seeing that increased consumption always accompanies prosperity, infer that consumption is in itself beneficial—is the cause of prosperity, instead of its collateral effect; and hence, on witnessing a fire or the mad extravagance of some spendthrift, they console themselves with the reflection that such things are "good for trade." Dangerous voters, these, if sound political knowledge is a needful qualification.

Similarly diffused among the middle ranks is a notion that the withdrawal of a large part of the funds of the community by the non-producing classes is no real detriment to the rest; for that as the money thus abstracted is subsequently spent among the rest, it eventually comes to the same thing as though it had not been abstracted at all. Even a professed political economist—Dr.

Chalmers—maintains that the revenues of landowners form no deduction from the means of society, seeing that the expenditure of such revenues consists "in a transference to the industrious of sustenance and support for their services": which proposition amounts to this—that it matters not in the end whether A and his servants, B, C, and D, live on the produce of their own industry or on the produce of other men's industry![5]

Another mistake current alike among rich and poor is that the speculations of corn dealers are injurious to the public. So indignant are many well-meaning men at what they conceive to be a practice of intolerable cruelty that it is scarcely possible to make them see how perfect freedom of trade is nationally advantageous in this, as in all other cases. Their anger blinds them to the fact that, were not the price raised immediately after a deficient harvest by the purchases of these large factors, there would be nothing to prevent the people from consuming food at their ordinary rate; which would end in the inadequate supply being eaten up long before the ripening of the next crop. They do not perceive that this mercantile operation is analogous in its effect to putting the crew of a vessel on diminished rations when the stock of provisions is found insufficient to last out the voyage. A somewhat serious error, this, for electors to labor under; especially as many of them would prevent the buying up of corn by legal penalties!

What crude theories prevail also respecting the power of a legislature to encourage different branches of industry—"agricultural interests" and other "interests." It is not farmers only who labor under the mistake that their occupation can be made permanently more prosperous than the rest by act of Parliament; educated townspeople, too, participate in the delusion, quite forgetting that the greater profitableness artificially given to any

---

[5]No doubt the belief which Dr. Chalmers combats—viz., that the landlord's revenue is wholly consumed by him—is an erroneous one; for, as he points out, the greater portion of it goes to maintain those who directly or indirectly minister to the landlord's wants: but Dr. Chalmers overlooks the fact that, did the landlord not exist, the services which such now render to him in return for "sustenance and support" would be rendered to those producers from whom the landlord's revenue originally came; and that in the loss of these services society suffers.

particular trade inevitably draws into that trade such an increased number of competitors as quickly to reduce its proffered advantages to the general level, and even for a time below that level. Is not the educator wanted behind the counter and on the farm as well as in the workshop?

Note again the wild ideas entertained on currency questions. We smile at the simplicity which in times past led a famine-pinched populace to ascribe the high price of bread to the covetousness of bakers and millers; yet there is no little analogy between such a theory and that which attributes national distress to bad monetary arrangements. Just as the poor man, when made to feel the scarcity of food by having to pay double the usual sum for a loaf, straightway taxed the seller of the loaf with the evil, so do many traders to whom commercial depression comes in the shape of a difficulty in getting advances from their bankers, or cash for their bills of exchange, conclude that the "circulating medium" is in fault; being ignorant, like their hungry prototypes, that the primary cause of the mischief is a deficiency in the national stock of food or other commodities. To suppose that a state of general privation can be cured by the issue of bank notes is to err with the projector of perpetual motion, who hopes to make power out of nothing.

Thus the tu quoque argument, which we found so completely to neutralize the inference drawn from the alleged immorality of the laboring classes, is a not much less cogent answer to the objection urged against the extension of the suffrage on the ground of popular ignorance. If, because they are deficient in information, the people should continue unenfranchised, then for a like reason should the existing electoral body be disfranchised. If the two classes are to have their relative degrees of competence to wield political power determined by comparing the amounts of their knowledge—their political knowledge, mind—then the advantage on the side of the present holders of such power is quite insufficient to give them an exclusive claim to it. As we have just seen, a great proportion of them are in error on the most important public questions—on the nature of wealth, on what things are "good for trade," on the relationship of producers and non-producers, on dealings in the people's food, on the "encouragement" of trade, on the influences of currency, and so forth. Where, then, is their great superiority over the non-electors? Have many artisans mistaken excessive competition for the cause of an evil instead of taking it for what it is—the symptom of one? Why, they are countenanced in this error by not a few of the educated. Do workingmen hold wrong opinions concerning machinery? So likewise do nearly all the farmers and no small number of tradesmen. Is the false impression that manufacturers can raise or lower wages at will prevalent among the masses? It is widely entertained, too, by their richer neighbors. How, then, can the ignorance of the people be urged as a reason for refusing them votes?

**9.** THOSE WHO CUT SHORT THE ARGUMENTS IN FAVOR OF DEMOCracy by saying that it has been tried and found wanting would do well to consider whether the governments they refer to really were democratic ones—whether a true democracy has ever been known—whether such a thing can be found even now. Of arrangements simulating it, the world has seen not a few. But that democracy itself has ever existed—existed, that is, for a sufficient length of time to admit of its fruits being judged—or that it was possible for it so to have existed during the past condition of humanity, is denied. A return to definitions settles the matter at once. A democracy, properly so called, is a political organization modeled in accordance with the law of equal freedom. And if so, those cannot be called democracies under which, as under the Greek and Roman governments, from four fifths to eleven twelfths of the people were slaves. Neither can those be called democracies which, like the constitutions of medieval Italy, conferred power on the burghers and nobles only. Nor can those even be called democracies which, like the Swiss states, have always treated a certain unincorporated class as political outlaws. Enlarged aristocracies these should be termed; not democracies. No matter whether they be a minority or a majority to whom power is denied, the exclusion of them is in spirit the same, and the definition of a democracy is equally broken. The man who steals a penny we call dishonest, as well as the man who steals a pound; and we do so because his act equally testifies to a certain defect of character. Similarly we must consider a government aristocratic, be the class it excludes large or small.

They, however, make the strangest mistake who, referring as they commonly do to the United States, urge the existence of slavery as itself an argument against democracy. Put in a definite form, this would aptly serve the logician as a specimen absurdity. A pseudo-democracy is found not democratic enough, and it is therefore inferred that democracy is a bad thing! While some Autolycus is eulogizing honesty and quoting himself as a sample of it, he is detected in the act of picking his neighbor's pocket; whereupon it is argued that honesty ought forthwith to be repudiated! With his mouth full of "noble sentiments," and leading a seemingly moral life, a Joseph Surface deceives his friends; and, on its being discovered that he is a villain, there arises the exclamation, "What a shocking thing is this morality!"

But, passing over what might further be said concerning the alleged failure of democracies, let it be granted that they have failed; let it be granted that there have from time to time been forms of government approaching to the democratic—nay, that in the course of revolutions the thing itself has had a transient existence; let all this be granted, it still proves nothing. For which is it among the endeavors of man that does not at first fail? Is not perseverance through a series of defeats the natural history of success? Does not the process we pass through in learning to walk afford us a type of all human experiences? Though we see a child make hundreds of bootless attempts to maintain its balance, we do not conclude that it is doomed to remain forever upon all fours. Nor do we, in the conduct of its education, cease telling it to "try again" because it has many times fallen short of a desired achievement. Doubtless it would be unwise to base an argument upon the assumed analogy between the growth of the individual and of the state (though, both being governed by the same laws of human development, there is probably a genuine analogy between them); but the simile may fairly be employed to hint that the failure of past efforts made by society to preserve the erect attitude of democracy by no means shows that such an attitude is not the proper one.

And, in fact, our theory anticipates such failures. We have already seen that a high form of government is rendered practicable only by a high type of character, that freedom can increase only as fast as control becomes needless, that the perfect man alone can realize the perfect state. A democracy, therefore, being the highest form that a government can assume—indicative, if not of the ultimate phase of civilization, still of the penultimate one—must of necessity fail in the hands of barbarous and semi-barbarous men.

While, then, it is maintained that nearly all these alleged failures of democracy are not failures of democracy at all but of something else, it is argued that the fact of those comparatively genuine democracies set up during revolutions, lapsing rapidly back into pre-existing arrangements, is in nowise at variance with our position.

**10.** WHETHER IN ANY GIVEN CASE A DEMOCRACY IS PRACTICABLE IS a question that will always find its own solution. The physiologist shows us that in an animal organism the soft parts determine the forms of the hard ones, and it is equally true that in the social organism the seemingly fixed framework of laws and institutions is molded by the seemingly forceless thing—character. Social arrangements are the bones to that body, of which the national morality is the life; and they will grow into free, healthy shapes or into sickly and cramped ones, according as that morality, that life, is vigorous or otherwise.

The vital principle of society we have seen to be the law of equal freedom; and we have further seen that in the compound faculty originating a moral sense there exists an agent enabling men to appreciate, to love, and to act up to this law (Chapters IV and V). We have seen that to realize the Divine idea—greatest happiness—the human constitution must be such as that each man confining himself within his own sphere of activity shall leave intact the similar spheres of activity of others (Chapter III); and we have further seen that an instinct of our own freedom and a sympathy which makes us respect the like freedom of our fellows compose a mechanism capable of establishing this state of things. If these feelings are undeveloped, a people's beliefs, laws, customs, and manners will be aggressive in their character: let them act with due force, and the organization of the community, equally with the conduct of its members, will be in harmony with the social law. Political forms indicate the degree of efficiency with which this mental mechanism works; are in a manner supplementary to such mechanism; are bad and coercive if it is defective; become ameliorated in proportion as it acts well. And thus democracy, as one of the higher social forms, is of necessity identified, both in origin and practicability, with a dominant moral sense. This fact has been already more than once hinted, but it will be desirable now to examine more attentively than heretofore the grounds on which it is alleged.

Observe first, then, that in the earlier stages of civilization, before the process of adaptation has yet produced much effect, the desire for political equality does not exist. There were no agitations for representative government among the Egyptians, or the Persians, or the Assyrians; with them all disputes were as to who should be tyrant. By the Hindus a similar state of things is exhibited to the present hour. The Russians, too, are still under this phase; and, in their utter carelessness of civil liberty, shun anyone who preaches justice and condemns tyranny, as a perverse malcontent. The like mental condition was shown during the earlier stages of our own progress. In the Middle Ages fealty to a feudal lord was accounted a duty, and the assertion of personal freedom a crime. Rights of man were not then dreamed of. Revolutions were nothing but dynastic quarrels; not what they have been in later times—attempts to make governments more popular. And if, after glancing at the changes that have taken place between the far past and the present, we reflect upon the character of modern ideas and agitations, on declarations of rights, liberty of the press, slave emancipation, removal of religious disabilities, Reform Bills, Chartism, etc., and consider how through all of them there runs a kindred spirit, and how this spirit is manifesting itself with constantly increasing intensity and universality, we shall see that these facts imply some moral change; and explicable as they are by the growth of this compound faculty responding to the law of equal freedom, it is reasonable to consider them as showing the mode in which such faculty seeks to place social arrangements in harmony with that law; or, in other words, as illustrating the efforts of the moral sense to realize the democratic state.

If a democracy is produced by this agency, so also is it rendered practicable by it. The popular form of government as contrasted with the monarchical, is professedly one which places less restraint upon the individual. In speaking of it we use such terms as free institutions, civil liberty, self-government, all implying this. But the diminution of external restraint can take place only at the same rate as the increase of internal restraint. Conduct has to be ruled either from without or from within. If the rule from within is not efficient, there must exist a supplementary rule from without. If, on the other hand, all men are properly ruled from within, government becomes needless, and all men are perfectly free. Now the chief faculty of self-rule being the moral sense (Chapter V), the degree of freedom in their institutions which any given people can bear will be proportionate to the diffusion of this moral sense among them. And only when its influence greatly predominates can so large an installment of freedom as a democracy become possible.

Lastly, the supremacy of this same faculty affords the only guarantee for the stability of a democracy. On the part of the people it gives rise to what we call a jealousy of their liberties—a watchful determination to resist anything like encroachment upon their rights; while it generates among those in power such a respect for these rights as checks any desire they may have to aggress. Conversely, let the ruled be deficient in the instinct of freedom, and they will be indifferent to the gradual usurpation of their privileges so long as it entails no immediate inconvenience upon them; and the rulers in such case, being deficient in sympathetic regard for these privileges, will be, to a like extent, unscrupulous in usurping. Let us observe in detail the different modes in which men thus contradistinguished comport themselves under a representative form of government. Among a people not yet fitted for such a form, citizens, lacking the impulse to claim equal power with each other, become careless in the exercise of their franchise, doubt whether it is of any use to them, and even pride themselves on not interfering in public affairs.⁰ Provided their liberties are but indirectly affected, they will watch the passing of the most insidious measures with vacant unconcern. It is only barefaced aggressions that they can perceive to be aggressions at all. Placing as they do but little value upon their privileges, they are readily bribed. When threatened, instead of assuming that attitude of dogged resistance which the instinct of freedom dictates, they truckle. If tricked out of a right of citizenship, they are quite indifferent about getting it again, and indeed, when the exercise of it conflicts with any immediate interest, are glad to give it up—will even petition, as in times past did many of the corporate towns, both in England and Spain, that they may be excused from electing representatives. Meanwhile, in accordance with that law of social homogeneity lately dwelt upon, those in authority are in a like ratio ready to encroach. They intimidate, they bribe, they plot, and by degrees establish a comparatively coercive government. On the other hand, among a people sufficiently endowed with the faculty responding to the law of equal freedom, no such retrograde process is possible. The man of genuinely democratic feeling loves liberty as a miser loves gold, for its own sake and quite irrespective of its advantages (p. 88). What he thus highly values he sleeplessly watches; he quickly detects any attempt at diminution of it; and he opposes aggression the moment it commences. Should any assume undue prerogatives, he straightway steps up to them and demands their authority for so doing. Transactions that seem in the remotest degree underhand awaken his suspicions, which are not to be laid so long as anything remains unexplained. He scents out an abuse with instinctive sagacity and, having found one, never rests until it is abolished. If in any proposed arrangement there be a latent danger to the liberties of himself and others—any germ of irresponsible power—he instantly discovers it and refuses his consent. He is alarmed by such a proposal as the disfranchisement of a constituency by the legislature, for it at once occurs to him that the measure thus leveled against one may be leveled against many. To call that responsible government under

⁰Instance the behavior of the Prussian electors since the late revolution.

which a cabinet minister can entangle the nation in a quarrel about some paltry territory before they know anything of it, he sees to be absurd. It needs no chain of reasoning to show him that the assumption, by a delegated assembly, of the power to lengthen its own existence from three years to seven is an infraction of the representative principle; he feels that it is so; and no plausible professions of patriotism, no boasting of honorable intentions, can check his opposition to the setting up of so dangerous a precedent. Still more excited is he when applied to for grants of public money, with the understanding that on a future occasion he shall be told how they have been spent. Flimsy excuses about "exigencies of the state," and the like, cannot entrap him into so glaring an act of self-stultification. He listens to them frowningly and, maintaining as he does that the protection of men's rights is the chief, or rather the sole, "exigency of the state," sternly negatives the request. Thus is he ever on the watch to extirpate incipient oppression; to nip abuses in the bud; or, if such an expression is allowable, to stop encroachment before it begins. And when a community consists of men animated by the spirit thus exemplified, the continuance of liberal institutions is certain.

Political freedom, therefore, is, as we say, an external result of an internal sentiment—is alike, in origin, practicability, and permanence, dependent on the moral sense; and it is only when this is supreme in its influence that so high a form of social organization as a democracy can be maintained.

**11.** AND THUS WE ARRIVE AT THE TRUE ANSWER TO THAT QUESTION at present so widely agitated: Is a purely popular form of government practicable now? For, as the sentiment by which a state of perfect political liberty is generated is also the one by which it is upheld, there immediately suggests itself the corollary that, when the sentiment is strong enough to generate it, it is strong enough to uphold it. Whenever, therefore, a people *calmly* arrives at the conclusion that democratic institutions are right; whenever they *dispassionately* determine that they shall be adopted; or, in other words, whenever the circumstances show that the setting up of such institutions is not an accident, but results from the ascendancy of the aforesaid sentiment; then, and then alone, are such institutions permanently possible.

In the opinion, now happily so prevalent, that the pacific mode of working out political changes is the only efficient one, we have a collateral expression of this truth. Men see that freedom achieved by the sword is uniformly lost again, but that it is lasting when gained by peaceful agitation. Hence they very properly infer the propriety of carrying reforms solely by means which the moral law recognizes—means which do not involve violations of it. Right as this conclusion may be, however, it is not philosophically understood. Men do not see why the thing is so. There is no truth in the usual supposition that the loss of liberties obtained by violence is a kind of retribution. It is not that bloodshed vitiates the free institutions it may help to set up; nor is it that when peacefully established such institutions are preserved by virtue of their being so established; but it is that the manner in which the change is wrought *indicates the national character* and proves it to be respectively unfit or fit for the new social form. A brief examination of the moral conditions implied by these different kinds of evolution will show this.

When an old regime is overthrown by force, no guarantee is given that the new one put in its place will satisfy the wants of the age. The occurrence is simply a demonstration that the miseries inflicted under this old regime were no longer bearable. To repeat the saying of Sully, quoted by Burke, and which is perfectly true when applied to convulsions of this nature, "It is never from the desire to attack that the people rise, but from impatience under suffering." Now anger against an agent inflicting pain is a passion, exhibited by brutes as well as by men; and a social revolution wrought out by such a motive power is not likely to leave behind it a state of things specially adapted to the people's circumstances. That sudden display of ill temper with which a man dashes on the ground something that has given him much provocation, and yet the loss of which he will subsequently regret, serves in some measure to illustrate the conduct of a people thus excited. They are irritated, and justly so; the

hold which authority has had over them is weakened; that sentiment of power worship—that loyalty, as we term it—which was
but the index of a certain adaptation between their characters
and the rule they had lived under, is for the time being in abeyance; is silenced, drowned in the rising tide of their wrath; and
when, after they had destroyed the old framework of things,
another becomes needful, it is very improbable that the one set
up during this temporary state of excitement will be one really
in harmony with their natural characters. Nay, indeed, it is sure
to be out of harmony with their natural characters; for consider,
the institutions they set up will bear the impress of the feeling
then prevalent—a feeling widely different from that previously
exhibited, and also from that which will come uppermost again
by and by. Stimulated by transpiring events, the germs of those
sentiments destined someday to establish genuine political freedom assume a precocious activity—seem much stronger and
more general than they really are; while, on the contrary, those
sentiments which upheld the preceding state of things are almost wholly dormant. The improvised form of government
exactly answers to this exceptional condition of mind and might
work could that condition be maintained; but as fast as the
popular feeling ebbs back into its ordinary channels, so fast does
the incongruity between the new arrangements and the old
character make itself felt; and so fast is the retrogression.

On viewing the facts, through the foregoing theory of moral-
sense agency, it becomes still more manifest that free institutions obtained by violence are of necessity premature. For what
are the requisite antecedents to one of these social convulsions?
They are the torments of a widespread and deep-seated injustice. And of what character is this injustice the exponent? Evidently a character deficient in those sentiments which deter
men from aggression—a character in which the faculties of the
social man are as yet imperfectly developed—a character, that is,
by which the law of equal freedom is not duly responded to.
Hence the unscrupulous trespasses on the one part and the
culpable submission on the other, which, by their accumulated
results, have induced so terrible a crisis. Well, though by a revolution the people may remake their government, they cannot

remake themselves. Slightly changed, perhaps, they may be in the passing through a period of such fiery excitement; but, in the main, they are still the men they were. The old process will consequently repeat itself. The storm of passion having died away, there will again begin these encroachments and this indifference; and they will continue until, by a gradual imposition of fresh bonds, the nation has been reduced, not, indeed, to a condition as bad as before, but to a condition not greatly in advance of it.

Of political ameliorations pacifically wrought out, exactly the opposite is predicable. These appertain to a higher phase of civilization. In the first place, they presuppose the popular suffering to be of a comparatively mild type—no longer unbearable, maddening; and, other things equal, this indicates a diminished amount of injustice; and a diminished amount of injustice implies a more prevalent and energetic moral sense. Thus the very antecedents of a peaceful agitation serve in some measure to ensure the success of the free institutions obtained by it. But it is in the process by which one of these bloodless revolutions is brought about that the existence of the needful popular character is most clearly evinced. For in what consists the vitality of such a movement? What is the secret power that originates it, to which its growth is due, and by the help of which it triumphs? Manifestly this feeling that responds to the law of equal freedom. These pertinacious demands for political equality are simply the signs of its increasing activity. Not hunger, nor the anxiety to escape from torture, nor the desire for vengeance, is now the transforming force, but a calm unswerving determination to get human liberties recognized. The carrying out one of these battles of opinion to a successful issue through long delays and discouragements, through ridicule and misrepresentation, implies a perennial source of energy quite different from mere insurrectionary rage. In place of a passing gust of anger, a persistent and ever-strengthening sentiment is here the acting agent. Agitation is its gymnasium. Men in whom it predominates cultivate it in the rest. They address it in speeches; they write articles to it; they convene meetings for its manifestation. It is aroused by denunciations of injustice; it is appealed to in the name of conscience; it is conjured by all that is fair and upright and equitable. Pictures of the slave and the tyrant are exhibited to excite its abhorrence; a state of pure freedom is described to it as the one to be loved and hoped for; and it is made sensible of the sacredness of human rights. After men's minds have been for many years thus exercised and stimulated, a sufficiently intense manifestation of feeling is produced, and then comes the reform. But this feeling, mark, proceeds from that same combination of faculties by which, as we have seen, free institutions are upheld and made practicable. One of these agitations, therefore, is a kind of apprenticeship to the liberties obtained by it. The power to get freedom becomes the measure of the power to use it. The law of social forms is that they shall be expressive of national character; they come into existence bearing its impress, and they live only so long as it supplies them with vitality. Now a general dissatisfaction with old arrangements is a sign that the national character requires better ones; and for the people in pursuit of these better ones to have organized associations, maintained lecturers, and for session after session to have wearied the legislature with petitions—to have continued this, too, until the accumulated force of opinion has become irresistible, is to have given conclusive proof that the change brought about is really in harmony with the wants of the age. The new institutions do not now express an *exceptional* state of the popular mind, but express its *habitual* state, and hence are certain to be fitted to it.

**12.** HERE, THEN, IS ENCOURAGEMENT FOR TIMID REFORMERS. MEN of true insight need none of these detailed considerations to steady their convictions by. The mathematician does not call for a pair of compasses to test a proved theorem with; nor does the man with healthy faith wait for more evidence after he hears what the moral law says. It is enough for him that a thing is *right*. He will never believe that the carrying out of what is right by right means can be injurious. And this is the only spirit worthy to be named religious. But as, unhappily, the many are not endowed with so trusting a belief, it is requisite to back the dictates of equity with supplementary arguments. The moral infidelity of the expediency school requires meeting. And it is to those infected by it that the above considerations are commended, as showing that they need not fear to exhibit whatever sympathy with democratic principles they possess—need not fear to throw their energies at once into the popular cause—for when *equitable* institutions are *equitably* obtained, they must necessarily prosper.

**13.** THUS THE CLAIM DEDUCIBLE FROM THE LAW OF EQUAL FREEDOM—the claim possessed by each citizen to like political power with the rest—is not counterbalanced by any of those prudential considerations commonly urged against it. We find that, so long as selfishness makes government needful at all, it must make every government corrupt, save one in which all men are represented. The assertion that conceding universal suffrage would be creating a comparatively immoral constituency proves to be quite unwarrantable, seeing that all classes are immoral, and, when numbers and circumstances are taken into account, apparently in an equal degree. A glance at the evidence shows that popular ignorance also is a two-edged objection; for, in the knowledge which may be supposed needful for the right use of votes, the mass of those inside the pale of the constitution are about as deficient as those outside of it. The argument that purely representative institutions have been tried and have failed is not only based upon inapplicable instances, but would prove nothing if substantiated. Lastly, in this, as in other cases, it turns out that the possibility of fulfilling the injunctions of the moral law is proportionate to the advance men have made toward the moral state, political arrangements inevitably adjusting themselves to the popular character. So that while we may say to the ardent democrats, "Be sure that a democracy will be attained whenever the people are good enough for one," we may on the other hand say to those of little faith, "Fear not that a democracy, when peacefully attained, can be attained too soon."

## CHAPTER XXI

## *The Duty of the State*

**1.** AS ALREADY SAID (PP. 185 AND 186), MORALITY STANDS TO-ward government only in the nature of a limitation—behaves negatively with regard to it, not positively—replies to all inquiries by silently indicating the conditions of existence, constitution, and conduct, under which alone it may be ethically tolerated. And thus, ignoring government altogether, the moral law can give us no direct information as to what a government ought to do—can merely say what it ought not to do. That we are left with no precise knowledge beyond this may indeed be inferred from a preceding chapter. For if, as was shown, every man has a right to secede from the state, and if, as a consequence, the state must be regarded as a body of men voluntarily associated, there remains nothing to distinguish it in the abstract from any other incorporated society—nothing to determine its specific function; and we may conceive its members assigning to it any function that does not involve a breach of the moral law.

Immediate guidance in this matter being thus impossible, we must follow such indirect ways of arriving at the truth as are open to us. The question is no longer one of pure ethics and is therefore incapable of solution by any exact methods: approximate ones only are available. Fortunately there are several of these; and converging as they do to the same conclusion, that conclusion assumes something like the character of certainty. Let us now successively employ them.

**2.** GOOD, AND PERFECT, AND COMPLETE ARE WORDS APPLICABLE to whatever is thoroughly fitted to its purpose, and by the word *moral* we signify the same property in a man. A thing which entirely answers its end cannot be improved; and a man whose nature leads him to a spontaneous fulfillment of the Divine will cannot be conceived better. To be quite self-sufficing—to have powers exactly commensurate with what ought to be done—is to be organically moral. Given the ordained object, happiness; given the conditions under which this happiness is to be compassed, and perfection consists in the possession of faculties exactly adapted to these conditions; while the moral law is simply a statement of that line of conduct by which the conditions are satisfied. Hence to the rightly constituted man all external help is needless—detrimental even. Just as the healthy body wants no crutch, tonic, or stimulus, but has within itself the means of doing everything required of it, so the normally developed character asks no artificial aids, and indeed repudiates them as preoccupying the sphere for the exercise of faculties which the hypothesis supposes it to have. When, on the other hand, man's constitution and the conditions of his existence are not in harmony, there arise external agencies to supply the place of deficient internal faculties. And these temporary substitutes, being supplementary to the faculties and assisting the imperfect man as they do to fulfill the law of his being—the moral law, as we call it—obtain a certain reflex authority from that law, varying with the degree in which they subserve its requirements. Whatever may be its special function, it is clear that government is one of these artificial aids, and the most important of them.

Or the case may perhaps be more clearly stated thus: If government has any duty at all, that duty must be to perform a service of some kind—to confer a benefit. But every possible benefit or service which can be rendered to a man is comprehended under the general expression of assisting him to fulfill the law of his being. Whether you feed the hungry, or cure the diseased, or defend the weak, or curb the vicious, you do but enable or constrain them to conform to the conditions of complete happiness more nearly than they would otherwise do. And causing conformity to the conditions of complete happiness is causing conformity to the moral law. If, therefore, all benefits that can be conferred on men are aids to the fulfillment of the moral law, the benefits to be conferred by government must be of this nature.

So much being conceded, let us next inquire how the moral law may be most essentially subserved. Practicability manifestly underlies performance. That which makes an act feasible must take precedence of the act itself. Before the injunction—Do this —there necessarily comes the postulate—It can be done. Before establishing a code for the right exercise of faculties, there must be established the condition which makes the exercise of faculties possible. Now, this condition which makes the exercise of faculties possible is power to pursue the objects on which they are to be exercised—the objects of desire; and this is what we otherwise call liberty of action—freedom. But that which makes the exercise of faculties possible is that which makes the fulfillment of the moral law possible. And freedom being thus the grand prerequisite to the fulfillment of the moral law, it follows that if a man is to be helped in fulfilling of the moral law, the first thing to be done is to secure to him this all-essential freedom. This aid must come before any other aid—is, in fact, that which renders any other aid practicable; for no faculty to which liberty of action is denied can be assisted in the performance of its function until liberty of action has been restored. Of all institutions, therefore, which the imperfect man sets up as supplementary to his nature, the chief one must have for its office to guarantee his freedom. But the freedom that can be guaranteed to each is bounded by the like freedom to be guaranteed to all others. This is necessitated both by the moral law and by the simultaneous claims made upon the institution itself by its clients. Hence we must infer that it is the function of this chief institution which we call a government to uphold the law of equal freedom.

To determine the duty of the state by reverting to a supposed understanding entered into by the founders of society—a social contract—we have already seen to be impracticable (p. 179). Men did not deliberately establish political arrangements, but grew into them unconsciously—probably had no conception of an associated condition until they found themselves in it. More-over, were the hypothesis of an original agreement reasonable, it could not help us; for it would be folly to assume that the duties imposed by a horde of savages on their chief, or council of chiefs, must necessarily be the duties of governments throughout all time. Nevertheless, if, instead of speculating as to what *might* have happened during the infancy of civilization, we consider what *must* have happened, something may be learned. On turning to page 182, the reader will find it argued at length that for men to have remained in the associated state implies that on the whole they found it preferable to the isolated one; which means that they obtained a greater sum total of gratification under it; which means that it afforded them fuller exercise for their faculties; which means that it offered a safer guarantee for such exercise—more security for their claims to life and property; that is, for their rights. But if men could have continued in the associated state only because on the average it insured their rights better than the previous one, then the insurance of their rights becomes the special duty which society in its corporate capacity has to perform toward individuals. That function by which a thing begins to exist we may safely consider its all-essential function. Now, while those many aids to gratification which civilization has brought us were yet undeveloped, society must have existed only because it protected its members in the pursuit of those things which afford satisfaction to the faculties. But to protect men in the pursuit of those things which afford satisfaction to the faculties is to maintain their rights. And if it was by maintaining the rights of its members that society began to be, then to maintain their rights must ever be regarded as its primary duty.

Further confirmation may be drawn from the universal practice of mankind in this matter. Widely as people have differed respecting the proper bounds of legislative superintendence, all have held them to include the defense of the subject against aggression. While, in various countries and times, a hundred different functions have been assigned to the state; while there have probably been no two governments that have entirely agreed in the number and nature of their functions; while the things specially attended to by some have been wholly neglected by others, and thereby proved nonessential, there is one office

—that of protector—which has been common to them all. Did this fact stand alone it might by a stretch of incredulity be construed into an accident. But coinciding as it does with the foregoing inferences drawn from the nature of man's constitution and the necessary origin of society, we may safely take it as a further evidence that the duty of the state is to protect, to enforce the law of equal freedom, to maintain men's rights— or, as we commonly express it, to administer justice.

**3.** THE QUESTION, WHAT IS THE THING TO BE DONE BY A GOVERNment? being answered, there arises the other, Which is the most efficient mode of doing it? To the proposition, the administration of justice is the special duty of the state, there hangs the corollary, the state ought to employ the best methods of fulfilling that duty; and this brings us to the inquiry: What are they?

By our hypothesis the connection of each individual with the community as politically organized must be voluntary. In virtue of its very office an institution which proposes to guarantee a man's freedom to exercise his faculties can only tender its services to him; cannot coerce him into the acceptance of them. If it does, it becomes self-contradicting—violates that very freedom which it proposes to maintain. Citizenship then being willingly assumed, we must inquire what agreement is thereby tacitly entered into between the state and its members. Two things are conceivable. There may either be an understanding that whoever applies to the judicial power for assistance shall defray the costs thereupon incurred by it on his behalf, or it may be provided that the payment of a constant contribution toward the expenses of this judicial power shall entitle the contributor to its services whenever he needs them. The first of these arrangements does not seem altogether practicable; the other is one to which existing systems partially assimilate. In either case, however, it is taken for granted that the parties will duly fulfill their promises; that equivalents of protection and taxation shall be exchanged; that, on the one side, if the individual chooses to avail himself of state guardianship, he shall not refuse his fair share of state burdens; and on the other, that when the state has imposed the burdens it shall not withhold the guardianship.

Self-evident as is this interpretation of the agreement which citizenship presupposes, judicial practice is but little guided by it. Our system of jurisprudence takes a very one-sided view of the matter. It is indeed stringent enough in enforcing the claim of the state against the subject; but as to the reciprocal claim of the subject against the state it is comparatively careless. That it recognizes the title of the taxpayer to protection is true; but it is also true that it does this but partially. From certain infringements of rights, arbitrarily classed as criminal, it is ready to defend every complainant; but against others, not so classed, it leaves everyone to defend himself. The most trifling injury, if inflicted in a specified manner, is cognizable by the magistrate, and redress may be obtained free of charge; but if otherwise inflicted, the injury, no matter how serious, must be passively borne, unless the sufferer has plenty of money and a sufficiency of daring. Let a man have his hat knocked over his eyes, and the law will zealously espouse his cause—will mulct his assailant in a fine and costs, and will do this without charge. But if, instead of having been bonneted, he has been wrongfully imprisoned, he is politely referred to a solicitor, with the information that the offense committed against him is actionable: which means that if rich he may play double or quits with Fate; and that if poor he must go without even this chance of compensation. Against picking of pockets, as ordinarily practiced, the ruling power grants its lieges gratuitous protection; but pockets may be picked in various indirect ways, and it will idly look on unless costly means are taken to interest it. It will rush to the defense of one who has been deprived of a few turnips by a half-starved tramp; but as to the estate on which these turnips grew, that may be stolen without risk, so long as the despoiled owner is left friendless and penniless.[1] Some complaints need only to be whispered, and it forthwith plays the

---

[1] It is true that a plaintiff who can swear that he is not worth £5 may sue *in forma pauperis*. But this privilege is almost a dead letter. Actions so instituted are usually found to fail, because those who conduct them, having to plead gratuitously, plead carelessly.

parts of constable, lawyer, judge, and jailer; while to others it turns a deaf ear unless they are made through its bribed hangers-on. Now it is the injured man's champion; and now it throws down its weapons to sit as umpire, while oppressor and oppressed run a tilt at each other. Over such-and-such portions of a citizen's rights it mounts guard and cries, "Who goes there?" to every intruder; but upon the rest anyone may trample without fear of being challenged by it.

To a man with perceptions unblunted by custom, this mode of carrying out the agreement subsisting between himself and the state would seem strange enough. It is not impossible that he might call the transaction a swindle; might argue that his property had been taken from him under false pretenses. "To what purpose," he might ask, "did I submit myself to your laws, if I am now to be denied the advantages promised in return? Have I not complied with all the stipulations? You demanded allegiance, and I gave it. You said money was needful, and I paid the uttermost farthing of your exactions, heavy as they were. You required me to fulfill certain civil functions, and I fulfilled them cheerfully. Yet now when I ask you to give me that for which I made these sacrifices, you shuffle. I supposed you were to act the part of an Argus-eyed and Briareus-armed guardian, ever watching over my interests, ever ready to step in and defend them; so that whether sleeping or waking, absorbed in business or immersed in pleasure, I might have the gratifying consciousness of being carefully shielded from injury. Now, however, I find not only that my rights may be trespassed upon in many ways without attracting your notice, but that even when I tell you I have been wronged and demand your interposition, you shut the door in my face and will not listen until I have exorbitantly fed some of the servants who have access to your private ear. What am I to understand by this? Is it that your revenue is insufficient to defray the cost of dispensing justice in all cases? If so, why not say as much, and let us increase it? Is it that you cannot accomplish what you profess? If so, declare candidly what you are able to do, and what not. But, at any rate, let us have some intelligible understanding, and not this jumble of contradictions—this conflict of promise and performance—this taking of the pay without doing the duty."

**4.** THAT MEN SHOULD SIT DOWN SO APATHETICALLY AS THEY DO under the present corrupt administration of justice is not a little remarkable. That we, with all our jealousy of abuses; with all our opportunities of canvassing, blaming, and amending the acts of the legislature; with all our readiness to organize and agitate; with the Anti-Corn Law, Slavery-Abolition, and Catholic-Emancipation victories fresh in remembrance; that we, the independent, determined, self-ruling English, should daily behold the giant abominations of our judicial system and yet do nothing to rectify them is really quite incomprehensible. It is not as though the facts were disputed; all men are agreed upon them. The dangers of law are proverbial. The names of its officers are used as synonyms for trickery and greediness. The decisions of its courts are typical of chance. In all companies you hear but one opinion, and each person confirms it by a fresh illustration. Now you are informed of £300 having been expended in the recovery of forty shillings' worth of property; and again of a cause that was lost because an affirmation could not be received in place of an oath. A right-hand neighbor can tell you of a judge who allowed an indictment to be objected to, on the plea that the words, "in the year of our Lord," were not inserted before the date; and another to your left narrates how a thief lately tried for stealing a guinea pig was acquitted, because a guinea pig was shown to be a kind of rat, and a rat could not be property. At one moment the story is of a poor man whose rich enemy has deliberately ruined him by tempting him into litigation; and at the next it is of a child who has been kept in prison for six weeks, in default of sureties for her appearance as witness against one who had assaulted her.[2] This gentleman has been cheated out of half his property but dared not attempt to recover it for fear of losing more; while his less prudent companion can parallel the experience of him who said that he had only twice been on the verge of ruin: once when he had lost a lawsuit, and once when he had gained one.

[2] The case occurred at Winchester in July 1849.

On all sides you are told of trickery and oppression and revenge, committed in the name of justice; of wrongs endured for want of money wherewith to purchase redress; of rights unclaimed because contention with the powerful usurper was useless; of chancery suits that outlasted the lives of the suitors; of fortunes swallowed up in settling a title; of estates lost by an informality. And then comes a catalogue of victims—of those who have trusted and been deceived; gray-headed men whose hard-earned savings went to fatten the attorney; threadbare and hollow-cheeked insolvents who lost all in the attempt to get their due; some who had been reduced to subsist on the charity of friends; others who had died the death of a pauper; with not a few whose anxieties had produced insanity, or who in their desperation had committed suicide. Yet, while all parties echo each other's exclamations of disgust, these iniquities continue unchecked!

**5.** THERE ARE NOT WANTING, HOWEVER, MEN WHO DEFEND THIS state of things—who actually argue that government should perform but imperfectly what they allow to be its special function. While, on the one hand, they admit that administration of justice is the vital necessity of civilized life, they maintain, on the other, that justice may be administered too well! "For," say they, "were law cheap, all men would avail themselves of it. Did there exist no difficulty in obtaining justice, justice would be demanded in every case of violated rights. Ten times as many appeals would be made to the authorities as now. Men would rush into legal proceedings on the slightest provocation; and litigation would be so enormously increased as to make the remedy worse than the disease."

Such is the argument; an argument involving either a gross absurdity or an unwarrantable assumption. For observe: when this great multiplication of law proceedings under a gratuitous administration of justice is urged as a reason why things should remain as they are, it is implied that the evils attendant upon the rectification of all wrongs would be greater than are the evils attendant upon submission to those wrongs. Either the great majority of civil aggressions must be borne in silence as now, or must be adjudicated upon as then; and the allegation is that the first alternative is preferable. But if ten thousand litigations are worse than ten thousand injustices, then one litigation is worse than one injustice. Which means that, as a general principle, an appeal to the law for protection is a greater evil than the trespass complained of. Which means that it would be better to have no administration of justice at all! If for the sake of escaping this absurdity it be assumed that, as things now are, all *great* wrongs are rectified, that the costliness of law prevents insignificant ones only from being brought into court, and that consequently the above inference cannot be drawn—then, either denial is given to the obvious fact that, by the poverty they inflict, many of the greatest wrongs incapacitate their victims from obtaining redress, and to the obvious fact that the civil injuries suffered by the masses, though *absolutely* small, are *relatively* great; or else it is taken for granted that on nine tenths of the population, who are too poor to institute legal proceedings, no civil injuries of moment are ever inflicted!

Nor is this all. It is not necessarily true that making the law easy of access would increase litigation. An opposite effect might be produced. The prophecy is vitiated by that very common mistake of calculating the result of some new arrangement on the assumption that all other things would remain as they are. It is taken for granted that under the hypothetical regime just as many transgressions would occur as at present. Whereas any candid observer can see that most of the civil offenses now committed are committed *in consequence* of the inefficiency of our judicial system;

"FOR SPARING JUSTICE FEEDS INIQUITY."

It is the difficulty that he knows there will be in converting him which tempts the knave to behave knavishly. Were not the law so expensive and so uncertain, dishonest traders would never risk the many violations of it they now do. The trespasses of the wealthy against the poor would be rare were it not that the aggrieved have practically no remedy. Mark how, to the man who contemplates wronging his fellow, our legal system holds out promises of impunity. Should his proposed victim be one of small means, there is the likelihood that he will not be able to carry on a lawsuit: here is encouragement. Should he possess enough money, why, even then, having, like most people, a great dread of litigation, he will probably bear his loss unresistingly: here is further encouragement. Lastly, our plotter remembers that, should his victim venture an action, judicial decisions are very much matters of accident, and that the guilty are often rescued by clever counsel: here is still more encouragement. And so, all things considered, he determines to chance it. Now, he would never decide thus were legal protection efficient. Were the administration of law prompt, gratuitous, and certain, those probabilities and possibilities which now beckon him on to fraudulent acts would vanish. Civil injuries wittingly committed would almost cease. Only in cases where both parties sincerely believed themselves right would judicial arbitration be called for; and the number of such cases is comparatively small. Litigation, therefore, so far from *increasing* on justice being made easy of obtainment, would probably *decrease*.

**6.** BUT, AFTER ALL, IT IS NOT THE SETTING UP OF THIS OR THAT system of jurisprudence which causes the intercourse of men with each other to be equitable or otherwise. The matter lies deeper. As with forms of government, so with forms of law; it is the national character that decides. The power of an apparatus primarily depends, not on the ingenuity of its design, but on the strength of its materials. Be his plan never so well devised—his arrangement of struts and ties and bolts never so good, his balance of forces never so perfect—yet if our engineer has not considered whether the respective parts of his structure will bear the strain to be put upon them, we must call him a bungler. Similarly with the institution maker. If the people with whom he has to deal are not of the requisite quality, no cleverness in his contrivance will avail anything. Let us never forget that institutions are *made* of men; that men are the struts, ties, and bolts out of which they are framed; and that, dovetail and brace them together as we may, it is their nature which must finally determine whether the institutions can stand. Always there will be some *line of least resistance* along which, if the humanity they are wrought out of be not strong enough, they will give way; and, having given way, will sink down into a less trying attitude. Thus it is, among other things, with judicial mechanisms. No matter how admirably devised, their results will be good only in proportion as the nation is good. The instrumentalities by which they are to act—judges, juries, constables, witnesses, jailers, and the rest—must be units of the people; will, on the average, be marked by the same imperfections as the people; and though the system they are set to work out be perfect, yet will the badness of their characters degrade its acts down to a level with the general conduct of society.

That justice can be well administered only in proportion as men become just is a fact too generally overlooked. "If they had but trial by jury!" says someone, moralizing on the Russians. But they can't have it. It could not exist among them. Even if established it would not work. They lack that substratum of honesty and truthfulness on which alone it can stand. To be of use, this, like any other institution, must be born of the popular character. It is not trial by jury that produces justice, but it is the sentiment of justice that produces trial by jury, as the organ through which it is to act; and the organ will be inert unless the sentiment is there. These social forms which we regard as so potential are things of quite secondary importance. What mattered it that the Roman plebeians were endowed with certain privileges, when the patricians prevented them from exercising those privileges by ill treatment carried even to the death? What mattered it that our statute book contained equitable provisions, and that officers were appointed to enforce them, when there needed a Magna Charta to demand that justice should neither be sold, denied, nor delayed? What matters it even now that all men are declared equal before the law, when magistrates are swayed by class sympathies and treat a gentleman more leniently than an artisan? If we think that we can rectify the relationships of men at will, we deceive ourselves. What Sir James Mackintosh says of constitutions— that they are not made, but grow—applies to all social arrangements. It is not true that once upon a time men said, "Let there be law," and there was law. Administration of justice was originally impracticable, Utopian, and has become more and more practicable only as men have become less savage. The old system of settling disputes by personal contest and the new system of settling them by state arbitration have coexisted throughout all ages; the one little by little usurping the place of the other, outgrowing it. It was only after some advance had been made that the civil power could get recognized at all as a maintainer of rights. The feudal baron with castle and retainers maintained his own rights and would have considered himself disgraced by asking legal aid. Even after he had agreed to regard his suzerain as umpire, it was still in the lists, and by the strength of his arm and his lance, that he made good his cause. And when we remember that equally among lords and laborers this practice lingers even now—that we have still duels, which it is thought dishonorable for a gentleman to avoid by applying to a magistrate—that we have still pugilistic fights, which the people try to hide from the police—we are taught that it is impossible for a judicial system to become efficient faster than men become good. It is only after public morality has gained a certain ascendancy that the civil power gets strong enough to perform its simplest functions. Before this it cannot even put down banditti; border forays continue in spite of it; and it is bearded in its very strongholds, as, among ourselves, by the thieves of Whitefriars but two centuries ago. Under early governments the officers of law are less friends than enemies. Legal forms are habitually used for purposes of oppression. Causes are decided by favoritism, bribery, and backstairs intrigue. The judicial apparatus breaks down under the work it has to do, and shows us in a Jonathan Wild, a Judge Jeffries, and even a Lord Chancellor Bacon how inevitably its several parts are rendered inoperative by a generally diffused wickedness.

Of course the efficiency of present and future systems of jurisprudence must be determined by the same influences. Of our own legal arrangements we may say what Emerson has well said of institutions generally—that they are about as good as the characters of men permit them to be. When we read of Orange magistrates who became aggressors rather than protectors; of policemen who conspire with each other to obtain convictions that they may be promoted; and of the late Palace Court, whose officers habitually favored the plaintiff, with the view of inducing men to enter suits there, we find that now, as of old, judicial protection is vitiated by the depravity of the age. Nevertheless, it is probable that we are ripe for something better than we have. The universal disgust with which law is regarded may be taken as evidence of this—as evidence, moreover, that a change is at hand. But it is not likely that the mode of administering justice lately pointed out as the proper one is immediately feasible; seeing that men, by not having yet even recognized it as theoretically right, show themselves considerably below the state to which it is natural. This, however, is no reason for not advocating its adoption. For what was said in the last chapter respecting an equitable form of government may be here said respecting an equitable system of law: that the power quietly to establish it is the measure of its practicability.

**7.** BY DISPERSING THAT HAZE OF POLITICAL SUPERSTITION through which the state and its appendages loom so large, the foregoing considerations suggest a somewhat startling question. For if, when men's savageness and dishonesty render the administration of justice most necessary, it is impossible; if it becomes possible only in proportion as men themselves become just; and if that same universal uprightness which permits the administration of justice to become perfect also makes it needless, as it evidently must, then we may naturally ask: Can the state really administer justice at all? Does it, looking at society as a whole, secure to the people any fuller enjoyment of their rights than they would have without it? May we not conclude that it takes away from men's liberties in one direction as much as it gives in another? Is it not a mere dead mechanism worked by a nation's moral sense, neither adding to, nor deducting from the force of that moral sense, and consequently unable to alter the sum total of its effects?

A strange idea, this, some will think: and so at first sight it seems. We have such a habit of regarding government in its

protective character and forgetting its aggressive one that to
ask whether the rights it secures are not about balanced by the
rights it violates seems almost laughable. Nevertheless, we shall
find that on drawing up a debtor and creditor account the absurdity of the doubt disappears. Passing over those ruling powers
of the East, which, in return for the small amount of security
they guarantee, are in the habit of confiscating, under one
pretense or other, any property not efficiently concealed by the
unfortunate owners, and which, in some cases, push their exactions so far as to have to give back for seed in the spring a part
of that crop they had taken from the husbandman at the
previous harvest; passing over, too, those Middle Age systems
of government under which protection, such as it was, had to
be purchased by the resignation of personal freedom, let us
institute as favorable a comparison as possible. Let us take the
relatively good governments we now know, and setting down
on the one side the benefits conferred, and on the other the
evils inflicted, let us strike a balance between them. Under the
head of obligations may be entered the efficient curb which our
police system puts upon offenses against person and property;
our courts of law, too, with all their defects, afford a partial
defense against civil injuries which needs setting down in the
estimate; and to these must be added what far outweigh them
both—that sense of habitual security and that consequent ability
fearlessly to carry on the business of life, which are produced
by the mere presence of an active civil power. Even after deducting from these a heavy discount on the score of shortcomings, there unquestionably remains a large surplus of benefit
for which the state may claim credit. Turn we now to the per
contra statement. As the first item on the list there stands that
gigantic injustice inflicted upon nineteen twentieths of the community by the usurpation of the soil—by the breach of their
rights to the use of the earth (Chapter IX). For this the civil
power is responsible—has itself been a party to the aggression
—has made it legal and still defends it as right. Next comes
the trespass committed against the many by subordinating them
to the few and forcing them to obey laws to which their consent
was never asked. Note again the tyrannies accompanying na-

tional defense—the impressments and militia drawings, the continuous abnegations of liberty in the persons of soldiers and sailors, ending not unfrequently in the sacrifice of their lives. Remember also how our rights are trenched upon by commercial restrictions, and how men are not only prevented from buying and selling where they please, but are debarred from following certain occupations until they have bought government permits. Nor let us forget the penalties that until lately so seriously transgressed religious freedom—penalties which, as the Anti-State-Church Association can show, have by no means disappeared. And all these, together with the many minor restrictions hedging us about, are accompanied by those never-ceasing incursions made upon our property by the tax gatherer and the officers of customs and excise, by poor-rate collectors and churchwardens. Measuring wrongs, as we must, by the degree in which they limit the exercise of faculties, let us now add up the two accounts and contrast their sum totals. On the one side, government partially saves us (only partially, mind) from those assaults, robberies, murders, cheatings, and kindred injuries to which, were there no such institution, the existing immorality of men would expose us. These we must imagine to be distributed over the community at large and over the life of each citizen, and then conceive to what average restriction on the free exercise of faculties they would be equivalent. On the other side, government itself transgresses men's liberties by the monopoly of land, by the usurpation of power, by restrictions on trade, by the slavery and death of thousands of soldiers, by the ruin of hundreds it ought to protect, by favoritism to creeds and classes, by the civil functions it makes imperative, by petty restraints too numerous to name, but above all by a remorseless taxation, which, affecting seven eights of the nation as it does by abstracting a large percentage from earnings already insufficient for necessaries, virtually obliterates, in great measure, the spheres needed for the development of their natures. We have now to suppose these manifold limitations to the free exercise of faculties averaged like the others, and then to ask ourselves whether the two averages are, or are not, equal. Is the question, after all, so very irrational? Is not the answer doubtful?

Nay, indeed; consider it rightly, and the answer is not at all doubtful. It is very certain that government can not alter the total amount of injustice committed. The absurdity is in supposing that it can—in supposing that by some ingenious artifice we may avoid the consequences of our own natures. The civil power no more does what to the careless eye it seems to do than the juggler really performs his apparent miracles. It is impossible for man to create force. He can only alter the mode of its manifestations, its direction, its distribution. The power that propels his steamboats and locomotives is not of his making; it was all lying latent in the coal. He telegraphs by an agent set free during the oxidation of zinc, but of which no more is obtained than is due to the number of atoms that have combined. The very energy he expends in moving his arm is generated by the chemical affinities of the food he eats. In no case can he do anything but avail himself of dormant forces. This is as true in ethics as in physics. Moral feeling is a force—a force by which men's actions are restrained within certain prescribed bounds—and no legislative mechanism can increase its results one iota. By how much this force is deficient, by so much must its work remain undone. In whatever degree we lack the qualities needful for our state, in the same degree must we suffer. Nature will not be cheated. Whoso should think to escape the influence of gravitation by throwing his limbs into some peculiar attitude would not be more deceived than are those who hope to avoid the weight of their depravity by arranging themselves into this or that form of political organization. Every jot of the evil must in one way or other be borne—consciously or unconsciously; either in a shape that is recognized or else under some disguise. No philosopher's stone of a constitution can produce golden conduct from leaden instincts. No apparatus of senators, judges, and police can compensate for the want of an internal governing sentiment. No legislative manipulation can eke out an insufficient morality into a sufficient one. No administrative sleight of hand can save us from ourselves.

But must not this imply that government is of no use whatever? Not at all. Although unable to alter the sum total of injustice to be supported, it can still alter its distribution. And this is what it really does. By its aid, men to a considerable extent equalize the evil they have to bear—spread it out more uniformly over the whole community and over the life of each citizen. Entire freedom to exercise the faculties, interrupted by entire deprivations of it, and marred by the perpetual danger of these deprivations, is exchanged for a freedom on which the restrictions are constant but partial. Instead of those losses of life, of limb, or of the means of subsistence, which, under a state of anarchy, all are liable to and many suffer, a political organization commits unversal aggressions of a comparatively mild type. Wrongs that were before occasional but crushing are now unceasing but bearable. The system is one of mutual assurance against moral disasters. Just as men, while they cannot prevent fires and shipwrecks, can yet guarantee each other against ruin from these by bearing them in common and distributing the injuries entailed over long periods of time; so, although by uniting together for judicial purposes men cannot diminish the amount of injustice to be borne, they can, and do, insure themselves against its otherwise fatal results.

**8.** WHEN WE AGREED THAT IT WAS THE ESSENTIAL FUNCTION OF the state to protect, to administer the law of equal freedom, to maintain men's rights, we virtually assigned to it the duty, not only of shielding each citizen from the trespasses of his neighbors, but of defending him, in common with the community at large, against foreign aggressions. An invading force may violate people's rights as much as, or far more than, an equal body of felons; and our definition requires that government shall resist transgression in the one case as much as in the other. Protection —this is what men seek by political combination; and whether it be against internal or external enemies matters not. Unquestionably war is immoral. But so likewise is the violence used in the execution of justice; so is all coercion. Ethical law is as certainly broken by the deeds of judicial authorities as by those of a defensive army. There is, in principle, no difference whatever between the blow of a policeman's baton and the thrust of a

soldier's bayonet. Both are infractions of the law of equal freedom in the persons of those injured. In either case we have force
sufficient to produce submission; and it matters not whether
that force be employed by a man in red or by one in blue.
Policemen are soldiers who act alone; soldiers are policemen
who act in unison. Government employs the first to attack in
detail ten thousand criminals who separately make war upon
society, and it calls in the last when threatened by a like number
of criminals in the shape of drilled troops. Resistance to foreign
foes and resistance to native ones having consequently the same
object—the maintenance of men's rights—and being effected by
the same means—force—are in their nature identical, and no
greater condemnation can be passed upon the one than upon
the other. The doings of the battlefield merely exhibit in a concentrated form that immorality which is inherent in government and attaches to all its functions. What is so manifest in its
military acts is true of its civil acts, that it uses wrong to put
down wrong.

Defensive warfare (and of course it is solely to this that the
foregoing argument applies) must therefore be tolerated as the
least of two evils. There are indeed some who unconditionally
condemn it and would meet invasion by non-resistance. To such
there are several replies.

First, consistency requires them to behave in like fashion to
their fellow citizens. They must not only allow themselves to be
cheated, assaulted, robbed, wounded, without offering active
opposition, but must refuse help from the civil power; seeing
that they who employ force by proxy are as much responsible
for that force as though they employed it themselves.

Again, such a theory makes pacific relationships between men
and nations look needlessly Utopian. If all agree not to aggress,
they must as certainly be at peace with each other as though
they had all agreed not to resist. So that, while it sets up so
difficult a standard of behavior, the rule of non-resistance is not
one whit more efficient as a preventive of war than the rule of
non-aggression.

Moreover, this principle of non-resistance is not deducible
from the moral law. The moral law says, Do not aggress. It can-

not say, Do not resist; for to say this would be to presuppose its own precepts broken. As explained at the outset (Chapter I), Morality describes the conduct of perfect men, and cannot include in its premises circumstances that arise from imperfection. That rule which attains to universal sway when all men are what they ought to be must be the right rule, must it not? And that rule which then becomes impossible of fulfillment must be the wrong one? Well, in an ideal state the law of non-aggression is obeyed by all—is the vital principle of everyone's conduct—is fully carried out, reigns, lives; whereas in such a state the law of non-resistance necessarily becomes a dead letter.

Lastly, it can be shown that non-resistance is absolutely wrong. We may not carelessly abandon our rights. We may not give away our birthright for the sake of peace. If it be a duty to respect other men's claims, so also is it a duty to maintain our own. That which is sacred in their persons is sacred in ours also. Have we not a faculty which makes us feel and assert our title to freedom of action at the same time that, by a reflex process, it enables us to appreciate the like title in our fellows? Did we not find that this faculty can act strongly on behalf of others only when it acts strongly on our own behalf (p. 91)? And must we assume that, while its sympathetic promptings are to be diligently listened to, its direct ones are to be disregarded? To suppose this is to suppose an incurable defect in our moral constitution—is to suppose that the very sentiment intended to lead us will itself mislead us. No, we may not be passive under aggression. In the due maintenance of our claims is involved the practicability of all our duties. Without liberty of action, without rights, we cannot fully exercise our faculties; and if we cannot fully exercise our faculties, we cannot fulfill the Divine will; and if we allow ourselves to be deprived of that without which we cannot fulfill the Divine will, we virtually neglect that will.

But how, if all coercion is immoral? Will it not follow that it is immoral to use violence in opposing a trespasser? Certainly. Then either alternative is wrong? Just so; the law of right conduct has been broken, and this dilemma is the consequence. Action and reaction are equal. The blow dealt at morality in the person of the injured cannot end with itself: there must be a corresponding recoil. The first evil gives rise to an equivalent second, whether it is met by resistance or not. The assertion looks strange—will perhaps be incredible to many; nevertheless, it must be made. And all we can say of this seeming paradox is that it shows how actions lapse into a moral chaos when once the equilibrium of men's relationships is destroyed.

Thus we find that the principle of non-resistance is not ethically true, but only that of non-aggression—that hence a government is justified in taking up a defensive attitude toward foreign enemies, and that the abstract criminality undoubtedly attaching to such a proceeding is the same criminality which pervades the administration of justice, is the same criminality of which government is itself a consequence.

**9.** OF INTERNATIONAL ARBITRATION WE MUST SAY, AS OF A FREE constitution or a good system of jurisprudence, that its possibility is a question of time. The same causes which once rendered all government impossible have hitherto forbidden this widest extension of it. A federation of peoples—a universal society—can exist only when man's adaptation to the social state has become tolerably complete. We have already seen (p. 177) that in the earliest stage of civilization, when the repulsive force is strong and the aggregative force weak, only small communities are possible; a modification of character causes these tribes, and satrapies, and *gentes*, and feudal lordships, and clans gradually to coalesce into nations; and a still further modification will allow of a still further union. That the time for this is now drawing nigh seems probable. We may gather as much from the favor with which such an arrangement is regarded. The recognition of its desirableness foreshadows its realization. In peace societies, in proposals for simultaneous disarmament, in international visits and addresses, and in the frequency with which friendly interventions now occur, we may see that humanity is fast growing toward such a consummation. Though hitherto impracticable, and perhaps impracticable at the present moment, a brotherhood of nations is being made practicable by the very efforts used to bring it about. These philanthropic enthusiasms, which the worldly-wise think so ridiculous, are essential parts of the process by which the desideratum is being wrought out. Perhaps no fact is more significant of the change going on than the spread of that non-resistance theory lately noticed. That we should find sprinkled among us men who, from the desire to receive this ultra-humane doctrine, do violence to their perceptions of what is due to themselves cannot but afford matter for congratulation. Unsound as the idea may be, its origin is good. It is a redundant utterance of that sympathy which transforms the savage man into the social man, the brutal into the benevolent, the unjust into the just; and, taken in conjunction with other signs of the times, prophesies that a better relationship between nations is approaching. Meanwhile, in looking forward to some all-embracing federal arrangement, we must keep in mind that the stability of so complicated a political organization depends not upon the fitness of one nation but upon the fitness of many.

CHAPTER XXII

---

## *The Limit of State Duty*

**1.** A FUNCTION TO EACH ORGAN AND EACH ORGAN TO ITS OWN function is the law of all organization. To do its work well, an apparatus must possess special fitness for that work; and this will amount to unfitness for any other work. The lungs cannot digest, the heart cannot respire, the stomach cannot propel blood. Each muscle and each gland must have its own particular nerve. There is not a fiber in the body but what has a channel to bring it food, a channel to take its food away, an agency for causing it to assimilate nutriment, an agency for stimulating it to perform its peculiar duty, and a mechanism to take away effete matter; not one of which can be dispensed with. Between creatures of the lowest type and creatures of the highest, we similarly find the essential difference to be that in the one the vital actions are carried on by a few simple agents, while in the other the vital actions are severally decomposed into their component parts, and each of these parts has an agent to itself. In organizations of another order the same principle is apparent. When the manufacturer discovered that by confining each of his employees wholly to one process he could immensely increase the productive powers of his establishment, he did but act upon this same rule of one function to one organ. If we compare the mercantile arrangements of a village with those of a city, we shall find that the hucksters of the one carry on many trades each, while every shopkeeper of the other confines himself to a single trade; showing us how a highly developed apparatus for the distribution of commodities is similarly distinguished by subdivision of duties. Language, too, exemplifies the same truth. Between its primitive state, in which it consisted of nothing but nouns, used vaguely to indicate all ideas indiscriminately, and its present state, in which it consists of numerous "parts of speech," the process of growth has been that of gradually separating words into classes serving different purposes; and just as fast as this process has advanced has language become capable of completely fulfilling its end.

May we not, then, suspect that the assigning of one function to one organ is the condition of efficiency in all instrumentalities? If, as far as we can see, such is the law not only of natural organizations but of what, in a superficial sense, we call artificial ones, does it not seem probable that it is the universal law? Will it not be the law of institutions? Will it not be the law of the state? Must we not expect that with a government, also, special adaptation to one end implies non-adaptation to other ends? And is it not likely that, by devolving on a government additional functions, the due discharge of its peculiar function will be sacrificed? And would not this imply that a government ought not to undertake such additional functions?

But laying aside analogy, let us inquire whether it is not the fact that, in assuming any office besides its original one, the state begins to lose the power of fulfilling that original one. What is it that we call the state? Men politically associated. How associated? Voluntarily. For what purpose? For mutual protection. Men voluntarily associated for mutual protection:

this, then, is our definition. Now, when rightly ordered, the conditions on which this voluntary association offers its services must be such as enable it to afford the greatest amount of protection possible. If otherwise—if it insists on nonessential conditions which prevent some men from accepting its services, or on conditions which unnecessarily compromise the liberty of those men who do accept its services—it manifestly fails to that extent in performing its function. Now the moment the state undertakes a second office it does all this. Men leagued together for a special object will never unanimously agree in the pursuit of any other object. So long as our joint-stock protection society confines itself to guaranteeing the rights of its members, it is pretty certain to be coextensive with the nation; for while such an organization is needed at all, most men will sacrifice something to secure its guardianship. But let an additional duty be assigned to it, and there will immediately arise more or less schism. The dissenting minority may in such case consist of two parties: the one comprising those who have so great a repugnance to the contemplated arrangement as to resolve upon seceding rather than consent to it, and a larger party consisting of those who grumble at the imposition of additional charges for the doing what they do not wish to be done but who think well to submit rather than give up the benefits of protection. Toward both these parties the state fails in its duty. The one it drives away by disadvantageous terms, and from the other it extracts sacrifices beyond what are needful for the performance of its original function; and by so doing becomes an aggressor instead of a protector. Observe how the case stands when put personally.

"Your taxes are heavier this year than last," complains a citizen to the government; "how is it?"

"The sums voted for these new schoolhouses and for the salaries of the masters and mistresses have increased the draft upon our exchequer," replies the government.

"Schoolhouses, masters and mistresses—what have I to do with these? You are not charging me with the cost of them, are you?"

"Yes."

"Why, I never authorized you to do so."

"True, but Parliament, or in other words the majority of the nation, has decided that the education of the young shall be entrusted to us and has authorized us to raise such funds as may be necessary for fulfilling this trust."

"But suppose I wish to superintend the education of my children myself?"

"You may do as you please, but you must pay for the privilege we offer, whether you avail yourself of it or not. Even if you have no children you must still pay."

"And what if I refuse?"

"Why, were we to act up to old precedents, we should punish you; but as things now stand, we shall content ourselves with giving notice that you have outlawed yourself."

"Nay, I have no wish to do that; I cannot at present dispense with your protection."

"Very well, then you must agree to our terms and pay your share of the new tax."

"See, now, what a dilemma you place me in. As I dare not relinquish the protection I entered into political combination to obtain, I must either give you a part of my property for nothing; or, should I make a point of having some equivalent, I must cease to do that which my natural affections prompt. Will you answer me a few questions?"

"Certainly."

"What is it that you, as a national executive, have been appointed for? Is it not to maintain the rights of those who employ you; or, in other words, to guarantee to each the fullest freedom for the exercise of his faculties compatible with the equal freedom of all others?"

"It has been so decided."

"And it has been also decided that you are justified in diminishing this freedom only to such extent as may be needful for preserving the remainder, has it not?"

"That is evidently a corollary."

"Exactly. And now let me ask what is this property, this money, of which in the shape of taxes you are demanding from me an additional amount? Is it not that which enables me to get food, clothing, shelter, recreation, or, to repeat the original expression, that on which I depend for the exercise of most of my faculties?"

"It is."

"Therefore, to decrease my property is to decrease my freedom to exercise my faculties, is it not?"

"Clearly."

"Then this new impost of yours will practically decrease my freedom to exercise my faculties?"

"Yes."

"Well, do you not now perceive the contradiction? Instead of acting the part of a protector, you are acting the part of an aggressor. What you were appointed to guarantee me and others you are now taking away. To see that the liberty of each man to pursue the objects of his desires is unrestricted, save by the like liberty of all, is your special function. To diminish this liberty by means of taxes or civil restraints more than is absolutely needful for performing such function is wrong because adverse to the function itself. Now your new impost does so diminish this liberty more than is absolutely needful, and it is consequently unjustifiable."

Thus we find, as was foretold, that whenever the state begins to exceed its office of protector it begins to lose protective power. Not a single supplementary service can it attempt without producing dissent; and in proportion to the amount of dissent so produced by it, the state defeats the end for which it was established. Let it undertake many additional duties, and there will be scarcely a man who does not object to being taxed on account of one or more of them—scarcely a man, therefore, to whom the state does not in some degree do the very opposite of what it is appointed to do. Now this thing which the state is appointed to do is the essential thing—the thing by which society is made possible; and these other things proposed to be done are nonessential, for society is possible without them. And as the essential ought not to be sacrificed to the nonessential, the state ought not to do anything but protect.

**2.** IT WILL PERHAPS BE URGED, HOWEVER, THAT THE EVIL DONE BY a government, when it thus oversteps its original duty, is only an apparent one; seeing that, though it diminishes men's spheres of action in one direction, it adds to them in another. All such supplementary functions, an objector may say, subserve in some way or other the wants of society; that is, they facilitate the satisfaction of men's desires; that is, they afford to men greater freedom for the exercise of their faculties. For if you argue that taking away a man's property diminishes his freedom to exercise his faculties, because it diminishes his means of exercising them, then you must in fairness admit that by procuring for him certain of the objects he desires, or by taking away the obstacles that lie between him and those objects, or by otherwise helping him to his ends, the state is increasing his power to exercise his faculties, and hence is practically increasing his freedom.

To all which the answer is that cutting away men's opportunities on one side, to add to them on another, is at best accompanied by a loss. Let us remember that the force by which a society, through its government, works out certain results is never increased by administrative mechanism, but that part of it escapes in friction. Government evidently cannot create any facilities for the exercise of faculties; all it can do is to redistribute them. It is easy to calculate what one of these artificial arrangements can effect. Set down the amount of power to satisfy his wants, which it takes from a citizen in extra taxes; deduct the serious waste occurring under official manipulations; and the remainder, transformed into some new shape, is all that can be returned to him. The transaction is consequently a losing one. So that, while in attempting to serve the public by undertaking supplementary functions a government fails in its duty toward all who dissent, it does not really compensate for this by additional advantages afforded to the rest, to whom it merely gives with one hand less than it takes away with the other.

**3.** BUT IN TRUTH THE TRANSACTION IS A YET MORE DETRIMENTAL one than it thus appears, for even the gift is a delusion—has a minus sign before it, unobserved, perhaps, by the many, but sufficiently visible to the analyst. The expediency philosophy of which this general state superintendence is a practical expression embodies the belief that government ought not only to guarantee men in the unmolested pursuit of happiness, but should provide the happiness for them and deliver it at their doors. Now no scheme could be more self-defeating, for no scheme could be more completely at variance with the constitution of things. Man, as briefly delineated at the outset (p. 19), consists of a congeries of faculties qualifying him for surrounding conditions. Each of these faculties, if normally developed, yields to him, when exercised, a gratification constituting part of his happiness; while, in the act of exercising it, some deed is done subserving the wants of the man as a whole, and affording to the other faculties the opportunity of performing in turn their respective functions and of producing, every one, its peculiar pleasure: so that, when healthily balanced, each subserves all, and all subserve each. We cannot live at all unless this mechanism works with tolerable efficiency; and we can live entirely—that is, can have entire happiness—only when the reciprocity between capacities and requirements is perfect. As before said, the complete man is the self-sufficing man—the man who is in every point fitted to his circumstances—the man in whom there are desires corresponding not only to all the acts which are immediately advantageous, but to those which are remotely so. Evidently, one who is thus rightly constituted cannot be helped. To do anything for him by some artificial agency is to supersede certain of his powers—is to leave them unexercised, and therefore to diminish his happiness. To healthily developed citizens, therefore, state aid is doubly detrimental. It injures them both by what it takes and by what it does. By the revenues required to support its agencies it absorbs the means on which certain of the faculties depend for their exercise; and by the agencies themselves it shuts out other faculties from their spheres of action.

"But men are not complete; they are not healthily developed; they have not capacities in harmony with their wants; and therefore, as matters stand, a government does not by its interpositions preoccupy offices which there are faculties to fill." Very true; but next to being what we ought to be, the most desirable thing is that we should become what we ought to be as fast as possible. We are undergoing the process of adaptation. We have

to lose the characteristics which fitted us for our original state
and to gain those which will fit us for our present state; and the
question to be asked respecting these mechanical remedies for
our deficiences is: Do they facilitate change? Certainly not. A
moment's thought will convince us that they retard it. No one
can need reminding that demand and supply is the law of life as
well as the law of trade, that strength will show itself only where
strength is called for, that an undeveloped capability can be
developed only under the stern discipline of necessity. Would
you draw out and increase some too feeble sentiment? Then you
must set it to do, as well as it can, the work required of it. It
must be kept ever active, ever strained, ever inconvenienced by
its incompetency. Under this treatment it will, in the slow lapse
of generations, attain to efficiency; and what was once its impossible task will become the source of a healthy, pleasurable,
and desired excitement. But let a state instrumentality be thrust
between such faculty and its work, and the process of adaptation
is at once suspended. Growth ceases, and in its place commences
retrogression. The embryo agency now superseded by some commission—some board and staff of officers—straightway dwindles;
for power is as inevitably lost by inactivity as it is gained by
activity. Hence, humanity no longer goes on molding itself into
harmony with the natural requirements of the social state, but
begins, instead, to assume a form fitting these artificial requirements. It is consequently stopped in its progress toward that
self-sufficingness characteristic of the complete man; or, in other
words, is prevented from fulfilling the conditions essential to
complete happiness. And thus, as before said, not only does a
government reverse its function by taking away more property
than is needful for protective purposes, but even what it gives in
return for the excess so taken is in essence a loss.

**4.** THERE IS INDEED ONE FACULTY, OR RATHER COMBINATION OF
faculties, for whose shortcomings the state, as far as in it lies,
may advantageously compensate—that, namely, by which society is made possible. It is clear that any being whose constitution is to be molded into fitness for new conditions of existence
must be placed under those conditions. Or, putting the proposi-

tion specifically, it is clear that man can become adapted to the
social state only by being retained in the social state. This
granted, it follows that as man has been, and is still, deficient in
those feelings which, by dictating just conduct, prevent the perpetual antagonism of individuals and their consequent disunion,
some artificial agency is required by which their union may be
maintained. Only by the process of adaptation itself can be
produced that character which makes social equilibrium spontaneous. And hence, while this process is going on, an instrumentality must be employed, first to bind men into an
associated state, and second to check all conduct endangering
the existence of that state. Such an instrumentality we have in
a government.

And now mark that whether we consider government from
this point of view, or from that previously occupied, our conclusions respecting it are in essence identical. For when government fulfills the function here assigned it, of retaining men in
the circumstances to which they are to be adapted, it fulfills the
function which we on other grounds assigned it—that of protector. To administer justice, to mount guard over men's rights,
to prevent aggression, is simply to render society possible, to
enable men to live together, to keep them in contact with their
new conditions. And seeing that the two definitions are thus at
root the same, we shall be prepared for the fact that, in whichever way we specify its duty, the state cannot exceed that duty
without defeating itself. For, if regarded as a protector, we find
that, the moment it does anything more than protect, it becomes an aggressor instead of a protector; and if regarded as a
help to adaptation, we find that, when it does anything more
than sustain the social state, it retards adaptation instead of
hastening it.

**5.** THUS MUCH FOR THE POSITIVE EVIDENCE: LET US NOW ENTER
upon the negative. The expediency philosophers say that government has other functions to fulfill besides that of upholding
men's rights. If so, what are they? To the assertion that the
boundary line of state duty as above drawn is at the wrong place,
the obvious rejoinder is: Show us where it should be drawn.

This appeal the expediency philosophers have never yet been able to answer. Their alleged definitions are no definitions at all. As was proved at the outset (p. 4), to say that government ought to do that which is "expedient," or to do that which will tend to produce the "greatest happiness," or to do that which will subserve the "general good," is to say just nothing; for there is infinite disagreement respecting the natures of these desiderata. A definition of which the terms are indefinite is an absurdity. While the practical interpretation of "expediency" remains a matter of opinion, to say that a government should do that which is "expedient" is to say that it should do what we think it should do!

Still then our demand is—a definition. Between the two extremes of its possible power—the *everything* and the *nothing* with which a government may be entrusted—where is the proper limitation? Of the innumerable fields of action lying open to an uncontrolled legislature, which shall it occupy? Shall it extend its interference to the fixing of creeds, as in the old times; or to overlooking modes of manufacture, farming operations, and domestic affairs, as it once did; or to commerce, as of late; to education, as now; to public health, as some wish; to dress, as in China; to literature, as in Austria; to charity, to manners, to amusements? If not to all of them, to which of them? Should the perplexed inquirer seek refuge in authority, he will find precedents not only for these but for many more such interferences. If, like those who disapprove of master tailors having their work done off the premises, or like those who want to prevent the produce of industrial prisons displacing that of free artisans, or like those who would restrain charity-school children from competing with seamstresses, he thinks it desirable to meddle with trade arrangements, there are plenty of exemplars for him. There is the law of Henry VII, which directed people at what fairs they should sell their goods; and that of Edward VI, which enacted a fine of £100 for a usurious bargain; and that of James I, which prescribed the quantity of ale to be sold for a penny; and that of Henry VIII, which made it penal to sell any pins but such as are "double headed, and have their head soldered fast to the shank, and well smoothed; the shank well shaven; the point well and round-filed and sharpened." He has the countenance, too, of those enactments which fixed the wages of labor; and of those which dictated to farmers, as in 1533, when the sowing of hemp and flax was made compulsory; and of those which forbad the use of certain materials, as that now largely consumed article, logwood, was forbidden in 1597. If he approves of so extended a superintendence, perhaps he would adopt M. Louis Blanc's idea that "government should be considered as the supreme regulator of production" and, having so adopted it, push state control as far as it was once carried in France, when manufacturers were pilloried for defects in the materials they employed and in the texture of their fabrics; when some were fined for weaving of worsted a kind of cloth which the law said should be made of mohair, and others because their camlets were not of the specified width; and when a man was not at liberty to choose the place for his establishment, nor to work at all seasons, nor to work for everybody. Is this considered too detailed an interference? Then perhaps greater favor will be shown to those German regulations by which a shoemaker is prevented from following his craft until an inspecting jury has certified to his competence; which disable a man who has chosen one calling from ever adopting another; and which forbid any foreign tradesman from settling in a German town without a license. And if work is to be regulated, is it not proper that work should be provided and the idle compelled to perform a due amount of it? In which case how shall we deal with our vagrant population? Shall we take a hint from Fletcher of Saltoun, who warmly advocated the establishment of slavery in Scotland as a boon to "so many thousands of our people who are at this day dying for want of bread"? or shall we adopt the analogous suggestion of Mr. Carlyle, who would remedy the distresses of Ireland by organizing its people into drilled regiments of diggers? The hours of labor too—what must be done about these? Having acceded to the petition of the factory workers, ought we not to entertain that of the journeymen bakers? And if that of the journeymen bakers, why not, as Mr. Cobden asks, consider the cases of the glass blowers, the nightmen, the iron founders, the Sheffield knife grinders, and indeed all other classes, including the hard-worked M.P.s themselves. And when employment has been provided, and the hours of labor fixed, and trade regulations settled, we must decide how far the state ought to look after people's minds and morals and health. There is this education question: having satisfied the prevalent wish for government schools with tax-paid teachers, and adopted Mr. Ewart's plan for town libraries and museums, should we not canvass the supplementary proposal to have national lecturers? And if this proposal is assented to, would it not be well to carry out the scheme of Sir David Brewster, who desires to have "men ordained by the State to the undivided functions of science"—"an intellectual priesthood," "to develop the glorious truths which time and space embosom"?[1] Then having established "an intellectual priesthood" to keep company with our religious one, a priesthood of physic such as is advocated by certain feeless medical men, and of which we have already the germ in our union doctors, would nicely complete the trio. And when it had been agreed to put the sick under the care of public officials, consistency would of course demand the adoption of Mr. G. A. Walker's system of government funerals, under which "those in authority" are "to take especial care" that "the poorest of our brethren" shall have "an appropriate and solemn transmission" to the grave, and are to grant in certain cases "gratuitous means of interment." Having carried out thus far the communist plan of doing everything for everybody, should we not consider the people's amusements, and, taking example from the opera subsidy in France, establish public ball-rooms, and gratis concerts, and cheap theaters, with state-paid actors, musicians, and masters of the ceremonies; using care at the same time duly to regulate the popular taste, as indeed in the case of the Art-Union subscribers our present government proposed to do? Speaking of taste naturally reminds us of dress, in which sundry improvements might be enforced; for instance, the abolition of hats: we should have good precedent either in Edward IV, who fined those wearing "any gown or mantell" not according to specification, and who limited the superfluity of people's boot toes; or in Charles II, who prescribed the material

[1] See Address to the British Association at Edinburgh, in 1850.

for his subjects' grave-clothes. The matter of health, too, would need attending to; and, in dealing with this, might we not profitably reconsider those ancient statutes which protected people's stomachs by restricting the expenses of their tables; or, remembering how injurious are our fashionable late hours, might we not advantageously take a hint from the old Norman practice and fix the time at which people should put out their fires and go to bed; or might we not with benefit act upon the opinion of M. Beausobre, a statesman, who said it was "proper to watch during the fruit season, lest the people eat that which is not ripe"? And then, by way of making the superintendence quite complete, would it not be well to follow the example of that Danish king who gave directions to his subjects how they should scour their floors and polish their furniture?

Multiply these questions into a volume full, add to them the endless subordinate ones to which in practice they must give rise, and some idea may be formed of the maze through which the expediency philosopher has to find his way. Where now is his clue? Again comes the inquiry: How does he propose to determine between what should be attempted and what should not? Which is his definition? If he would escape the charge of political empiricism, he must show us some scientific test by which he can in each case determine whether or not state superintendence is desirable. Between the one extreme of entire non-interference and the other extreme in which every citizen is to be transformed into a grown-up baby, "with bib and papspoon," there lie innumerable stopping places; and he who would have the state do more than protect is required to say where he means to draw the line, and to give us substantial reasons why it must be just there and nowhere else.

**6.** AFTER THE DIFFICULTY OF FINDING OUT THE THING TO BE DONE, there comes the other difficulty of finding out the way to do it. Let us excuse the expediency philosopher one half of his task—let us for the occasion assume something to be unanimously agreed to as a proper undertaking; and now suppose we inquire of him, How about your means of accomplishing it? Are you quite sure they will answer? Are you quite sure that your appa-

ratus will not break down under its work? Quite sure that it will
produce the result you wish? Quite sure that it will not produce
some very different result? Quite sure that you will not get into
one of those imbroglios that so many have lost themselves in?
There is no lack of warnings. "Let us put down usury," the
rulers of the Middle Ages said to themselves; they tried, and did
just the reverse of what they intended; for it has turned out that
"all regulations interfering with the interest of money render its
terms more rigorous and burdensome." "We will exterminate
Protestantism," whispered the continental Catholics to each
other; they tried, and instead of doing this they planted in England the germs of a manufacturing organization which has to a
great extent superseded their own. "It will be well to give the
laboring classes fixed settlements," thought the Poor Law legislators; and this thought having been acted out, there eventually
grew up the clearance system, with its overcrowded cottages and
non-resident labor gangs. "We must suppress these brothels,"
decided the authorities of Berlin in 1845; they did suppress
them, and in 1848 the registrar's books and the hospital returns
proved matters to be considerably worse than before.[2] "Suppose
we compel the London parishes to maintain and educate their
pauper children in the country," said statesmen in the time of
George III; "it would greatly tend to the *preservation of the
lives* of the infant parish poor": so they passed the 7 Geo. III., c.
39; and by and by there began the business of child-farming,
ending in the Tooting tragedy. Are not such warnings worthy of
attention? Or does the expediency philosopher value those facts
only which are embodied in Blue-books and Board of Trade
tables?

Then as to his administrative mechanisms—can he answer for
the satisfactory working of them? The common remark that
public business is worse managed than all other business is not
altogether unfounded. Today he will find it illustrated in the
doings of a department which makes a valuable estate like the
New Forest a loss to the country of £3,000 a year; which allowed Salcey Forest to be wholly cut down and made away with
by a dishonest agent and which, in 1848, had its accounts made

[2]Reports of Dr. Fr. J. Behrend. See *Medical Times*, March 16, 1850.

up to March 1839 only. Tomorrow he may read of Admiralty bunglings—of ships badly built, pulled to pieces, rebuilt, and patched—of nearly a million spent on iron war steamers which are now found not to stand cannon shot—and of a sluggishness which puts the national dockyards "about seven years" behind all others. Now the exposure is of an extravagance which builds jails at a cost of £1,200 per prisoner; and now of a carelessness which permits important legal records to rot among rubbish. Here is a sailor of whom the state remanded sixpence a month toward a hospital which was never provided, and whose pension from the Merchant-Seaman's Fund is nothing like what it would have been from an ordinary assurance society; and there, on the other hand, is a Mint moneyer who gets more than £4,000 a year for doing what a tithe of the amount would amply pay for. Official delay is seen in the snail-paced progress of the Museum Catalogue; official mismanagement in the building of Houses of Parliament not fit for speaking in; and official perversity in the opposition uniformly made to improvement by the Excise, the Customs, and the Post Office authorities. Does the expediency philosopher feel no apprehensions on contemplating such evidence? Or, as one specially professing to be guided by experience, does he think that on the whole experience is in his favor?

Perhaps he has not heard that of ten mechanical inventions usually some nine fail; and that, before the tenth can be made to answer, endless obstacles that had never been dreamed of have to be surmounted. Or, if he has heard this, does he think that the properties of humanity being so much easier to understand than those of iron and brass, and an institution constructed of living men being a simple thing as compared with an inanimate mechanism, legislative schemes are not likely thus to miscarry?

7. "IT IS A GROSS DELUSION TO BELIEVE IN THE SOVEREIGN POWER of political machinery," says M. Guizot. True; and it is not only a gross delusion, but a very dangerous one. Give a child exaggerated notions of its parent's power, and it will by and by cry for the moon. Let a people believe in government omnipotence,

and they will be pretty certain to get up revolutions to achieve impossibilities. Between their exorbitant ideas of what the state ought to do for them on the one side, and its miserable performances on the other, there will surely be generated feelings extremely inimical to social order—feelings which, by adding to the dissatisfaction otherwise produced, may occasion outbreaks that would not else have occurred.

But this belief in "the sovereign power of political machinery" is not born with men; they are taught it. And how are they taught it? Evidently by these preachers of universal legislative superintendence—by the pretensions of statesmen themselves—and by having seen, from their childhood, all kinds of functions undertaken by government officials. The idea which, in his critique upon the late events in France, M. Guizot calls a "gross delusion" is an idea which he, in common with others, has been practically inculcating. Following in the steps of his predecessors, he has kept in action, and in some cases even extended, that system of official supervision to which this idea owes its birth. Was it not natural that men, living under the regulation of legions of prefects, sub-prefects, inspectors, controllers, intendants, commissaries, and other civil employees to the number of 535,000—men who were educated by the government and taught religion by it—who had to ask its consent before they could stir from home—who could not publish a handbill without a permit from the authorities, nor circulate a newspaper after the censor's veto—who daily saw it dictating regulations for railways, inspecting and managing mines, building bridges, making roads, and erecting monuments—who were led to regard it as the patron of science, literature, and the fine arts, and as the dispenser of honors and rewards—who found it undertaking the manufacture of gunpowder, superintending the breeding of horses and sheep, playing the part of public pawn-broker, and monopolizing the sale of tobacco and snuff—who saw it attending to everything, from the execution of public works down to the sanitary inspection of prostitutes—was it not natural that men so circumstanced should acquire exalted ideas of state power? And, having acquired such ideas, were they not likely to desire the state to compass for them unattainable benefits; to get angry because it did not do this; and to attempt by violent means the enforcement of their wishes? Evidently the reply must be affirmative. And if so, it is not too much to say that this overstepping of the proper sphere of government, leading as it does to that "gross delusion," a belief in "the sovereign power of political machinery," is the natural forerunner of such schemes as those of Blanc and Cabet, and of that confusion which the attempt to realize them by state agency must produce.

There are other modes, too, in which social stability is endangered by this interference system. It is a very expensive system: the further it is carried, the larger become the revenues required; and we all know that heavy taxation is inseparable from discontent. Moreover, it is in its nature essentially despotic. In governing everything it unavoidably cramps men and, by diminishing their liberty of action, angers them. It galls by its infinity of ordinances and restrictions; it offends by professing to help those whom it will not allow to help themselves; and it vexes by its swarms of dictatorial officials, who are forever stepping in between men and their pursuits. Those regulations by which the French manufacturers were hampered during the last century, when the state decided on the persons to be employed, the articles to be made, the materials to be used, and the quantities of the products, when inspectors broke the looms and burnt the goods that were not made according to law, and when improvements were illegal and inventors were fined, had no small share in producing the great revolution. Nor, among the causes which conspired to overthrow the government of Louis Philippe, must we forget the irritation generated by an analogous supervision, under which a mine cannot be opened without the permission of the authorities; under which a bookseller or printer may have his business suspended by the withdrawal of his license; and under which it is penal to take a bucket of water out of the sea.

Thus, if we regard government as a means of upholding the social state, we find that, besides suffering a direct loss of power to perform its duty on attempting anything else, there are several subsidiary ways in which the assumption of additional functions endangers the fulfillment of its original function.

**8.** BUT WE HAVE NOT SUFFICIENTLY CONSIDERED THE INFINITE presumption discernible in this attempt at regulating all the doings of men by law. To make up for defects in the original constitution of things—this is the meaning of the scheme, nakedly stated. It is said of a certain personage that he wished he had been consulted when the world was being made, for he could have given good advice; and not a little historical celebrity has attached to this personage, in virtue of his so-thought unparalleled arrogance. Shallow, shallow! Why, the great majority of our statesmen and politicians do as much every day. Advice, indeed! They do not stop at advice. They actively interpose, take into their own hands matters that God seems to be mismanaging, and undertake to set them right! It is clear to them that social wants and relationships have been so carelessly provided for that without their vigilant management all will go wrong. As for any silent influences by which imperfections are in process of being removed, they do not believe in them. But by a commission, a staff of officers, and a parliamentary grant, every deficiency shall be made good, and the errors of Omniscience be rectified!

In truth it is a sad sight for anyone who has been what Bacon recommends—"a servant and interpreter of nature"—to see these political schemers, with their clumsy mechanisms, trying to supersede the great laws of existence. Such a one, no longer regarding the mere outside of things, has learned to look for the secret forces by which they are upheld. After patient study, this chaos of phenomena into the midst of which he was born has begun to generalize itself to him; and where there seemed nothing but confusion, he can now discern the dim outlines of a gigantic plan. No accidents, no chance, but everywhere order and completeness. One by one exceptions vanish, and all becomes systematic. Suddenly what had appeared an anomaly answers to some intenser thought, exhibits polarity, and ranges itself along with kindred facts. Throughout he finds the same vital principles, ever in action, ever successful, and embracing the minutest details. Growth is unceasing; and, though slow, all-powerful: showing itself here in some rapidly developing outline, and there, where the necessity is less, exhibiting only the fibrils of incipient organization. Irresistible as it is subtle, he sees in the worker of these changes a power that bears onward peoples and governments regardless of their theories and schemes and prejudices—a power which sucks the life out of their lauded institutions, shrivels up their state parchments with a breath, paralyzes long-venerated authorities, obliterates the most deeply graven laws, makes statesmen recant and puts prophets to the blush, buries cherished customs, shelves precedents, and which, before men are yet conscious of the fact, has wrought a revolution in all things and filled the world with a higher life. Always toward perfection is the mighty movement —toward a complete development and a more unmixed good, subordinating in its universality all petty irregularities and fallings back, as the curvature of the earth subordinates mountains and valleys. Even in evils, the student learns to recognize only a struggling beneficence. But, above all, he is struck with the inherent sufficingness of things and with the complex simplicity of those principles by which every defect is being remedied— principles that show themselves alike in the self-adjustment of planetary perturbations and in the healing of a scratched finger—in balancing of social systems and in the increased sensitiveness of a blind man's ear—in the adaptation of prices to produce and in the acclimatization of a plant. Day by day he sees a further beauty. Each new fact illustrates more clearly some recognized law or discloses some inconceived completeness: contemplation thus perpetually discovering to him a higher harmony and cherishing in him a deeper faith.

And now, in the midst of his admiration and his awe, the student shall suddenly see some flippant red-tapist get upon his legs and tell the world how he is going to put a patch upon nature! Here is a man who, in the presence of all the wonders that encompass him, dares to announce that he and certain of his colleagues have laid their heads together and found out a way to improve upon the Divine arrangements! Scarcely an idea have these meddlers got of what underlies the facts with which they propose to deal, as you shall soon find on sounding their philosophy; and yet, could they carry out their pretensions, we should see them self-appointed nurses to the universe! They have so little faith in the laws of things, and so much faith in themselves, that, were it possible, they would chain earth and sun together, lest centripetal force should fail! Nothing but a Parliament-made agency can be depended upon; and only when this infinitely complex humanity of ours has been put under their ingenious regulations and provided for by their supreme intelligence will the world become what it ought to be! Such, in essence, is the astounding creed of these creation menders.

**9.** CONSIDER IT THEN IN WHAT LIGHT WE MAY—MORALLY OR scientifically, with reference to its practicableness, or as a question of political prudence, or even in its bearings upon religious faith—we find this theory, that a government ought to undertake other offices besides that of protector, to be an untenable theory. It has been shown that if the maintaining of rights be regarded as the special function of the state, the state cannot fulfill any other function without a partial loss of power to fulfill its special one. When, from another point of view, the state is looked upon as an aid to adaptation, we still find that it cannot exceed its duty of guarding men's liberties without becoming a hindrance to adaptation instead of an aid. It turns out that to abolish the limit of legislative interposition now contended for is in fact to abolish all limits whatever—is to give the civil power a field of action to which no bounds can be fixed, save in some arbitrary and utterly unphilosophical way. Moreover, even could certain supplementary affairs, considered fit for government supervision, be duly distinguished from the rest, there would still be the fact that all experience shows government to be an incompetent manager of such supplementary affairs. It is further urged that the system of extended official control is bad because unfavorable to social stability. And, finally, that system is repudiated, as involving an absurd and even impious presumption.

Such, then, are the general arguments brought forward to prove that, while the state ought to protect, it ought to do nothing more than protect. By the abstract thinker they may perhaps be deemed conclusive. There are others, however, with whom they will weigh comparatively little; and, for the conviction of these, it will be needful to examine in detail each of the several cases in which legislative superintendence is commonly advocated. Let us now proceed to do this.

CHAPTER XXIII

## The Regulation of Commerce

**1.** ARRANGEMENTS WHICH ALTER THE NATURAL COURSE OF TRADE are of two kinds: they may be classed as either artificial stimuli or artificial restraints—bounties or restrictions.

Of bounties must here be said specially what was said in the last chapter of factitious advantages generally; namely, that a government cannot give them without indirectly reversing its function. Not being requisite for the due maintenance of the citizen's rights, the taking away of his property for the purpose of encouraging certain branches of production would be wrong even were collateral benefits given in exchange; and as, instead of affording him collateral benefits, the commercial derangements consequent upon it put additional limits to the exercise of his faculties, such a measure is doubly wrong. Now that the faith in mercantile bribes is nearly extinct, it is needless to enforce this abstract inference by any supplementary reasoning.

Of restrictions it scarcely needs saying that they are even more directly inequitable than bounties. Deducible as it is from the law of equal freedom, the right of exchange is as sacred as any other right (Chapter XIII) and exists as much between members of different nations as between members of the same nation. Morality knows nothing of geographical boundaries or distinctions of race. You may put men on opposite sides of a river or a chain of mountains, may else part them by a tract of salt water, may give them, if you like, distinct languages, and may even color their skins differently, but you cannot change their fundamental relationships. Originating as these do in the facts of man's constitution, they are unaltered by the accidents of external condition. The moral law is cosmopolite—is no respecter of nationalities; and between men who are the antipodes of each other, either in locality or anything else, there must still exist the same balance of rights as though they were next-door neighbors in all things.

Hence, in putting a veto upon the commercial intercourse of two nations, or in putting obstacles in the way of that intercourse, a government trenches upon men's liberties of action, and by so doing directly reverses its function. To secure for each man the fullest freedom to exercise his faculties, compatible with the like freedom of all others, we find to be the state's duty. Now trade prohibitions and trade restrictions not only do not secure this freedom, but they take it away. So that in enforcing them the state is transformed from a maintainer of rights into a violator of rights. If it be criminal in a civil power commissioned to shield us from murder to turn murderer itself; if it be criminal in it to play the thief, though set to keep off thieves, then must it be criminal in it to deprive men, in any way, of liberty to pursue the objects of desire, when it was appointed to insure them that liberty. Whether it kills, or robs, or enslaves, or shackles by trade regulations, its guilt is alike in kind and differs only in degree. In one extreme it wholly destroys the power to exercise the faculties; in the other it does this partially. And in strict ethics the same species of condemnation must be visited upon it in both cases.

**2.** NOT A FEW WILL BE STARTLED BY THIS VIEW OF THE MATTER. Let such reflect awhile upon the antecedents and associations of this trade ruling. They will find, on doing so, that it is allied in both origin and practice to all other forms of wrong. More than once it has been pointed out that as unjust customs and institutions derive their viciousness from a moral defect in the people living under them, they must be uniformly pervaded by that viciousness; that as social laws, creeds, and arrangements consist merely of solidified character, the same character will be shown in all the social laws, creeds, and arrangements which coexist; and, further, that any process of amelioration will affect them simultaneously. This truth was amply illustrated (pp. 144 and 159). We saw that tyranny in forms of government, tyranny in the conduct of lord to serf, tyranny in religious organizations and discipline, tyranny in the matrimonial relationship, and tyranny in the treatment of children regularly flourished together and regularly decreased at a like rate. In the same category we must now put tyranny in commercial laws. Sinking those minor irregularities which pervade all nature's processes, we shall find that from the days when exportation was a capital crime down to our own free-trade era there has been a constant ratio kept between the stringency of mercantile restraints and the stringency of other restraints, as there has between the increase of commercial liberty and the increase of general liberty.

A few facts will sufficiently exemplify this. Take as one the instance just alluded to, in which associated with autocratic rule in church, in state, and in feudal hall we find Edward III, for the purpose of making foreigners come and buy in our markets, prohibiting his subjects from sending abroad any staple goods "under penalty of death and confiscation," and further enacting "that the law should be unalterable either by himself or his successors." Observe, too, how this same despotic spirit was exhibited in the regulations requiring these continental traders to reside during their stay with certain inspectors commissioned to see the cargoes sold within a specified time, and the proceeds reinvested in English goods, and charged to transmit to the Exchequer periodical statements of each merchant's bargains—regulations, by the way, of which the abandonment was in after times lamented by the venerators of ancestral wisdom, much as the abolition of the sliding scale is mourned over by a certain party of our own day. Note again how, under the same regime, laborers were coerced into working for fixed wages; and then how, to keep the balance even, shopkeepers had the prices of provisions dictated to them. Mark further that when the most tyrannical of these ordinances fell into disuse, there still continued the less burdensome ones, such as those usury laws, orders to farmers, prescribings of the material for grave-clothes, instructions to manufacturers, etc., referred to in the last chapter. But without going into further detail—without enlarging upon the fact that those intolerable restraints once borne by the manufacturing classes of France were cotemporary with intense despotism at court and a still lingering feudalism in the provinces—without tracing the parallelism that exists between the political and commercial bondage, under which, in spite of their revolutions, the French still live—without pointing out at length the same connection of phenomena in Prussia, in Austria, and in other similarly ruled countries—without doing all this, the evidence adduced sufficiently shows that the oppressiveness of a nation's mercantile laws varies as the oppressiveness of its general arrangements and government. While, conversely, if we glance over the annals of progress and then contemplate the changes that have taken place within these few years, or which are yet in progress, we cannot but remark a similar kinship between the manifestations of a juster feeling in political organization, in ecclesiastical affairs, in the family, and in our commercial code.

Thus, trade restrictions are of the same race with irresponsible government and slavery. An obtuse perception of, and an insufficient sympathy with, the claims of man are the parents of all tyrannies and dishonesties, bear they what name they may. Interferences with the freedom of exchange are as certainly their progeny as are the worst violations of human rights; they are constantly found in the society of these; and though not popularly classed as crimes, they are in both origin and nature closely related to them.

**3.** THERE IS ANOTHER ASPECT UNDER WHICH THESE TRADE REGUlations, in common with many kindred contrivances for the management of social affairs, may be regarded. They are all in essence idolatrous. The worship of dead, powerless things made with human hands is not extinct, as people flatter themselves —cannot be extinct—never will be entirely extinct. The elements of man's nature are persistent; the change is in their ratios. Typical remains of every disposition must continue traceable even to the remotest future. If, on the one hand, it is an error to suppose that humanity has not altered at all, it is, on the other hand, an error to suppose that it has altered, or even will alter, so completely as to retain no traces of its bygone character.

Scientifically defined, idolatry is a mode of thought under which all causation is attributed to entities. It results from the first generalization of the undeveloped intellect, which, having constantly seen results produced by visible, tangible objects, infers that all results are so produced. In the mind of the savage every effect is believed to be due to a special worker, because special workers have been observed to precede effects in a multitude of instances. The laws of mental action necessitate that, as all known causes have presented themselves to him as personal agencies, all unknown causes must be conceived by him of the same nature. Hence the original fetishism. A stone thrown by an unseen hand, a piece of wood that, when heated, bursts into flame, or an animal found in the neighborhood of some natural catastrophe is at once assumed to be the acting power. Here is a phenomenon—a visible change of state in some observed object: past experience inevitably suggests that there is a worker of this change; past experience also inevitably suggests that such worker is an entity; the entity to which the character of worker is ultimately ascribed will be that which past experience points out as most probable; and, in the absence of other entities, this character of worker will attach to the wood that gives out the flame or to the stone that inflicts the blow. Thus the wood and stone, being looked upon as agents of unknown power capable of inflicting injury, are prayed to and propitiated.

From the very first, however, there begins an accumulation of facts calculated to undermine this theory of things and certain ultimately to overthrow it. For, while he regards all phenomena as the doings of living beings, the primitive man necessarily attributes to such beings qualities similar to those of the being he sees—men and brutes. Reasoning, as he must, from the known to the unknown, he is obliged to conceive the unknown generators of change to be like the known ones in all things; and we find that he represents them by forms either human, or bestial, or both, that he imagines their passions and habits to be like his own. Now an attribute, possessed in common by all the beings known to him, is that of irregular volition. He sees no creature whose acts are so uniform that he can say positively what its future behavior will be. Hence it happens that when certain natural events, originally ascribed by him to living agents—events such as the rising and setting of the sun and the falling of bodies to the earth—come to be perpetually repeated and follow the same antecedents without exception, his notion of personal agency is shaken. This perfect uniformity of action is at variance with his knowledge of all known beings—is at variance with his very conception of a being. And thus in respect to the most familiar sequences, experience silently forces upon him the idea of a constant course of procedure—or what we express by the word *law*; and a belief in *im*personal agency slowly supplants the original belief in personal agency. This revolution in his mode of thinking, though at first confined to the everyday instances of causation, extends in process of time to a wider and wider range of cases. The unceasing accumulation of facts which begins when increase of population provides a multitude of observers continually furnishes new illustrations of that uniformity of sequence which conflicts with the notion of special workers; and thus the domain of the so-called *supernatural* is step by step usurped by the so-called *natural*. Still, it is only in so far as uniformity of sequence is made abundantly manifest that the old theory is superseded. Though, among the Greeks, Thales taught that there were laws of matter, he nevertheless considered that a loadstone had a soul. Where the occurrence is unusual—that is, where the connection between antecedent and consequent is not familiar—that is, where circumstances do not discountenance the original belief in special workers, that belief is still held. Hence it happens that, long after all ordinary phenomena have come to be considered as due to the properties of things, or, in other words, to impersonal agency, such an event as an eclipse or an earthquake is explained as a dragon eating the sun or as a god turning over in his sleep; an epidemic is ascribed to witchcraft; a luminous whiff of marsh gas is regarded as a "will-o'-the-wisp"; a failure in the dairy or brewhouse is set down to fairy malice; and there are myths about Giants' Causeways and Devils' Bridges. Where the connection between cause and effect is very remote or obscure, as in matters of fortune and in certain bodily affections, this disposition to attribute power to entities continues even after science has made great progress; and thus we find that in our own day the old fetishism still lingers in the regard shown to crooked sixpences, wart charms, and omens.

It lingers, moreover, as already hinted, in less suspected forms. Many much-reverenced social instrumentalities also have originated in this primitive necessity of ascribing all causation to special workers—this inability to detach the idea of force from an individual something. Just in proportion as natural phenomena are recorded by any people as of personal instead of impersonal origin will the phenomena of national life be similarly construed; and, indeed, since moral sequences are less obvious than physical ones, they will be thus construed even more generally. The old belief that a king could fix the value of coinage, and the cry raised at the change of style—"Give us our eleven days"—obviously implied minds incapable of conceiving social affairs to be regulated by other than visible, tangible agencies. That there should be at work some unseen but universally diffused influence determining the buyings and sellings of citizens and the transactions of merchants from abroad, in a way the most advantageous to all parties, was an idea as foreign to such minds as was that of uniform physical causation to the primitive Greeks;[1] and, conversely, as the primitive Greeks could understand the operations of nature being performed by a number of presiding individualities, so to the people of the Middle Ages it was comprehensible that a proper production and distribution of commodities should be insured by acts of Parliament and government officials. While the due regulation of trade by a natural indestructible force was inconceivable to them, they could conceive trade to be duly regulated by a force resident in some material instrumentality put together by legislators, clothed in the robes of office, painted by

[1] See Grote's History.

court flatterers, and decorated with "jewels five words long."[2]

But with the complex phenomena of commerce, as with the simpler phenomena of the inorganic world, constancy of sequence has gradually undermined the theory that power dwells in entities. Irresistible evidence is at length establishing a belief in the law of supply and demand, as some thousands of years ago it established a belief in the law of gravitation. And the development of politico-economical science, being thus a further conquest of the faith in impersonal agencies over the faith in personal agencies, must be regarded as one of that series of changes which commenced with the first victory of natural philosophy over superstition.

**4.** FORTUNATELY IT IS NOW NEEDLESS TO ENFORCE THE DOCTRINE of commercial freedom by any considerations of policy. After making continual attempts to improve upon the laws of trade, from the time of Solon downward, men are at length beginning to see that such attempts are worse than useless. Political economy has shown us in this matter—what indeed it is its chief mission to show—that our wisest plan is to let things take their own course. An increasing sense of justice, too, has assisted in convincing us. We have here learned what our forefathers learned in some cases and what, alas, we have yet to learn in many more, that nothing but evil can arise from inequitable regulations. The necessity of respecting the principles of abstract rectitude—this it is that we have had another lesson upon. Look at it rightly and we shall find that all the Anti-Corn Law League did, with its lectures, its newspapers, its bazaars, its monster meetings, and its tons of tracts, was to teach people— what should have been very clear to them without any such teaching—that no good can come of violating men's rights. By bitter experience and a world of talk we have at length been made partially to believe as much. Be it true or not in other cases, we are now quite certain that it is true in trade. In respect to this at least we have declared that, for the future, we will obey the law of equal freedom.

[2] A metaphor that has been used to denote the pride with which the German officials regard their titles.

## CHAPTER XXIV

*Religious Establishments*

**1.** AS A MATTER OF ROUTINE, IT IS NEEDFUL HERE TO POINT OUT what the reader will have inferred from Chapter XXII, that, by devoting a portion of its revenues or a part of the nation's property to the propagation of Christianity or any other creed, a government necessarily commits a wrong. If, as with ourselves, such government forcibly takes a citizen's money for the support of a national church, it is guilty of infringing the rights it ought to maintain—of trespassing upon that freedom to exercise the faculties which it was commissioned to guard. For, as already shown, by diminishing a subject's liberty of action more than is needful for securing the remainder, the civil power becomes an aggressor instead of a protector. If, on the other hand, the right to ignore the state is recognized, as, in considering the question abstractedly, we must suppose it to be, then, by insisting upon conditions which drive some men to abandon its aid and which unnecessarily restrict the freedom of those who do not, the state fails to that extent in discharging its duty. Hence, specifically applying the principle lately set forth in general terms, we find that a government cannot undertake the teaching of a religious faith without either directly reversing its function or partially incapacitating itself for the performance of that function.

**2.** IN THE CONDUCT OF ENGLISH CHURCHMEN WE HAVE A CURIOUS illustration of the way in which men will readopt, when it is thinly disguised, a belief they had indignantly cast from them. That same Romish dogmatism, against which our clergy exclaim with such vehemence, they themselves defend when it is exercised on behalf of their own creed. Every state church is essentially popish. We also have a Vatican—St. Stephen's. It

is true that our archpriest is a composite one. It is true that
with us the triple tiara is separated into its parts—one for
monarch, one for peers, and one for commons. But this fact
makes no difference. In substance, popery is the assumption
of infallibility. It matters not in principle whether this assumption is made by one man or by an assembly of men. No doubt
the astounding announcement, "You must believe what we
say is right, and not what you think is right," comes less
offensively from the lips of a parliamentary majority than from
those of a single individual. But there still arises the question:
By what authority do these men assert this? Whence do *they*
derive their infallibility?

That in establishing any religion a government *does* claim
to be infallible scarcely needs proof. Before a church organization can be set to work, a distinct understanding as to what it
is to do must be arrived at. Before state-paid ministers can be
set to preach, it must first be decided *what* they are to preach.
And who is to say? Clearly the state. Either it must itself
elaborate a creed, or it must depute some man or men to do so.
It must in some way sift out truth from error, and cannot
escape the responsibility attending this. If it undertakes itself
to settle the doctrines to be taught, it is responsible. If it adopts
a ready-made set of doctrines, it is equally responsible. And if
it selects its doctrines by proxy, it is still responsible, both as
appointing those who choose for it, and as approving their
choice. Hence, to say that a government ought to set up and
maintain a system of religious instruction is to say that it ought
to pick out from among the various tenets that men hold, or
have held, those which are right; and that, when it has done
this—when it has settled between the Roman Catholic, the
Greek, the Lutheran, and the Anglican creeds, or between the
Puseyite, High Church, and Evangelical ones—when it has decided whether we should be baptized during infancy or at a
mature age, whether the truth is with Trinitarians or Unitar-
ians, whether men are saved by faith or by works, whether
pagans go to hell or not, whether ministers should preach in
black or white, whether confirmation is scriptural, whether or
not saints' days should be kept, and (as we have lately seen it

debating) whether baptism does or does not regenerate—when, in short, it has settled all those controversies which have split mankind into innumerable sects, it ought to assert that its judgment is incapable of error, is unquestionable, is beyond appeal. There is no alternative. Unless the state says this, it convicts itself of the most absurd inconsistency. Only on the supposition of infallibility can its ecclesiastical doings be made to seem tolerable. How else shall it demand rates and tithes of the dissenter? What answer can it make to his expostulations? "Are you quite sure about these doctrines of yours?" inquires the dissenter. "No," replies the state; "not quite sure, but nearly so." "Then it is just possible you may be wrong, is it not?" "Yes." "And it is just possible that I may be right, is it not?" "Yes." "Yet you threaten to inflict penalties upon me for nonconformity! You seize my goods; you imprison me if I resist; and all to force from me the means to preach up doctrines which you admit may be false, and by implication to preach down doctrines which you admit may be true! How do you justify this?" No reply. Evidently, therefore, if the state persists, the only position open to it is that its judgment *cannot* be mistaken—that its doctrines *cannot* be erroneous. And now observe that if it says this it stands committed to the whole Roman Catholic discipline as well as to its theory. Having a creed that is beyond the possibility of doubt, and being commissioned to disseminate that creed, the state is in duty bound to employ the most efficient means of doing this—is bound to put down all adverse teachers, as usurping its function and hindering the reception of its unquestionable doctrine—is bound to use as much force as may be needful for doing this—is bound, therefore, to imprison, to fine, and, if necessary, to inflict severer penalties, so that error may be exterminated and truth be triumphant. There is no halfway. Being charged to put men in the way to heaven, it cannot without sin permit some to be led the other way. If, rather than punish a few on earth, it allows many to be eternally damned for mischief, it is manifestly culpable. Evidently it must do all or it must do nothing. If it does not claim infallibility, it cannot in reason set up a national religion; and if, by setting up a national religion, it does claim infallibility, it ought to coerce all men into the belief of that religion. Thus, as we said, every state church is essentially popish.

**3.** BUT THERE HAS BEEN GRADUALLY DAWNING UPON THOSE WHO think the conviction that a state church is not so much a religious as a political institution. "Who does not see," inquires Locke, speaking of the clergy, "that these men are more *ministers of the government* than *ministers of the gospel?*" Probably in Locke's time there were few who did see this, but there are now many. Nor, indeed, is the fact altogether denied, as you shall hear from some politic supporter of religious establishments during an after-dinner confidence. "Between ourselves," will whisper such a one, "these churches and parsons and all the rest of it are not for sensible men such as you and I; we know better; we can do without all that; but there must be something of the kind to keep the people in order."[1] And then he will go on to show what influential restraints religious services are; how they encourage subordination and contentment; and how the power which the clergy obtain over their parishioners strengthens the hands of the civil ruler. That some such view widely prevails may be gathered from the acts and proposals of our statesmen. How otherwise can we understand that avowed willingness in the political leaders of all parties to endow the Roman Catholic Church in Ireland if the religious public of England would let them? Or what but a political motive can that state's lieutenant—the East India Company—have for giving an annual subsidy of 23,000 rupees to the temple of Juggernaut, reimbursing itself by a tax upon the pilgrims? Or why else should the Ceylon government take upon itself to be curator of Buddha's tooth and to commission the Buddhist priests?[2]

**4.** OF THE CLERGY WHO, ON THE OTHER HAND, COMMONLY ADVOcate a state church as being needful for the upholding of religion, it may be said that by doing this they condemn their

[1] The writer has himself been thus addressed.
[2] See letter of Sir Colin Campbell to Lord Stanley, May 2, 1845.

own case, pass sentence upon their creed as worthless, and bring themselves in guilty of hypocrisy. What! Will they allow this faith, which they value so highly, to die a natural death if they are not paid for propagating it? Must all these people, about whose salvation they profess such anxiety, be left to go to perdition if livings and canonries and bishoprics are abolished? Has that apostolic inspiration of which they claim to be the inheritors brought with it so little apostolic zeal that there would be no preaching were it not for parsonages and tithes? Do they who, on ordination, declared themselves "inwardly moved by the Holy Ghost," now find that they are inwardly moved only by the chink of gold? This would be called slander coming from any but themselves. And then their flocks—what say they of these? Do these care so little for the faith they have been taught that its maintenance cannot be entrusted to them? After centuries of church culture, has Christianity got so little root in men's hearts that but for government watering pots it must wither away? Are we to understand that these perpetual prayers and sacraments, these homilies and exhortations, these visitings and scripture readings have not even generated as much enthusiasm as can keep itself alive? Have ten thousand sermons a week done so little that the hearers will not contribute a sum sufficient for the sustentation of a ministry? Why, if this be true, what is the system good for? These advocates do but open their briefs, and then straightway argue themselves out of court. They labor to prove either how powerless is the faith they teach, or how miserably they teach it! The sum and substance of their plea for the state propagation of this creed is that it has failed in animating its ministers with its own spirit of self-sacrifice, and failed to arouse in its devotees a spark of its own generosity!

5. IT IS NEEDLESS, HOWEVER, IN THIS YEAR OF GRACE 1850, WITH its Gorham controversies and Puseyite divisions, with its Romish and Rationalist secessions, with confusion inside the church and a hostile association outside, to debate the question at greater length. Events are proving to most of the reflective— even to many of the clergy themselves—that a state support of any particular faith is wrong and that in England, at least, it

must shortly cease. For those who do not yet see this there are already volumes of argument to which addition is almost superfluous. The conclusions above come to that the state cannot establish a religion without assuming infallibility, and that to argue an establishment of it needful is to condemn the religion itself, will sufficiently enforce, for present purposes, our abstract proposition.

CHAPTER XXV

*Poor Laws*

**1.** IN COMMON WITH ITS OTHER ASSUMPTIONS OF SECONDARY offices, the assumption by a government of the office of reliever-general to the poor is necessarily forbidden by the principle that a government cannot rightly do anything more than protect. In demanding from a citizen contributions for the mitigation of distress—contributions not needed for the due administration of men's rights—the state is, as we have seen, reversing its function and diminishing that liberty to exercise the faculties which it was instituted to maintain. Possibly, unmindful of the explanations already given, some will assert that by satisfying the wants of the pauper a government is in reality extending his liberty to exercise his faculties, inasmuch as it is giving him something without which the exercise of them is impossible; and that hence, though it decreases the rate payer's sphere of action, it compensates by increasing that of the rate receiver. But this statement of the case implies a confounding of two widely different things. To enforce the fundamental law—to take care that every man has freedom to do all that he wills, provided he infringes not the equal freedom of any other man—this is the special purpose for which the civil power exists. Now insuring to each the right to pursue within the specified limits the objects of his desires, without let or hindrance, is quite a separate thing from insuring him satisfaction. Of two individuals, one may use his liberty of action successfully—may achieve the gratifications he seeks after, or accumulate what is equivalent to many of them—property; while the other, having like privileges, may fail to do so. But with these results the state has no concern. All that lies within its commission is to see that each man is allowed to use such powers and opportunities as he possesses; and if it takes from him who has prospered to give to him who has not, it violates its duty toward the one to do more than its duty toward the other. Or, repeating the idea elsewhere expressed (p. 249), it breaks down the vital law of society, that it may effect what social vitality does not call for.

**2.** THE NOTION POPULARIZED BY COBBETT, THAT EVERYONE HAS a right to a maintenance out of the soil, leaves those who adopt it in an awkward predicament. Do but ask them to specify, and they are set fast. Assent to their principle; tell them you will assume their title to be valid; and then, as a needful preliminary to the liquidation of their claim, ask for some precise definition of it; inquire, "What is a maintenance?" They are dumb. "Is it," say you, "potatoes and salt, with rags and a mud cabin? Or is it bread and bacon in a two-roomed cottage? Will a joint on Sundays suffice? Or does the demand include meat and malt liquor daily? Will tea, coffee, and tobacco be expected? And if so, how many ounces of each? Are bare walls and brick floors all that is needed? Or must there be carpets and paper hangings? Are shoes considered essential? Or will the Scotch practice be approved? Shall the clothing be of fustian? If not, of what quality must the broadcloth be? In short, just point out where, between the two extremes of starvation and luxury, this something called a maintenance lies." Again they are dumb. You expostulate. You explain that nothing can be done until the question is satisfactorily answered. You show that the claim must be reduced to a detailed, intelligible shape before a step can be taken toward its settlement. "How else," you ask, "shall we know whether enough has been awarded or whether too much?" Still they are dumb. And, indeed, there is no possible reply for them. Opinions they may offer in plenty; but not a precise, unanimous answer. One thinks that a bare subsistence is all

that can fairly be demanded. Here is another who hints at
something beyond mere necessaries. A third maintains that a
few of the enjoyments of life should be provided for. And some
of the more consistent, pushing the doctrine to its legitimate
result, will rest satisfied with nothing short of community of
property. Who now shall decide among these conflicting
notions? Or, rather, how shall their propounders be brought to
an agreement? Can any one of them prove that his definition is
tenable and the others not? Yet he must do this if he would
make out a case. Before he can prosecute his claim against
society, in the high court of morality, he must "file his bill of
particulars." If he accomplishes this he is entitled to a hearing.
If not, he must evidently be non-suited.

The right to labor—that French translation of our Poor Law
doctrine—may be similarly treated. A criticism parallel to the
foregoing would place its advocates in a parallel dilemma. But
there is another way in which the fallacy of this theory, either
in its English or its continental form, may be made manifest—
a way that may here be fitly employed.

And first let us make sure of the meaning wrapped up in
this expression—right to labor. Evidently if we would avoid
mistakes we must render it literally—right to *the* labor; for the
thing demanded is not the liberty of laboring: this, no one disputes; but it is the opportunity of laboring, the having remunerative employment provided, which is contended for.
Now, without dwelling upon the fact that the word *right* as
here used bears a signification quite different from its legitimate
one; that it does not here imply something inherent in man, but
something depending upon external circumstances—not something possessed in virtue of his faculties, but something springing out of his relationship to others; not something true of him
as a solitary individual, but something which can be true of him
only as one of a community; not something antecedent to
society, but something necessarily subsequent to it; not something expressive of a claim to *do*, but of a claim to be *done unto*
—without dwelling upon this, let us take the expression as it
stands and see how it looks when reduced to its lowest terms.
When the artisan asserts his right to have work provided for

him, he presupposes the existence of some power on which devolves the duty of providing such work. What power is this? The government, he says. But the government is not an original power; it is a deputed one—is subject, therefore, to the instruction of its employer, must do only that which its employer directs, and can be held responsible for nothing save the performance of its employer's behests. Now who is its employer? Society. Strictly speaking, therefore, the assertion of our artisan is that it is the duty of society to find work for him. But he is himself a member of society—is consequently a unit of that body who ought, as he says, to find work for every man—has hence a share in the duty of finding work for every man. While, therefore, it is the duty of all other men to find work for him, it is his duty to help in finding work for all other men. And hence, if we indicate his fellows alphabetically, his theory is that A, B, C, D, and the rest of the nation are bound to employ him; that he is bound, in company with B, C, D, and the rest, to employ A; that he is bound, in company with A, C, D, and the rest, to employ B; is bound, with A, B, D, and the rest, to employ C; with A, B, C, and the rest, to employ D; and so on with each individual of the half score or score millions of whom the society may be composed!

Thus do we see how readily imaginary rights are distinguishable from real ones. They need no disproof: they disprove themselves. The ordeal of a definition breaks the illusion at once. Bubble-like, they will bear a cursory glance, but disappear in the grasp of anyone who tries to lay hold of them.

Meanwhile we must not overlook the fact that, erroneous as are these Poor Law and communist theories—these assertions of a man's right to a maintenance and of his right to have work provided for him—they are, nevertheless, nearly related to a truth. They are unsuccessful efforts to express the fact that whoso is born on this planet of ours thereby obtains some interest in it, may not be summarily dismissed again, may not have his existence ignored by those in possession. In other words, they are attempts to embody that thought which finds its legitimate utterance in the law—all men have equal rights to the use of the earth (Chapter IX). The prevalence of these crude ideas is natural enough. A vague perception that there is something wrong about the relationship in which the great mass of mankind stand to the soil and to life was sure eventually to grow up. After getting from under the grosser injustice of slavery, men could not help beginning in course of time to feel what a monstrous thing it was that nine people out of ten should live in the world on sufferance, not having even standing room, save by allowance of those who claimed the earth's surface (p. 103). Could it be right that all these human beings should not only be without claim to the necessaries of life—should not only be denied the use of those elements from which such necessaries are obtainable—but should further be unable to exchange their labor for such necessaries, except by leave of their more fortunate fellows? Could it be that the majority had thus no better title to existence than one based upon the good will or convenience of the minority? Could it be that these landless men had "been mis-sent to this earth, where all the seats were already taken?" Surely not. And if not, how ought matters to stand? To all which questions, now forced upon men's minds in more or less definite shapes, there come, among other answers, these theories of a right to a maintenance and a right of labor. While, therefore, they must be rejected as untenable, we may still recognize in them the imperfect utterances of the moral sense in its efforts to express equity.

**3.** THE WRONG DONE TO THE PEOPLE AT LARGE BY ROBBING THEM of their birthright—their heritage in the earth—is, indeed, thought by some a sufficient excuse for a Poor Law, which is regarded by such as an instrumentality of distributing compensation. There is much plausibility in this construction of the matter. But as a defense of national organizations for the support of paupers, it will not bear criticism. Even were there no better reason for demurring to the supposed compromise, it might still be objected that to counterbalance one injury by inflicting another, and to perpetuate these mutual injuries without knowing whether they are or are not equivalents, is at best a very questionable policy. Why organize a diseased state? Sometime or other this morbid constitution of things, under which the greater part of the body politic is cut off from direct access to the source of life, must be changed. Difficult, no doubt, men will find it to establish a normal condition. There is no knowing how many generations may pass away before the task is accomplished. But accomplished it will eventually be. All arrangements, however, which disguise the evils entailed by the present inequitable relationship of mankind to the soil postpone the day of rectification. "A generous Poor Law" is openly advocated as the best means of pacifying an irritated people. Workhouses are used to mitigate the more acute symptoms of social unhealthiness. Parish pay is hush money. Whoever, then, desires the radical cure of national maladies, but especially of this atrophy of one class and hypertrophy of another, consequent upon unjust land tenure, cannot consistently advocate any kind of compromise.

But a Poor Law is *not* the means of distributing compensation. Neither in respect of those from whom it comes, nor in respect of those to whom it goes, does pauper relief fulfill the assumed purpose. According to the hypothesis, poors' rates should bear wholly upon the land. But they do not. And at least that part of them which bears upon the land should come from the usurpers or their descendants. But it does not. According to the hypothesis, the burden should not fall upon the innocent. But it does; for poors' rates were imposed after landed property had in many cases changed hands by purchase. According to the hypothesis, the burden should not fall upon those already defrauded. But it does; for the majority of ratepayers belong to the non-landowning class. According to the hypothesis, all men kept out of their inheritance should receive a share of this so-called compensation. But they do not; for only here and there one gets any of it. In no way, therefore, is the theory carried out. The original depredators are beyond reach. The guiltless are taxed in their place. A large proportion of those already robbed are robbed afresh. And of the rest, only a few receive the proceeds.

**4.** THE USUAL REASON ASSIGNED FOR SUPPORTING A POOR LAW IS that it is an indispensable means of mitigating popular suffering.

Given by a churchman, such a reason is natural enough; but coming, as it often does, from a dissenter, it is strangely inconsistent. Most of the objections raised by the dissenter to an established religion will tell with equal force against established charity. He asserts that it is unjust to tax him for the support of a creed he does not believe. May not another as reasonably protest against being taxed for the maintenance of a system of relief he disapproves? He denies the right of any bishop or council to choose for him which doctrines he shall accept and which he shall reject. Why does he not also deny the right of any commission or vestry to choose for him who are worthy of his charity and who are not? If he dissents from a national church on the ground that religion will be more general and more sincere when voluntarily sustained, should he not similarly dissent from a Poor Law on the ground that spontaneous beneficence will produce results both wider and better? Might not the corruption which he points out as neutralizing the effects of a state-taught creed be paralleled by those evils of pauperism accompanying a state provision for the poor? Should not his nonconformity in respect to *faith* be accompanied by nonconformity in respect to *good works*? Certainly his present opinions are incongruous beyond all reconciling. He resists every attempt to interfere with the *choice* of his religion, but submits to despotic dictation as to the *exercise* of that religion. While he denies the right of a legislature to explain the *theory*, he yet argues the necessity of its direction in the *practice*. It is inconceivable that these positions can be harmonized. Whoso believes that spiritual destitution is to be remedied only by a national church may with some show of reason propose to deal with physical destitution by an analogous instrumentality. But the advocate of voluntaryism is bound to stand by his principle in the one case as much as in the other.

**5.** WHETHER THE SUFFERINGS OF THE UNFORTUNATE SHALL BE soothed in obedience to the gentle whisperings of benevolence or whether fear of the harsh threats of law shall be the motive for relieving them is indeed a question of no small importance. In deciding how misery is best alleviated we have to consider, not only what is done for the afflicted, but what is the reactive effect upon those who do it. The relationship that springs up between benefactor and beneficiary is, for this present state of the world, a refining one. Having power to muzzle awhile those propensities of the savage which yet linger in us—corrective as it is of that cold, hard state of feeling in which the everyday business of life is pursued—and drawing closer as it does those links of mutual dependence which keep society together, charity is in its nature essentially civilizing. The emotion accompanying every generous act adds an atom to the fabric of the ideal man. As no cruel thing can be done without character being thrust a degree back toward barbarism, so no kind thing can be done without character being moved a degree forward toward perfection. Doubly efficacious, therefore, are all assuagings of distress instigated by sympathy; for not only do they remedy the particular evils to be met, but they help to mold humanity into a form by which such evils will one day be precluded.

Far otherwise is it with law-enforced plans of relief. These exercise just the opposite influence. "The quality of mercy (or pity) is not strained," says the poet. But a Poor Law tries to make men pitiful by force. "It droppeth as the gentle rain from heaven," continues the poet. By a Poor Law it is wrung from the unwilling. "It blesses him that gives, and him that takes," adds the poet. A Poor Law makes it curse both; the one with discontent and recklessness, the other with complainings and often-renewed bitterness.

This turning of balm into poison must have been remarked by the most careless. Watch a ratepayer when the collector's name is announced. You shall observe no kindling of the eye at some thought of happiness to be conferred—no relaxing of the mouth as though selfish cares had for the moment been forgotten—no softening of the voice to tell of compassionate emotion: no, none of these; but rather shall you see contracted features, a clouded brow, a sudden disappearance of what habitual kindliness of expression there may be; the taxpaper is glanced over half in fear and half in vexation; there are grumblings about the short time that has elapsed since the last rate; the purse comes slowly from the pocket; every coin is grudgingly parted with; and after the collector (who is treated with bare civility) has made his exit, some little time passes before the usual equanimity is regained. Is there anything in this to remind us of the virtue which is "twice blessed"? Note again how this act-of-Parliament charity perpetually supersedes men's better sentiments. Here is a respectable citizen with enough and to spare: a man of some feeling; liberal, if there is need; generous even if his pity is excited. A beggar knocks at his door, or he is accosted in his walk by some wayworn tramp. What does he do? Does he listen, investigate, and, if proper, assist? No; he commonly cuts short the tale with, "I have nothing for you, my good man; you must go to your parish." And then he shuts the door or walks on, as the case may be, with evident unconcern. Should it strike him the next moment that there was something very woebegone in the petitioner's look, this uncomfortable thought is met by the reflection that so long as there is a Poor Law he cannot starve and that it will be time enough to consider his claims when he applies for relief. Thus does the consciousness that there exists a legal provision for the indigent act as an opiate to the yearnings of sympathy. Had there been no ready-made excuse, the behavior would probably have been different. Commiseration, pleading for at least an inquiry into the case, would most likely have prevailed; and, in place of an application to the board of guardians, ending in a pittance coldly handed across the pay table to be thanklessly received, might have commenced a relationship good for both parties—a generosity humanizing to the one, and a succor made doubly valuable to the other by a few words of consolation and encouragements, followed, it may be, by a lift into some self-supporting position.

In truth there could hardly be found a more efficient device for estranging men from each other and decreasing their fellow feeling than this system of state almsgiving. Being kind by proxy! Could anything be more blighting to the finer instincts? Here is an institution through which, for a few shillings periodically paid, the citizen may compound for all kindness owing from him to his poorer brothers. Is he troubled with twinges of conscience? Here is an anodyne for him, to be had by subscribing so much in the pound on his rental. Is he indifferent as to the welfare of others? Why, then, in return for punctual payment of rates he shall have absolution for hardness of heart. Look; here is the advertisement: "Gentlemen's benevolence done for them, in the most businesslike manner, and on the lowest terms. Charity doled out by a patent apparatus, warranted to save all soiling of fingers and offenses to the nose. Good works undertaken by contract. Infallible remedies for self-reproach always on hand. Tender feelings kept easy at per annum."

And thus we have the gentle, softening, elevating intercourse that should be habitually taking place between rich and poor superseded by a cold, hard, lifeless mechanism bound together by dry parchment acts and regulations, managed by commissioners, boards, clerks, and collectors, who perform their respective functions as tasks, and kept a-going by money forcibly taken from all classes indiscriminately. In place of the music breathed by feelings attuned to kind deeds, we have the harsh creaking and jarring of a thing that cannot stir without creating discord—a thing whose every act, from the gathering of its funds to their final distribution, is prolific of grumblings, discontent, anger—a thing that breeds squabbles about authority, disputes as to claims, browbeatings, jealousies, litigations, corruption, trickery, lying, ingratitude—a thing that supplants, and therefore makes dormant, men's nobler feelings, while it stimulates their baser ones.

And now mark how we find illustrated in detail the truth elsewhere expressed in the abstract, that whenever a government oversteps its duty—the maintaining of men's rights—it inevitably retards the process of adaptation. For what faculty is it whose work a Poor Law so officiously undertakes? Sympathy. The very faculty above all others needing to be exercised. The faculty which distinguishes the social man from the savage. The faculty which originates the idea of justice—which makes men regardful of each other's claims—which renders society possible. The faculty of whose growth civilization is a history, on whose increased strength the future ameliorations of man's state mainly depend, and by whose ultimate supremacy human morality, freedom, and happiness will be secured. Of this faculty Poor Laws partially supply the place. By doing which they diminish the demands made upon it, limit its exercise, check its development, and therefore retard the process of adaptation.

**6.** PERVADING ALL NATURE, WE MAY SEE AT WORK A STERN DISCIpline, which is a little cruel that it may be very kind. That state of universal warfare maintained throughout the lower creation, to the great perplexity of many worthy people, is at bottom the most merciful provision which the circumstances admit of. It is much better that the ruminant animal, when deprived by age of the vigor which made its existence a pleasure, should be killed by some beast of prey than that it should linger out a life made painful by infirmities and eventually die of starvation. By the destruction of all such, not only is existence ended before it becomes burdensome, but room is made for a younger generation capable of the fullest enjoyment; and, moreover, out of the very act of substitution happiness is derived for a tribe of predatory creatures. Note further that their carnivorous enemies not only remove from herbivorous herds individuals past their prime, but also weed out the sickly, the malformed, and the least fleet or powerful. By the aid of which purifying process, as well as by the fighting, so universal in the pairing season, all vitiation of the race through the multiplication of its inferior samples is prevented; and the maintenance of a constitution completely adapted to surrounding conditions, and therefore most productive of happiness, is insured.

The development of the higher creation is a progress toward a form of being capable of a happiness undiminished by these drawbacks. It is in the human race that the consummation is to be accomplished. Civilization is the last stage of its accomplishment. And the ideal man is the man in whom all the conditions of that accomplishment are fulfilled. Meanwhile the well-being of existing humanity and the unfolding of it into this ultimate perfection are both secured by that same beneficent, though severe, discipline to which the animate creation at large is subject: a discipline which is pitiless in the working out of good: a felicity-pursuing law which never swerves for the avoidance of partial and temporary suffering. The poverty of the incapable, the distresses that come upon the imprudent, the starvation of the idle, and those shoulderings aside of the weak by the strong, which leave so many "in shallows and in miseries," are the decrees of a large, far-seeing benevolence. It seems hard that an unskilfullness which with all his efforts he cannot overcome should entail hunger upon the artisan. It seems hard that a laborer incapacitated by sickness from competing with his stronger fellows should have to bear the resulting privations. It seems hard that widows and orphans should be left to struggle for life or death. Nevertheless, when regarded not separately, but in connection with the interests of universal humanity, these harsh fatalities are seen to be full of the highest beneficence—the same beneficence which brings to early graves the children of diseased parents and singles out the low-spirited, the intemperate, and the debilitated as the victims of an epidemic.

There are many very amiable people—people over whom in so far as their feelings are concerned we may fitly rejoice—who have not the nerve to look this matter fairly in the face. Disabled as they are by their sympathies with present suffering, from duly regarding ultimate consequences, they pursue a course which is very injudicious and in the end even cruel. We do not consider it true kindness in a mother to gratify her child with sweetmeats that are certain to make it ill. We should think it a very foolish sort of benevolence which led a surgeon to let his patient's disease progress to a fatal issue rather than inflict pain by an operation. Similarly, we must call those spurious philanthropists, who, to prevent present misery, would entail greater misery upon future generations. All defenders of a Poor Law must, however, be classed among such. That rigorous necessity which, when allowed to act on them, becomes so sharp a spur to the lazy and so strong a bridle to the random, these paupers' friends would repeal, because of the wailings it here and there produces. Blind to the fact that under the natural order of things, society is constantly excreting its unhealthy, imbecile, slow, vacillating, faithless members, these unthinking, though well-meaning, men advocate an interference which not only

stops the purifying process but even increases the vitiation—
absolutely encourages the multiplication of the reckless and incompetent by offering them an unfailing provision, and discour-
ages the multiplication of the competent and provident by
heightening the prospective difficulty of maintaining a family.
And thus, in their eagerness to prevent the really salutary sufferings that surround us, these sigh-wise and groan-foolish people
bequeath to posterity a continually increasing curse.

Returning again to the highest point of view, we find that
there is a second and still more injurious mode in which law-
enforced charity checks the process of adaptation. To become fit
for the social state, man has not only to lose his savageness, but
he has to acquire the capacities needful for civilized life. Power
of application must be developed; such modification of the intellect as shall qualify it for its new tasks must take place; and,
above all, there must be gained the ability to sacrifice a small
immediate gratification for a future great one. The state of
transition will of course be an unhappy state. Misery inevitably
results from incongruity between constitution and conditions.
All these evils, which afflict us and seem to the uninitiated the
obvious consequences of this or that removable cause, are unavoidable attendants on the adaptation now in progress. Humanity is being pressed against the inexorable necessities of its new
position—is being molded into harmony with them and has to
bear the resulting unhappiness as best it can. The process must
be undergone, and the sufferings must be endured. No power on
earth, no cunningly devised laws of statesmen, no world-rectify-
ing schemes of the humane, no communist panaceas, no reforms
that men ever did broach or ever will broach can diminish them
one jot. Intensified they may be, and are; and in preventing their
intensification, the philanthropic will find ample scope for exertion. But there is bound up with the change a normal amount
of suffering, which cannot be lessened without altering the very
laws of life. Every attempt at mitigation of this eventuates in
exacerbation of it. All that a Poor Law or any kindred institution can do is partially to suspend the transition—to take off for
a while from certain members of society the painful pressure
which is effecting their transformation. At best this is merely to

postpone what must ultimately be borne. But it is more than this: it is to undo what has already been done. For the circumstances to which adaptation is taking place cannot be superseded without causing a retrogression—a partial loss of the adaptation previously effected; and as the whole process must sometime or other be passed through, the lost ground must be gone over again and the attendant pain borne afresh. Thus, besides retarding adaptation, a Poor Law adds to the distress inevitably attending it.

At first sight these considerations seem conclusive against all relief to the poor—voluntary as well as compulsory; and it is no doubt true that they imply a condemnation of whatever private charity enables the recipients to elude the necessities of our social existence. With this condemnation, however, no rational man will quarrel. That careless squandering of pence which has fostered into perfection a system of organized begging; which has made skillful mendicancy more profitable than ordinary manual labor; which induces the simulation of palsy, epilepsy, cholera, and no end of diseases and deformities; which has called into existence warehouses for the sale and hire of imposter's dresses; which has given to pity-inspiring babes a market value of 9d. per day—the unthinking benevolence which has generated all this cannot but be disapproved by everyone. Now it is only against this injudicious charity that the foregoing argument tells. To that charity which may be described as helping men to help themselves it makes no objection—countenances it, rather. And in helping men to help themselves, there remains abundant scope for the exercise of a people's sympathies. Accidents will still supply victims on whom generosity may be legitimately expended. Men thrown upon their backs by unforeseen events, men who have failed for want of knowledge inaccessible to them, men ruined by the dishonesty of others, and men in whom hope long delayed has made the heart sick may, with advantage to all parties, be assisted. Even the prodigal, after severe hardship has branded his memory with the unbending conditions of social life to which he must submit, may properly have another trial afforded him. And although by these ameliorations the process of adaptation must be remotely interfered with, yet in the majority of cases it will not be so much retarded in one direction as it will be advanced in another.

**7.** OBJECTIONABLE AS WE FIND A POOR LAW TO BE, EVEN UNDER the supposition that it does what it is intended to do—diminish present suffering—how shall we regard it on finding that in reality it does no such thing—cannot do any such thing? Yet, paradoxical as the assertion looks, this is absolutely the fact. Let the observer cease to contemplate so fixedly one side of the phenomenon—pauperism and its relief—and begin to examine the other side—rates and the *ultimate* contributors of them— and he will discover that to suppose the sum total of distress diminishable by act-of-Parliament bounty is a delusion. A statement of the case in terms of labor and produce will quickly make this clear.

Here, at any specified period, is a given quantity of food and things exchangeable for food, in the hands or at the command of the middle and upper classes. A certain portion of this food is needed by these classes themselves and is consumed by them at the same rate, or very near it, be there scarcity or abundance. Whatever variation occurs in the sum total of food and its equivalents must therefore affect the remaining portion not used by these classes for personal sustenance. This remaining portion is given by them to the people in return for their labor, which is partly expended in the production of a further supply of necessaries and partly in the production of luxuries. Hence, by how much this portion is deficient, by so much must the people come short. Manifestly a redistribution by legislative or other agency cannot make that sufficient for them which was previously insufficient. It can do nothing but change the parties by whom the insufficiency is felt. If it gives enough to some who else would not have enough, it must inevitably reduce certain others to the condition of not having enough. And thus, to the extent that a Poor Law mitigates distress in one place, it unavoidably produces distress in another.

Should there be any to whom this abstract reasoning is unsatisfactory, a concrete statement of the case will, perhaps, remove their doubts. A poors' rate collector takes from the citizen a sum of money equivalent to bread and clothing for one or more paupers. Had not this sum been so taken, it would either have been used to purchase superfluities, which the citizen now does without, or it would have been paid by him into a bank and lent by the banker to a manufacturer, merchant, or tradesman; that is, it would ultimately have been given in wages either to the producer of the superfluities or to an operative, paid out of the banker's loan. But this sum having been carried off as poors' rate, whoever would have received it as wages must now to that extent go without wages. The food which it represented having been taken to sustain a pauper, the artisan to whom that food would have been given in return for work done must now lack food. And thus, as at first said, the transaction is simply a change of the parties by whom the insufficiency of food is felt.

Nay, the case is even worse. Already it has been pointed out that by suspending the process of adaptation a Poor Law increases the distress to be borne at some future day; and here we shall find that it also increases the distress to be borne now. For be it remembered that of the sum taken in any year to support paupers, a large portion would otherwise have gone to support laborers employed in new reproductive works—land drainage, machine building, etc. An additional stock of commodities would by and by have been produced, and the number of those who go short would consequently have been diminished. Thus the astonishment expressed by some that so much misery should exist, notwithstanding the distribution of fifteen millions a year by endowed charities, benevolent societies, and Poor Law unions, is quite uncalled for; seeing that the larger the sum gratuitously administered, the more intense will shortly become the suffering. Manifestly, out of a given population, the greater the number living on the bounty of others, the smaller must be the number living by labor; and the smaller the number living by labor, the smaller must be the production of food and other necessaries; and the smaller the production of necessaries, the greater must be the distress.

**8.** WE FIND, THEN, THAT THE VERDICT GIVEN BY THE LAW OF STATE duty against a public provision for the indigent is enforced by sundry independent considerations. A critical analysis of the alleged rights, for upholding which a Poor Law is defended, shows them to be fictitious. Nor does the plea that a Poor Law is a means of distributing compensation for wrongs done to the disinherited people turn out to be valid. The assumption that only by law-administered relief can physical destitution be met proves to be quite analogous to the assumption that spiritual destitution necessitates a law-administered religion; and consistency requires those who assert the sufficiency of voluntary effort in the one case to assert it in the other also. The substitution of a mechanical charity for charity prompted by the heart is manifestly unfavorable to the growth of men's sympathies, and therefore adverse to the process of adaptation. Legal bounty further retards adaptation by interposing between the people and the conditions to which they must become adapted, so as partially to suspend those conditions. And, to crown all, we find not only that a Poor Law must necessarily fail to diminish popular suffering, but that it must inevitably increase that suffering, both directly by checking the production of commodities, and indirectly by causing a retrogression of character, which painful discipline must at some future day make good.

CHAPTER XXVI

## *National Education*

**1.** IN THE SAME WAY THAT OUR DEFINITION OF STATE DUTY FORbids the state to administer religion or charity, so likewise does it forbid the state to administer education. Inasmuch as the taking away, by government, of more of a man's property than is needful for maintaining his rights is an infringement of his rights and therefore a reversal of the government's function toward him, and inasmuch as the taking away of his property to educate his own or other people's children is not needful for the maintaining of his rights, the taking away of his property for such a purpose is wrong.

Should it be said that the rights of the children are involved and that the state interposition is required to maintain these, the reply is that no cause for such interposition can be shown until the children's rights have been violated, and that their rights are not violated by a neglect of their education. For, as repeatedly explained, what we call rights are merely arbitrary subdivisions of the general liberty to exercise the faculties; and that only can be called an infringement of rights which actually diminishes this liberty—cuts off a previously existing power to pursue the objects of desire. Now the parent who is careless of a child's education does not do this. The liberty to exercise the faculties is left intact. Omitting instruction in no way takes from a child's freedom to do whatsoever it wills in the best way it can, and this freedom is all that equity demands. Every aggression, be it remembered—every infraction of rights—is necessarily *active*; while every neglect, carelessness, omission is as necessarily *passive*. Consequently, however wrong the non-performance of a parental duty may be, however much it is condemned by that secondary morality—the morality of beneficence (pp. 62 and 63)—it does not amount to a breach of the law of equal freedom and cannot therefore be taken cognizance of by the state.

**2.** WERE THERE NO DIRECT DISPROOF OF THE FREQUENTLY ALleged right to education at the hands of the state, the absurdities in which it entangles its assertors would sufficiently show its invalidity. Conceding for a moment that the government is bound to educate a man's children, then what kind of logic will demonstrate that it is not bound to feed and clothe them? If there should be an act-of-Parliament provision for the development of their minds, why should there not be an act-of-Parliament provision for the development of their bodies? If the mental wants of the rising generation ought to be satisfied by the state, why not their physical ones? The reasoning which is held to establish the right to intellectual food will equally well establish the right to material food; nay, will do more—will prove that children should be altogether cared for by government. For if the benefit, importance, or necessity of education be assigned as a sufficient reason why government should educate, then may the benefit, importance, or necessity of food, clothing, shelter, and warmth be assigned as a sufficient reason why government should administer these also. So that the alleged right cannot be established without annulling all parental responsibility whatever.

Should further refutation be thought needful, there is the ordeal of a definition. We lately found this ordeal fatal to the assumed right to a maintenance; we shall find it equally fatal to this assumed right to education. For what is an education? Where, between the teaching of a dame-school and the most comprehensive university curriculum, can be drawn the line separating that portion of mental culture which may be justly claimed of the state from that which may not be so claimed? What peculiar quality is there in reading, writing, and arithmetic which gives the embryo citizen a right to have them imparted to him, but which quality is not shared in by geography, and history, and drawing, and the natural sciences? Must calculation be taught because it is useful? Why, so is geometry, as the carpenter and mason will tell us; so is chemistry, as we may gather from dyers and bleachers; so is physiology, as is abundantly proved by the ill-health written in so many faces. Astronomy, mechanics, geology, and the various connate sciences—should not these be taught, too? They are all useful. Where is the unit of measure by which we may determine the respective values of different kinds of knowledge? Or, assuming them determined, how can it be shown that a child may claim from the civil power knowledge of such-and-such values but not knowledge of certain less values? When those who demand a state education can say exactly how much is due—can agree upon what the young have a right to, and what not—it will be time to listen. But until they accomplish this impossibility, their plea cannot be entertained.

**3.** A SAD SNARE WOULD THESE ADVOCATES OF LEGISLATIVE TEACHing betray themselves into could they substantiate their doctrine. For what is meant by saying that a government ought to educate the people? Why should they be educated? What is the education for? Clearly, to fit the people for social life—to make them good citizens. And who is to say what are good citizens? The government: there is no other judge. And who is to say how these good citizens may be made? The government: there is no other judge. Hence the proposition is convertible into this—a government ought to mold children into good citizens, using its own discretion in settling what a good citizen is and how the child may be molded into one. It must first form for itself a definite conception of a pattern citizen; and, having done this, must elaborate such system of discipline as seems best calculated to produce citizens after that pattern. This system of discipline it is bound to enforce to the uttermost. For if it does otherwise, it allows men to become different from what in its judgment they should become, and therefore fails in that duty it is charged to fulfill. Being thus justified in carrying out rigidly such plans as it thinks best, every government ought to do what the despotic governments of the Continent and of China do. That regulation under which, in France, "private schools cannot be established without a license from the minister, and can be shut up by a simple ministerial order," is a step in the right direction but does not go far enough, seeing that the state cannot permit its mission to be undertaken by others without endangering the due performance of it. The forbidding of all private schools whatever, as until recently in Prussia, is nearer the mark. Austrian legislation, too, realizes with some consistency the state-education theory. By it a tolerably stringent control over the mental culture of the nation is exercised. Much thinking being held at variance with good citizenship, the teaching of metaphysics, political economy, and the like, is discouraged. Some scientific works are prohibited. And a reward is offered for the apprehension of those who circulate Bibles—the authorities in the discharge of their function preferring to entrust the interpretation of that book to their employees, the Jesuits. But in China alone is the idea carried out with logical completeness. There the government publishes a list of works which may be read; and, considering obedience the supreme virtue, authorizes such only as are friendly to despotism. Fearing the unsettling effects of innovation, it allows nothing to be taught but what proceeds from itself. To the end of producing pattern citizens, it exerts a stringent discipline over all conduct. There are "rules for sitting, standing, walking, talking, and bowing, laid down with the greatest precision. Scholars are prohibited from chess, football, flying kites, shuttlecock, playing on wind instruments, training beasts, birds, fishes, or insects—all which amusements, it is said, dissipate the mind and debase the heart."

Now a minute dictation like this, which extends to every action and will brook no nay, is the legitimate realization of this state-education theory. Whether the government has got erroneous conceptions of what citizens ought to be, or whether the methods of training it adopts are injudicious, is not the question. According to the hypothesis, it is commissioned to discharge a specified function. It finds no ready-prescribed way of doing this. It has no alternative, therefore, but to choose that way which seems to it most fit. And as there exists no higher authority, either to dispute or confirm its judgment, it is justified in the absolute enforcement of its plans, be they what they may. As from the proposition that government ought to teach religion there springs the other proposition, that government must decide what is religious truth and how it is to be taught, so the assertion that government ought to educate necessitates the further assertion that it must say what education is and how it shall be conducted. And the same rigid popery, which we found to be a logical consequence in the one case (p. 275), follows in the other also.

**4.** THERE ARE FEW SAYINGS MORE TRITE THAN THIS, THAT LOVE of offspring is one of our most powerful passions. To become a parent is an almost universal wish. The intensity of affection exhibited in the glistening eye, the warm kiss, and the fondling caress, in the untiring patience and the ever-ready alarm of the mother, is a theme on which philosophers have written and poets have sung in all ages. Everyone has remarked how commonly the feeling overmasters all others. Observe the self-gratulation with which maternity witnesses her first-born's unparalleled achievements. Mark the pride with which the performances of each little brat are exhibited to every visitor as indicating a precocious genius. Consider again the deep interest which in later days a father feels in his children's mental welfare, and the anxiety he manifests to get them on in life; the promptings of his natural affection being ofttimes sharpened by the reflection that the comfort of his old age may, perchance, be dependent upon their success.

Now "servants and interpreters of nature" have usually supposed these feelings to be of some use. Hitherto they have always thought that the gratification accruing to a mother from the forwardness of her little ones serves as a stimulus to the proper culture of their minds, that the honor which the father expects to derive from the distinction of his sons acts as an incentive to their improvement, and that the anticipation by parents of the distress which ill-trained children may one day entail constitutes an additional spur to the proper management of them. In these strong affections and mutual dependencies observers believed they saw an admirably arranged chain of influences calculated to secure the mental and physical development of successive generations, and in the simplicity of their faith had concluded that these divinely appointed means were fully sufficient for this purpose. It would appear, however, according to the state-educationists, that they have been mistaken. It seems that this apparatus of feelings is wholly insufficient to work out the desideratum, that this combination of affections and interests was not provided for such a purpose, or, what is the same thing, that it has no purpose at all. And so, in default of any natural provision for supplying the exigency, legislators exhibit to us the design and specification of a state machine, made up of masters, ushers, inspectors, and councils, to be worked by a due proportion of taxes, and to be plentifully supplied with raw material, in the shape of little boys and girls, out of which it is to grind a population of well-trained men and women who shall be "useful members of the community"!

**5.** BUT IT IS ARGUED THAT PARENTS, AND ESPECIALLY THOSE whose children most need instructing, do not know what good instruction is. "In the matter of education," says Mr. Mill, "the intervention of government is justifiable; because the case is one in which the interest and judgment of the consumer are not sufficient security for the goodness of the commodity."

It is strange that so judicious a writer should feel satisfied with such a worn-out excuse. This alleged incompetency on the part of the people has been the reason assigned for all state interferences whatever. It was on the plea that buyers were unable to tell good fabrics from bad that those complicated regulations which encumbered the French manufacturers were established. The use of certain dyes here in England was prohibited because of the insufficient discernment of the people. Directions for the proper making of pins were issued, under the idea that experience would not teach the purchasers which were best. Those examinations as to competency which the German handicraftsmen undergo are held needful as safeguards to the consumers. A stock argument for the state teaching of religion has been that the masses cannot distinguish false religion from true. There is hardly a single department of life over which, for similar reasons, legislative supervision has not been, or may not be, established. Here is Mr. H. Hodson Rugg, M.R.C.S., publishing a pamphlet to point out the injury inflicted upon poor ignorant householders by the adulteration of milk, and proposing as a remedy that there shall be government officers to test the milk and to confiscate it when not good, police to inspect the ventilation of cow sheds and to order away invalid cattle, and a government cow infirmary, with veterinary surgeon attached. Tomorrow someone else may start up to tell us that bad bread is still more injurious than bad milk, equally common, quite as difficult to distinguish, and that, consequently, bakehouses ought to be overlooked by the authorities. Next there will be wanted officials with hydrometers and chemical reagents to dabble in the vats of the porter breweries. In the wake of these must, of course, follow others commissioned to watch the doings of wine merchants. And so on, until, in the desire to have all processes of production duly inspected, we approach a condition somewhat like that of the slave states, in which, as they say, "one half of the community is occupied in seeing that the other half does its duty." And for each additional interference the plea may be, as it always has been, that "the interest and judgment of the consumer are not sufficient security for the goodness of the commodity."

Should it be said that the propriety of legislative control depends upon circumstances, that respecting some articles the judgment of the consumer is sufficient while respecting other articles it is not, and that the difficulty of deciding upon its quality places education among these last, the reply again is that the same has been said on behalf of all meddlings in turn. Plenty of trickeries, plenty of difficulties in the detection of fraud, plenty of instances showing the inability of purchasers to protect themselves are quoted by the advocates of each proposed recourse to official regulation; and in each case it is urged that here, at any rate, official regulation is required. Yet does experience disprove these inferences one after another, teaching us that, in the long run, the interest of the consumer is not only an efficient guarantee for the goodness of the things consumed, but the best guarantee. Is it not unwise, then, to trust for the hundredth time in one of these plausible but deceptive conclusions? Is it not rational, rather, to infer that, however much appearances are to the contrary, the choice of the commodity—education—like the choice of all other commodities, may be safely left to the discretion of buyers?

Still more reasonable will this inference appear on observing that the people are not, after all, such incompetent judges of education as they seem. Ignorant parents are generally quick enough to discern the effects of good or bad teaching; will note them in the children of others and act accordingly. Moreover, it is easy for them to follow the example of the better instructed and choose the same schools. Or they may get over the difficulty by asking advice; and there is generally someone both able and willing to give the uneducated parent a trustworthy answer to his inquiry about teachers. Lastly, there is the test of price. With education, as with other things, price is a tolerably safe index of value; it is one open to all classes, and it is one which the poor instinctively appeal to in the matter of schools, for it is notorious that they look coldly at very cheap or gratuitous instruction.

But even admitting that, while this defect of judgment is not virtually so extreme as is alleged, it is nevertheless great, the need for interference is still denied. The evil is undergoing rectification, as all analogous ones are or have been. The rising generation will better understand what good education is than their parents do, and their descendants will have clearer conceptions of it still. Whoso thinks the slowness of the process a sufficient reason for meddling must, to be consistent, meddle in all other things, for the ignorance which in every case serves as an excuse for state interposition is of very gradual cure. The errors both of consumers and producers often take generations to set right. Improvements in the carrying on of commerce, in manufactures, and especially in agriculture, spread almost imperceptibly. Take rotation of crops for an example. And if this tardiness is a valid argument for interference in one case, why not in others? Why not have farms superintended by government, because it may take a century for farmers generally to adopt the plans suggested by modern science?

Did we duly realize the fact that society is a growth, and not a manufacture—a thing that makes itself, and not a thing that can be artificially made—we should fall into fewer mistakes, and we should see that among other imperfections this incompetence of the masses to distinguish good instruction from bad is being outgrown.

**6.** WHEN IN THE MATTER OF EDUCATION "THE INTEREST AND judgment of the consumer" are said not to be "sufficient security for the goodness of the commodity," and when it is argued that government superintendence is therefore needful, a very questionable assumption is made: the assumption, namely, that "the interest and judgment" of a government are sufficient security. Now there is good reason to dispute this—nay, even to assert that, taking the future into account, they offer much less security.

The problem is how best to develop minds: a problem among the most difficult—may we not say, *the* most difficult? Two things are needful for its solution. First, to know what minds should be fashioned into. Next, to know how they may be so fashioned. From the work to be done, turn we now to the proposed doers of it. Men of education (as the word goes) they no doubt are; well-meaning, many of them; thoughtful, some; philosophical, a few; men, however, for the most part born with silver spoons in their mouths and prone to regard human affairs as reflected in these—somewhat distortedly. Very comfortable lives are led by the majority of them, and hence "things as they are" find favor in their eyes. For their tastes—they are shown in the subordination of national business to the shooting of grouse and the chasing of foxes. For their pride—it is in wide estates or long pedigrees; and should the family coat of arms bear some such ancient motto as "Strike hard," or "Furth fortune, and fill the fetters," it is a great happiness. As to their ideal of society, it is either a sentimental feudalism, or it is a state, something like the present, under which the people shall be respectful to their betters and "content with that station of life to which it has pleased God to call them"; or it is state-arranged with the view of making each laborer the most efficient producing tool, to the end that the accumulation of wealth may be the greatest possible. Add to this that their notions of moral discipline are shown in the maintenance of capital punishment and in the sending of their sons to schools where flogging is practiced and where they themselves were brought up. Now could the judgment of such respecting the commodity—education—be safely relied on? Certainly not.

Still less might their "interest" be trusted. Though at variance with that of the people, it would inevitably be followed in preference. The self-seeking which, consciously or unconsciously, sways rulers in other cases, would sway them in this likewise—could not fail to do so—while the character of men is what it is. With taxation unequally distributed, with such a glaringly unjust apportionment of representatives to population, with a nepotism that fills lucrative places with Greys and Elliots, with a staff of a hundred animals more than are wanted, with lavish pensions to the undeserving, with a system of retrenchment which discharges common men and retains officers, and with such votes as those given by the military, the naval, the landed, and the clerically related members of Parliament, we may be quite sure that a state education would be administered for the advantage of those in power rather than for the advantage of the nation. To hope for anything else is to fall into the old error of looking for grapes from thorns. Nothing can be more truly Utopian than expecting that, with men and things as they are, the influences which have vitiated all other institutions would not vitiate this one.

Thus, even were it true that in the matter of education "the interest and judgment of the consumer are not sufficient security for the goodness of the commodity," the wisdom of superseding them by the "interest and judgment" of a government is by no means obvious. It may, indeed, be said that the argument proves only the unfitness of existing governments to become national teachers, and not the unfitness of a government normally consti-tuted; whereas the object of inquiry being to determine what a government *should* do, the hypothesis must be that the govern-ment is what it *should* be. To this the reply is that the nature of the allegation to be met necessitates a descent to the level of present circumstances. It is on the defective "interest and judg-ment" of the people, as they now are, that the plea for legisla-tive superintendence is based; and, consequently, in criticizing this plea we must take government as it now is. We cannot rea-son as though government were what it should be, since, before it can become so, any alleged deficiency of "interest and judg-ment" on the part of the people must have disappeared.

**7.** THE IMPOLICY OF SETTING UP A NATIONAL ORGANIZATION FOR cultivating the popular mind and commissioning the govern-ment to superintend this organization is further seen in the general truth that every such organization is in spirit conserva-tive and not progressive. All institutions have an instinct of self-preservation growing out of the selfishness of those connected with them. Being dependent for their vitality upon the continu-ance of existing arrangements, they naturally uphold these.

Their roots are in the past and the present; never in the future. Change threatens them, modifies them, eventually destroys them; hence to change they are uniformly opposed. On the other hand, education, properly so called, is closely associated with change, is its pioneer, is the never-sleeping agent of revolution, is always fitting men for higher things and unfitting them for things as they are. Therefore, between institutions whose very existence depends upon man continuing what he is and true education, which is one of the instruments for making him something other than he is, there must always be enmity.

From the time of the Egyptian priesthood downward, the conduct of corporations, whether political, ecclesiastical, or educational, has given proof of this. Some 300 years B.C., unlicensed schools were forbidden by the Athenian senate. In Rome, the liberty of teaching was attacked twice before the Christian Era; and again, afterward, by the Emperor Julian. The existing continental governments show, by their analogous policy, how persistent the tendency is. In the universality of censorships we see the same fact further illustrated. The celebrated saying of the Empress Catharine to her Prime Minister well exhibits the way in which rulers regard the spread of knowledge. And whenever governments have undertaken to educate, it has been with the view of forestalling that spontaneous education which threatened their own supremacy. Witness the case of China, where diligently impressed ideas, such as "Oh! How magnificent are the affairs of government!" "Oh! What respect is due to the officers of government!" sufficiently indicate the intention. Witness, again, the case of Austria, where, in accordance with the will of the Emperor Francis, the training of the popular mind was entrusted to the Jesuits, that they might "counteract the propagandism of liberty, by the propagandism of superstition."[1] Nor have there been wanting signs of a like spirit here in Eng-

[1]And not without success, according to Mr. Wilde, who (writing before the late revolution) tells us, by way of panegyric upon the Austrian system of education, that the people "sigh not for a state of political liberty about which they know nothing. The government wisely preventing their minds from being inflamed by those blisters upon society that have written and preached our own countrymen into the fever of discontent and disaffection, the effects of which are now so visible in Great Britain." (!)

land. That attempt in Cobbett's day to put down cheap literature, by an act which prevented weekly publications from being
sold for less than sixpence, unmistakably indicated it. It was
again exhibited in the reluctance with which the newspaper
stamp duty was reduced, when resistance had become useless.
And we may still see it in the double-facedness of a legislature
which professes to favor popular enlightenment and yet continues to raise a million and a quarter sterling yearly from "taxes
on knowledge."

How unfriendly all ecclesiastical bodies have been to the
spread of education everyone knows. The obstinacy shown by
the Brahman in fighting against the truths of modern science,
the fanaticism with which the Mohammedan doctor ignores all
books but the Koran, and the prejudice fostered by the religious
institutions of our own country against the very name of philosophy are kindred illustrations of the conduct which this self-
conserving instinct produces. In that saying of the monks, "We
must put down printing, or printing will put down us," the universal motive was plainly expressed; as it was, again, through
the mouth of that French bishop who denounced the Bell and
Lancaster systems as inventions of the devil. Nor let anyone
conclude that the educational zeal latterly manifested by church
clergy indicates a new animus. Those who remember the bitterness with which Sunday schools were at first assailed by them,
and those who mark how keenly they now compete with dis-
senters for the children of the poor, can see clearly enough that
they are endeavoring to make the best of a necessity—that,
having a more or less defined consciousness of the inevitability
of educational progress, they wish to educate the people in
allegiance to the Church.

Still more manifest becomes this obstructive tendency on considering that the very organizations devised for the spreading of
knowledge may themselves act as suppressors of it. Thus it is
said that Oxford was one of the last places in which the New-
tonian philosophy was acknowledged. We read again, in the life
of Locke, that "there was a meeting of the heads of houses at
Oxford, where it was proposed to censure and discourage the
reading of this essay (On the Human Understanding); and after

various debates, it was concluded that without any public censure each head of a house shall endeavour to prevent its being read in his own college." At Eton, too, in Shelley's time, "Chemistry was a forbidden thing," even to the banishment of chemical treatises. So uniformly has it been the habit of these endowed institutions to close the door against innovations, that they are among the last places to which anyone looks for improvements in the art of teaching, or a better choice of subjects to be taught. The attitude of the universities toward natural science has been that of contemptuous non-recognition. College authorities have long resisted, either actively or passively, the making of physiology, chemistry, geology, etc., subjects of examination; and only of late, under pressure from without, and under the fear of being supplanted by rival institutions, have new studies been gingerly taken to.

Now, although *vis inertiæ* may be very useful in its place, although the resistance of office holders has its function, although we must not quarrel with this instinct of self-preservation which gives to institutions their vitality because it also upholds them through a lingering decrepitude, we may yet wisely refuse to increase its natural effect. It is very necessary to have in our social economy a conservative force as well as a reforming one, that there may be progress for the *resultant*; but it is highly impolitic to afford the one an artificial advantage over the other. To establish a state education is to do this, however. The teaching organization itself, and the government which directs it, will inevitably lean to things as they are; and to give them control over the national mind is to give them the means of repressing aspirations after things as they should be. Just that culture which seems compatible with their own preservation will these institutions allow, while just that culture which, by advancing society, threatens to sap their own foundations, or, in other words, just that culture which is most valuable, they will oppose.

The sanguine will perhaps hope that, though this has been the rule hitherto, it will not be the rule in future. Let them not deceive themselves. So long as men pursue private advantage at the expense of the common weal—that is to say, so long as government is needful at all—so long will this be true. Less marked the tendency will no doubt be in proportion as men are less unjustly selfish. But to whatever extent they lack perfect conscientiousness, to the same extent will vested interests sway them, and to the same extent will institutions resist change.

**8.** DID THE READER EVER WATCH A BOY IN THE FIRST HEAT OF A gardening fit? The sight is an amusing and not uninstructive one. Probably a slice of a border—some couple of square yards or so—has been made over to him for his exclusive use. No small accession of dignity, and not a little pride of proprietorship, does he exhibit. So long as the enthusiasm lasts, he never tires of contemplating his territory; and every companion and every visitor with whom the liberty can be taken is pretty sure to be met with the request, "Come and see my garden." Note chiefly, however, with what anxiety the growth of a few scrubby plants is regarded. Three or four times a day will the little urchin rush out to look at them. How provokingly slow their progress seems to him. Each morning on getting up he hopes to find some marked change; and lo, everything appears just as it did the day before. When *will* the blossoms come out? For nearly a week has some forward bud been promising him the triumph of a first flower, and still it remains closed. Surely there must be something wrong! Perhaps the leaves have stuck fast. Ah! That is the reason, no doubt. And so ten to one you shall someday catch our young florist very busily engaged in pulling open the calyx and, it may be, trying to unfold a few of the petals.

Somewhat like this childish impatience is the feeling exhibited by not a few state-educationists. Both they and their type show a lack of faith in natural forces—almost an ignorance that there are such forces. In both there is the same dissatisfaction with the ordained rate of progress. And by both, artificial means are used to remedy what are conceived to be nature's failures. Within these few years men have all at once been awakened to the importance of instructing the people. That to which they were awhile since indifferent or even hostile has suddenly become an object of enthusiasm. With all the ardor of recent

converts, with all a novice's inordinate expectations, with all the
eagerness of a lately aroused desire do they await the hoped-for
result; and, with the unreasonableness ever attendant upon such
a state of mind, are dissatisfied because the progress from general ignorance to universal enlightenment has not been completed in a generation. One would have thought it sufficiently
clear to everybody that the great changes taking place in this
world of ours are uniformly slow. Continents are upheaved at
the rate of a foot or two in a century. The deposition of a delta
is the work of tens of thousands of years. The transformation of
barren rock into life-supporting soil takes countless ages. If any
think society advances under a different law, let them read. Has
it not required the whole Christian Era to abolish slavery in
Europe—as far, at least, as it is abolished? Did not a hundred
generations live and die while picture writing grew into printing? Have not science and commerce and mechanical skill increased at a similarly tardy pace? Yet are men disappointed that
a pitiful fifty years has not sufficed for thorough popular enlightenment! Although within this period an advance has been made
far beyond what the calm thinker would have expected—far
beyond what the past rate of progress in human affairs seemed
to prophesy—yet do these so impatient people summarily condemn the voluntary system as a failure! A natural process—a
process spontaneously set up, a process of self-unfolding which
the national mind had commenced—is pooh-poohed because it
has not wrought a total transformation in the course of what
constitutes but a day in the life of humanity! And then, to make
up for nature's incompetency, the unfolding must be hastened
by legislative fingerings!

**9.** THERE IS, INDEED, ONE EXCUSE FOR ATTEMPTS TO SPREAD EDU-
cation by artificial means; namely, the anxiety to diminish
crime, of which education is supposed to be a preventive. "We
hold," says Mr. Macaulay, "that whoever has the right to hang
has the right to educate."[2] And in a letter relative to the Man-
chester district system, Miss Martineau writes, "Nor can I see
that political economy objects to the general rating for educa-

[2]Quoted from a speech at Edinburgh.

tional purposes. As a mere police-tax this rating would be a very cheap affair. It would cost us much less than we now pay for juvenile depravity." In both which remarks this prevalent belief is implied.

Now, with all respect to the many high authorities holding it, the truth of this belief may be disputed. We have no evidence that education, as commonly understood, is a preventive of crime. Those perpetually reiterated newspaper paragraphs, in which the ratios of instructed to uninstructed convicts are so triumphantly stated, prove just nothing. Before any inference can be drawn, it must be shown that these instructed and un-instructed convicts come from two *equal* sections of society, alike *in all other respects* but that of knowledge—similar in rank and occupation, having similar advantages, laboring under similar temptations. But this is not only not the truth; it is nothing like the truth. The many ignorant criminals belong to a most unfavorably circumstanced class, while the few educated ones are from a class comparatively favored. As things stand, it would be equally logical to infer that crime arises from going without animal food, or from living in badly ventilated rooms, or from wearing dirty shirts; for were the inmates of a jail to be catechized, it would doubtless be found that the majority of them had been placed in these conditions. Ignorance and crime are not cause and effect; they are coincident results of the same cause. To be wholly untaught is to have moved among those whose incentives to wrong-doing are strongest; to be partially taught is to have been one of a class subject to less urgent temptations; to be well taught is to have lived almost beyond the reach of the usual motives for transgression. Ignorance, therefore (at least in the statistics referred to), simply indicates the presence of crime-producing influences, and can no more be called the cause of crime than the falling of a barometer can be called the cause of rain.

So far indeed from proving that morality is increased by education, the facts prove, if anything, the reverse. Thus we are told, in a report by the Rev. Joseph Kingsmill, head chaplain of Pentonville Prison, that the proportion borne by the educated to the uneducated convicts is fully as high as that which exists between the educated and the uneducated classes in the general population; although, as just explained, we might reasonably expect that, having had fewer temptations, the educated convicts would bear a smaller ratio to their class. Again, it has been shown from government returns "that the number of juvenile offenders in the metropolis has been steadily increasing every year since the institution of the Ragged School Union; and that whereas the number of criminals who cannot read and write has decreased from 24,856 (in 1844) to 22,968 (in 1848)—or no less than 1,888 in that period—the number of those who can read and write imperfectly has increased from 33,337 to 36,229—or 2,857—in the same time."—*Morning Chronicle*, April 25, 1850. Another contributor to the series of articles on "Labour and the Poor," from which the above statement is quoted, remarks that "the mining population (in the north) are exceedingly low in point of education and intelligence; and yet they contradict the theories generally entertained upon the connection of ignorance with crime, by presenting the least criminal section of the population of England."—*Morning Chronicle*, December 27, 1849. And speaking of the women employed in the ironworks and collieries throughout South Wales, he says, "Their ignorance is absolutely awful; yet the returns show in them a singular immunity from crime."—*Morning Chronicle*, March 21, 1850.

If these testimonies are thought insufficient, they may be enforced by that of Mr. Fletcher, who has entered more elaborately into this question than perhaps any other writer of the day. Summing up the results of his investigations, he says:

"1. In comparing the gross commitments for criminal offences with the proportion of instruction in each district, there is found to be a small balance in favour of the most instructed districts in the years of most industrial depression (1842-'3-'4), but a greater one against them in the years of less industrial depression (1845-'6-'7); while in comparing the more with the less instructed portions of each district, the final result is against the former at both periods, though fourfold at the latter what it is at the former.

"2. No correction for the ages of the population in different districts, to meet the excess of criminals at certain younger periods of life, will change the character of this superficial evidence against instruction; every legitimate allowance of the kind having already been made in arriving at these results.

"3. Down to this period, therefore, the comparison of the criminal and educational returns of this, any more than of any other country of Europe, has afforded no sound statistical evidence in favour, and as little against, the moral effects associated with instruction, as actually disseminated among the people."[3]

To all which evidence may be added that of Messrs. Gurrea and Dupin, who have shown that the most highly educated districts in France are the most criminal districts.

The fact is that scarcely any connection exists between morality and the discipline of ordinary teaching. Mere culture of the intellect (and education as usually conducted amounts to little more) is hardly at all operative upon conduct. Creeds pasted upon the memory, good principles learned by rote, lessons in right and wrong will not eradicate vicious propensities, though people, in spite of their experience as parents and as citizens, persist in hoping they will. All history, both of the race and of individuals, goes to prove that in the majority of cases precepts do not act at all. And where they seem to act, it is not by them, but by pre-existing feelings which respond to them, that the effects are really produced. Intellect is not a power, but an instrument—not a thing which itself moves and works, but a thing which is moved and worked by forces behind it. To say that men are ruled by reason is as irrational as to say that men are ruled by their eyes. Reason *is* an eye—the eye through which the desires see their way to gratification. And educating it only makes it a better eye—gives it a vision more accurate and more comprehensive—does not at all alter the desires subserved by it. However far-seeing you make it, the passions will still determine the directions in which it shall be turned—the objects on which it shall dwell. Just those ends which the instincts or sentiments propose will the intellect be employed to accomplish, culture of it having done nothing but increase the ability to accomplish them. Probably some will urge that enlightening men enables

[3]Summary of the Moral Statistics of England and Wales, by Joseph Fletcher, Esq., Barrister-at-Law, one of Her Majesty's Inspectors of Schools.

them to discern the penalties which naturally attach to wrong-doing, and in a certain sense this is true. But it is only superficially true. Though they may learn that the grosser crimes commonly bring retribution in one shape or other, they will not learn that the subtler ones do. Their sins will merely be made more Machiavellian. If, as Coleridge says, "a knave is a fool with a circumbendibus," then by instructing the knave you do but make the circumbendibus a wider one. Did much knowledge and piercing intelligence suffice to make men good, then Bacon should have been honest and Napoleon should have been just. Where the character is defective, intellect, no matter how high, fails to regulate rightly, because predominant desires falsify its estimates. Nay, even a distinct foresight of evil consequences will not restrain when strong passions are at work. How else does it happen that men will get drunk, though they know drunkenness will entail on them suffering, and disgrace, and (as with the poor) even starvation? How else is it that medical students, who know the diseases brought on by dissolute living better than other young men, are just as reckless, and even more reckless? How else is it that the London thief, who has been at the treadmill a dozen times, will steal again as soon as he is at liberty? How else is it that people who have all their lives long been taught Christianity will not behave as Christians, though they believe that dire penalties are entailed by behaving otherwise?

It is indeed strange that with the facts of daily life before them in the street, in the countinghouse, and in the family, thinking men should still expect education to cure crime. If armies of teachers, regarded with a certain superstitious reverence, have been unable to purify society in all these eighteen centuries, it is hardly likely that other armies of teachers, not so regarded, will be able to do it. If natural persuasion, backed by supernatural authority, will not induce men to do as they would be done by, it is hardly likely that natural persuasion alone will induce them. If hopes of eternal happiness and terrors of eternal damnation fail to make human beings virtuous, it is hardly likely that the commendations and reproofs of the schoolmaster will succeed.

There is, in fact, a quite sufficient reason for failure—no less a reason than the impossibility of the task. The expectation that crime may presently be cured, whether by state education, or the silent system, or the separate system, or any other system, is one of those Utopianisms fallen into by people who pride themselves on being practical. Crime is incurable, save by that gradual process of adaptation to the social state which humanity is undergoing. Crime is the continual breaking out of the old unadapted nature—the index of a character unfitted to its conditions—and only as fast as the unfitness diminishes can crime diminish. To hope for some prompt method of putting down crime is in reality to hope for some prompt method of putting down all evils—laws, governments, taxation, poverty, caste, and the rest; for they and crime have the same root. Reforming men's conduct without reforming their natures is impossible; and to expect that their natures may be reformed otherwise than by the forces which are slowly civilizing us is visionary. Schemes of discipline or culture are of use only in proportion as they organically alter the national character, and the extent to which they do this is by no means great. It is not by humanly devised agencies, good as these may be in their way, but it is by the never-ceasing action of circumstances upon men—by the constant pressure of their new conditions upon them—that the required change is mainly effected.

Meanwhile it may be remarked that whatever moral benefit can be effected by education must be effected by an education which is emotional rather than perceptive. If, in place of making a child understand that this thing is right and the other wrong, you make it feel that they are so—if you make virtue loved and vice loathed—if you arouse a noble desire and make torpid an inferior one—if you bring into life a previously dormant sentiment—if you cause a sympathetic impulse to get the better of one that is selfish—if, in short, you produce a state of mind to which proper behavior is natural, spontaneous, instinctive, you do some good. But no drilling in catechisms, no teaching of moral codes can effect this. Only by repeatedly awakening the appropriate emotions can character be changed. Mere ideas received by the intellect, meeting no response from within—having no roots there—are quite inoperative upon conduct and are quickly forgotten upon entering into life.

Perhaps it will be said that a discipline like this now described as the only efficient one might be undertaken by the state. No doubt it might. But from all legislative attempts at emotional education may Heaven defend us!

**10.** YET ANOTHER OBJECTION REMAINS. JUST AS WE FOUND, ON close examination, by Poor Laws a government cannot really cure distress but can only shift it from one section of the community to another (p. 293), so, astounding as the assertion looks, we shall find that a government cannot in fact educate at all but can only educate some by uneducating others. If, before agitating the matter, men had taken the precaution to define education, they would probably have seen that the state can afford no true help in the matter. But having unfortunately neglected to do this, they have confined their attention solely to the education given at school and have forgotten to inquire how their plans bear upon the education which commences when school days end. It is not indeed that they do not know this discipline of daily duty to be valuable—more valuable, in fact, than the discipline of the teacher. You may often hear them remark as much. But, with the eagerness usual among schemers, they are so absorbed in studying the *action* of their proposed mechanism as to overlook its *reaction*.

Now, of all qualities, which is the one men most need? To the absence of what quality are popular distresses mainly attributable? What is the quality in which the improvident masses are so deficient? Self-restraint—the ability to sacrifice a small present gratification for a prospective great one. A laborer endowed with due self-restraint would never spend his Saturday-night's wages at the public house. Had he enough self-restraint, the artisan would not live up to his income during prosperous times and leave the future unprovided for. More self-restraint would prevent imprudent marriages and the growth of a pauper population. And were there no drunkenness, no extravagance, no reckless multiplication, social miseries would be trivial.

Consider next how the power of self-restraint is to be increased. By a sharp experience alone can anything be done. Those in whom this faculty needs drawing out—*educating* must be left to the discipline of nature and allowed to bear the pains attendant on their defect of character. The only cure for imprudence is the suffering which imprudence entails. Nothing but bringing him face to face with stern necessity and letting him feel how unbending, how unpitying, are her laws can improve the man of ill-governed desires. As already shown (p. 290), all interposing between humanity and the conditions of its existence—cushioning off consequences by Poor Laws or the like—serves but to neutralize the remedy and prolong the evil. Let us never forget that the law is adaptation to circumstances, be they what they may. And if, rather than allow men to come in contact with the real circumstances of their position, we place them in artificial—in false—circumstances, they will adapt themselves to these instead; and will, in the end, have to undergo the miseries of a readaptation to the real ones.

Of all incentives to self-restraint, perhaps none is so strong as the sense of parental responsibility. And if so, to diminish that sense is to use the most effectual means of preventing self-restraint from being developed. We have ample proof of this in the encouragement of improvident marriages by a Poor Law; and the effect which a Poor Law produces by relieving men from the final responsibility of maintaining their children must be produced in a smaller degree by taking away the responsibility of educating their children. The more the state undertakes to do for his family, the more are the expenses of the married man reduced, at the cost of the unmarried man, and the greater becomes the temptation to marry. Let not any think that the offer of apparently gratuitous instruction for his offspring would be of no weight with the workingman deliberating on the propriety of taking a wife. Whoever has watched the freaks which strong passion plays in the councils of the intellect has marked how it will bully into silence the weaker feelings that opposes it; how it will treat slightingly the most conclusive adverse evidence, while, in urging the goodness of its own cause, "trifles light as air are confirmations strong as proofs of Holy

Writ"—whoever has marked this can hardly doubt that, in the deliberations of such a one, the prospect of public training for children would in no small degree affect the decision. Nay, indeed, it would afford a positive reason for giving way to his desires. Just as a man at an expensive dinner will eat more than he knows is good for him, on the principle of having his money's worth, so would the artisan find one excuse for marrying in the fact that, unless he did so, he would be paying education rates for nothing.

Nor is it only thus that a state education would encourage men to obey present impulses. An influence unfavorable to the increase of self-control would be exercised by it throughout the whole of parental life. That powerful restraint which the anxiety to give children schooling now imposes upon the improvident tendencies of the poor would be removed. Many a man who, as things are, can but just keep the mastery over some vicious or extravagant propensity, and whose most efficient curb is the thought that if he gives way it must be at the sacrifice of that book learning which he is ambitious to give his family, would fall were this curb weakened—would not only cease to improve in power of self-control as he is now doing, but would probably retrograde and bequeath his offspring to a lower instead of a higher phase of civilization.

Hence, as was said, a government can educate in one direction only by uneducating in another—can confer knowledge only at the expense of character. It retards the development of a quality universally needed—one in the absence of which poverty and recklessness and crime must ever continue; and all that it may give a smattering of information.

What a contrast is there between these futile contrivances of men and the admirable, silent-working mechanisms of nature! Nature, with a perfect economy, turns all forces to account. She makes action and reaction alike useful. This strong affection for progeny becomes in her hands the agent of a double culture, serving at once to fashion parent and child into the desired form. And beautiful is it to see how the most powerful of instincts is made the means of holding men under a discipline to which, perhaps, nothing else could make them submit.

Yet this skillfully devised arrangement statesmen propose to dislocate, confidently opining that their own patent apparatus will answer a great deal better!

**11.** THUS, IN THE PRESENT, AS IN OTHER CASES, WE FIND THE dictate of the abstract law enforced by secondary considerations. The alleged right to education at the hands of the state proves to be untenable; first, as logically committing its supporters to other claims too absurd for consideration; and again, as being incapable of definition. Moreover, could the claim be established, it would imply the duty of government despotically to enforce its system of discipline, and the duty of the subject to submit. That education ought not to be dealt in after the same manner as other things, because in its case "the interest and judgment of the consumer are not sufficient security for the goodness of the commodity," is a plea with most suspicious antecedents; having been many times employed in other instances, and many times disproved. Neither is the implied assumption that the "interest and judgment" of a government *would* constitute a sufficient security admissible. On the contrary, experience proves that the interests of a government and of all the institutions it may set up are directly opposed to education of the most important kind. Again, to say that legislative teaching is needful because other teaching has failed presupposes a pitiably narrow view of human progress; and, further, involves the strange skepticism that, though natural agencies have brought the enlightenment of mankind to its present height and are even now increasing it at an unparalleled rate, they will no longer answer. The belief that education is a preventive of crime, having no foundation either in theory or fact, cannot be held an excuse for interference. And, to crown all, it turns out that the institution so much longed for is a mere dead machine which can only give out in one form the power it absorbs in another, minus the friction—a thing which cannot stir toward effecting this kind of education without abstracting the force now accomplishing that—a thing, therefore, which cannot educate at all.

## CHAPTER XXVII

## *Government Colonization*

**1.** A COLONY BEING A COMMUNITY, TO ASK WHETHER IT IS RIGHT for the state to found and govern colonies is practically to ask whether it is right for one community to found and govern other communities. And this question not being one in which the relationships of a society to its own authorities are alone involved, but being one into which there enter the interests of parties external to such society, is in some measure removed out of the class of questions hitherto considered. Nevertheless, our directing principle affords satisfactory guidance in this case as well as in the others.

That a government cannot undertake to administer the affairs of a colony and to support for it a judicial staff, a constabulary, a garrison, and so forth, without trespassing against the parent society, scarcely needs pointing out. Any expenditure for these purposes, be it like our own some three and a half millions sterling a year or but a few thousands, involves a breach of state duty. The taking from men property beyond what is needful for the better securing of their rights, we have seen to be an infringement of their rights. Colonial expenditure cannot be met without property being so taken. Colonial expenditure is therefore unjustifiable.

An objector might indeed allege that, by maintaining in a settlement a subordinate legislature, the parent legislature does but discharge toward the settlers its original office of protector, and that the settlers have a claim to protection at its hands. But the duty of a society toward itself—that is, of a government toward its subjects—will not permit the assumption of such a responsibility. For, as it is the function of a government to administer the law of equal freedom, it cannot, without reversing its function, tax one portion of its subjects at a higher rate than is needful to protect them, that it may give protection to another portion below prime cost; and to guard those who emigrate, at the expense of those who remain, is to do this. Manifestly, the guardianship which a nation in its corporate capacity extends to each of its members is limited by conditions. The citizen must defray his share of the expenses, must agree to perform certain political duties, and must reside within specified geographical boundaries. If he prefers to go elsewhere, it may be presumed that he has duly considered, on the one hand, the benefits promised by his contemplated emigration, and, on the other, the evils attending loss of citizenship, and that the prospective advantages of a change preponderate. At any rate, he cannot show that, by refusing to send out officers to the antipodes to take care of him, society violates a recognized or implied contract.

Moreover, colonial government, properly so called, cannot be carried on without transgressing the rights of the colonists. For if, as generally happens, the colonists are dictated to by authorities sent out from the mother country, then the law of equal freedom is broken in their persons, as much as by any other kind of autocratic rule. If, again, they are allowed to administer their own affairs, the parent state retaining only a veto power, there is still injustice in the assumption of greater freedom by the members of the old community than is conceded to those of the new one. And if the new community is as completely self-governed as the old one, then, politically speaking, it is not a colony at all, but a separate nation. In one way, however, legislative union between a parent state and its colonies may be maintained without breach of the law; namely, by making them integral parts of one empire, severally represented in a united assembly commissioned to govern the whole. But theoretically just as such an arrangement may be, and even carried out though it is by France, it is still too palpably impolitic for serious consideration. To propose that, while the English joined in legislating for the people of Australia, of the Cape, of New Zealand, of Canada, of Jamaica, and of the rest, these should in turn legislate for the English, and for each other, is much like proposing that the butcher should superintend the classification of the draper's goods, the draper draw up a tariff of prices for the grocer, and the grocer instruct the baker in making bread.

Hence, the political union of a parent state with a colony is inadmissible; seeing that, as usually maintained, such union necessarily infringes the rights of the members of both communities, and seeing that it cannot be made just without at the same time being made absurdly unfit.

**2.** IT WAS EXCEEDINGLY COOL OF POPE ALEXANDER VI TO PARCEL out the unknown countries of the earth between the Spaniards and Portuguese, granting to Spain all discovered and undiscovered heathen lands lying west of a certain meridian drawn through the Atlantic, and to Portugal those lying east of it. Queen Elizabeth, too, was somewhat cool when she empowered Sir Humphrey Gilbert "to discover and take possession of remote and heathen countries," and "to exercise rights, and royalties, and jurisdiction, in such countries and seas adjoining." Nor did Charles II show less coolness when he gave to Winthrop, Mason, and others power to "kill, slay, and destroy, by all fitting ways, enterprises, and means whatsoever, all and every such person or persons as shall at any time hereafter attempt or enterprise the destruction, invasion, detriment, or annoyance of the inhabitants" of the proposed plantation of Connecticut. Indeed, all colonizing expeditions down to those of our own day, with its American annexations, its French occupations of Algiers and Tahiti, and its British conquests of Sind, and of the Punjab, have borne a very repulsive likeness to the doings of buccaneers. As usual, however, these unscrupulous acts have brought deserved retributions. Insatiate greediness—a mere blind impulse to clutch whatever lies within reach —has generated very erroneous beliefs and betrayed nations into most disastrous deeds. "Men are rich in proportion to their acres," argued politicians. "An increase of estate is manifestly equivalent to an increase of wealth. What, then, can be clearer than that the acquirement of new territory must be a national advantage?" So, misled by the analogy and spurred on by acquisitiveness, we have continued to seize province after province, in utter disregard of the losses uniformly entailed by them. In fact, it has been inconceivable that they do entail losses. That the addition of anything must enrich seems so self-evident a truth that it has never struck men to ask what happens when the thing added is a minus quantity. And even now, though doubt is beginning to dawn upon the public mind, the instinctive desire to keep hold is too strong to permit a change of policy. Our predicament is like that of the monkey in the fable, who, putting his hand into a jar of fruit, grasps so large a quantity that he cannot get his hand out again and is obliged to drag the jar about with him, never thinking to let go what he has seized. When we shall attain to something more than the ape's wisdom remains to be seen. Happily the old piratical spirit is on the decline. A conquest is no longer gloried in as a national aggrandizement. Our last Indian annexation was lamented as an unfortunate necessity. Experience is fast teaching us that distant dependencies are burdens, and not acquisitions. And thus this earliest motive for state colonization—the craving for wider possessions—will very soon be destroyed by the conviction that territorial aggression is as impolitic as it is unjust.

**3.** WHILE THE MERE PROPENSITY TO THIEVE—COMMONLY KNOWN under some grandiloquent alias, disguised by glittering falsehoods, and made sublime in men's eyes by the largeness of its aims—has been the real prompter of colonizing invasions, from those of Cortez and Pizarro downward, the ostensible purpose of them has been either the spread of religion or the extension of commerce. In modern days the latter excuse has been the favorite one. To obtain more markets—this is what people have said aloud to each other—was the object aimed at. And, though second to the widening of empire, it has been to the compassing of this object that colonial legislation has been mainly directed. Let us consider the worth of such legislation.

Those holy men of whom the Middle Ages were so prolific seem to have delighted in exhibiting their supernatural powers on the most trifling occasions. It was a common feat with them, when engaged in church building, magically to lengthen a beam which the carpenter had made too short. Some were in the constant habit of calling down fire from heaven to light their candles. When at a loss where to deposit his habiliments, St. Goar of Treves would transform a sunbeam into a hat peg. And it is related of St. Columbanus that he wrought a miracle to keep the grubs from his cabbages. Now, although these examples of the use of vast means for the accomplishment of insignificant ends are not quite paralleled by the exertions of governments to secure colonial trade, the absurdity attaching to both differs only in degree. An expenditure of power ridiculously disproportionate to the occasion is their common characteristic. In the one case, as in the other, an unnatural agency is employed to effect what a natural agency would effect as well. Trade is a simple enough thing that will grow up wherever there is room for it. But, according to statesmen, it must be created by a gigantic and costly machinery. That trade only is advantageous to a country which brings, in return for what is directly and indirectly given, a greater worth of commodities that could otherwise be obtained. But statesmen recognize no such limit to its benefits. Every new outlet for English goods, kept open at no matter what cost, they think valuable. Here is some scrubby little island or wild territory—unhealthy, or barren, or inclement, or uninhabited even—which, by right of discovery, conquest, or diplomatic maneuvering, may be laid hands on. Possession is forthwith taken; a high-salaried governor is appointed; officials collect round him; then follow forts, garrisons, guardships; from these by and by come quarrels with neighboring peoples, incursions, war; and these again call for more defensive works, more force, more money. And to all protests against this reckless expenditure, the reply is, "Consider how it extends our commerce." If you grumble at the sinking of £800,000 in fortifying Gibraltar and Malta, at the outlay of £130,000 a year for the defense of the Ionian Islands, at the maintenance of 1,200 soldiers in such a good-for-nothing place as the Bermudas, at the garrisoning of St. Helena, Hong Kong, Helgoland, and the rest, you are told that all this is needful for the protection of our commerce. If you object to the expenditure of £110,000 per annum on the government of

Ceylon, it is thought a sufficient answer that Ceylon buys manufactures from us to the gross value of £240,000 yearly. Any criticisms you may pass upon the policy of retaining Canada, at an annual cost of £800,000, are met by the fact that this amounts to only 30 per cent upon the sum which the Canadians spend on our goods.[1] Should you, under the fear that the East India Company's debt may someday be saddled upon the people of England, lament the outlay of £17,000,000 over the Afghan war, the sinking of £1,000,000 a year in Sind, and the swallowing up of untold treasure in the subjugation of the Punjab, there still comes the everlasting excuse of more trade. A Bornean jungle, the deserts of Kaffraria, and the desolate hills of the Falkland Islands are all occupied upon this plea. The most profuse expenditure is forgiven, if but followed by an insignificant demand for merchandise; even though such demand be but for the supply of a garrison's necessities—glass for barrack windows, starch for officers' shirts, and lump sugar for the governor's table—all of which you shall find carefully included in Board of Trade Tables and rejoiced over as constituting an increase in our exports.

**4.** BUT NOT ONLY DO WE EXPEND SO MUCH TO GAIN SO LITTLE, we absolutely expend it for nothing; nay, indeed, in some cases to achieve a loss. All profitable trade with colonies will come without the outlay of a penny for colonial administration—must flow to us naturally; and whatever trade will not flow to us naturally is not profitable, but the reverse. If a given settlement deals solely with us, it does so from one or two causes: either we make the articles its inhabitants consume at a lower rate than any other nation, or we oblige its inhabitants to buy those articles from us, though they might obtain them for less elsewhere. Manifestly, if we can undersell other producers, we should still exclusively supply its markets, were the settlement independent. If we cannot undersell them, it is equally certain that we are indirectly injuring ourselves and the settlers too; for, as McCulloch says: "Each country has some natural or

[1]For these and other such facts, see Sir W. Molesworth's speeches delivered during the sessions of 1848 and 1849.

acquired capabilities that enable her to carry on certain branches of industry more advantageously than anyone else. But the fact of a country being undersold in the markets of her colonies shows conclusively that, instead of having any superiority, she labours under a disadvantage, as compared with others, in the production of the peculiar articles in demand in them. And hence, in providing a forced market in the colonies for articles that we should not otherwise be able to dispose of, we really engage a portion of the capital and labour of the country in a less advantageous channel than that into which it would naturally have flowed." And if to the injury we do ourselves by manufacturing goods which we could more economically buy is added the injury we suffer in pacifying the colonists, by purchasing from them commodities obtainable on better terms elsewhere, we have before us the twofold loss which these much-coveted monopolies entail.

Thus are we again taught how worthy of all reverence are the injunctions of equity and how universal is their applicability. Just that commercial intercourse with colonies which may be had without breaking these injunctions brings gain, while just that commercial intercourse which cannot be so had brings loss.

**5.** PASSING FROM HOME INTERESTS TO COLONIAL INTERESTS, WE still meet nothing but evil results. It is a prettily sounding expression, that of mother-country protection, but a very delusive one. If we are to believe those who have known the thing rather than the name, there is but little of the maternal about it. In the Declaration of American Independence we have a candid statement of experience on this point. Speaking of the king, the personification of the parent state, the settlers say:

"He has obstructed the administration of justice, by refusing his assent to laws for establishing judiciary powers.

"He has erected a multitude of new offices, and sent hither swarms of officers to harass our people, and eat out their subsistence.

"He has kept among us in times of peace standing armies, without the consent of our legislatures.

"He has combined with others to subject us to a jurisdiction foreign to our constitution and unacknowledged by our laws; giving his assent to their pretended acts of legislation:—

"For quartering large bodies of armed troops among us.

"For protecting them by a mock trial from punishment for any murders which they should commit on the inhabitants of these states.

"For cutting off our trade with all parts of the world.

"For imposing taxes upon us without our consent.

"For depriving us in many cases of the benefits of trial by jury," etc., etc., etc.

Now, though tyrannies so atrocious as these do not commonly disgrace colonial legislation in the present day, we have but to glance over the newspapers published in our foreign possessions to see that the arbitrary rule of the Colonial Office is no blessing. Chronic irritation, varying in intensity from that of which petitions are symptomatic to that exhibited in open rebellions, is habitually present in these forty-six scattered dependencies which statesmen have encumbered us with. Two outbreaks in fifteen years pretty plainly hint the feeling of the Canadas—a feeling still extant and growing, as recent events testify. Within the same period the Cape Boers have revolted thrice; and we have just had a tumultuous agitation and a violent paper war about convicts. In the West Indies there is universal discontent. Jamaica advices tell of stopped supplies and state machinery at a deadlock. Guiana sends like news. Here are quarrels about retrenchment; there, insurrectionary riots; and anger is everywhere. The name of Ceylon calls to mind the insolence of a titled governor on the one side, and on the other the bitterness of insulted colonists. In the Australian settlements, criminal immigration has been the sore subject; while from New Zealand there come protests against official despotism. All winds bring the same tale of a negligence caring for no expostulations, impertinence without end, blunderings, disputes, delays, corruption. Canadians complain of having been induced by a proffered privilege to sink their capital in flour mills, which subsequent legislation made useless. With an ever-varying amount of protection, sugar planters say they do not know what to be at. South Africa bears witness to a mis-management that at one time makes enemies of the Griquas and at another entails a Kaffir war. The emigrants of New Zealand lament over a seat of government absurdly chosen, money thrown away upon useless roads, and needful works left undone. South Australia is made bankrupt by its governor's extravagance; lands are apportioned so as to barbarize the settlers by dispersion, and laborers are sent out in excess and left to beg. Our Chinese trade gets endangered by the insulting behavior of military officers to the natives; and the authorities of Labuan make their first settlement in a pestilential swamp.

Nevertheless, these odd results of mother-country protection need not surprise us, if we consider by whom the duties of maternity are discharged. Dotted here and there over the earth, at distances varying from one thousand to fourteen thousand miles, and to and from some of which it takes three quarters of a year to send a question and get back an answer, are forty-six communities, consisting of different races, placed in different circumstances. And the affairs of these numerous, far-removed communities—their commercial, social, political, and religious interests—are to be cared for by whom? By six functionaries and their twenty-three clerks sitting at desks in Downing Street! Being at the rate of 0:13 of a functionary and half a clerk to each settlement!

Is it not, then, sufficiently clear that this state colonization is as indefensible on the score of colonial welfare as on that of home interests? May we not reasonably doubt the propriety of people on one side of the earth being governed by officials on the other? Would not these transplanted societies probably manage their affairs better than we can do it for them? At any rate, our benevolent anxiety on their behalf may be at rest, should it turn out that they would willingly dispense with our superintendence. All that the most romantic generosity can require from us is the tender of our good offices; and should these be declined, our consciences may feel fully discharged of any assumed duty. Now on polling the inhabitants of each colony on the question whether England should continue legislating for them or not, we should be pretty certain to get the answer that, were it the same thing to us, they would much rather legislate for themselves.

**6.** GREAT, HOWEVER, AS ARE THE EVILS ENTAILED BY GOVERNMENT colonization upon both parent state and settlers, they look insignificant when compared with those it inflicts upon the aborigines of the conquered countries. The people of Java believe that the souls of Europeans pass at death into the bodies of tigers; and it is related of a Hispanolian chief that he hoped not to go to heaven when he heard there were Spaniards there. Significant facts, these: darkly suggestive of many an unrecorded horror. But they hint nothing worse than history tells of. Whether we think of the extinct West Indian tribes who were worked to death in mines, or of the Cape Hottentots whose masters punished them by shooting small shot into their legs, or of those nine thousand Chinese whom the Dutch massacred one morning in Batavia, or of the Arabs lately suffocated in the caves of Dahra by the French, we do but call to mind solitary samples of the treatment commonly received by subjugated races from so-called Christian nations. Should anyone flatter himself that we English are guiltless of such barbarities, he may soon be shamed by a narrative of our doings in the East. The Anglo-Indians of the last century—"birds of prey and of passage," as they were styled by Burke—showed themselves only a shade less cruel than their prototypes of Peru and Mexico. Imagine how black must have been their deeds, when even the directors of the Company admitted that "the vast fortunes acquired in the inland trade have been obtained by a scene of the most tyrannical and oppressive conduct that was ever known in any age or country." Conceive the atrocious state of society described by Vansittart, who tells us that the English compelled the natives to buy or sell at just what rates they pleased, on pain of flogging or confinement. Judge to what a pass things must have come when, in describing a journey, Warren Hastings says, "Most of the petty towns and serais were deserted at our approach." A cold-blooded treachery was the established policy of the authorities. Princes were betrayed into war with each other; and one of them, having been helped to overcome his antagonist, was then himself dethroned for some alleged misdemeanor. Always some muddied stream was at hand as a pretext for official wolves. Dependent chiefs holding coveted lands were impoverished by exorbitant demands for tribute; and their ultimate inability to meet these demands was construed into a treasonable offense, punished by deposition. Even down to our own day kindred iniquities are continued.[2] Down to our own day, too, are continued the grievous salt monopoly, and the pitiless taxation that wrings from the poor ryots nearly half the produce of the soil. Down to our own day continues the cunning despotism which uses native soldiers to maintain and extend native subjection—a despotism under which, not many years since, a regiment of sepoys was deliberately massacred for refusing to march without proper clothing. Down to our own day the police authorities league with wealthy scamps and allow the machinery of the law to be used for purposes of extortion. Down to our own day so-called gentlemen will ride their elephants through the crops of impoverished peasants and will supply themselves with provisions from the native villages without paying for them. And down to our own day it is common with the people in the interior to run into the woods at sight of a European!

No one can fail to see that these cruelties, these treacheries, these deeds of blood and rapine, for which European nations in general have to blush, are mainly due to the carrying on of colonization under state management, and with the help of state funds and state force. It is quite needless to point to the recent affair at Wairau in New Zealand, or to the Kaffir war, or to our perpetual aggressions in the East, or to colonial history at large, in proof of this, for the fact is self-evident. A schoolboy, made overbearing by the consciousness that there is always a big brother to take his part, typifies the colonist, who sees in his mother country a bully ever ready to back and defend him. Unprotected emigrants, landing among a strange race and feeling themselves the weaker party, are tolerably certain to behave well, and a community of them is likely to grow up in amicable relationship with the natives. But let these emigrants be fol-

[2]See Sir Alexander Burns' despatches.

lowed by regiments of soldiers, let them have a fort built and cannons mounted, let them feel that they have the upper hand, and they will no longer be the same men. A brutality will come out which the discipline of civilized life had kept under, and not unfrequently they will prove more vicious than they even knew themselves to be. Various evil influences conspire with their own bad propensities. The military force guarding them has a strong motive to foment quarrels, for war promises prize money. To the civil employees, conquest holds out a prospect of more berths and quicker promotion—a fact which must bias them in favor of it. Thus an aggressive tendency is encouraged in all—a tendency which is sure to show itself in acts and to betray the colonists into some of those atrocities that disgrace civilization.

**7.** AS THOUGH TO ROUND OFF THE ARGUMENT MORE COMPLETELY, history presents us with proof that while government colonization is accompanied by endless miseries and abominations, colonization naturally carried on is free from these. Notwithstanding the misconduct he is accused of, to William Penn belongs the honor of having shown men that the kindness, justice, and truth of its inhabitants are better safeguards to a colony than troops and fortifications and the bravery of governors. In all points Pennsylvania illustrates the equitable, as contrasted with the inequitable, mode of colonizing. It was founded not by the state, but by private individuals. It needed no mother-country protection, for it committed no breaches of the moral law. Its treaty with the Indians, described as "the only one ever concluded which was not ratified by an oath, and the only one that was never broken," served it in better stead than any garrison. For the seventy years during which the Quakers retained the chief power, it enjoyed an immunity from that border warfare, with its concomitant losses and fears and bloodshed, to which other settlements were subject. On the other hand, its people maintained a friendly and mutually beneficial intercourse with the natives; and, as a natural consequence of complete security, made unusually rapid progress in material prosperity.

That a like policy would have been similarly advantageous in other cases may reasonably be inferred. No one can doubt, for instance, that, had the East India Company been denied military aid and state-conferred privileges, both its own affairs and the affairs of Hindustan would have been in a far better condition than they now are. Insane longing for empire would never have burdened the Company with the enormous debt which at present paralyzes it. The energy that has been expended in aggressive wars would have been employed in developing the resources of the country. Unenervated by monopolies, trade would have been much more successful. The native rulers, influenced by a superior race on friendly terms with them, would have facilitated improvements; and we should not have seen, as now, rivers unnavigated, roads not bridged or metaled, and the proved capabilities of the soil neglected. Private enterprise would long ago have opened up these sources of wealth, as in fact it is at length doing, in spite of the discouragements thrown in its way by conquest-loving authorities. And had the settlers thus turned their attention wholly to the development of commerce and conducted themselves peaceably, as their defenseless state would have compelled them to do, England would have been better supplied with raw materials, the markets for her goods would have enlarged, and something appreciable toward the civilization of the East would have been accomplished.

**8.** IN MANY WAYS, THEN, DOES EXPERIENCE ENFORCE THE VERDICT pronounced by the law of state duty against state colonization. It turns out that extension of empire is not synonymous with increase of wealth; but that, on the contrary, aggressions bred of the desire for territorial gain entail loss. The notion that we secure commercial benefits by legislative connection with colonies is a proved delusion. At best we throw away the whole sum which colonial government costs us; while we may, and often do, incur further loss by establishing an artificial trade. The plea for protection to the settlers must be abandoned, seeing that this so-called protection is in practice oppression, and seeing that the settlers, from whose judgment on the matter

there is no appeal, hint very plainly their wish to dispense with
it. As for the aborigines, it is manifest that the cruelties inflicted on them have been mainly due to the backing of emigrants by the parent state. And, lastly, we have conclusive
proof not only that voluntary colonization is practicable, but
that it is free from those many evils attendant upon colonization managed by a government.

CHAPTER XXVIII

## Sanitary Supervision

**1.** THE CURRENT IDEAS RESPECTING LEGISLATIVE INTERFERENCE IN
sanitary matters do not seem to have taken the form of a
definite theory. The Eastern Medical Association of Scotland
does indeed hold "that it is the duty of the state to adopt measures for protecting the health as well as the property of its subjects"; and the *Times* lately asserted that "the Privy Council is
chargeable with the health of the Empire";[1] but no considerable
political party has adopted either of these dogmas by way of
a distinct confession of faith. Nevertheless, the opinions that
widely prevail on questions of sewage, water supply, ventilation,
and the like, fully commit their advocates to the belief these
dogmas embody.

That it comes within the proper sphere of government to repress nuisances is evident. He who contaminates the atmosphere
breathed by his neighbor is infringing his neighbor's rights. Men,
having equal claims to the free use of the elements, having faculties which need this free use of the elements for their due
exercise, and having that exercise more or less limited by whatever makes the elements more or less unusable, are obviously
trespassed against by anyone who unnecessarily vitiates the elements and renders them detrimental to health, or disagreeable
to the senses; and in the discharge of its function as protector,

[1] See *Times*, October 17, 1848.

a government is obviously called upon to afford redress to those
so trespassed against.

Beyond this, however, it cannot lawfully go. As already shown
in several kindred cases, for a government to take from a citizen
more property than is needful for the efficient defense of that
citizen's rights is to infringe his rights; is, consequently, to do
the opposite of what it, the government, is commissioned to
do for him—or, in other words, is to do wrong. And hence all
taxation for sanitary superintendence, coming, as it does, within
this category, must be condemned.

**2.** THIS THEORY, OF WHICH BOARDS OF HEALTH AND THE LIKE ARE
embodiments, is not only inconsistent with our definition of
state duty, but is further open to strictures similar to, and
equally fatal with, those made in analogous cases. If by saying
"that it is the duty of the state to adopt measures for protecting
the health of its subjects" it is meant (as it is meant by the
majority of the medical profession) that the state should interpose between quacks and those who patronize them, or between
the druggist and the artisan who wants a remedy for his cold—
if it is meant that to guard people against empirical treatment
the state should forbid all unlicensed persons from prescribing
—then the reply is that to do so is directly to violate the moral
law. Men's rights are infringed by these, as much as by all other
trade interferences. The invalid is at liberty to buy medicine and
advice from whomsoever he pleases; the unlicensed practitioner
is at liberty to sell these to whomsoever will buy. On no pretext
whatever can a barrier be set up between them without the law
of equal freedom being broken; and least of all may the government, whose office it is to uphold that law, become a trans-
gressor of it.

Moreover, this doctrine, that it is the duty of the state to
protect the health of its subjects, cannot be established, for the
same reason that its kindred doctrines cannot; namely, the impossibility of saying how far the alleged duty shall be carried out.
Health depends upon the fulfillment of numerous conditions.
—can be "protected" only by insuring that fulfillment; if, therefore, it is the duty of the state to protect the health of its sub-

jects, it is its duty to see that all the conditions of health are fulfilled by them. Shall this duty be consistently discharged? If so, the legislature must enact a national dietary; prescribe so many meals a day for each individual; fix the quantities and qualities of food, both for men and women; state the proportion of fluids, when to be taken, and of what kind; specify the amount of exercise and define its character; describe the clothing to be employed; determine the hours of sleep, allowing for the difference of age and sex; and so on with all other particulars necessary to complete a perfect synopsis for the daily guidance of the nation; and to enforce these regulations it must employ a sufficiency of duly qualified officials empowered to direct everyone's domestic arrangements. If, on the other hand, a universal supervision of private conduct is not meant, then there comes the question: Where, between this and no supervision at all, lies the boundary up to which supervision is a duty? To which question no answer can be given.

**3.** THERE IS A MANIFEST ANALOGY BETWEEN COMMITTING TO government guardianship the physical health of the people and committing to it their moral health. The two proceedings are equally reasonable, may be defended by similar arguments, and must stand or fall together. If the welfare of men's souls can be fitly dealt with by acts of Parliament, then the welfare of their bodies can be fitly dealt with likewise. He who thinks the state commissioned to administer spiritual remedies may consistently think that it should administer material ones. The disinfecting of society from vice may naturally be quoted as a precedent for disinfecting it from pestilence. Purifying the haunts of men from noxious vapors may be held quite as legitimate as purifying their moral atmosphere. The fear that false doctrines may be instilled by unauthorized preachers has its analogue in the fear that unauthorized practitioners may give deleterious medicines or advice. And the persecutions once committed to prevent the one evil countenance the penalties used to put down the other. Contrariwise, the arguments employed by the dissenter to show that the moral sanity of the people is not a matter for state superintendence are applicable, with a slight change of terms, to their physical sanity also.

Let no one think this analogy imaginary. The two notions are not only theoretically related; we have facts proving that they tend to embody themselves in similar institutions. There is an evident inclination on the part of the medical profession to get itself organized after the fashion of the clerisy. Moved as are the projectors of a railway, who, while secretly hoping for salaries, persuade themselves and others that the proposed railway will be beneficial to the public—moved as all men are under such circumstances, by nine parts of self-interest gilt over with one part of philanthropy—surgeons and physicians are vigorously striving to erect a medical establishment akin to our religious one. Little do the public at large know how actively professional publications are agitating for state-appointed overseers of the public health. Take up the *Lancet,* and you shall find articles written to show the necessity of making Poor Law medical officers independent of Boards of Guardians by appointing them for life, holding them responsible only to central authority, and giving them handsome salaries from the Consolidated Fund. The *Journal of Public Health* proposes that "every house on becoming vacant be examined by a competent person as to its being in a condition adapted for the safe dwelling in of the future tenants"; and to this end would raise by fees, chargeable on the landlords, "a revenue adequate to pay a sufficient staff of inspectors four or five hundred pounds a year each." A non-professional publication, echoing the appeal, says, "No reasonable man can doubt that if a proper system of ventilation were rendered imperative upon landlords, not only would the cholera and other epidemic diseases be checked, but the general standard of health would be raised." While the *Medical Times* shows its leanings by announcing, with marked approbation, that "the Ottoman government has recently published a decree for the appointment of physicians to be paid by the state," who "are bound to treat gratuitously all—both rich and poor—who shall demand advice."

More or less distinctly expressed in these passages there is an unmistakable wish to establish an organized, tax-supported class charged with the health of men's bodies, as the clergy

are charged with the health of their souls. And whoever has
watched how institutions grow—how by little and little a very
innocent-looking infancy unfolds into a formidable maturity,
with vested interests, political influence, and a strong instinct
of self-preservation—will see that the germs here peeping forth
are quite capable, under favorable circumstances, of developing
into such an organization. He will see further that favorable
circumstances are not wanting—that the prevalance of unem-
ployed professional men, with whom these proposals for sanitary inspectors and public surgeons mostly originate, is likely
to continue; and that, continuing, it will tend to multiply the
offices it has created, much in the same way that the super-
abundance of clergy multiplies churches. He will even anticipate that, as the spread of education is certain to render the
pressure upon the intellectual labor market still more intense
than it now is, there will by and by be a yet greater stimulus
to the manufacture of berths—a yet greater tendency on the
part of all who want genteel occupations for their sons to countenance this manufacture—and, therefore, a yet greater danger
of the growth of a medical establishment.

**4.** THE MOST SPECIOUS EXCUSE FOR NOT EXTENDING TO MEDI-
cal advice the principles of Free Trade is the same as that given
for not leaving education to be diffused under them; namely,
that the judgment of the consumer is not a sufficient guarantee
for the goodness of the commodity. The intolerance shown by
orthodox surgeons and physicians toward unordained followers
of their calling is to be understood as arising from a desire to
defend the public against quackery. Ignorant people say they
cannot distinguish good treatment from bad or skillful advisers
from unskillful ones; hence it is needful that the choice should
be made for them. And then, following in the track of priest-
hoods, for whose persecutions a similar defense has always been
set up, they agitate for more stringent regulations against unlicensed practitioners, and descant upon the dangers to which
men are exposed by an unrestricted system. Hear Mr. Wakley.
Speaking of a recently revived law relating to chemists and druggists, he says, "It must have the effect of checking, to a vast

extent, that frightful evil called counter practice, exercised by unqualified persons, which has so long been a disgrace to the operation of the laws relating to medicine in this country, and which, doubtless, has been attended with a dreadful sacrifice of human life." (*Lancet*, September 11, 1841.) And again, "There is not a chemist and druggist in the empire who would refuse to prescribe in his own shop in medical cases, or who would hesitate day by day to prescribe simple remedies for the ailments of infants and children. . . . We had previously considered the evil to be of enormous magnitude, but it is quite clear that we had under-estimated the extent of the danger to which the public are exposed." (*Lancet*, October 16, 1841.)

Anyone may discern through these ludicrous exaggerations much more of the partisan than of the philanthropist. But let that pass. And without dwelling upon the fact that it is strange a "dreadful sacrifice of human life" should not have drawn the attention of the people themselves to this "frightful evil"— without doing more than glance at the further fact that nothing is said of those benefits conferred by "counter practice," which would at least form a considerable set-off against this "evil of enormous magnitude"—let it be conceded that very many of the poorer classes are injured by druggists' prescriptions and quack medicines. The allegation having been thus, for argument's sake, admitted in full, let us now consider whether it constitutes a sufficient plea for legal interference.

Inconvenience, suffering, and death are the penalties attached by nature to ignorance, as well as to incompetence—are also the means of remedying these. And whoso thinks he can mend matters by dissociating ignorance and its penalties lays claim to more than Divine wisdom and more than Divine benevolence. If there seems harshness in those ordinations of things which, with unfaltering firmness, punish every breach of law—if there seems harshness in those ordinations of things which visit a slip of the foot with a broken limb, which send lingering agonies to follow the inadvertent swallowing of a noxious herb, which go on quietly, age after age, giving fevers and agues to dwellers in marshes, and which now and then sweep away by pestilence tens of thousands of unhealthy livers—if there seems harshness in such ordinations, be sure it is apparent only, and not real. Partly by weeding out those of lowest development and partly by subjecting those who remain to the never-ceasing discipline of experience, nature secures the growth of a race who shall both understand the conditions of existence and be able to act up to them. It is impossible in any degree to suspend this discipline by stepping in between ignorance and its consequences, without, to a corresponding degree, suspending the progress. If to be ignorant were as safe as to be wise, no one would become wise. And all measures which tend to put ignorance upon a par with wisdom inevitably check the growth of wisdom. Acts of Parliament to save silly people from the evils which putting faith in empirics may entail upon them do this, and are therefore bad. Unpitifying as it looks, it is best to let the foolish man suffer the appointed penalty of his foolishness. For the pain—he must bear it as well as he can; for the experience—he must treasure it up and act more rationally in future. To others as well as to himself will his case be a warning. And by multiplication of such warnings there cannot fail to be generated in all men a caution corresponding to the danger to be shunned. Are there any who desire to facilitate the process? Let them dispel error; and, provided they do this in a legitimate way, the faster they do it, the better. But to guard ignorant men against the evils of their ignorance, to divorce a cause and consequence which God has joined together, to render needless the intellect put into us for our guidance—to unhinge what is, in fact, the very mechanism of existence—must necessarily entail nothing but disasters.

Who, indeed, after pulling off the colored glasses of prejudice and thrusting out of sight his pet projects, can help seeing the folly of these endeavors to protect men against themselves? A sad population of imbeciles would our schemers fill the world with, could their plans last. A sorry kind of human constitution would they make for us—a constitution lacking the power to uphold itself and requiring to be kept alive by superintendence from without—a constitution continually going wrong and needing to be set right again—a constitution even tending to self-destruction. Why, the whole effort of nature is to get rid of such to clear the world of them and make room for better. Nature demands that every being shall be self-sufficing. All that are not so, nature is perpetually withdrawing by death. Intelligence sufficient to avoid danger, power enough to fulfill every condition, ability to cope with the necessities of existence—these are qualifications invariably insisted on. Mark how the diseased are dealt with. Consumptive patients, with lungs incompetent to perform the duties of lungs, people with assimilative organs that will not take up enough nutriment, people with defective hearts that break down under excitement of the circulation, people with any constitutional flaw preventing the due fulfillment of the conditions of life are continually dying out and leaving behind those fit for the climate, food, and habits to which they are born. Even the less imperfectly organized, who, under ordinary circumstances, can manage to live with comfort, are still the first to be carried off by epidemics; and only such as are robust enough to resist these—that is, only such as are tolerably well adapted to both the usual and incidental necessities of existence—remain. And thus is the race kept free from vitiation. Of course this statement is in substance a truism, for no other arrangement of things is conceivable. But it is a truism to which most men pay little regard. And if they commonly overlook its application to body, still less do they note its bearing upon mind. Yet it is equally true here. Nature just as much insists on fitness between mental character and circumstances as between physical character and circumstances; and radical defects are as much causes of death in the one case as in the other. He on whom his own stupidity, or vice, or idleness entails loss of life must, in the generalizations of philosophy, be classed with the victims of weak viscera or malformed limbs. In his case, as in the others, there exists a fatal non-adaptation; and it matters not in the abstract whether it be a moral, an intellectual, or a corporeal one. Beings thus imperfect are nature's failures, and are recalled by her laws when found to be such. Along with the rest they are put upon trial. If they are sufficiently complete to live, they do live, and it is well they should live. If they are not sufficiently complete to live, they die, and it is best they should die. Whether the incompleteness be in strength, or agility, or perception, or foresight, or self-control is not heeded in the rigorous proof they are put to. But if any faculty is unusually deficient, the probabilities are that, in the long run, some disastrous or, in the worst cases, fatal result will follow. And, however irregular the action of this law may appear—however it may seem that much chaff is left behind which should be winnowed out, and that much grain is taken away which should be left behind—yet due consideration must satisfy everyone that the *average* effect is to purify society from those who are, *in some respect or other*, essentially faulty.

Of course, in so far as the severity of this process is mitigated by the spontaneous sympathy of men for each other, it is proper that it should be mitigated: albeit there is unquestionably harm done when sympathy is shown, without any regard to ultimate results. But the drawbacks hence arising are nothing like commensurate with the benefits otherwise conferred. Only when this sympathy prompts to a breach of equity; only when it originates an interference forbidden by the law of equal freedom; only when, by so doing, it suspends in some particular department of life the relationship between constitution and conditions, does it work pure evil. Then, however, it defeats its own end. Instead of diminishing suffering, it eventually increases it. It favors the multiplication of those worst fitted for existence, and, by consequence, hinders the multiplication of those best fitted for existence—leaving, as it does, less room for them. It tends to fill the world with those to whom life will bring most pain, and tends to keep out of it those to whom life will bring most pleasure. It inflicts positive misery, and prevents positive happiness.

**5.** TURNING NOW TO CONSIDER THESE IMPATIENTLY AGITATED schemes for improving our sanitary condition by act of Parliament, the first criticism to be passed upon them is that they are altogether needless, inasmuch as there are already efficient influences at work gradually accomplishing every desideratum.

Seeing, as do the philanthropic of our day, like the congenitally blind to whom sight has just been given—looking at things through the newly opened eyes of sympathy—they form very crude and very exaggerated notions of the evils to be dealt with. Some, anxious for the enlightenment of their fellows, collect statistics exhibiting a lamentable amount of ignorance, publish these, and the lovers of their kind are startled. Others dive into the dens where poverty hides itself, and shock the world with descriptions of what they see. Others, again, gather together information respecting crime and make the benevolent look grave by their disclosures. Whereupon, in their horror at these revelations, men keep thoughtlessly assuming that the evils have lately become greater, when in reality it is they who have become more observant of them. If few complaints have hitherto been heard about crime, and ignorance, and misery, it is not that in times past these were less widely spread, for the contrary is the fact, but it is that our forefathers were comparatively indifferent to them—thought little about them and said little about them. Overlooking which circumstance, and forgetting that social evils have been undergoing a gradual amelioration—an amelioration likely to progress with increasing rapidity—many entertain a needless alarm lest fearful consequences should ensue if these evils are not immediately remedied, and a visionary hope that immediate remedy of them is possible.

Such are the now prevalent feelings relative to sanitary reform. We have had a multitude of blue-books, Board of Health reports, leading articles, pamphlets, and lectures descriptive of bad drainage, overflowing cesspools, festering graveyards, impure water, and the filthiness and humidity of low lodging houses. The facts thus published are thought to warrant, or rather to demand, legislative interference. It seems never to be asked whether any corrective process is going on. Although everyone knows that the rate of mortality has been gradually decreasing and that the value of life is higher in England than elsewhere—although everyone knows that the cleanliness of our towns is greater now than ever before and that our spontaneously grown sanitary arrangements are far better than those existing on the Continent, where the stinks of Cologne, the uncovered drains of

Paris, the water tubs of Berlin,[2] and the miserable footways of the German towns show what state management effects—although everyone knows these things, yet it is perversely assumed that by state management only can the remaining impediments to public health be removed. Surely the causes which have brought the sewage, the paving and lighting, and the water supply of our towns to their present state have not suddenly ceased. Surely that amelioration which has been taking place in the condition of London for these two or three centuries may be expected to continue. Surely the public spirit which has carried out so many urban improvements since the Municipal Corporations Act gave greater facilities can carry out other improvements. Surely, if all that has been done toward making cities healthy has been done not only without government aid but in spite of government obstructions—in spite, that is, of the heavy expense of local acts of Parliament—we may reasonably suppose that what remains to be done can be done in the same way, especially if the obstructions are removed. One would have thought that less excuse for meddling existed now than ever. Now that so much has been effected; now that spontaneous advance is being made at an unparalleled rate; now that the laws of health are beginning to be generally studied; now that people are reforming their habits of living; now that the use of baths is spreading; now that temperance and ventilation and due exercise are getting thought about—to interfere now, of all times, is surely as rash and uncalled for a step as was ever taken.

And then to think that, in their hot haste to obtain by law healthier homes for the masses, men should not see that the natural process already commenced is the only process which can eventually succeed. The Metropolitan Association for Improving the Dwellings of the Labouring Classes is doing all that is possible in the matter. It is endeavoring to show that, under judicious management, the building of salubrious habitations for the poor becomes a profitable employment of capital. If it shows this, it will do all that needs to be done; for capital will

[2]For putting out fires in Berlin they depend on open tubs of water that stand about the city at certain points, ready to be dragged where they are wanted.

quickly flow into investments offering good returns. If it does not show this—if, after due trial, it finds that these Model Lodging Houses do not pay and that better accommodation than the working people now have can be obtained for them only by diminishing the interest on money sunk in building—then not all the acts of Parliament that can be passed between now and doomsday will improve matters one jot. These plans for making good ventilation imperative; insisting upon water supply and fixing the price for it, as Lord Morpeth's Bill would have done; having empty houses cleansed before reoccupation and charging the owners of them for inspection—these plans for coercing landlords into giving additional advantages for the same money are nothing but repetitions of the old proposal that the "three-hooped pot shall have ten hoops," and are just as incapable of realization. The first result of an attempt to carry them out would be a diminution of the profits of house owners. The interest on capital invested in houses no longer being so high, capital would seek other investments. The building of houses would cease to keep pace with the growth of population. Hence would arise a gradual increase in the number of occupants to each house. And this change in the ratio of houses to people would continue until the demand for houses had raised the profits of the landlord to what they were, and until, by over-crowding, new sanitary evils had been produced to parallel the old ones.[3] If, by building in larger masses and to a greater

[3]Such results have actually been brought about by the Metropolitan Buildings Act. While this act has introduced some reform in the better class of houses (although to nothing like the expected extent, for the surveyors are bribed, and moreover the fees claimed by them for inspecting every trifling alteration operate as penalties on improvement), it has entailed far more evil, just where it was intended to confer benefit. An architect and surveyor describes it as having worked after the following manner. In those districts of London consisting of inferior houses, built in that insubstantial fashion which the New Building Act was to mend, there obtains an average rent, sufficiently remunerative to landlords whose houses were run up economically before the New Building Act passed. This existing average rent fixes the rent that must be charged in these districts for new houses of the same accommodation—that is, the same number of rooms—for the people they are built for do not appreciate the extra safety of living within walls strengthened with hoop-iron bond. Now it turns out upon trial that houses built in accordance with the present regulations and let at this established

height, such an economy can be achieved in ground rent, the cost of outer walls, and of roofing, as to give more accommodation at the same expense as now (which happily seems probable), then the fact only needs proving, and, as before said, the competition of capital for investment will do all that can be done; but if not, the belief that legislative coercion can make things better is a fit companion to the belief that it can fix the price of bread and the rate of wages.

Let those who are anxious to improve the health of the poor through the indirect machinery of law bring their zeal to bear *directly* upon the work to be done. Let them appeal to men's sympathies, and again to their interests. Let them prove to people of property that the making of these reforms will pay. Let them show that the productive powers of the laborer will be increased by bettering his health, while the poors' rate will be diminished. Above all, let them demand the removal of those obstacles which existing legislation puts in the way of sanitary improvement.[4] Their efforts thus directed will really promote

---

rate bring in nothing like a reasonable return. Builders have consequently confined themselves to erecting houses in better districts (where the possibility of a profitable competition with pre-existing houses shows that those pre-existing houses were tolerably substantial), and have ceased to erect dwellings for the masses, except in the suburbs, where no pressing sanitary evils exist. Meanwhile, in the inferior districts above described, has resulted an increase of overcrowding—half a dozen families in a house—a score lodgers to a room. Nay, more than this has resulted. That state of miserable dilapidation into which these abodes of the poor are allowed to fall is due to the absence of competition from new houses. Landlords do not find their tenants tempted away by the offer of better accommodation. Repairs, being unnecessary for securing the largest amount of profit, are not made. And the fees demanded by the surveyor, even when an additional chimney pot is put up, supply ready excuses for doing nothing. Thus, while the New Building Act has caused some improvement where improvement was not greatly needed, it has caused none where it was needed, but has instead generated evils worse than those it was to remove. In fact, for a large percentage of the very horrors which our sanitary agitators are now trying to cure by law, we have to thank previous agitators of the same school!

[4]Writing before the repeal of the brick duty, the *Builder* says, "It is supposed that one fourth of the cost of a dwelling which lets for 2s. 6d. or 3s. a week is caused by the expense of the title deeds and the tax on wood and bricks used in its construction. Of course the owner of such property must be remunerated, and he therefore charges 7½d. or 9d. a week to cover these burdens." Mr. C. Gatliff, secretary to the Society for Improving the Dwell-

progress. Whereas their efforts as now directed are either need-less or injurious.

**6.** THESE ENDEAVORS TO INCREASE THE SALUBRITY OF TOWN LIFE by law are not only open to the criticism that the natural forces already at work render them unnecessary and to the additional criticism that some of the things strained after are impossible of legislative achievement, but it must further be observed that even the desiderata which acts of Parliament will reach can be so reached only through very faulty instrumentalities. It is, in this case, as in many others, the peculiarity of what are oddly styled "practical measures" that they supersede agencies which are answering well by agencies which are not likely to answer well. Here is a heavy charge of inefficiency brought against the drains, cesspools, stink traps, etc., of England in general, and London in particular. The evidence is voluminous and conclu-sive, and by common consent a verdict of proven is returned. Citizens look grave and determine to petition Parliament about it. Parliament promises to consider the matter, and after the usual amount of debate says, "Let there be a Board of Health." Whereupon petitioners rub their hands and look out for great things. They have unbounded simplicity, these good citizens. Legislation may disappoint them fifty times running without at all shaking their faith in its efficiency. They hoped that church abuses would be rectified by the Ecclesiastical Commission; the poor curates can say whether that hope has been realized. Backed by an act of Parliament, the Poor Law Commissioners were to have eradicated able-bodied pauperism; yet, until checked by the recent prosperity, the poors' rates have been rapidly rising to their old level. The New Building Act was to

---

ings of the Working Classes, describing the effect of the window tax, says, "They are now paying upon their institution in St. Pancras the sum of £162 16s. in window duties, or 1 per cent per annum upon the original outlay. The average rental paid by the Society's tenants is 5s. 6d. per week, and the window duty deducts from this 7¼d. per week."—Deputation to Lord Ashley, see *Times*, January 31, 1850. Mr. W. Voller, a master tailor, says, "I lately inserted one of Dr. Arnott's ventilators in the chimney of the workshop, little thinking I should be called upon by Mr. Badger, our dis-trict surveyor, for a fee of 25s."—*Morning Chronicle*, February 4, 1850.

have given the people of London better homes; whereas, as we lately saw, it has made worse the homes that most wanted improving. Men were sanguine of reforming criminals by the silent system, or the separate system; but, if we are to judge by the disputes of their respective advocates, neither of these plans is very successful. Pauper children were to have been made into good citizens by industrial education; from all quarters, however, come statements that a very large percentage of them get into jail, or become prostitutes, or return to the workhouse. The measures enjoined by the Vaccination Act of 1840 were to have exterminated smallpox; yet the Registrar-General's reports show that the deaths from smallpox have been increasing. And thus does year after year add to those abortive schemes, of which so many have been quoted (pp. 43, 258). Yet scarcely a doubt seems to arise respecting the competency of legislators to do what they profess. From the times when they tried to fix the value of money down to our own day, when they have but just abandoned the attempt to fix the price of corn, statesmen have been undertaking all kinds of things, from regulating the cut of boot toes up to preparing people for Heaven, and have been constantly failing, or producing widely different results from those intended. Nevertheless, such inexhaustible faith have men that, although they see this, and although they are daily hearing of imbecilities in public departments—of Admiralty Boards that squander three millions a year in building bad ships and breaking them up again, of Woods and Forests Commissioners who do not even know the rental of the estates they manage, of bungling excise chemists who commit their chiefs to losing prosecutions, for which compensation has to be made—yet government needs but to announce another plausible project, and men straightway hurrah and throw up their caps, in the full expectation of getting all that is promised.

But the belief that Boards of Health and the like will never effect what is hoped needs not wholly rest either upon abstract considerations or upon our experience of state instrumentalities in general. We have one of these organizations at work, and, as far as may be at present judged, it has done anything but answer people's expectations. To condemn it because choked sewers and open gully holes and filthy alleys remain much as they were would perhaps be unreasonable, for time is needed to rectify evils so widely established. But there is one test by which we may fairly estimate its efficiency; viz., its conduct before and during the late pestilence. It had more than a year's notice that the cholera was on its way here. There were two whole sessions of Parliament intervening between the time when a second invasion from that disease was foreseen and the time when the mortality was the highest. The Board of Health had, therefore, full opportunity to put forth its powers and to get greater powers if it wanted them. Well, what was the first step that might have been looked for from it? Shall we not say the suppression of intramural interments? Burying the dead in the midst of the living was manifestly hurtful; the evils attendant on the practice were universally recognized; and to put it down required little more than a simple exercise of authority. If the Board of Health believed itself possessed of authority sufficient for this, why did it not use that authority when the advent of the epidemic was rumored? If it thought its authority not great enough (which can hardly be, remembering what it ultimately did), then why did it not obtain more? Instead of taking either of these steps, however, it occupied itself in considering future modes of water supply and devising systems of sewage. While the cholera was approaching, the Board of Health was cogitating over reforms, from which the most sanguine could not expect any considerable benefit for years to come. And then, when the enemy was upon us, this guardian in which men were putting their trust suddenly bestirred itself and did what, for the time being, made worse the evils to be remedied. As was said by a speaker at one of the medical meetings held during the height of the cholera, the Commissioners of Public Health had adopted the very means likely to produce the complaint. Instead of taking their measures years ago, they had stirred up all sorts of abominations now. They had removed dung hills and cesspools and added fuel tenfold to the fire that existed. Never since he could recollect had there been such accumulations of abominable odors as since the Health of Towns Commission had attempted to purify the atmosphere. At length, when, in

spite of all that had been done (or, perhaps, partly in consequence of it), the mortality continued to increase, the closing of
graveyards was decided upon, in the hope, as we must suppose,
that the mortality would thereby be checked. As though, when
there were hundreds of thousands of bodies decomposing, the
ceasing to add to them would immediately produce an appreciable effect!

If to these facts we add the further one, that notwithstanding
the directions issued for prophylactic treatment and the system
of domiciliary visits, the cholera carried off a greater number
than before, we have some reason for thinking that this sanitary
guardianship did no good, but, it may be, even harm.

Should it be said that the Board of Health is badly constituted or has not sufficient power, and that had a better organization been given to it we should have seen different results, the
reply is that the almost invariable occurrence of some such fatal
hitch is one of the reasons for condemning these interferences.
There is always some provoking *if* in the way. *If* the established
clergy were what they should be, a state church might do some
good. *If* parish relief were judiciously administered, a Poor Law
would not be so bad a thing. And *if* a sanitary organization
could be made to do just what it is intended to do, something
might be said in its favor.

**7.** EVEN COULD STATE AGENCY COMPASS FOR OUR TOWNS THE
most perfect salubrity, it would be in the end better to remain as
we are rather than obtain such a benefit by such means. It is
quite possible to give too much even for a great desideratum.
However valuable good bodily health may be, it is very dearly
purchased when mental health goes in exchange. Whoso thinks
that government can supply sanitary advantages for nothing, or
at the cost of more taxes only, is woefully mistaken. They must
be paid for with character as well as with taxes. A full equivalent
must be given in other coin than gold, and even more than an
equivalent.

Let it be again remembered that men cannot *make* force. All
they can do is to avail themselves of force already existing, and
employ it for working out this or that purpose. They cannot in-

crease it; they cannot get from it more than its specific effect; and as much as they expend of it for doing one thing must they lack of it for doing other things. Thus it is now becoming a received doctrine that what we call chemical affinity, heat, light, electricity, magnetism, and motion are all manifestations of the same primordial force; that they are severally convertible into each other; and, as a corollary, that it is impossible to obtain in any one form of this force more than its equivalent in the previous form. Now this is equally true of the agencies acting in society. It is quite possible to divert the power at present working out one result to the working out of some other result. You may transform one kind of influence into another kind. But you cannot make more of it, and you cannot have it for nothing. You cannot, by legislative maneuvering, get increased ability to achieve a desired object, except at the expense of something else. Just as much better as this particular thing is done, so much worse another thing be done.

Or, changing the illustration and regarding society as an organism, we may say that it is impossible artificially to use up social vitality for the more active performance of one function without diminishing the activity with which other functions are performed. So long as society is let alone, its various organs will go on developing in due subordination to each other. If some of them are very imperfect and make no appreciable progress toward efficiency, be sure it is because still more important organs are equally imperfect and because, the amount of vital force pervading society being limited, the rapid growth of these involves cessation of growth elsewhere. Be sure, also, that whenever there arises a special necessity for better performance of any one function, or for the establishment of some new function, nature will respond. Instance in proof of this the increase of particular manufacturing towns and seaports, or the formation of incorporated companies. Is there a rising demand for some commodity of general consumption? Immediately the organ secreting that commodity becomes more active, absorbs more people, begins to enlarge, and secretes in greater abundance. Instrumentalities for the fulfillment of other social requirements—for the supply of religious culture, education, and

so forth—are similarly provided: the less needful being postponed to the more needful; just as the several parts of the
embryo are developed in the order of their subservience to life.
To interfere with this process by producing premature development in any particular direction is inevitably to disturb the due
balance of organization by causing somewhere else a corresponding atrophy. Let it never be forgotten that at any given time the
amount of a society's vital force is fixed. Dependent as is that
vital force upon the degree of adaptation that has taken place,
upon the extent to which men have acquired fitness for co-
operative life, upon the efficiency with which they can combine
as elements of the social organism, we may be quite certain that,
while their characters remain constant, nothing can increase its
total quantity. We may be also certain that this total quantity
can produce only its exact equivalent of results, and that no
legislators can get more from it, although by wasting it they
may, and always do, get less.

Already, in treating of Poor Laws and national education, we
have examined in detail the reaction by which these attempts at
a multiplication of results are defeated. In the case of sanitary
administrations, a similar reaction may be traced; showing itself,
among other ways, in the checking of all social improvements
that demand popular enterprise and perseverance. Under the
natural order of things, the unfolding of an intelligent, self-
helping character must keep pace with the amelioration of
physical circumstances—the advance of the one with the exertions put forth to achieve the other—so that in establishing
arrangements conducive to robustness of body, robustness of
mind must be insensibly acquired. Contrariwise, to whatever
extent activity of thought and firmness of purpose are made less
needful by an artificial performance of their work, to that same
extent must their increase and the dependent social improvements be retarded.

Should proof of this be asked for, it may be found in the contrast between English energy and continental helplessness. English engineers (Manby, Wilson, and Co.) established the first
gasworks in Paris after the failure of a French company, and
many of the gasworks throughout Europe have been constructed

by Englishmen. An English engineer (Miller) introduced steam navigation on the Rhone; another English engineer (Pritchard) succeeded in ascending the Danube by steam after the French and Germans had failed. The first steamboats on the Loire were built by Englishmen (Fawcett and Preston); the great suspension bridge at Pesth has been built by an Englishman (Tierney Clarke); and an Englishman (Vignolles) is now building a still greater suspension bridge over the Dnieper; many continental railways have had Englishmen as consulting engineers; and in spite of the celebrated Mining College at Freyburg, several of the mineral fields along the Rhine have been opened up by English capital employing English skill. Now why is this? Why were our coaches so superior to the diligences and eilwagen of our neighbors? Why did our railway system develop so much faster? Why are our towns better drained, better paved, and better supplied with water? There was originally no greater mechanical aptitude and no greater desire to progress in us than in the connate nations of northern Europe. If anything, we were comparatively deficient in these respects. Early improvements in the arts of life were imported. The germs of our silk and woolen manufactures came from abroad. The first waterworks in London were erected by a Dutchman. How happens it, then, that we have now reversed the relationship? How happens it that, instead of being dependent on continental skill and enterprise, our skill and enterprise are at a premium on the Continent? Manifestly the change is due to difference of discipline. Having been left in a greater degree than others to manage their own affairs, the English people have become self-helping and have acquired great practical ability. While conversely that comparative helplessness of the paternally governed nations of Europe, illustrated in the above facts and commented upon by Laing in his *Notes of a Traveller* and by other observers, is a natural result of the state-superintendence policy—is the reaction attendant on the action of official mechanisms—is the atrophy corresponding to some artificial hypertrophy.

**8.** ONE APPARENT DIFFICULTY ACCOMPANYING THE DOCTRINE NOW contended for remains to be noticed. If sanitary administration by the state be wrong because it implies a deduction from the citizen's property greater than is needful for maintaining his rights, then is sanitary administration by municipal authorities wrong also for the same reason. Be it by general government or by local government, the levying of compulsory rates for drainage, and for paving and lighting is inadmissible, as indirectly making legislative protection more costly than necessary, or, in other words, turning it into aggression (p. 249); and if so, it follows that neither the past, present, nor proposed methods of securing the health of towns are equitable.

This seems an awkward conclusion; nevertheless, as deducible from our general principle, we have no alternative but to take to it. How streets and courts are rightly to be kept in order remains to be considered. Respecting sewerage, there would be no difficulty. Houses might readily be drained on the same mercantile principle that they are now supplied with water. It is highly probable that in the hands of a private company the resulting manure would not only pay the cost of collection but would yield a considerable profit. But if not, the return on the invested capital would be made up by charges to those whose houses were drained: the alternative of having their connections with the main sewer stopped, being as good a security for payment as the analogous ones possessed by water and gas companies. Paving and lighting would properly fall to the management of house owners. Were there no public provision for such conveniences, house owners would quickly find it their interest to furnish them. Some speculative building society having set the example of improvement in this direction, competition would do the rest. Dwellings without proper footway before them and with no lamps to show the tenants to their doors would stand empty when better accommodation was offered. And good paving and lighting having thus become essential, landlords would combine for the more economical supply of them.

To the objection that the perversity of individual landlords and the desire of others to take unfair advantage of the rest would render such an arrangement impracticable, the reply is that in new suburban streets not yet taken to by the authorities such an arrangement is, to a considerable extent, already carried

out and would be much better carried out but for the consciousness that it is merely temporary. Moreover, no adverse inference
could be drawn were it even shown that for the present such an
arrangement is impracticable. So, also, was personal freedom
once. So once was representative government, and is still with
many nations. As repeatedly pointed out, the practicability of
recognizing men's rights is proportionate to the degree in which
men have become moral. That an organization dictated by the
law of equal freedom cannot yet be fully realized is no proof of
its imperfection: is proof only of our imperfection. And as by
diminishing this the process of adaptation has already fitted us
for institutions which were once too good for us, so will it go on
to fit us for others that may be too good for us now.

**9.** WE FIND, THEN, THAT BESIDES BEING AT VARIANCE WITH THE
moral law, and besides involving absurdities, the dogma that it is
the duty of the state to protect the health of its subjects may be
successfully combated on grounds of policy. It turns out, upon
examination, to be near akin to the older dogma that it is the
duty of the state to provide for the spiritual welfare of its subjects—must, if consistently followed out, necessitate a coextensive organization—and must, for aught their appears to the
contrary, produce analogous results. Of the sufferings consequent upon unrestrained empiricism, it may safely be said that
they are not so great as is represented; and that in as far as they
do exist, they are among the penalties nature has attached to
ignorance or imbecility, and cannot be dissociated from it without ultimately entailing much greater sufferings. The anxiety to
improve by legislative measures the salubrity of our towns is
deprecated on the ground that natural causes insure the continuance of progress—insure further sanitary reforms, just as
they insure advancement in the arts of life, the development of
manufactures and commerce, and the spread of education.
Moreover, it appears that such of these measures as are directed
to the improvement of habitations aim at what laws either cannot do or what is being done much better without them; and to
the rest it is objected that they are not likely to accomplish the
proposed end—a belief founded upon the results of all analo-

gous legislation and confirmed by the little experience we have
at present had of sanitary legislation itself. Further, it is argued
that even could the hoped-for advantages be fully realized they
would be purchased at too great a cost, seeing that they could be
obtained only by an equivalent retardation in some still more
important department of social progress.

## CHAPTER XXIX

# Currency, Postal Arrangements, etc.

**1.** SO CONSTANTLY HAVE THE IDEAS CURRENCY AND GOVERNMENT
been associated, so universal has been the control exercised by
law-givers over monetary systems, and so completely have men
come to regard this control as a matter of course, that scarcely
anyone seems to inquire what would result were it abolished.
Perhaps in no case is the necessity of state superintendence so
generally assumed; and in no case will the denial of that necessity cause so much surprise. Yet must the denial be made.

That laws interfering with currency cannot be enacted without a reversal of state duty is obvious; for either to forbid the
issue or enforce the receipt of certain notes or coin in return for
other things is to infringe the right of exchange—is to prevent
men making exchanges which they otherwise would have made,
or to oblige them to make exchanges which they otherwise
would not have made—is, therefore, to break the law of equal
freedom in their persons (Chapter XXIII). If there be truth in
our general principle, it must be impolitic as well as wrong to do
this. Nor will those who infer as much be deceived, for it may
be shown that all such dictation is not only needless but necessarily injurious.

The monetary arrangements of any community are ultimately
dependent, like most of its other arrangements, on the morality
of its members. Among a people altogether dishonest, every
mercantile transaction must be effected in coin or goods, for

promises to pay cannot circulate at all where, by the hypothesis, there is no probability that they will be redeemed. Conversely, among perfectly honest people paper alone will form the circulating medium; seeing that, as no one of such will give promises to pay more than his assets will cover, there can exist no hesitation to receive promises to pay in all cases; and metallic money will be needless, save in nominal amount to supply a measure of value. Manifestly, therefore, during any intermediate state, in which men are neither altogether dishonest nor altogether honest, a mixed currency will exist; and the ratio of paper to coin will vary with the degree of trust individuals can place in each other. There seems no evading this conclusion. The greater the prevalence of fraud, the greater will be the number of transactions in which the seller will part with his goods only for an equivalent of intrinsic value; that is, the greater will be the number of transactions in which coin is required, and the more will the metallic currency preponderate. On the other hand, the more generally men find each other trustworthy, the more frequently will they take payment in notes, bills of exchange, and checks, the fewer will be the cases in which gold and silver are called for, and the smaller will be the quantity of gold and silver in circulation.

Thus, self-regulating as is a currency when let alone, laws cannot improve its arrangements, although they may and continually do, derange them. That the state should compel everyone who has given promises to pay, be he merchant, private banker, or shareholder in a joint-stock bank, duly to discharge the responsibilities he has incurred, is very true. To do this, however, is merely to maintain men's rights—to administer justice—and therefore comes within the state's normal function. But to do more than this—to restrict issues or forbid notes below a certain denomination—is no less injurious than inequitable. For, limiting the paper in circulation to an amount smaller than it would otherwise reach, inevitably necessitates a corresponding increase of coin; and as coin is locked-up capital, on which the nation gets no interest, a needless increase of it is equivalent to an additional tax equal to the additional interest lost.

Moreover, even under such restrictions, men must still depend mainly upon each other's good faith and enlightened self-interest; seeing that only by requiring the banker to keep sufficient specie in his coffers to cash all the notes he has issued can complete security be given to the holders of them; and to require as much is to destroy the motive for issuing notes. It should be remembered, too, that even now the greater part of our paper currency is wholly unguaranteed. Over the bills of exchange in circulation,[1] which represent liabilities three times as great as are represented by notes, no control is exercised. For the honoring of these there exists no special security, and the multiplication of them is without any limit, save that natural one above mentioned—the credit men find it safe to give each other.

Lastly, we have experience completely to the point. While in England banking has been perpetually controlled, now by privileging the Bank of England, now by limiting banking partnerships, now by prohibiting banks of issue within a specified circle, and now by restricting the amounts issued; while "we have never rested for many years together without some new laws, some new regulations, dictated by the fancy and theory fashionable at particular periods"[2]; and while "by constant interference we have prevented public opinion, and the experience of bankers themselves, adapting and molding their business to the best and safest course,"[3] there has existed in Scotland for nearly two centuries a wholly uncontrolled system—a complete free trade in currency. And what have been the comparative results? Scotland has had the advantage, both in security and economy. The gain in security is proved by the fact that the proportion of bank failures in Scotland has been far less than in England. Though "by law there has never been any restriction against any one issuing notes in Scotland; yet, in practice, it has ever been impossible for any unsound or unsafe paper to obtain currency."[4]

[1]Though not literally currency, bills of exchange, serving in many cases to effect mercantile transactions which would otherwise be effected in money, to that extent perform its function.
[2]Capital, Currency, and Banking, by James Wilson, Esq., M. P.
[3]Ibid.
[4]Ibid.

And thus the natural guarantee in the one case has been more efficient than the legislative one in the other. The gain in economy is proved by the fact that Scotland has carried on its business with a circulation of £3,500,000, while in England the circulation is from £50,000,000 to £60,000,000; or, allowing for difference of population, England has required a currency three times greater than Scotland.

When, therefore, we find a priori reason for concluding that in any given community the due balance between paper and coin will be spontaneously maintained; when we also find that three fourths of our own paper circulation is self-regulated, that the restrictions on the other fourth entail a useless sinking of capital, and further, that facts prove a self-regulated system to be both safer and cheaper, we may fairly say, as above, that legislative interference is not only needless but injurious.

If evil arises when the state takes upon itself to regulate currency, so also does evil arise when it turns banker. True, no direct breach of duty is committed in issuing notes; for the mere transfer of promises to pay to those who will take them necessitates neither infringement of men's rights nor the raising of taxes for illegitimate purposes. And did the state confine itself to this, no harm would result; but when as in practice it makes its notes, or, rather, those of its proxy, legal tender, it both violates the law of equal freedom and opens the door to abuses that were else impossible. Having enacted that its agent's promises to pay shall be taken in discharge of all claims between man and man, there readily follows, when occasion calls, the further step of enacting that these promises to pay shall be taken in discharge of all claims on its agent. This done, further liabilities are incurred without difficulty, for they can be liquidated in paper. Paper continues to be issued without limit, and then comes depreciation; which depreciation is virtually an additional taxation, imposed without the popular consent—a taxation which, if directly imposed, would make men realize the extravagance of their national expenditure and condemn the war necessitating it. Seeing, then, that there could never occur depreciation and its concomitant evils were there no notes made inconvertible by act of Parliament, and seeing that there could never exist any motive to make notes legally inconvertible, save for purposes of state banking, there is good reason to consider state banking injurious. Should it be urged that, for the occasional evils it entails, state banking more than compensates by the habitual supply of many millions' worth of notes whose place could not be supplied by other notes of equal credit, it is replied that had the Bank of England no alliance with the state[5] its notes would still circulate as extensively as now, provided its proprietors continued their solicitude (so constantly shown at the half-yearly meetings) to keep their assets more than three millions above their liabilities.

There is a third capacity in which a government usually stands related to the currency; viz., as a manufacturer of coins. That in theory a government may carry on the trade of stamping bullion without necessarily reversing its proper function is admitted. Practically, however, it never does so without collaterally transgressing. For the same causes which prevent it from profitably competing with private individuals in other trades must prevent it from profitably competing with them in this—a truth which inquiry into the management of the mint will sufficiently enforce. And if so, a government can manufacture coins without loss, only by forbidding everyone else to manufacture them. By doing this, however, it diminishes men's liberty of action in the same way as by any other trade restriction—in short, does wrong. And, ultimately, the breach of the law of equal freedom thus committed results in society having to pay more for its metallic currency than would otherwise be necessary.

Perhaps to many it will seem that by a national mint alone can the extensive diffusion of spurious coinage be prevented. But those who suppose this forget that under a natural system there would exist the same safeguards against such an evil as at present. The ease with which bad money is distinguished from good is the ultimate guarantee for genuineness; and this guaran-

---

[5]The alliance consists in this, that on the credit of a standing debt of £14,000,000, due from the government to the Bank, the Bank is allowed to issue notes to that amount (besides further notes on other security), and hence to the extent of this debt the notes have practically a government guarantee.

tee would be as efficient then as now. Moreover, whatever additional security arises from the punishment of "smashers" would still be afforded; seeing that to bring to justice those who by paying in base coin obtain goods "under false pretenses" comes within the state's duty. Should it be urged that in the absence of legislative regulations there would be nothing to prevent makers from issuing new mintages of various denominations and degrees of fineness, the reply is that only when some obvious public advantage was to be obtained by it could a coin differing from current ones get into circulation. Were private mints now permitted, the proprietors of them would be obliged to make their sovereigns like existing ones, because no others would be taken. For the size and weight, they would be tested by gauge and balance, as now (and for a while with great caution). For the fineness, it would be guaranteed by the scrutiny of other makers. Competing firms would assay each other's issues whenever their appeared the least reason to think them below the established standard and, should their suspicions prove correct, would quickly find some mode of diffusing the information. Probably a single case of exposure and the consequent ruin would ever after prevent attempts to circulate coins of inferior fineness.[6]

It is not unlikely that many readers, though unprepared with definite replies to these reasonings, will still doubt their correctness. That the existing monetary system—an actual working system, seemingly kept going by the state—would be benefited by the withdrawal of state control is a belief which the strongest arguments will in most cases fail to instill. Custom will bias men in this case, much as in another case it does the vine growers of France, who, having long been instructed by state-commissioned authorities when to commence the vintage, believe that such dictation is beneficial. So much more does a realized fact influ-

---

[6]While these sheets are passing through the press, facts which he is not now at liberty to quote have been communicated to the writer conclusively proving the superior economy of a coin manufacture conducted by private individuals; together with other facts suggesting the obvious truth that the debasement of coinage, from which our forefathers suffered so much, was made possible only by legal compulsion—would never have been possible had the currency been left to itself.

ence us than an imagined one, that had the baking and sale of bread been hitherto carried on by government agents, probably the supply of bread by private enterprise would scarcely be conceived possible, much less advantageous. The philosophical free-trader, however, remembering this effect of habit over the convictions, remembering how innumerable have been the instances in which legislative control was erroneously thought necessary, remembering that in this very matter of currency men once considered it requisite "to use the most ferocious measures to bring as much foreign bullion as possible into the country, and to prevent any going out," remembering how *that* interference, like others, proved not only needless but injurious—remembering thus much, the philosophical free-trader will infer that in the present instance, also, legislative control is undesirable. Reasons for considering trade in money an exception to the general rule will weigh but little with him, for he will recollect that similar reasons have been assigned for restricting various trades and disproved by the results. Rather will he conclude that as, in spite of all prophecies and appearances to the contrary, entire freedom of exchange has been beneficial in other cases, so, despite similar prophecies and adverse appearances, will it be beneficial in this case.

**2.** WHAT WAS LATELY SAID RESPECTING THE STAMPING OF BULLION may here be repeated respecting the carrying of letters; viz., that it is not intrinsically at variance with state duty, for it does not in the abstract necessitate any infringement of men's rights, either directly or by taxes raised for nonprotective purposes. Nevertheless, just as we found reason to think that government could not continue to manufacture coin unless by preventing private individuals from doing the same, we shall also find reason to think that it would cease to carry letters did it not forbid competition. And if so, a government cannot undertake postal functions without reversing its essential function.

Evidence that private enterprise *would* supersede state agency in this matter, were it allowed the opportunity, is deducible not only from our general experience of the inferiority of government in the capacity of manufacturer-trader, or manager of business, but from facts immediately bearing upon the question. Thus we must remember that the efficiency to which our postal system has actually attained is not due to its being under public administration, but is due to pressure from without. Changes have been forced upon the authorities, not introduced by them. The mail-coach system was established, and for a length of time managed, by a private individual and lived down official opposition. The reform originated by Mr. Rowland Hill was strenuously resisted; and it is generally reported that even now official perversity prevents his plans from being fully carried out. Whereas, seeing that the speculative spirit of trade is not only ready but eager to satisfy social wants, it is probable that under a natural state of things modern postal improvements would have been willingly adopted, if not forestalled. Should it be alleged that private enterprise would not be competent to so gigantic an undertaking, it is replied that already there are extensive organizations of analogous character which work well. The establishments of our large carriers ramify throughout the whole kingdom, while we have a Parcels' Delivery Company, coextensive in its sphere with the London District Post and quite as efficient. Private agencies for communicating information beat public ones even now, wherever they are permitted to compete with them. The foreign expresses of our daily papers are uniformly before the government expresses. Copies of a royal speech or statements of an important vote are diffused throughout the country by the press with a rapidity exceeding that even achieved by the Post Office; and if expedition is shown in the stamping and sorting of letters, it is far surpassed by the expedition of parliamentary reporting. Moreover, much of the postal service itself is already performed by private agency. Not only are our internal mails carried by contract, but nearly all our external ones also; and where they are carried by government they are carried at a great loss. In proof of which assertion it needs but to quote the fact that the Peninsular and Oriental Steam Navigation Company offers to secure for us a direct monthly communication with Australia; two communications, monthly, from Southampton to Alexandria; two communications, monthly, from Suez to Ceylon, Singapore, and China; and two communications, monthly, from Calcutta to Singapore and China; besides performing the service twice a month between Suez and Bombay, and all for the same sum of money which the latter service alone (Suez to Bombay) now costs the governments of India and Great Britain.

If, then, public letter-carrying has been brought to its existing efficiency by the thought, enterprise, and urgency of private persons, in spite of official resistance; if organizations similar to our postal ones already exist and work well; if, as conveyors of intelligence by other modes than the mail, trading bodies uniformly excel the state; if much of the mail service itself is performed by such trading bodies, and that, too, on the largest scale, with incomparably greater economy than the state can perform it with, there is nothing unreasonable in the conclusion that, were it permitted, commercial enterprise would generate a letter-carrying system as efficient as, if not more efficient than, our present one. It is true that many obstacles stand in the way of such a result. But because it is now scarcely possible to see our way over these, it does not at all follow that they may not be surmounted. There are moral inventions as well as physical ones. And it frequently happens that the instrumentalities which ultimately accomplish certain social desiderata are as little foreseen as are the mechanical appliances of one generation by the previous one. Take the Railway Clearing House for an example. Hence it is not too much to expect that under the pressure of social necessity, and the stimulus of self-interest, satisfactory modes of meeting all such difficulties would be discovered.

However, any doubts which may still be entertained on the point do not militate against our general principle. It is clear that the restriction put upon the liberty of trade, by forbidding private letter-carrying establishments, is a breach of state duty. It is also clear that were that restriction abolished a natural postal system would eventually grow up, could it surpass in efficiency our existing one. And it is further clear that if it could not surpass it, the existing system might rightly continue; for, as at first said, the fulfillment of postal functions by the state is not *intrinsically* at variance with the fulfillment of its essential function.

**3.** THE EXECUTION BY GOVERNMENT OF WHAT ARE COMMONLY called public works, as lighthouses, harbors of refuge, etc., implying, as it does, the imposition of taxes for other purposes than maintaining men's rights, is as much forbidden by our definition of state duty as is a system of national education or a religious establishment. Nor is this unavoidable inference really an inconvenient one, however much it may at first seem so. The agency by which these minor wants of society are now satisfied is not the only agency competent to satisfy them. Wherever there exists a want, there will also exist an impulse to get it fulfilled, and this impulse is sure, eventually, to produce action. In the present case, as in others, that which is beneficial to the community as a whole will become the private interest of some part of the community to accomplish. And as this private interest has been so efficient a provider of roads, canals, and railways, there is no reason why it should not be an equally efficient provider of harbors of refuge, lighthouses, and all analogous appliances. Even were there no classes whose private interests would be obviously subserved by executing such works, this inference might still be defended. But there are such classes. Shipowners and merchants have a direct and ever-waking motive to diminish the dangers of navigation; and, were they not taught by custom to look for state aid, would themselves quickly unite to establish safeguards. Or, possibly, they would be anticipated by a combination of Marine Insurance Offices (themselves protective institutions, originated by self-interest). But inevitably, in some way or other, the numerousness of the parties concerned and the largeness of the capital at stake would guarantee the taking of all requisite precautions. That enterprise which built the docks of London, Liverpool, and Birkenhead, which is enclosing the Wash, which so lately bridged the Atlantic by steam, and which is now laying down the electric telegraph across the Channel, might safely be trusted to provide against the contingencies of coast navigation.

# SOCIAL STATICS

---

## Part IV

## CHAPTER XXX

## *General Considerations*

**1.** SOCIAL PHILOSOPHY MAY BE APTLY DIVIDED (AS POLITICAL economy has been) into statics and dynamics; the first treating of the equilibrium of a perfect society, the second of the forces by which society is advanced toward perfection. To determine what laws we must obey for the obtainment of complete happiness is the object of the one, while that of the other is to analyze the influences which are making us competent to obey these laws. Hitherto we have concerned ourselves chiefly with the statics, touching upon the dynamics only occasionally for purposes of elucidation. Now, however, the dynamics claim special attention. Some of the phenomena of progress already referred to need further explanation, and many others associated with them remain to be noticed. There are also sundry general considerations not admissible into foregoing chapters, which may here be fitly included.

**2.** AND FIRST LET US MARK THAT THE COURSE OF CIVILIZATION could not possibly have been other than it has been. Whether a perfect social state might have been at once established, and why, if it might have been, it was not, why for unnumbered ages the world was filled with inferior creatures only, and why mankind was left to make it fit for human life by clearing it of these, are questions that need not be discussed here. But given an unsubdued earth; given the being—man—appointed to overspread and occupy it; given the laws of life what they are; and no other series of changes than that which has taken place could have taken place.

For be it remembered that the ultimate purpose of creation—

the production of the greatest amount of happiness—can be fulfilled only under certain fixed conditions (p. 62). Each member of the race fulfilling it must not only be endowed with faculties enabling him to receive the highest enjoyment in the act of living, but must be so constituted that he may obtain full satisfaction for every desire, without diminishing the power of others to obtain like satisfaction: nay, to fulfill the purpose perfectly, must derive pleasure from seeing pleasure in others. Now, for beings thus constituted to multiply in a world already tenanted by inferior creatures—creatures that must be dispossessed to make room—is a manifest impossibility. By the definition such beings must lack all desire to exterminate the races they are to supplant. They must, indeed, have a repugnance to exterminating them, for the ability to derive pleasure from seeing pleasure involves the liability to pain from seeing pain; the sympathy by which either of these results is effected simply having for its function to reproduce observed emotions, irrespective of their kind. Evidently, therefore, having no wish to destroy—to destroy giving them, on the contrary, disagreeable sensations—these hypothetical beings, instead of subjugating and overspreading the earth, must themselves become the prey of pre-existing creatures in whom destructive desires predominate. How, then, are the circumstances of the case to be met? Evidently the aboriginal man must have a constitution adapted to the work he has to perform, joined with a dormant capability of developing into the ultimate man when the conditions of existence permit. To the end that he may prepare the earth for its future inhabitants —his descendants—he must possess a character fitting him to clear it of races endangering his life, and races occupying the space required by mankind. Hence he must have a desire to kill, for it is the universal law of life that to every needful act must attach a gratification, the desire for which may serve as a stimulus (p. 19). He must further be devoid of sympathy or must have but the germ of it, for he would otherwise be incapacitated for his destructive office. In other words, he must be what we call a savage and must be left to acquire fitness for social life as fast as the conquest of the earth renders social life possible.

Whoever thinks that a thoroughly civilized community could

be formed out of men qualified to wage war with the pre-existing occupants of the earth—that is, whoever thinks that men might behave sympathetically to their fellows, while behaving unsympathetically to inferior creatures—will discover his error on looking at the facts. He will find that human beings are cruel to one another in proportion as their habits are predatory. The Indian, whose life is spent in the chase, delights in torturing his brother man as much as in killing game. His sons are schooled into fortitude by long days of torment, and his squaw made prematurely old by hard treatment. The treachery and vindictiveness which Bushmen or Australians show to one another and to Europeans are accompaniments of that never-ceasing enmity existing between them and the denizens of the wilderness. Among partially civilized nations the two characteristics have ever borne the same relationship. Thus the spectators in the Roman amphitheaters were as much delighted by the slaying of gladiators as by the death struggles of wild beasts. The ages during which Europe was thinly peopled and hunting a chief occupation were also the ages of feudal violence, universal brigandage, dungeons, tortures. Here in England a whole province depopulated to make game preserves and a law sentencing to death the serf who killed a stag show how great activity of the predatory instinct and utter indifference to human happiness coexisted. In later days, when bull-baiting and cockfighting were common pastimes, the penal code was far more severe than now; prisons were full of horrors; men put in the pillory were mal-treated by the populace; and the inmates of lunatic asylums, chained naked to the wall, were exhibited for money and tormented for the amusement of visitors. Conversely, among ourselves a desire to diminish human misery is accompanied by a desire to ameliorate the condition of inferior creatures. While the kindlier feeling of men is seen in all varieties of philanthropic effort, in charitable societies, in associations for improving the dwellings of the laboring classes, in anxiety for popular education, in attempts to abolish capital punishment, in zeal for temperance reformation, in ragged schools, in endeavors to protect climbing boys, in inquiries concerning "labor and the poor," in emigration funds, in the milder treatment of children, and so on, it also shows itself in societies for the prevention of cruelty of animals, in acts of Parliament to put down the use of dogs for purpose of draft, in the condemnation of steeplechases and *battues*, in the late inquiry why the pursuers of a stag should not be punished as much as the carter who maltreats his horse, and lastly, in vegetarianism. Moreover, to make the evidence complete, we have the fact that men, partially adapted to the social state, retrograde on being placed in circumstances which call forth the old propensities. The barbarizing of colonists who live under aboriginal conditions is universally remarked. The back settlers of America, among whom unavenged murders, rifle duels, and lynch law prevail—or, better still, the trappers, who, leading a savage life, have descended to savage habits, to scalping, and occasionally even to cannibalism—sufficiently exemplify it.

But, indeed, without collecting from so wide a field illustrations of the truth that the behavior of men to the lower animals and their behavior to each other bear a constant relationship, it becomes clear that such is the fact, on observing that the same impulses govern in either case. The blind desire to inflict suffering distinguishes not between the creatures who exhibit that suffering, but obtains gratification indifferently from the agonies of beast and human being—delights equally in worrying a brute and in putting a prisoner to the rack. Conversely, the sympathy which prevents its possessor from inflicting pain that he may avoid pain himself, and which tempts him to give happiness that he may have happiness reflected back upon him, is similarly undistinguishing. As already said, its function is simply to reproduce in one being the emotions exhibited by other beings; and everyone must have noticed that it extracts pleasure from the friskiness of a newly unchained dog or excites pity for an ill-used beast of burden as readily as it generates fellow feeling with the joys and sorrows of men.

So that only by giving us some utterly different mental constitution could the process of civilization have been altered. Assume that the creature scheme is to be wrought out by natural means, and it is necessary that the primitive man should be one whose happiness is obtained at the expense of the happiness of other beings. It is necessary that the ultimate man should be one who can obtain perfect happiness without deducting from the happiness of others. After accomplishing its appointed purpose, the first of these constitutions has to be molded into the last. And the manifold evils which have filled the world for these thousands of years—the murders, enslavings, and robberies —the tyrannies of rulers, the oppressions of class, the persecutions of sect and party, the multiform embodiments of selfishness in unjust laws, barbarous customs, dishonest dealings, exclusive manners, and the like—are simply instances of the disastrous working of this original and once needful constitution, now that mankind has grown into conditions for which it is not fitted—are nothing but symptoms of the suffering attendant upon the adaptation of humanity to its new circumstances.

**3.** BUT WHY, IT MAY BE ASKED, HAS THIS ADAPTATION GONE ON SO slowly? Judging from the rapidity with which habits are formed in the individual, and seeing how those habits, or rather the latent tendencies toward them, become hereditary, it would seem that the needful modification should have been completed long ago. How, then, are we to understand the delay?

The answer is that the new conditions to which adaptation has been taking place have themselves grown up but slowly. Only when a revolution in circumstances is at once both marked and permanent does a decisive alteration of character follow. If the demand for increase of power in some particular faculty is great and unceasing, development will go on with proportionate speed. And, conversely, there will be an appreciable dwindling in a faculty altogether deprived of exercise. But the conditions of human life have undergone no changes sudden enough to produce these immediate results.

Thus, note in the first place that the warfare between man and the creatures at enmity with him has continued up to the present time, and over a large portion of the globe is going on now. Note, further, that where the destructive propensities have almost fulfilled their purpose and are on the eve of losing their gratification, they make to themselves an artificial sphere of exercise by game-preserving and are so kept in activity after they

would otherwise have become dormant. But note, chiefly, that
the old predatory disposition is in a certain sense self-main-
tained. For it generates between men and men a hostile relationship similar to that which it generates between men and inferior
animals, and by doing so provides itself a lasting source of excitement. This happens inevitably. The desires of the savage,
acting, as we have seen, indiscriminately, necessarily lead him to
perpetual trespasses against his fellows and, consequently, to
endless antagonisms—to quarrels of individuals, to fightings of
tribes, to feuds of clan with clan, to wars of nations. And thus
being by their constitutions made mutual foes, as well as foes to
the lower races, men keep alive in each other the old propensities after the original need for them has in great measure ceased.

Hitherto, then, human character has changed but slowly because it has been subject to two conflicting sets of conditions.
On the one hand, the discipline of the social state has been
developing it into the sympathetic form; while on the other
hand, the necessity for self-defense, partly of man against brute,
partly of man against man, and partly of societies against each
other, has been maintaining the old unsympathetic form. And
only where the influence of the first set of conditions has ex-
ceeded that of the last, and then only in proportion to the excess, has modification taken place. Among tribes who have kept
each other's anti-social characteristics in full activity by constant
conflict, no advance has been possible. But where warfare
against man and beast has ceased to be continuous, or where it
has become the employment of but a portion of the people, the
effects of living in the associated state have become greater than
the effects of barbarizing antagonisms, and progress has resulted.

Regarded thus, civilization no longer appears to be a regular
unfolding after a specific plan, but seems rather a development
of man's latent capabilities under the action of favorable circumstances; which favorable circumstances, mark, were certain sometime or other to occur. Those complex influences underlying the
higher orders of natural phenomena, but more especially those
underlying the organic world, work in subordination to the law
of probabilities. A plant, for instance, produces thousands of
seeds. The greater part of these are destroyed by creatures that

live upon them, or fall into places where they cannot germinate. Of the young plants produced by those which do germinate, many are smothered by their neighbors; others are blighted by insects or eaten up by animals; and in the average of cases, only one of them produces a perfect specimen of its species, which, escaping all dangers, brings to maturity seeds enough to continue the race. Thus is it also with every kind of creature. Thus is it also, as M. Quetelet has shown, with the phenomena of human life. And thus was it even with the germination and growth of society. The seeds of civilization existing in the aboriginal man, and distributed over the earth by his multiplication, were certain in the lapse of time to fall here and there into circumstances fit for their development; and, in spite of all blightings and uprootings, were certain, by sufficient repetition of these occurrences, ultimately to originate a civilization which should outlive all disasters and arrive at perfection.

**4.** WHILE THE CONTINUANCE OF THE OLD PREDATORY INSTINCT after the fulfillment of its original purpose has retarded civilization by giving rise to conditions at variance with those of social life, it has subserved civilization by clearing the earth of inferior races of men. The forces which are working out the great scheme of perfect happiness, taking no account of incidental suffering, exterminate such sections of mankind as stand in their way, with the same sternness that they exterminate beasts of prey and herds of useless ruminants. Be he human being or be he brute, the hindrance must be got rid of. Just as the savage has taken the place of lower creatures, so must he, if he has remained too long a savage, give place to his superior. And, observe, it is necessarily to his superior that, in the great majority of cases, he does give place. For what are the prerequisites to a conquering race? Numerical strength or an improved system of warfare, both of which are indications of advancement. Numerical strength implies certain civilizing antecedents. Deficiency of game may have necessitated agricultural pursuits, and so made the existence of a larger population possible; or distance from other tribes may have rendered war less frequent, and so have prevented its perpetual decimations; or accidental superiority over neighboring tribes may have led to the final subjugation and enslaving of these: in any of which cases the comparatively peaceful condition resulting must have allowed progress to commence. Evidently, therefore, from the very beginning, the conquest of one people over another has been, in the main, the conquest of the social man over the anti-social man; or, strictly speaking, of the more adapted over the less adapted.

In another mode, too, the continuance of the unsympathetic character has indirectly aided civilization while it has directly hindered it; namely, by giving rise to slavery. It has been observed—and, as it seems, truly enough—that only by such stringent coercion as is exercised over men held in bondage could the needful power of continuous application have been developed. Devoid of this, as from his habits of life the aboriginal man necessarily was (and as, indeed, existing specimens show), probably the severest discipline continued for many generations was required to make him submit contentedly to the necessities of his new state. And if so, the barbarous selfishness which maintained that discipline must be considered as having worked a collateral benefit, though in itself so radically bad.

Let not the reader be alarmed. Let him not fear that these admissions will excuse new invasions and new oppressions. Nor let anyone who fancies himself called upon to take nature's part in this matter, by providing discipline for idle Negroes or others, suppose that these dealings of the past will serve for precedents. Rightly understood, they will do no such thing. That phase of civilization during which forcible supplantings of the weak by the strong and systems of savage coercion are on the whole advantageous, is a phase which spontaneously and necessarily gives birth to these things. It is not in pursuance of any calmly reasoned conclusions respecting nature's intention that men conquer and enslave their fellows—it is not that they smother their kindly feelings to subserve civilization; but it is that as yet constituted they care little what suffering they inflict in the pursuit of gratification, and even think the achievement and exercise of mastery honorable. As soon, however, as there arises a perception that these subjugations and tyrannies are not right, as soon as the sentiment to which they are repugnant becomes sufficiently powerful to suppress them, it is time for them to cease. The question altogether hinges upon the amount of moral sense possessed by men; or, in other words, upon the degree of adaptation to the social state they have undergone. Unconsciousness that there is anything wrong in exterminating inferior races, or in reducing them to bondage, presupposes an almost rudimentary state of men's sympathies and their sense of human rights. The oppressions they then inflict and submit to are not, therefore, detrimental to their characters—do not retard in them the growth of the social sentiments, for these have not yet reached a development great enough to be offended by such doings. And hence the aids given to civilization by clearing the earth of its least advanced inhabitants, and by forcibly compelling the rest to acquire industrial habits, are given without moral adaptation receiving any corresponding check. Quite otherwise is it, however, when the flagitiousness of these gross forms of injustice begins to be recognized. Then the times give proof that the old regime is no longer fit. Further progress cannot be made until the newly felt wrong has been done away or diminished. Were it possible under such circumstances to uphold past institutions and practices (which, happily, it is not), it would be at the expense of a continual searing of men's consciences. The feelings whose predominance gives possibility to an advanced social state would be constantly repressed, kept down on a level with the old arrangements, to the stopping of all further progress; and before those who have grown beyond one of these probationary states could reinstitute it, they must resume that inferior character to which it was natural. Before a forced servitude could be again established for the industrial discipline of eight hundred thousand Jamaica blacks, the thirty millions of English whites who established it would have to retrograde in all things—in truthfulness, fidelity, generosity, honesty, and even in material condition; for to diminish men's moral sense is to diminish their fitness for acting together and, therefore, to render the best producing and distributing organizations impracticable. Another illustration, this, of the perfect economy of nature.

While the injustice of conquests and enslavings is not perceived, they are on the whole beneficial; but as soon as they are felt to be at variance with the moral law, the continuance of them retards adaptation in one direction more than it advances it in another: a fact which our new preacher of the old doctrine that might is right may profitably consider a little.

**5.** CONTRASTED AS ARE THEIR UNITS, PRIMITIVE COMMUNITIES and advanced ones must essentially differ in the principles of their structure. Like other organisms, the social organism has to pass in the course of its development through temporary forms, in which sundry of its functions are fulfilled by appliances destined to disappear as fast as the ultimate appliances become efficient. Associated humanity has larval appendages analogous to those of individual creatures. As in the common *Triton* of our ponds, the external lungs or branchiae dwindle away when the internal lungs have grown to maturity; and as during the embryo stage of the higher vertebrata temporary organs appear, serve their purpose awhile, and are subsequently reabsorbed, leaving only signs of their having been; so, in the earlier forms of the body politic, do there exist institutions which after answering their ends for a time are superseded and become extinct.

But deciduous institutions imply deciduous sediments. Dependent as they are upon popular character, established political systems cannot die out until the feeling which upholds them dies out. Hence during man's apprenticeship to the social state there must predominate in him some impulse corresponding to the arrangements requisite; which impulse diminishes as the probationary organization made possible by it merges into the ultimate organization. The nature and operation of this impulse now demand our attention.

**6.** "I HAD SO GREAT A RESPECT FOR THE MEMORY OF HENRY IV," said the celebrated French robber and assassin, Cartouche, "that had a victim I was pursuing taken refuge under his statue on the Pont Neuf, I would have spared his life." An apt illustration, this, of the coexistence of profound hero worship with the extremest savageness, and of the means hero worship affords whereby the savage may be ruled. The necessity for some such sentiment to bind men together while they are as yet unsympathetic has been elsewhere shown. For the anti-social man to be transformed into the social man, he must live in the social state. But how can a society be maintained when, by the hypothesis, the aggressive desires of its members are destructive of it? Evidently its members must possess some counterbalancing tendency which shall keep them in the social state despite the incongruity, which shall make them submit to the restraint imposed, and which shall diminish as adaptation to the new circumstances renders restraint less needful. Such counterbalancing tendency we have in this same sentiment of hero worship; a sentiment which leads men to prostrate themselves before any manifestation of power, be it in chief, feudal lord, king, or constitutional government, and makes them act in subordination to that power.

Facts illustrating this alleged connection between strength of hero worship and strength of the aggressive propensities, together with other facts illustrating the simultaneous decline of both, were given when the matter was first discussed (p. 177). Now, however, we may appropriately examine the evidence in detail. The proposition is that in proportion as the members of a community are barbarous—that is, in proportion as they show a lack of moral sense by seeking gratification at each other's expense—in the same proportion will they show depth of reverence for authority. What, now, are the several indications of deficient moral sense? First on the list stands disregard of human life; next, habitual violation of personal liberty; next to that, theft, and the dishonesty akin to it. Each of these, if the foregoing theory be true, we ought to find most prevalent where the awe of power is most profound.

Well, is it not a fact that groveling submission to despotic rule flourishes side by side with the practice of human sacrifices, infanticide, and assassination? We find suttees and thuggee among a race who have ever been abject slaves. In some of the Pacific isles, where the immolation of children to idols and the burying of parents alive are common, "so high is the reverence for hereditary chieftainship that it is often connected with the idea of Divine power." Complete absolutism uniformly coexists with cannibalism. We read of human hecatombs in connection with the extremest prostration of subjects to rulers. In Madagascar, where men are put to death on the most trifling occasions, and where the coast is decorated with skulls stuck on poles, the people are governed on the severest maxims of feudal law, by absolute chieftains under an absolute monarch. The head-hunting Dyaks of Borneo have petty tyrants over them. There is autocratic government, too, for the bloodthirsty Mongolian races. Both positive and negative proof of this association is given by Mr. Grote, where he says, "In no city of historical Greece did there prevail either human sacrifice or deliberate mutilations, such as cutting off the nose, ears, hands, feet, etc., or castration, or selling of children into slavery, or polygamy, or *the feeling of unlimited obedience toward one man*; all of them customs, which might be pointed out as existing amongst the contemporary Carthaginians, Egyptians, Persians, Thracians," etc. If we consult medieval history, there, along with loyalty strongly manifested, are the judicial combats, right of private war, constant wearing of arms, religious martyrdoms and massacres, etc., to prove that life was held in less respect than now. Glancing over modern Europe, we find the assassinations of Italy, the cruelty of the Croats and Czechs, and the Austrian butcheries illustrating the relationship. While, among ourselves, diminished reverence for authority has occurred simultaneously with diminished sanguinariness in our criminal code.

That infringements of personal liberty are greatest where awe of power is greatest is in some sort a truism, seeing that forced servitude, through which alone extensive violations of human liberty can be made, is impossible, unless the sentiment of power worship is strong. Thus, the ancient Persians could never have allowed themselves to be considered the private property of their monarchs had it not been for the overwhelming influence of this sentiment. But that such submission is associated with a defect of moral sense is best seen in the acknowledged truth that readiness to cringe is accompanied by an equal readiness to tyrannize. Satraps lorded it over the people as their king over them. The Helots were not more coerced by their Spartan masters than these in turn by their oligarchy. Of the servile Hindus we are told that "they indemnify themselves for their passiveness to their superiors by their tyranny, cruelty, and violence to those in their power." During the feudal ages, while the people were bondsmen to the nobles, the nobles were vassals to their kings, their kings to the Pope. In Russia, at the present moment, the aristocracy are dictated to by their emperor much as they themselves dictate to their serfs. And when to these facts we add the significant one elsewhere dwelt upon (pp. 144 and 159), that the treatment of women by their husbands and children by their parents has been tyrannical in proportion as the servility of subjects to rulers has been extreme, we have sufficient proof that hero worship is strongest where there is least regard for human freedom.

Equally abundant evidence exists that the prevalence of theft is similarly associated with a predominance of the loyalty-producing faculty. Books of travels give proof that among uncivilized races pilfering and the irresponsible power of chiefs coexist. The same association of dishonesty and submissiveness is found among more advanced peoples. It is so with the Hindus, with the Singhalese, and with the inhabitants of Madagascar. The piracy of the Malays and of the Chinese, and the long-continued predatory habits of the Arab races, both on land and sea, exist in conjunction with obedience to despotic rule. "One quality," says Kohl, "which the Lettes show, with all enslaved tribes, is a great disposition to thieving." The Russians, to whom worship of their emperor is a needful luxury, confess openly that they are cheats and laugh over the confession. The Poles, whose servile salutation is, "I throw myself under your feet," and among whom nobles are cringed to by the Jews and citizens, and these again by the people, are certainly not noted for probity. Turning to the superior races, we find that they, too, have passed through phases in which this same relationship of characteristics was strongly marked. Thus, the times when fealty of serfs to feudal barons was strongest were times of universal rapine. "In Germany a very large proportion of the rural nobility lived by robbery," their castles being built with a special view to this occupation, and that even by ecclesiastics.[1] Burghers were fleeced, towns were now and then sacked, and Jews were tortured for their money. Kings were as much thieves as the rest. They laid violent hands upon the goods of their vassals, like John of England and Philip Augustus of France; they cheated their creditors by debasing the coinage; they impressed men's horses without paying for them; and they seized the goods of traders, sold them, and pocketed a large part of the proceeds. Meantime, while freebooters overran the land, pirates covered the sea, the Cinque Ports and St. Malo's being the headquarters of those infesting the English Channel.

Between these days and ours, the gradual decline of loyalty —as shown in the extinction of feudal relationships, in the abandonment of divine right of kings, in the reduction of monarchical power, and in the comparative leniency with which treason is now punished—has accompanied an equally gradual increase of honesty and of regard for people's lives and liberties. By how much men are still deficient in respect for each other's rights, by so much are they still penetrated with respect for authority; and we may even trace in existing parties the constant ratio preserved between these characteristics. It has been shown, for instance, that the unskilled laborers of the metropolis, who, instead of entertaining violently democratic opinions, appear to have no political opinions whatever, or, if they think at all, rather lean toward the maintenance of "things as they are," and part of whom, (the coal whippers) are extremely proud of their having turned out to a man on the tenth of April, 1848, and become special constables for the "maintenance of law and order" on the day of the great Chartist Demonstration—it has been shown that these same unskilled laborers constitute the most immoral class. The Criminal-Returns prove them to be nine times as dishonest, five times as drunken, and nine times as savage (shown by the assaults) as the rest of the community. Of like import is the observation respecting convicts, quoted

[1]"An Archbishop of Cologne having built a fortress of this kind, the governor inquired how he was to maintain himself, no revenue having been assigned for that purpose. The prelate only desired him to remark, that the castle was situated near the junction of four cross roads."—Hallam's Middle Ages.

and confirmed by Captain Maconochie, that "a good prisoner (*i.e.*, a submissive one) is usually a bad man."[2] If, again, we turn over the newspapers which circulate among court satellites, and chronicle the movements of the *haut-ton*, which ascribe national calamities to the omission of a royal title from a new coin and which apologize for continental despots, we read in them excuses for war and standing armies, sneerings at "peace-mongers," defenses of capital punishment, condemnations of popular enfranchisement, diatribes against freedom of exchange, rejoicings over territorial robberies, and vindications of church-rate seizures: showing that, where belief in the sacredness of authority most lingers, belief in the sacredness of life, of liberty, and of property is least displayed.

**7.** THE FACT THAT DURING CIVILIZATION HERO WORSHIP AND moral sense vary inversely is simply the obverse of the fact already hinted, that society is possible so long only as they continue to do this. Where there is insufficient reverence for the Divine Law, there must be supplementary reverence for human law; otherwise there will be complete lawlessness or barbarism. Evidently, if men are to live together, the absence of internal power to rule themselves rightly toward each other necessitates the presence of external power to enforce such behavior as may make association tolerable; and this power can become operative only by being held in awe. So that wild races deficient in the allegiance-producing sentiment cannot enter into a civilized state at all, but have to be supplanted by others that can. And it must further follow that, if in any community loyalty diminishes at a greater rate than equity increases, there will arise a tendency toward social dissolution—a tendency which the populace of Paris threaten to illustrate.

How needful the continuance of a savage selfishness renders the continuance of a proportionate amount of power worship may be perceived daily. Listen to the chattings of men about their affairs, examine into trade practices, read over business correspondence, or get a solicitor to detail his conversations with clients: you will find that in most cases conduct depends, not

[2]See pamphlets on the Mark System of Discipline.

upon what is right, but upon what is legal. Provided they "keep o' the windy side of the law," the great majority are but little restrained by regard for strict rectitude. The question with your everyday man of the world is not, "May the claimant justly require thus much of me?" but rather "Is it so nominated in the bond?" If "an action will lie," such a one will commonly enough take proceedings to obtain what he knows himself not equitably entitled to, and if "the law allows it and the court awards it" will pocket all he can get without scruple. When we find doings like these regarded as matters of course, and those guilty of them passing for respectable men, when we thus find that so many will deal fairly by their fellows only on compulsion, we discover how requisite is the sentiment from which the compelling instrumentality derives its power.

Without doubt this sentiment has begotten many gigantic evils, some of which it still nurtures. The various superstitions that have prevailed and that still prevail as to the great things legislature can do and the disastrous meddlings growing out of these superstitions are due to it. The veneration which produces submission to a government unavoidably invests that government with proportionately high attributes; for being in essence a worship of power, it can be strongly drawn out toward that only which either has great power or is believed to have it. Hence, the old delusions that rulers can fix the value of money, the rate of wages, and the price of food. Hence, the still current fallacies about mitigating distress, easing monetary pressures, and curing overpopulation by law. Hence, also, the monstrous, though generally received doctrine that a legislature may equitably take people's property to such extent, and for such purposes, as it thinks fit—for maintaining state churches, feeding paupers, paying schoolmasters, founding colonies, etc. And hence, lastly, the astounding belief that an act of Parliament can abrogate one of nature's decrees—can, for instance, render it criminal in a trader to buy goods in France and bring them here to sell, while the moral law says it is criminal to prevent him! As though conduct could be made right or wrong by the votes of some men sitting in a room in Westminster! Yet, in spite of all this, in spite of the false theories and mischievous interferences, the numberless oppressions, disasters, and miseries in one way or other traceable to it, we must admit that this power worship has fulfilled, and does still fulfill, a very important function, and that it may advantageously last as long as it can.

**8.** THAT IT CANNOT LAST LONGER THAN NEEDFUL MAY BE READILY proved. In a way equally simple and perfect it is made to decline as fast as it can be done without. The very feeling, during whose minority it exercises regency over men, becomes the destroyer of its power. Between the temporary ruler and the ultimate rightful one there is an unceasing conflict in which the wane of influence on the one side is necessitated by its growth on the other.

For, as already shown (p. 89), the sense of rights, by whose sympathetic excitement men are led to behave justly toward each other, is the same sense of rights by which they are prompted to assert their own claims, their own liberty of action, their own freedom to exercise their faculties and to resist every encroachment. This impulse brooks no restraint, save that imposed by fellow feeling, and disputes all assumption of extra privilege by whomsoever made. Consequently, it is in perpetual antagonism with a sentiment which delights in subserviency. "Reverence this authority," suggests power worship. "Why should I? Who set it over me?" demands instinct of freedom. "Obey," whispers the one. "Rebel," mutters the other. "I will do what Your Highness bids," says the one with bated breath. "Pray, sir," shouts the other, "who are you, that you should dictate to me?" "This man is Divinely appointed to rule over us, and we ought therefore to submit," argues the one. "I tell you, no," replies the other; "we have Divinely endorsed claims to freedom, and it is our duty to maintain them." And thus the controversy goes on: conduct during each phase of civilization being determined by the relative strengths of the two feelings. While yet too feeble to be operative as a social restraint, moral sense, by its scarcely heard protest, does not hinder a predominant hero worship from giving possibility to the most stringent despotism. Gradually, as it grows strong enough to deter men from the grosser trespasses upon each other, does it also grow strong enough to struggle successfully against that excess of coercion no longer required. And when it shall finally have attained sufficient power to give men, by its reflex function, so perfect a regard for each other's rights as to make government needless, then will it also, by its direct function, give men so wakeful a jealousy of their own rights as to make government impossible. A further example, this, of the admirable simplicity of nature. The same sentiment which fits us for freedom, itself makes us free.

Of course the institutions of any given age exhibit the compromise made by these contending moral forces at the signing of their last truce. Between the state of unlimited government arising from supremacy of the one feeling and the state of no government arising from supremacy of the other lie intermediate forms of social organization, beginning with "despotism tempered by assassination," and ending with that highest development of the representative system, under which the right of constituents to instruct their delegates is fully admitted—a system which, by making the nation at large a deliberative body and reducing the legislative assembly to an executive, carries self-government to the fullest extent compatible with the existence of a ruling power. Of necessity the mixed constitutions that characterize this transition period are in the abstract absurd. The two feelings answering to the popular and monarchical elements, being antagonistic, give utterance to antagonistic ideas. And to suppose that these can be consistently united is to suppose that yes and no can be reconciled. The monarchical theory is that the people are in duty bound to submit themselves with all humility to a certain individual—ought to be loyal to him—ought to give allegiance to him, that is—ought to subordinate their wills to his will. Contrariwise, the democratic theory—either as specifically defined or as embodied in our own constitution under the form of a power to withhold supplies and in the legal fiction that the citizen assents to the laws he has to obey—is that the people ought not to be subject to the will of one, but should fulfill their own wills. Now these are flat contradictions which no reasoning can harmonize. If a king may rightfully claim obedience, then should that obedience be entire; else there starts up the unanswerable question: Why must we obey in this and not in that? But if men should mainly rule themselves, then should they rule themselves altogether. Otherwise it may be asked: Why are they their own masters in such-and-such cases and not in the rest?

Nevertheless, though these mixed governments, combining as they do two mutually destructive hypotheses, are utterly irrational in principle, they must of necessity exist, so long as they are in harmony with the mixed constitution of the partially adapted man. And it seems that the radical incongruity pervading them cannot be recognized by men while there exists a corresponding incongruity in their own natures: a good illustration of the law that opinion is ultimately determined by the feelings and not by the intellect.

**9.** HOW COMPLETELY, INDEED, CONCEPTIONS OF RIGHT AND wrong in these matters depend upon the balance of impulses existing in men may be worth considering a moment. And first, observe that no tracing out of actions to their final good or bad consequences is, by itself, capable of generating approbation, or reprobation, of those actions. Could it do this, men's moral codes would be high or low, according as they made these analyses well or ill; that is, according to their intellectual acuteness. Whence it would follow that in all ages and nations men of equal intelligence should have like ethical theories, while contemporaries should have unlike ones, if their reflective powers are unlike. But facts do not answer to these inferences. On the contrary, they point to the law above specified. Both history and daily experience prove to us that men's ideas of rectitude correspond to the sentiments and instincts predominating in them (pp. 24, 141, 312). We constantly read of tyrants defending their claims to unlimited sway as being Divinely authorized. The rights of rival princes were of old asserted by their respective partisans and are still asserted by modern legitimists with the same warmth that the most ardent democrat asserts the rights of man. To those living in the feudal times, so unquestionable seemed the duty of serfs to obey their lords that Luther (no doubt acting conscientiously) urged the barons to vengeance on the rebellious peasants, calling on all who could "to stab them, cut them down, and dash their brains out, as if they were mad dogs." Moreover, we shall find that absence of the ethical sentiment completely disables the mind from realizing the abstract title of the human being to freedom. Thus, with all his high reasoning powers, Plato could conceive of nothing better for his ideal republic than a system of class despotism; and, indeed, up to his time, and long after it, there seems to have existed no man who saw anything wrong in slavery. It is narrated of Colonel D'Oyley, the first governer of Jamaica, that within a few days after having issued an order "for the distribution to the army of 1,701 Bibles," he signed another order for the payment "of the summe of twenty pounds sterling, out of the impost money, to pay for fifteen doggs, brought by John Hoy, for the hunting of the Negroes." The holding of slaves by ministers of religion in America is a parallel fact. We read that the Chinese cannot understand why European women are treated with respect, and that they attribute the circumstance to the exercise of demoniacal arts by them over the men. Here and there among ourselves, analogous phenomena may be detected. For example, Dr. Moberly of Winchester College has written a book to defend fagging, which he says, as a system of school government, gives "more security of essential deep-seated goodness than any other which can be devised." Again, in a recent pamphlet signed "A Country Parson," it is maintained that "you must convert the Chartist spirit as you would reform the drunkard's spirit, by showing that it is a rebellion against the laws of God." But the strangest peculiarity exhibited by those deficient in sense of rights—or rather that which looks the strangest to us—is their inability to recognize their own claims. We are told, for instance, by Lieutenant Bernard,[3] that in the Portuguese settlements on the African coast the free Negroes are "taunted by the slaves as having no white man to look after them, and see them righted when oppressed"; and it is said that in America the slaves themselves look down upon the free blacks and call them rubbish. Which anomalous-looking facts are, however, easily conceivable when we remember

[3]*Three Years' Cruise in the Mozambique Channel.*

that here in England, in this nineteenth century, most women defend that state of servitude in which they are held by men.

To account, by any current hypothesis, for the numberless disagreements in men's ideas of right and wrong here briefly exemplified seems scarcely possible. But on the theory that opinion is a resultant of moral forces whose equilibrium varies with every race and epoch—that is, with every phase of adaptation—the rationale is self-evident. Nor, indeed, considering the matter closely, does it appear that society could ever hold together were not opinion thus dependent upon the balance of feelings. For were it otherwise, races yet needing coercive government might reason their way to the conclusion that coercive government was bad, as readily as more advanced races. The Russians might see despotism to be wrong, and free institutions to be right, as clearly as we do. And did they see this, social dissolution would ensue; for it is not conceivable that they would any longer remain contented under that stringent rule needed to keep them in the social state.

**10.** THE PROCESS BY WHICH A CHANGE OF POLITICAL ARRANGE-ments is effected, when the incongruity between them and the popular character becomes sufficient, must be itself in keeping with that character and must be violent or peaceful accordingly. There are not a few who exclaim against all revolutions wrought out by force of arms, forgetting that the quality of a revolution, like that of an institution, is determined by the natures of those who make it. Moral suasion is very admirable; good for us; good, indeed, for all who can be induced to use it. But to suppose that, in the earlier stages of social growth, moral suasion can be employed, or, if employed, would answer, is to overlook the conditions. Stating the case mechanically, we may say that as in proportion to their unfitness for associated life the framework within which men are restrained must be strong, so must the efforts required to break up that framework, when it is no longer fit, be convulsive. The existence of a government which does not bend to the popular will—a despotic government—presupposes several circumstances which make any change but a violent one impossible. First, for coercive rule to have been practicable, implies in the people a predominance of that awe of power ever indicative of still lingering savageness. Moreover, with a large amount of power worship present, disaffection can take place only when the cumulative evils of misgovernment have generated great exasperation. Add to which that as abundance of the sentiment upholding external rule involves lack of the sentiments producing internal rule, no such check to excesses as that afforded by a due regard for the lives and claims of others can be operative. And where there are comparatively active destructive propensities, extreme anger, and deficient self-restraint, violence is inevitable. Peaceful revolutions occur under quite different circumstances. They become possible only when society, no longer consisting of members so antagonistic, begins to cohere from its own internal organization and need not be kept together by unyielding external restraints; and when, by consequence, the force required to effect change is less. They become possible only when men, having acquired greater adaptation to the social state, will neither inflict on each other nor submit to such extreme oppressions, and when, therefore, the causes of popular indignation are diminished. They become possible only when character has grown more sympathetic and when, as a result of this, the tendency toward angry retaliation is partially neutralized. Indeed, the very idea that reforms may and ought to be effected peacefully implies a large endowment of the moral sense. Without this, such an idea cannot even be conceived, much less carried out; with this, it may be both.

Hence, we must look upon social convulsions as upon other natural phenomena which work themselves out in a certain inevitable, unalterable way. We may lament the bloodshed—may wish it had been avoided; but it is folly to suppose that, the popular character remaining the same, things could have been managed differently. If such-and-such events had not occurred, say you, the result would have been otherwise; if this or that man had lived, he would have prevented the catastrophe. Do not be thus deceived. These changes are brought about by a power far above individual wills. Men who seem the prime movers are merely the tools with which it works; and were they absent, it would quickly find others. Incongruity between character and institutions is the disturbing force, and a revolution is the act of restoring equilibrium. Accidental circumstances modify the process but do not perceptibly alter the effect. They precipitate; they retard; they intensify or ameliorate; but, let a few years elapse, and the same end is arrived at, no matter what the special events passed through.

That these violent overturnings of early institutions fail to do what their originators hope, and that they finally result in the setting up of institutions not much better than those superseded, is very true (p. 219). But it is not the less true that the modifications they effect can be effected in no other way. Non-adaptation necessitates a bad mode of making changes as well as a bad political organization. Not only must the habitual rule it calls for be severe, but even small ameliorations of this cannot be obtained without much suffering. Conversely, the same causes which render a better social state possible render the successive modifications of it easier. These occur under less pressure, with smaller disturbance, and more frequently; until, by a gradual diminution in the amounts and intervals of change, the process merges into one of uninterrupted growth.

**11.** THERE IS ANOTHER FORM UNDER WHICH CIVILIZATION CAN be generalized. We may consider it as a progress toward that constitution of man and society required for the complete manifestation of everyone's individuality. To be that which he naturally is—to do just what he would spontaneously do—is essential to the full happiness of each, and therefore to the greatest happiness of all. Hence, in virtue of the law of adaptation, our advance must be toward a state in which this entire satisfaction of every desire, or perfect fulfillment of individual life, becomes possible. In the beginning it is impossible. If uncontrolled, the impulses of the aboriginal man produce anarchy. Either his individuality must be curbed or society must dissolve. With ourselves, though restraint is still needful, the private will of the citizen, not being so destructive of order, has more play. And further progress must be toward increased sacredness of personal claims and a subordination of whatever limits them.

There are plenty of facts illustrating the doctrine that under primitive governments the repression of individuality is greatest, and that it becomes less as we advance. Referring to the people of Egypt, Assyria, China, and Hindustan, as contrasted with those of Greece, Mr. Grote says, "The religious and political sanction, sometimes combined and sometimes separate, determined for every one his mode of life, his creed, his duties, and his place in society, without leaving any scope for the will or reason of the individual himself." The ownership of people by rulers, from its pure form under Darius, through its various modifications down to the time of "*L'état c'est moi*," and as even still typified among ourselves in the expression, "my subjects," must be considered as a greater or less merging of many individualities into one. The parallel relationships of slaves or serfs to their master, and of the family to its head, have implied the same thing. In short, all despotisms, whether political or religious, whether of sex, of caste, or of custom, may be generalized as limitations of individuality, which it is in the nature of civilization to remove.

Of course, in advancing from the one extreme, in which the state is everything and the individual nothing, to the other extreme, in which the individual is everything and the state nothing, society must pass through many intermediate phases. Aristocracy and democracy are not, as they have been called, separate and conflicting principles; but they and their various mixtures with each other and with monarchy mark the stages in this progress toward complete individuality. Nor is it only by amelioration of governmental forms that the growth of private claims as opposed to public ones is shown. It is shown, too, by the alteration in voluntary unions—in political parties, for instance; the manifest tendency of which is toward dissolution, by internal divisions, by diminution of power over their members, by increasing heterogeneity of opinion—that is, by the spread of a personal independence fatal to them. Still better do the changes in religious organizations illustrate this law. That multiplication of sects which has been going on in these latter times with increasing rapidity, and which is now so abundantly exemplified by the severing of the Establishment into Evangelical, High Church, and Puseyite; again, by the Free

Church secession; again, by the schism of the Methodists; again, by Unitarian differences; again, by the splitting off of numberless local congregations not to be classed; and, again, by the preaching that identity of opinion should not be the bond of union—the universal tendency to separate thus exhibited is simply one of the ways in which a growing assertion of individuality comes out. Ultimately, by continual subdivision, what we call sects will disappear; and in place of that artificial uniformity, obtained by stamping men after an authorized pattern, there will arise one of nature's uniformities—a general similarity, with infinitesimal differences.

**12.** FROM THE POINT OF VIEW NOW ARRIVED AT, WE MAY DIScern how what is termed in our artificial classifications of truth *morality* is essentially one with physical truth—is, in fact, a species of transcendental physiology. That condition of things dictated by the law of equal freedom; that condition in which the individuality of each may be unfolded without limit, save the like individualities of others; that condition toward which, as we have just seen, mankind is progressing, is a condition toward which the whole creation tends. Already it has been incidentally pointed out that only by entire fulfillment of the moral law can life become complete (p. 156); and now we shall find that all life whatever may be defined as a quality, of which aptitude to fulfill this law is the highest manifestation.

A theory of life developed by Coleridge has prepared the way for this generalization. "By life," says he, "I everywhere mean the true idea of life, or that most general form under which life manifests itself to us, which includes all other forms. This I have stated to be the *tendency to individuation*; and the degrees or intensities of life to consist in the progressive realizations of this tendency." To make this definition intelligible, a few of the facts sought to be expressed by it must be specified—facts exemplifying the contrast between low and high types of structure, and low and high degrees of vitality.

Restricting our illustrations to the animal kingdom, and beginning where the vital attributes are most obscure, we find, for instance, in the genus *Porifera* creatures consisting of nothing but amorphous semi-fluid jelly, supported upon horny fibers (sponge). This jelly possesses no sensitiveness, has no organs, absorbs nutriment from the water which permeates its mass, and, if cut in pieces, lives on, in each part, as before. So that this "gelatinous film," as it has been called, shows little more individuality than a formless lump of inanimate matter, for, like that, it possesses no distinction of parts, and, like that also, has no greater completeness than the pieces it is divided into. In the compound polyps which stand next, and with which Coleridge commences, the progress toward individuality is manifest, for there is now distinction of parts. To the originally uniform gelatinous mass with canals running through it, we have superadded, in the *Alcyonidae*, a number of digestive sacks, with accompanying mouths and tentacles. Here is, evidently, a partial segregation into individualities—a progress toward separateness. There is still complete community of nutrition, while each polyp has a certain independent sensitiveness and contractility. From this stage onward there appear to be several routes; one through the *Corallidae*, in which the polyp-bearing mass surrounds a calcareous axis, up to the *Tubiporidae*, in which the polyps, no longer united, inhabit separate cells, seated in a common calcareous framework. But Coleridge has overlooked the remarkable mode in which these communist polyps are linked with higher individual organisms by the transitional arrangement seen in the common *Hydrae*, or fresh-water polyps of our ponds. These creatures (which are in structure similar to the separate members of the compound animal above described) multiply by gemmation—that is, by the budding out of young ones from the body of the parent. "During the first period of the formation of these sprouts, they are evidently continuous with the general substance from which they arise; and even when considerably perfected, and possessed of an internal cavity and tentacula, their stomachs freely communicate with that of their parent. . . . As soon as the newly-formed hydra is capable of catching prey, it begins to contribute to the support of its parent; the food which it captures passing through the aperture at its base into the body of the original polyp. At length, when the young is fully formed, and ripe for independent existence, the point of union between the two becomes more and more slender, until a slight effort on the part of either is sufficient to detach them, and the process is completed. . . . Sometimes six or seven gemmæ have been observed to sprout at once from the same hydra; and although the whole process is concluded in twenty-four hours, not unfrequently a third generation may be observed springing from the newly-formed polyps even before their separation from their parent; eighteen have in this manner been seen united into one group."[4] Now here is a creature which cannot be strictly called either simple or compound. Nominally, it is an individual; practically, it never is so. In the alcyonide polyp many individuals are permanently united together; in this genus they are temporarily united, in so far as particular individuals are concerned, but otherwise permanently so; for there is always a group, though that group keeps changing its members. Indeed, may we not say that the "tendency to individuation" is here most visible; seeing that the Hydrae are, as it were, perpetually striving to become individuals, without succeeding? And may we not further say that in the gradually decreasing recurrence of this budding, and the simultaneous appearance of a higher method of reproduction by ova (which in the Bryozoa coexists with a comparatively languid gemmation), this "tendency to individuation" is still further manifested?

After complete separateness of organisms has been arrived at, the law is still seen in successive improvements of structure. By greater individuality of parts, by greater distinctness in the nature and functions of these, are all creatures possessing high vitality distinguished from inferior ones. Those Hydrae just referred to, which are mere bags, with tentacles round the orifice, may be turned inside out with impunity: the stomach becomes skin, and the skin stomach. Here, then, is evidently no specialty of character; the duties of stomach and skin are performed by one tissue, which is not yet individualized into two separate parts, adapted to separate ends. The contrast between this state and that in which such a distinction exists will suffi-

[4] A General Outline of the Animal Kingdom, by Professor T. R. Jones, F.G.S.

ciently explain what is meant by individuation of organs. How clearly this individuation of organs is traceable throughout the whole range of animal life may be seen in the successive forms which the nervous system assumes. Thus, in the *Acrita*, a class comprehending all the genera above mentioned, "no nervous filaments or masses have been discovered, and the neurine or nervous matter is supposed to be diffused in a molecular condition through the body."[5] In the class next above this, the *Nematoneura*, we find the first step toward individuation of "the nervous system: the nervous matter is distinctly aggregated into filaments."[6] In the *Homogangliata*, it is still further concentrated into a number of small equal-sized masses—ganglia. In the *Heterogangliata*, some of these small masses are collected together into larger ones. Finally, in the *Vertebrata*, the greater part of the nervous centers are united to form a brain. And with the rest of the body there has simultaneously taken place just the same process of condensation into distinct systems—muscular, respiratory, nutritive, excretive, absorbent, circulatory, etc.—and of these again into separate parts, with special functions.

The changes of vital manifestation associated with and consequent upon these changes of structure have the same significance. To possess a greater variety of senses, of instincts, of powers, of qualities—to be more complex in character and attributes—is to be more completely distinguishable from all other created things; or to exhibit a more marked individuality. For, manifestly, as there are some properties which all entities, organic and inorganic, have in common; namely, weight, mobility, inertia, etc.; and as there are additional properties which all organic entities have in common; namely, powers of growth and multiplication; and as there are yet further properties which the higher organic entities have in common; namely, sight, hearing, etc.; then those still higher organic entities possessing characteristics not shared in by the rest thereby differ from a larger number of entities than the rest, and differ in more points—that is, are more separate, more individual. Ob-

[5]*Ibid.*
[6]*Ibid.*

serve, again, that the greater power of self-preservation shown by beings of superior type may also be generalized under this same term—a "tendency to individuation." The lower the organism, the more is it at the mercy of external circumstances. It is continually liable to be destroyed by the elements, by want of food, by enemies; and eventually is so destroyed in nearly all cases. That is, it lacks power to preserve its individuality, and loses this either by returning to the form of inorganic matter or by absorption into some other individuality. Conversely, where there is strength, sagacity, swiftness (all of them indicative of superior structure), there is corresponding ability to maintain life, to prevent the individuality from being so easily dissolved, and therefore the individuation is more complete.

In man we see the highest manifestation of this tendency. By virtue of his complexity of structure, he is furthest removed from the inorganic world in which there is least individuality. Again, his intelligence and adaptability commonly enable him to maintain life to old age—to complete the cycle of his existence; that is, to fill out the limits of this individuality to the full. Again, he is self-conscious; that is, he recognizes his own individuality. And, as lately shown, even the change observable in human affairs, is still toward a greater development of individuality—may still be described as "a tendency to individuation."

But note lastly, and note chiefly, as being the fact to which the foregoing sketch is introductory, that what we call the moral law—the law of equal freedom—is the law under which individuation becomes perfect, and that ability to recognize and act up to this law is the final endowment of humanity—an endowment now in process of evolution. The increasing assertion of personal rights is an increasing demand that the external conditions needful to a complete unfolding of the individuality shall be respected. Not only is there now a consciousness of individuality and an intelligence whereby individuality may be preserved, but there is a perception that the sphere of action requisite for due development of the individuality may be claimed, and a correlative desire to claim it. And when the change at present going on is complete—when each possesses

an active instinct of freedom, together with an active sympathy
—then will all the still existing limitations to individuality, be
they governmental restraints or be they the aggressions of men
on one another, cease. Then none will be hindered from duly
unfolding their natures; for while everyone maintains his own
claims, he will respect the like claims of others. Then there
will no longer be legislative restrictions and legislative burdens;
for by the same process these will have become both needless
and impossible. Then for the first time in the history of the
world will there exist beings whose individualities can be ex-
panded to the full in all directions. And thus, as before said, in
the ultimate man perfect morality, perfect individuation, and
perfect life will be simultaneously realized.

**13.** YET MUST THIS HIGHEST INDIVIDUATION BE JOINED WITH
the greatest mutual dependence. Paradoxical though the assertion looks, the progress is at once toward complete separateness
and complete union. But the separateness is of a kind consistent
with the most complex combinations for fulfilling social wants;
and the union is of a kind that does not hinder entire development of each personality. Civilization is evolving a state of
things and a kind of character in which two apparently conflicting requirements are reconciled. To achieve the creative
purpose—the greatest sum of happiness—there must on the one
hand exist an amount of population maintainable only by the
best possible system of production; that is, by the most elaborate subdivision of labor; that is, by the extremest mutual dependence: while on the other hand, each individual must have
the opportunity to do whatever his desires prompt. Clearly
these two conditions can be harmonized only by that adaptation humanity is undergoing—that process during which all
desires inconsistent with the most perfect social organization
are dying out and other desires corresponding to such an organization are being developed. How this will eventuate in producing at once perfect individuation and perfect mutual dependence may not be at once obvious. But probably an illustration
will sufficiently elucidate the matter. Here are certain domestic
affections which can be gratified only by the establishment of

relationships with other beings. In the absence of those beings, and the consequent dormancy of the feelings with which they are regarded, life is incomplete—the individuality is shorn of its fair proportions. Now as the normal unfolding of the conjugal and parental elements of the individuality depends on having a family, so, when civilization becomes complete, will the normal unfolding of all other elements of the individuality depend upon the existence of the civilized state. Just that kind of individuality will be acquired which finds in the most highly organized community the fittest sphere for its manifestation, which finds in each social arrangement a condition answering to some faculty in itself, which could not, in fact, expand at all if otherwise circumstanced. The ultimate man will be one whose private requirements coincide with public ones. He will be that manner of man who, in spontaneously fulfilling his own nature, incidentally performs the functions of a social unit, and yet is only enabled so to fulfill his own nature by all others doing the like.

**14.** HOW TRULY, INDEED, HUMAN PROGRESS IS TOWARD GREATER mutual dependence, as well as toward greater individuation, how truly the welfare of each is daily more involved in the welfare of all, and how truly, therefore, it is the interest of each to respect the interests of all may, with advantage, be illustrated at length, for it is a fact of which many seem woefully ignorant. Men cannot break that vital law of the social organism—the law of equal freedom—without penalties in some way or other coming round to them. Being themselves members of the community, they are affected by whatever affects it. Upon the goodness or badness of its state depends the greater or less efficiency with which it administers to their wants, and the less or greater amount of evil it inflicts upon them. Through those vicious arrangements that hourly gall them, they feel the cumulative result of all sins against the social law, their own sins included. And they suffer for these sins, not only in extra restraints and alarms, but in the extra labor and expense required to compass their ends.

That every trespass produces a reaction, partly general and partly special—a reaction which is extreme in proportion as the trespass is great—has been more or less noticed in all ages. Thus the remark is as old as the time of Thales, that tyrants rarely die natural deaths. From his day to ours, the thrones of the East have been continually stained with the blood of their successive occupants. The early histories of all European states and the recent history of Russia illustrate the same fact; and if we are to judge by his habits, the present Czar lives in constant fear of assassination. Nor is it true that those who bear universal sway and seem able to do as they please can really do so. They limit their own freedom in limiting that of others; their despotism recoils and puts them also in bondage. We read, for instance, that the Roman emperors were the puppets of their soldiers. "In the Byzantine palace," says Gibbon, "the emperor was the first slave of the ceremonies he imposed." Speaking of the tedious etiquette of the time of Louis le Grand, Madame de Maintenon remarks, "Save those only who fill the highest stations, I know of none more unfortunate than those who envy them. If you could only form an idea of what it is!" The same reaction is felt by slave owners. Some of the West India planters have acknowledged that before Negro emancipation they were the greatest slaves on their estates. The Americans, too, are shackled in various ways by their own injustice. In the South, the whites are self-coerced, that they may coerce the blacks. Marriage with one of the mixed race is forbidden; there is a slave-owning qualification for senators; a man may not liberate his own slaves without leave; and only at the risk of lynching dare any one say a word in favor of abolition.

It is indeed becoming clear to most that these gross transgressions return upon the perpetrators—that "this even-handed justice commends the ingredients of our poisoned chalice to our own lips"; but it is not yet clear to them that the like is true of those lesser transgressions they are themselves guilty of. Probably the modern maintainers of class power can see well enough that their feudal ancestors paid somewhat dearly for keeping the masses in thralldom. They can see that, what with armor and hidden mail, what with sliding panels, secret passages, dimly lighted rooms, precautions against poison, and constant fears of surprise and treachery, these barons had but uncomfortable lives of it at the best. They can see how delusive was the notion that the greatest wealth was to be obtained by making serfs of the people. They can see that in Jacqueries and Gallician massacres, when bondsmen glut their vengeance by burning castles and slaughtering the inmates, there arrive fatal settlements of long-standing balances. But they cannot see that their own inequitable deeds, in one way or other, come home to them. Just as these feudal nobles mistook the evils they suffered under for unalterable ordinations of nature, never dreaming that they were the reflex results of tyranny, so do their descendants fail to perceive that many of their own unhappinesses are similarly generated.

And yet, while in some cases it is scarcely possible to trace the secret channels through which our misbehavior to others returns upon us, there are other cases in which the reaction is palpable. An audience rushing out of a theater on fire, and in their eagerness to get before each other jamming up the doorway so that no one can get through, offers a good example of unjust selfishness defeating itself. An analogous result may be witnessed at the American ordinaries, where the attempts of greedy guests to get more than a fair share have generated a competition in fast eating which not only frustrates these attempts but entails on all immediate loss of enjoyment and permanent ill-health. In such cases it is clear enough that by trespassing upon the claims of others men hurt themselves also. The reaction is here direct and immediate. In all other cases, however, reaction is equally sure, though it may come round by some circuitous route, or after a considerable lapse of time, or in an unrecognized form. The country squire who thinks it a piece of profound policy to clear his estate of cottages, that he may saddle some other place with the paupers, forgets that landowners in neighboring parishes will eventually defeat him by doing the same; or that if he is so situated as to settle his laborers upon towns, the walking of extra miles to and fro must gradually lower the standard of a day's work, raise the cost of cultivation, and, in the end, decrease rent. Nor does he see that by the overcrowded bedrooms and neg-

lected drainage and repairs to which this policy leads, he is
generating debility or disease and raising his poors' rates in one
way, while he lowers them in another. The Dorsetshire farmer
who pays wages in tailings of wheat charged above market price
imagines he is economizing. It never occurs to him that he loses
more than the difference by petty thefts, by the destruction of
his hedges for fuel, by the consequent pounding of his cattle,
and by the increase of county rates, for the prosecution of rob-
bers and poachers. It seems very clear to the tradesman that all
extra profit made by adulterating goods is so much pure gain;
and for a while, perhaps, it may be. By and by, however, his
competitors do as he does—are in a measure compelled to do so
—and the rate of profit is then brought down to what it was
before. Meanwhile the general practice of adulteration has been
encouraged, has got into other departments, has deteriorated the
articles our shopkeeper buys; and thus, in his capacity of consumer, he suffers from the vicious system he has helped to
strengthen. When during Negro apprenticeship the West India
planters had to value slaves who wished to buy themselves off
before "the Queen's free," they no doubt thought it cunning to
make oath to a higher worth per day than the true one. But
when, a while after, having to pay wages, they had their own
estimates quoted to them and found that the Negroes would
take nothing less, they probably repented of their dishonesty. It
is often long before these recoils come; but they do come, nevertheless. See how the Irish landlords are at length being punished
for their rack-renting, their evictions, their encouragement of
middlemen, and their utter recklessness of popular welfare.
Note, too, how for having abetted those who wronged the
native Irish, England has to pay a penalty, in the shape of loans
which are not refunded and in the misery produced by the
swarms of indigent immigrants, who tend to bring down her
own people to their level. Thus, be they committed by many or
by few—be they seen in efforts to despoil foreigners by restric-
tive duties or in a tradesman's trickeries—breaches of equity are
uniformly self-defeating. While men continue social units, they
cannot transgress the life principle of society without disastrous
consequences somehow or other coming back upon them.

**15.** NOT ONLY DOES THE ULTIMATE WELFARE OF THE CITIZEN DE-
mand that he should himself conform to the moral law; it
equally concerns him that everyone should conform to it. This
interdependence which the social state necessitates makes all
men's business his business, in a more or less indirect way. To
people whose eyes do not wander beyond their ledgers, it seems
of no consequence how the affairs of mankind go. They think
they know better than to trouble themselves with public matters, making enemies and damaging their trade. Yet if they are
indeed so selfish as to care nothing about their fellow creatures,
while their own fleshpots are well filled, let them learn that they
have pounds, shillings, and pence interest at stake. Mere pocket
prudence should induce them to further human welfare, if no
higher motive will. To help in putting things on a juster footing
will eventually pay. The diffusion of sound principles and the
improvement of public morality end in diminishing household
expenses. Can they not see that when buying meat and bread
and groceries they have to give something toward maintaining
prisons and police? Can they not see that in the price of a coat
they are charged a large percentage to cover the tailor's bad
debts? Every transaction of their lives is in some way hampered
by the general immorality. They feel it in the rate of interest
demanded for capital, which (neglecting temporary variations)
is high in proportion as men are bad.[7] They feel it in the amount
of attorneys' bills; or in having to suffer robbery, lest the law
should commit on them greater robbery. They feel it in their
share of the two and a half millions a year which our metallic
currency costs. They feel it in those collapses of trade which
follow extensive gambling speculations. It seems to them an
absurd waste of time to help in spreading independence among
men; and yet, did they call to mind how those railway shares
which they bought at a premium went down to a ruinous discount because the directors cringed to a rich bully, they would
learn that the prevalence of a manly spirit may become of

[7]When dishonesty and improvidence are extreme, capital cannot be had
under 30 to 40 per cent, as in the Burmese empire, or in England, in the
time of King John.—See Mill's *Political Economy*.

money value to them. They suppose themselves unconcerned in the quarrels of neighboring nations; and yet, on examination, they will find that a Hungarian war, by the loans it calls for, or a Danish blockade by its influence upon our commerce, more or less remotely affects their profits in whatever secluded nook of England they may live. Their belief is that they are not at all interested in the good government of India; and yet a little reflection would show them that they continually suffer from those fluctuations of trade consequent upon the irregular and insufficient supply of cotton from America—fluctuations which would probably have ceased had not India been exhausted by its rulers' extravagance. Not interested? Why, even the better education of the Chinese is of moment to them, for Chinese prejudice shuts out English merchants. Not interested? Why, they have a stake in the making of American railways and canals, for these ultimately affect the price of bread in England. Not interested? Why, the accumulation of wealth by every people on the face of the earth concerns them; for while it is the law of capital to overflow from those places where it is abundant to those where it is scarce, rich nations can never fully enjoy the fruits of their own labor until other nations are equally rich. The well ordering of human affairs in the remotest and most insignificant communities is beneficial to all men; the ill ordering of them calamitous to all men. And though the citizen may be but slightly acted upon by each particular good or evil influence at work within his own society, and still more slightly by each of those at work within other societies—although the effect on him may be infinitesimal, yet it is on the cumulative result of myriads of these infinitesimal influences that his happiness or misery depends.

**16.** STILL MORE CLEARLY SEEN IS THIS ULTIMATE IDENTITY OF personal interests and social interests when we discover how essentially *vital* is the connection between each person and the society of which he is a unit. We commonly enough compare a nation to a living organism. We speak of "the body politic," of the functions of its several parts, of its growth, and of its diseases, as though it were a creature. But we usually employ these expressions as metaphors, little suspecting how close is the analogy and how far it will bear carrying out. So completely, however, is a society organized upon the same system as an individual being, that we may almost say there is something more than analogy between them. Let us look at a few of the facts.

Observe first that the parallel gains immensely in reasonableness when we learn that the human body is itself compounded of innumerable microscopic organisms, which possess a kind of independent vitality, which grow by imbibing nutriment from the circulating fluids, and which multiply, as the infusorial monads do, by spontaneous fission. The whole process of development, beginning with the first change in the ovum and ending with the production of an adult man, is fundamentally a perpetual increase in the number of these cells by the mode of fissiparous generation. On the other hand, that gradual decay witnessed in old age is in essence a cessation of this increase. During health the vitality of these cells is subordinated to that of the system at large; and the presence of insubordinate cells implies disease. Thus, smallpox arises from the intrusion of a species of cell foreign to that community of cells of which the body consists, and which, absorbing nourishment from the blood, rapidly multiplies by spontaneous division until its progeny have diffused themselves throughout the tissues; and if the excreting energies of the constitution fail to get rid of these aliens, death ensues. In certain states of body, indigenous cells will take on new forms of life, and by continuing to reproduce their like give origin to parasitic growths, such as cancer. Under the microscope, cancer can be identified by a specific element known as the cancer cell. Besides those modifications of cell vitality which constitute malignant diseases, there occasionally happens another in which cells, without any change in their essential nature, rebel against the general governing force of the system; and instead of ceasing to grow, while yet invisible to the naked eye, expand to a considerable size, sometimes even reaching several inches in diameter. These are called *Hydatids* or *Acephalocysts*,[8] and have, until lately, been taken for internal

[8]"The primitive forms of all tissues are free cells, which grow by imbibition, and which develop their like from their nucleus of hyaline. All the animal tissues result from transformations of these cells. It is to such cells

parasites or entozoa. Still closer appears the relationship between tissue cells and the lowest independent organisms, on
finding that there exists a creature called the Gregarina, very
similar in structure to the Hydatid, but which is admitted to be
an entozoon. Consisting as it does of a cell membrane enclosing
fluid and a solid nucleus, and multiplying as it does by the spontaneous fission of this nucleus and subsequent division of the
cell walls, the Gregarina differs from a tissue-cell merely in size,
and in not forming part of the organ containing it.[9] Thus there

that the acephalocyst bears the closest analogies in physical, chemical, and
vital properties. . . . We may, with some truth, say that the human body
is primarily composed or built up of acephalocysts; microscopical, indeed,
and which, under natural and healthy conditions, are metamorphosed into
cartilage, bone, nerve, muscular fibre, etc. When, instead of such change,
the organic cells grow to dimensions which make them recognizable to the
naked eye, such development of acephalocysts, as they are then called, is
commonly connected in the human subject with an enfeeblement of the
controlling plastic force, which, at some of the weaker points of the frame,
seems unable to direct the metamorphosis of the primitive cells along the
right road to the tissues they were destined to form, but permits them to
retain, as it were, their embryo condition, and to grow by the imbibition of
the surrounding fluid, and thus become the means of injuriously affecting or
destroying the tissues which they should have supported and repaired. I
regard the different Acephalocysts, therefore, as merely so many forms or
species of morbid or dropsical cells."—Professor Owen's Hunterian Lectures.

[9]"Schleiden has viewed these Gregarinæ as essentially single organic cells,
and would refer them to the lowest group of plants. And here, indeed, we
have a good instance of the essential unity of the organic division of matter.
It is only the power of self-contraction of tissue, and its solubility in acetic
acid, which turn the scale in favour of the animality of the Gregarinæ; they
have no mouth and no stomach, which have commonly been deemed the
most constant organic characteristics of an animal.

"1846, Henle and others have questioned the title of the Gregarina to be
regarded as an organic species or individual at all, or as any thing more than
a monstrous cell: thus applying it to my idea, propounded in 1843, of the
true nature of the acephalocyst.

"1848, Kollicker has recently published an elaborate memoir on the
genus, in which good and sufficient grounds are given for concluding that
the Gregarina not merely resembles, but actually is an animated cell; it
stands on the lowest step of the animal series, parallel with that of the
single-celled species of the vegetable kingdom. The Gregarina consists, as
Schleiden and others have well shown, of a cell-membrane, of the fluid and
granular contents of the cell, and of the nucleus with (occasional) nucleoli.
The nucleus is the hardest part, resisting pressure longest, like that of the
Polygastrian. It divides, and its division is followed by spontaneous fission."
—Ibid.

may coexist in the same organism cells of which that organism is constituted others which should have helped to build it up but which are subordinate or partially separate, and others which are naturally separate and simply reside in its cavities. Hence we are warranted in considering the body as a commonwealth of monads, each of which has independent powers of life, growth, and reproduction; each of which unites with a number of others to perform some function needful for supporting itself and all the rest; and each of which absorbs its share of nutriment from the blood. And when thus regarded, the analogy between an individual being and a human society, in which each man, while helping to subserve some public want, absorbs a portion of the circulating stock of commodities brought to his door, is palpable enough.

A still more remarkable fulfillment of this analogy is to be found in the fact that the different kinds of organization which society takes on in progressing from its lowest to its highest phase of development are essentially similar to the different kinds of animal organization. Creatures of inferior type are little more than aggregations of numerous like parts—are molded on what Professor Owen terms the principle of vegetative repetition; and in tracing the forms assumed by successive grades above these, we find a gradual diminution in the number of like parts and a multiplication of unlike ones. In the one extreme there are but few functions, and many similar agents to each function; in the other, there are many functions, and few similar agents to each function. Thus the visual apparatus in a fly consists of two groups of fixed lenses, numbering in some species 20,000. Every one of these lenses produces an image; but as its field of view is extremely narrow, and as there exists no power of adaptation to different distances, the vision obtained is probably very imperfect. While the mammal, on the other hand, possesses but two eyes, each of these includes numerous appendages. It is compounded of several lenses, having different forms and duties. These lenses are capable of various focal adjustments. There are muscles for directing them to the right and to the left, to the ground and to the sky. There is a curtain (the iris) to regulate the quantity of light admitted. There is a gland

to secrete, a tube to pour out, and a drain to carry off the lubri-
cating fluid. There is a lid to wipe the surface, and there are
lashes to give warning on the approach of foreign bodies. Now
the contrast between these two kinds of visual organ is the contrast between all lower and higher types of structure. If we
examine the framework employed to support the tissues, we find
it consisting in the *Annelida* (the common worm, for instance)
of an extended series of rings. In the *Myriapoda*, which stand
next above the *Annelida*, these rings are less numerous and
more dense. In the higher *Myriapoda* they are united into a
comparatively few large and strong segments, while in the
*Insecta* this condensation is carried still further. Speaking of
analogous changes in the crustaceans, the lowest of which is
constructed much as the centipede, and the highest of which
(the crab) has nearly all its segments united, Professor Jones
says, "And even the steps whereby we pass from the Annelidan
to the Myriapod, and from thence to the Insect, the Scorpion,
and the Spider, seem to be repeated as we thus review the progressive development of the class before us." Mark again that
these modifications of the exo-skeleton are completely paralleled
by those of the endo-skeleton. The vertebra are numerous in fish
and in the ophidian reptiles. They are less numerous in the
higher reptiles; less numerous still in the quadrupeds; fewest of
all in man: and while their number is diminished, their forms
and the functions of their appendages are varied, instead of
being, as in the eel, nearly all alike. Thus, also, is it with loco-
motive organs. The spines of the echinus and the suckers of the
star fish are multitudinous. So likewise are the legs of the centipede. In the crustaceans we come down to fourteen, twelve, and
ten; in the arachnidans and insects to eight and six; in the lower
mammalia to four; and in man to two. The successive modifications of the digestive cavity are of analogous nature. Its lowest
forms is that of a sack with but one opening. Next it is a tube
with two openings having different offices. And in higher creatures, this tube, instead of being made up of absorbents from
end to end—that is, instead of being an aggregation of like parts
—is modified into many unlike ones, having different structures
adapted to the different stages into which the assimilative func-

tion is now divided. Even the classification under which man, as forming the genus *Bimana*, is distinguished from the most nearly related genus *Quadrumana* is based on a diminution in the number of organs that have similar forms and duties.

Now just this same coalescence of like parts and separation of unlike ones—just this same increasing subdivision of functions—takes place in the development of society. The earliest social organisms consist almost wholly of repetitions of one element. Every man is a warrior, hunter, fisherman, builder, agriculturist, toolmaker. Each portion of the community performs the same duties with every other portion; much as each portion of the polyp's body is alike stomach, skin, and lungs. Even the chiefs, in whom a tendency toward separateness of function first appears, still retain their similarity to the rest in economic respects. The next stage is distinguished by a segregation of these social units into a few distinct classes—soldiers, priests, and laborers. A further advance is seen in the sundering of these laborers into different castes having special occupations, as among the Hindus. And, without further illustration, the reader will at once perceive that from these inferior types of society up to our own complicated and more perfect one the progress has ever been of the same nature. While he will also perceive that this coalescence of like parts, as seen in the concentration of particular manufactures in particular districts, and this separation of agents having separate functions, as seen in the more and more minute division of labor, are still going on.

Significant of the alleged analogy is the further fact consequent upon the above, that the sensitiveness exhibited by societies of low and high structure differs in degree, as does the sensitiveness of similarly contrasted creatures. That peculiar faculty possessed by inferior organisms of living on in each part after being cut in pieces is a manifest corollary to the other peculiarity just described; namely, that they consist of many repetitions of the same elements. The ability of the several portions into which a polyp has been divided to grow into complete polyps obviously implies that each portion contains all the organs needful to life; and each portion can be thus constituted only when those organs recur in every part of the original body.

Conversely, the reason why any member of a more highly organized being cannot live when separated from the rest is that it does not include all the vital elements but is dependent for its supplies of nutriment, nervous energy, oxygen, etc., upon the members from which it has been cut off. Of course, then, the earliest and latest forms of society, being similarly distinguished in structure, will be similarly distinguished in susceptibility of injury. Hence it happens that a tribe of savages may be divided and subdivided with little or no inconvenience to the several sections. Each of these contains every element which the whole did—is just as self-sufficing and quickly assumes the simple organization constituting an independent tribe. Hence, on the contrary, it happens that in a community like our own no part can be cut off or injured without all parts suffering. Annihilate the agency employed in distributing commodities, and much of the rest would die before another distributing agency could be developed. Suddenly sever the manufacturing portion from the agricultural portion, and the one would expire outright, while the other would long linger in grievous distress. This interdependence is daily shown in commercial changes. Let the factory hands be put on short time, and immediately the colonial produce markets of London and Liverpool are depressed. The shopkeeper is busy or otherwise, according to the amount of the wheat crop. And a potato blight may ruin dealers in consols.

Thus do we find not only that the analogy between a society and a living creature is borne out to a degree quite unsuspected by those who commonly draw it, but also that the same definition of life applies to both. This union of many men into one community, this increasing mutual dependence of units which were originally independent, this gradual segregation of citizens into separate bodies with reciprocally subservient functions, this formation of a whole consisting of numerous essential parts, this growth of an organism of which one portion cannot be injured without the rest feeling it, may all be generalized under the law of individuation. The development of society, as well as the development of man and the development of life generally, may be described as a tendency to individuate—*to become a thing*. And rightly interpreted, the manifold forms of progress going on around us are uniformly significant of this tendency.

Returning now to the point whence we set out, the fact that public interests and private ones are essentially in unison cannot fail to be more vividly realized when so vital a connection is found to subsist between society and its members. Though it would be dangerous to place implicit trust in conclusions founded upon the analogy just traced, yet harmonizing as they do with conclusions deducible from everyday experience, they unquestionably enforce these. When, after observing the reactions entailed by breaches of equity, the citizen contemplates the relation in which he stands to the body politic; when he learns that it has a species of life and conforms to the same laws of growth, organization, and sensibility that a being does; when he finds that one vitality circulates through it and him, and that while social health, in a measure, depends upon the fulfillment of some function in which he takes part, his happiness depends upon the normal action of every organ in the social body—when he duly understands this, he must see that his own welfare and all men's welfare are inseparable. He must see that whatever produces a diseased state in one part of the community must inevitably inflict injury upon all other parts. He must see that his own life can become what it should be only as fast as society becomes what it should be. In short, he must become impressed with the salutary truth that no one can be perfectly free till all are free; no one can be perfectly moral till all are moral; no one can be perfectly happy till all are happy.

CHAPTER XXXI

## Summary

**1.** BY BRINGING WITHIN NARROW COMPASS THE EVIDENCES THAT have been adduced in support of the Theory of Equity now before him, the reader will be aided in coming to a final judgment upon it.

At the head of these evidences stands the fact that, from

whatever side we commence the investigation, our paths alike
converge toward the principle of which this theory is a development. If we start with an a priori inquiry into the conditions
under which alone the Divine Idea—greatest happiness—can be
realized, we find that conformity to the law of equal freedom is
the first of them (Chapter III). If, turning to man's constitution, we consider the means provided for achieving greatest
happiness, we quickly reason our way back to this same condition, seeing that these means cannot work out their end unless
the law of equal freedom is submitted to (Chapter IV). If, pursuing the analysis a step further, we examine how subordination
to the law of equal freedom is secured, we discover certain faculties by which that law is responded to (Chapter V). If, again,
we contemplate the phenomena of civilization, we perceive that
the process of adaptation under which they may be generalized
can never cease until men have become instinctively obedient to
this same law of equal freedom (Chapter II). To all which positive proofs may also be added the negative one, that to deny this
law of equal freedom is to assert divers absurdities (Chapter
VI).

**2.** FURTHER CONFIRMATION MAY BE FOUND IN THE CIRCUMSTANCE
that pre-existing theories which are untenable as they stand are
yet absorbed, and the portion of truth contained in them assimi-
lated, by the theory now proposed. Thus the production of the
greatest happiness, though inapplicable as an immediate guide
for men, is nevertheless the true end of morality, regarded from
the Divine point of view, and as such forms part of the present
system (Chapter III). The moral-sense principle, also, while
misapplied by its propounders, is still based on fact; and, as was
shown, harmonizes, when rightly interpreted, with what seem
conflicting beliefs, and unites with them to produce a complete
whole. Add to this that the philosophy now contended for includes, and affords a wider application to, Adam Smith's doctrine of sympathy (p. 89); and, lastly, that it gives the finishing
development to Coleridge's "Idea of Life" (p. 391).

**3.** THE POWER WHICH THE PROPOSED THEORY POSSESSES OF RE-
ducing the leading precepts of current morality to a scientific

form, and of comprehending them, in company with sundry less acknowledged precepts, under one generalization, may also be quoted as additional evidence in its favor. Not as heretofore by considering whether, on the whole, manslaughter is productive of unhappiness, or otherwise—not by inquiring if theft is, or is not, expedient—not by asking in the case of slavery what are its effects on the common weal—not by any such complex and inexact processes, neither by the disputable decisions of unaided moral sense, are we here guided; but by undeniable inferences from a proved first principle. Nor are only the chief rules of right conduct and the just ordering of the connubial and parental relationships thus determined for us; this same first principle indirectly gives distinct answers respecting the proper constitution of governments, their duties, and the limits to their action. Out of an endless labyrinth of confused debate concerning the policy of these or those public measures, it opens short and easily discerned ways; and the conclusions it leads to are enforced, both generally by an abundant experience of the fallacy of expediency decisions, and specially by numerous arguments bearing on each successive question. Underlying, therefore, as this first principle does, so wide a range of duty, and applied as it is by a process of mental admeasurement nearly related to the geometrical—namely, by ascertaining the *equality* or *inequality* of moral quantities (p. 100)—we may consider that a system of ethics synthetically developed from it partakes of the character of an exact science; and, as doing this, possesses additional claims to our confidence.

**4.** AGAIN, THE INJUNCTIONS OF THE MORAL LAW, AS NOW INTERpreted, coincide with and anticipate those of political economy. Political economy teaches that restrictions upon commerce are detrimental; the moral law denounces them as wrong (Chapter XXIII). Political economy tells us that loss is entailed by a forced trade with colonies; the moral law will not permit such a trade to be established (Chapter XXVII). Political economy says it is good that speculators should be allowed to operate on the food markets as they see well; the law of equal freedom (contrary to the current notion) holds them justified in doing this and condemns all interference with them as inequitable. Penalties upon usury are proved by political economy to be injurious; by the law of equal freedom they are prohibited as involving an infringement of rights. According to political economy, machinery is beneficial to the people rather than hurtful to them; in unison with this the law of equal freedom forbids all attempts to restrict its use. One of the settled conclusions of political economy is that wages and prices cannot be artificially regulated; meanwhile it is an obvious inference from the law of equal freedom that no artificial regulation of them is morally permissible. We are taught by political economy that to be least injurious taxation must be direct; coincidentally we find that direct taxation is the only kind of taxation against which the law of equal freedom does not unconditionally protest (p. 187). On sundry other questions, such as the hurtfulness of tamperings with currency, the futility of endeavors permanently to benefit one occupation at the expense of others, the impropriety of legislative interference with manufacturing processes, etc., the conclusions of political economy are similarly at one with the dictates of this law. And thus the labored arguments of Adam Smith and his successors are forestalled, and for *practical* purposes made needless, by the simplest deductions of fundamental morality: a fact which, perhaps, will not be duly realized until it is seen that the inferences of political economy are true only because they are discoveries by a roundabout process of what the moral law commands.

**5.** MOREOVER, THE PROPOSED THEORY INCLUDES A PHILOSOPHY OF civilization. While in its ethical aspect it ignores evil, yet in its psychological aspect it shows how evil disappears. While, as an abstract statement of what conduct should be it assumes human perfection—is, in fact, the law of that perfection—yet, as a rationale of moral phenomena, it explains why conduct is becoming what it should be and why the process through which humanity has passed was necessary.

Thus we saw that the possession by the aboriginal man of a constitution enabling him to appreciate and act up to the principles of pure rectitude would have been detrimental, and indeed fatal (p. 368). We saw that in accordance with the law of adaptation the faculties responding to those principles began to unfold as soon as the conditions of existence called for them. From time to time it has been shown that the leading incidents of progress indicate the continued development of these faculties. That supremacy of them must precede the realization of the perfect state has been implied in numerous places. And the influence by which their ultimate supremacy is insured has been pointed out (Chapter II).

So that though one side of the proposed theory, in exhibiting the conditions under which alone the Divine Idea may be realized, overlooks the existing defects of mankind; the other side, in exhibiting the mental properties requisite for fulfilling these conditions, shows what civilization essentially is, why it was needful, and explains for us its leading traits.

**6.** FINALLY, THERE IS THE FACT, LATELY ALLUDED TO, THAT moral truth, as now interpreted, proves to be a development of physiological truth; for the so-called moral law is in reality the law of complete life. As more than once pointed out, a total cessation in the exercise of faculties is death; whatever partially prevents their exercise produces pain or partial death; and only when activity is permitted to all of them does life become perfect. Liberty to exercise the faculties being thus the first condition of life, and the extension of that liberty to the furthest point possible being the condition of the highest life possible, it follows that the liberty of each, limited only by the like liberty of all, is the condition of complete life as applied to mankind at large.

Nor is this true of mankind in their individual capacities only: it is equally true of them in their corporate capacity; seeing that the vitality which a community exhibits is high or low according as this condition is or is not fulfilled. For, as the reader no doubt observed in the course of our late analysis, those superior types of social organization, characterized by the mutual dependence of their respective parts, are possible only in as far as their respective parts can confide in each other; that is, only in as far as men behave justly to their fellows; that is, only in as far as they obey the law of equal freedom.

Hence, broadly generalizing, as it does, the prerequisites of existence, both personal and social; being on the one hand the law under which each citizen may attain complete life, and on the other hand being, not figuratively, but literally, the vital law of the social organism; being the law under which perfect individuation, both of man and of society, is achieved; being, therefore, the law of that state toward which creation tends, the law of equal freedom may properly be considered as a law of nature.

**7.** HAVING NOW BRIEFLY REVIEWED THE ARGUMENTS—HAVING called to mind that our first principle is arrived at by several independent methods of inquiry; that it unfolds into a system uniting in one consistent whole theories, some of which seem conflicting and others unrelated; that it not only gives a scientific derivation to the leading precepts of morality but includes them along with the laws of state duty under one generalization; that it utters injunctions coinciding with those of political economy; that civilization is explicable as the evolution of a being capable of conforming to it; that, as the law of complete life, it is linked with those physical laws of which life is the highest product; and lastly, that it possesses such multiplied relationships because it underlies the manifestations of life—having called to mind these things, the reader will perhaps find the rays of evidence thus brought to a focus sufficient to dissipate the doubts that may hitherto have lingered with him.

CHAPTER XXXII

## *Conclusion*

**1.** A FEW WORDS ARE NEEDFUL RESPECTING THE ATTITUDE TO BE assumed toward the doctrines that have been enunciated. Probably many will eagerly search out excuses for disregarding the restraints set up by the moral law as herein developed. The old habit of falling back upon considerations of expediency—a habit which men followed long before it was apotheosized by Paley—will still have influence. Although it has been shown that the system of deciding upon conduct by direct calculation of results is a fallacious one, although the plea that, however proper certain rules of action may be, occasional exceptions are necessary has been found hollow (Lemma II), yet we may anticipate further apologies for disobedience on the score of "policy." Among other reasons for claiming latitude, it will very likely be urged that, whereas the perfect moral code is confessedly beyond the fulfillment of imperfect men, some other code is needful for our present guidance. Not what is theoretically right, but what is the best course practicable under existing circumstances, will probably be insisted on as the thing to be discovered. Some again may argue that whichever line of conduct produces the greatest benefit as matters stand, if not positively right, is still relatively so; and is, therefore, for the time being, as obligatory as the abstract law itself. Or it will perhaps be said that if, with human nature what it now is, a sudden rearrangement of society upon the principles of pure equity would produce disastrous results it follows that, until perfection is reached, some discretion must be used in deciding how far these principles shall be carried out. And thus may we expect to have expediency reasserted as at least the temporary law, if not the ultimate one. Let us examine these positions in detail.

**2.** TO SAY THAT THE IMPERFECT MAN REQUIRES A MORAL CODE which recognizes his imperfection and allows for it seems at first sight reasonable. But it is not really so. Wherever such a code differs from the perfect code, it must so differ in being less stringent; for as it is argued that the perfect code requires so modifying as to become possible of fulfillment by existing men, the modification must consist in omitting its hardest injunctions. So that instead of saying, "Do not transgress at all," it is proposed, in consideration of our weakness, to say, "Transgress only in such-and-such cases." Stated thus, the proposition almost condemns itself; seeing that it makes morality countenance acts which are confessedly immoral.

Passing by this, however, suppose we inquire what advantage

is promised by so lowering the standard of conduct. Can it be supposed that men will on the whole come nearer to a full discharge of duty when the most difficult part of this duty is not insisted on? Hardly; for while performance so commonly falls below its aim, to bring down its aim to the level of possibility must be to make performance fall below possibility. Is it that any evil will result from endeavoring after a morality of which we are as yet but partially capable? No; on the contrary, it is only by perpetual aspiration after what has been hitherto beyond our reach that advance is made. And where is the need for any such modification? Whatever inability exists in us will of necessity assert itself; and in actual life our code will be virtually lowered in proportion to that inability. If men cannot yet entirely obey the law, why, they cannot, and there is an end of the matter; but it does not follow that we ought therefore to stereotype their incompetency by specifying how much is possible to them and how much is not. Nor, indeed, could we do this were it desirable. Only by experiment is it to be decided in how far each individual can conform; and the degree of conformity achievable by one is not the same as that achievable by others, so that one specification would not answer for all. Moreover, could an average be struck, it would apply only to the time being and would be inapplicable to the time immediately succeeding. Hence a system of morals which shall recognize man's present imperfections and allow for them cannot be devised, and would be useless if it could be devised.

**3.** THOSE WHO, BY WAY OF EXCUSING A LITTLE POLITIC DISOBEDIence, allege their anxiety to be practical will do well to weigh their words a little. By "practical" is described some mode of action productive of benefit; and a plan which is specially so designated, as contrasted with others, is one assumed to be, on the whole, more beneficial than such others. Now this that we call the moral law is simply a statement of the conditions of beneficial action. Originating in the primary necessities of things, it is the development of these into a series of limitations within which all conduct conducive to the greatest happiness must be confined. To overstep such limitations is to disregard these necessities of things—to fight against the constitution of nature. In other words, to plead the desire of being practical, as a reason for transgressing the moral law, is to assume that in the pursuit of benefit we must break through the bounds within which only benefit is obtainable.

What an insane notion is this that we can advantageously devise, and arrange, and alter in ignorance of the inherent conditions of success; or that, knowing these conditions, we may slight them! In the field and the workshop we show greater wisdom. We have learned to respect the properties of the substances with which we deal. Weight, mobility, inertia, cohesion are universally recognized—are virtually, if not scientifically, understood to be essential attributes of matter; and none but the most hopeless of simpletons disregard them. In morals and legislation, however, we behave as though the things dealt with had no fixed properties, no attributes. We do not inquire respecting this human nature what are the laws under which its varied phenomena may be generalized, and accommodate our acts to them. We do not ask what constitutes life, or wherein happiness properly consists, and choose our measures accordingly. Yet, is it not unquestionable that of man, of life, of happiness, certain primordial truths are predicable which necessarily underlie all right conduct? Is not gratification uniformly due to the fulfillment of their functions by the respective faculties? Does not each faculty grow by exercise and dwindle from disuse? And must not the issue of every scheme of legislation or culture primarily depend upon the regard paid to these facts? Surely it is but reasonable, before devising measures for the benefit of society, to ascertain what society is made of. Is human nature constant, or is it not? If so, why? If not, why not? Is it in essence always the same? Then what are its permanent characteristics? Is it changing? Then what is the nature of the change it is undergoing? What is it becoming, and why? Manifestly the settlement of these questions ought to precede the adoption of "practical measures." The result of such measures cannot be matter of chance. The success or failure of them must be determined by their accordance or discordance with certain fixed principles of things. What folly is it, then, to ignore these fixed

principles! Call you that "practical" to begin your twelfth book
before learning the axioms?

**4.** BUT IF WE ARE NOT AS YET CAPABLE OF ENTIRELY FULFILLING
the perfect law, and if our inability renders needful certain
supplementary regulations, then are not these supplementary
regulations, in virtue of their beneficial effects, ethically justifiable? And if the abolition of them, on the ground that they
conflict with abstract morality, would be disadvantageous, then
are they not of higher authority, for the time being, than the
moral law itself? Must not the *relatively* right take precedence
of the *positively* right?

The confident air with which this question seems to claim an
affirmative answer is somewhat rashly assumed. It is not true
that the arrangement best adapted to the time possesses, in
virtue of its adaptation, any independent authority. Its authority
is not original, but derived. Whatsoever respect is due to it is
due to it only as a partial embodiment of the moral law. The
whole benefit conferred by it is attributable to the fulfillment of
that portion of the moral law which it enforces. For consider the
essential nature of all advantages obtained by any such arrangement. The use of every institution is to aid men in the achievement of happiness. Happiness consists in the due exercise of
faculties. Hence an institution suited to the time must be one
which in some way or other insures to men more facility for the
exercise of faculties—that is, greater freedom for such exercise—
than they would enjoy without it. Thus, if it be asserted of a
given people that a despotism is at present the best form of
government for them, it is meant that the exercise of faculties is
less limited under a despotism than it would be limited under
the anarchical state entailed by any other form of government;
and that, therefore, despotism gives to such a people an amount
of liberty to exercise the faculties greater than they would possess in its absence. Similarly, all apologies that can be made for a
narrow suffrage, for censorship of the press, for restraint by pass-
ports, and the like, resolve themselves into assertions that the
preservation of public order necessitates these restrictions; that
social dissolution would ensue on their abolition; that there

would arise a state of universal aggression by men on each other; or, in other words, that the law of equal freedom is less violated by the maintenance of these restrictions than it would be violated were they repealed.

If, then, the only excuse to be made for measures of temporary expediency is that they get the commands of the moral law fulfilled better than any other measures can, their authority may no more be compared with that of the moral law itself than the authority of a servant with that of a master. While a conductor of force is inferior to a generator of it, while an instrument is inferior to the will which guides it, so long must an institution be inferior to the law whose ends it subserves, and so long must such institution bend to that law as the agent to his principal.

And here let it be remarked that we shall avoid much confusion by ceasing to use the word *right* in any but its legitimate sense; that, namely, in which it describes conduct purely moral. *Rightness* expresses of actions what *straightness* does of lines, and there can no more be two kinds of right action than there can be two kinds of straight line. If we would keep our conclusions free from ambiguity, we must reserve the term we employ to signify absolute rectitude solely for this purpose. And when it is needful to express the claims of imperfect, though beneficial, institutions, we must speak of them, not as "relatively right," or "right for the time being," but as the *least wrong* institutions now possible.

**5.** THE ADMISSION THAT SOCIAL ARRANGEMENTS CAN BE CONformed to the moral law only in as far as the people are themselves moral will probably be thought a sufficient plea for claiming liberty to judge how far the moral law may safely be acted upon. For if congruity between political organization and popular character is necessary; and if, by consequence, a political organization in advance of the age will need modification to make it fit the age; and if this process of modification must be accompanied by great inconvenience and even suffering; then it would seem to follow that for the avoidance of these evils our endeavor should be at first to adapt such organization to the age. That is to say, men's ambition to realize an ideal excellence must be checked by prudential considerations.

"Progress, and at the same time resistance"—that celebrated saying of M. Guizot, with which the foregoing position is in substance identical—no doubt expresses a truth; but not at all the order of truth usually supposed. To look at society from afar off, and to perceive that such-and-such are the principles of its development, is one thing; to adopt these as rules for our daily government will turn out on examination to be quite a different thing. Just as we saw that it is very possible for the attainment of greatest happiness to be from one point of view the recognized end of morality and yet to be of no value for immediate guidance (Chapter III.), so it is very possible for "progress, and at the same time resistance," to be a law of social life without being a law by which individual citizens may regulate their actions.

That the aspiration after things as they should be needs restraining by an attachment to things as they are is fully admitted. The two feelings answer to the two sides of our present mixed nature—the side on which we continue adapted to old conditions of existence, and the side on which we are becoming adapted to new ones. Conservatism defends those coercive arrangements which a still-lingering savageness makes requisite. Radicalism endeavors to realize a state more in harmony with the character of the ideal man. The strengths of these sentiments are proportionate to the necessity for the institutions they respond to. And the social organization proper for a given people at a given time will be one bearing the impress of these sentiments in the ratio of their prevalence among that people at that time. Hence the necessity for a vigorous and constant manifestation of both of them. While, on the one hand, love of what is abstractedly just indignation against every species of aggression and enthusiasm on behalf of reform are to be rejoiced over, we must, on the other hand, tolerate as indispensable these displays of an antagonistic tendency; be they seen in the detailed opposition to every improvement or in the puerile sentimentalisms of Young England, or even in some frantic effort to bring back the age of hero worship. Of all these nature has need, so long as they represent sincere beliefs. From time to time the struggle eventuates in change; and by composition of forces there is produced a *resultant*, embodying the right amount of movement in the right direction. Thus understood, then, the theory of "progress, and at the same time resistance," is correct.

Mark now, however, that for this resistance to be beneficial it must come from those who think the institutions they defend really the best, and the innovations proposed absolutely wrong. It must not come from those who secretly approve of change but think a certain opposition to it expedient. For if the true end of this conflict of opinion is to keep social arrangements in harmony with the average character of the people, and if (rejecting that temporary kind of opinion generated by revolutionary passion) the *honest* opinion held by each man of any given state of things is not an intellectual accident, but indicates a preponderating fitness or unfitness of that state of things to his moral condition (pp. 215, 382), then it follows that only by a universal manifestation of *honest* opinions can harmony between social arrangements and the average popular character be preserved. If, concealing their real sympathies, some of the movement party join the stationary party, merely with the view of preventing too rapid an advance, they must inevitably disturb the adaptation between the community and its institutions. So long as the natural conservatism ever present in society is left to restrain the progressive tendency, things will go right; but add to this natural conservatism an artificial conservatism—a conservatism not founded on love of the old, but on a theory that conservatism is needful—and the proper ratio between the two forces is destroyed; the *resultant* is no longer in the right direction; and the effect produced by it is more or less vitiated. While, therefore, there is truth in the belief that "progress, and at the same time resistance," is the law of social change, there is a fatal error in the inference that resistance should be factitiously created. It is a mistake to suppose this is the kind of resistance called for; and, as M. Guizot's own experience testifies, it is a further mistake to suppose that anyone can say how far resistance should be carried.

But, indeed, without entering upon a criticism like this, the man of moral insight sees clearly enough that no such self-contradicting behavior can answer. Successful methods are always genuine, sincere. The affairs of the universe are not carried on after a system of benign double-dealing. In nature's doings all things show their true qualities—exert whatsoever of influence is really in them. It is manifest that a globe built up partly of semblances instead of facts would not be long on this side of chaos. And it is certain that a community composed of men whose acts are not in harmony with their innermost beliefs will be equally unstable. To know in our hearts that some proposed measure is essentially right, and yet to say by our deeds that it is not right, will never prove really beneficial. Society cannot prosper by lies.

**6.** AND YET IT WILL STILL BE THOUGHT UNREASONABLE TO DENY discretionary power in this matter. Neglecting prudential considerations in the endeavor to put society on a purely equitable basis will probably be demurred to as implying an entire abandonment of private judgment. It must be confessed that it does so. But whoso urges this objection may properly ask himself how much his private judgment, as applied to such a subject, is worth?

What is the question he proposes to solve? Whether it is, or is not, the time for some desired change to be made? Whether the people are, or are not, fit for some higher social form than they have hitherto lived under? Where now are his qualifications for answering this question? Has he ever seen the millions for whom he would prescribe? Some tenth part of them, perhaps. How many of these does he recognize? Probably of one or two thousand he can tell you the names and occupations. But with how many of these is he acquainted? Several hundreds, it may be. And of what fraction of them does he personally know the characters? They are numbered by tens. Then it must be by what he reads in books and newspapers, witnesses at meetings, and hears in conversation that he judges? Partly so; from the salient points of character thus brought under his notice, he infers the rest. Does he then find his inferences trustworthy? On the contrary, when he goes among men he has read of or heard described, it usually turns out that he has got quite a wrong impression of them. Does this evidence from which he judges lead all persons to like conclusions? No; with the same sources of information open to them, others form opinions of the people widely different from those he holds. Are his own convictions constant? Not at all; he continually meets with facts which prove that he had generalized on insufficient data, and which compel a revision of his estimate. Nevertheless, may it not be that by averaging the characters of those whom he personally knows he can form a tolerably correct opinion of those whom he does not know? Hardly; seeing that of those whom he personally knows his judgments are generally incorrect. Very intimate friends occasionally astound him by quite unexpected behavior; even his nearest relatives—brothers, sisters, and children—do so; nay, indeed, he has but a limited acquaintance with himself, for though from time to time he imagines very clearly how he shall act under certain new circumstances, it commonly happens that when placed in these circumstances his conduct is quite different from that which he expected.

Now of what value is the judgment of so circumscribed an intelligence upon the question: Is the nation ready for such-and-such measures of reform, or is it not? Here is one who professes to say of some thirty millions of people how they will behave under arrangements a little freer than existing ones. Yet nine tenths of these people he has not even seen, can identify only a few thousands of them, personally knows but an infinitesimal fraction, and knows these so imperfectly that on some point or other he finds himself mistaken respecting nearly all of them. Here is one who cannot say even of himself how certain untried conditions will affect *him*, and yet who thinks he can say of a whole nation how certain untried conditions will affect *it!* Surely there is in this a most absurd incongruity between pretension and capability.

When the contrast between present institutions and projected ones is very great—when, for example, it is proposed to change at once from pure despotism to perfect freedom—we may, indeed, prophesy with certainty that the result will not fulfill expectation. For while the success of institutions depends on their fitness to popular character, and while it is impossible for popular character to undergo a great change all at once, it must follow that suddenly to substitute for existing institutions others of a quite opposite nature will necessitate unfitness and, therefore, failure. But it is not in cases like this that the power of judging is contended for. As elsewhere shown (p. 387), one of these extreme changes is never consequent upon that peaceful expression of opinion presupposed by the hypotheses that the citizen should be cautious in advocating reform; on the contrary, it is always a result of some revolutionary passion which no considerations of policy can control. Only when an amelioration is being peaceably discussed and agitated for—that is, only when the circumstances prove its advent at hand—can the proposed discretion be exercised; and then does the right use of this discretion imply an acquaintance with the people accurate enough to say of them, "Now they are not fit"; and again, "Now they are fit"—an acquaintance which it is preposterous to assume; an acquaintance which nothing short of omniscience can possess.

Who, then, is to find out when the time for any given change has arrived? No one; it will find itself out. For us to perplex ourselves with such questions is both needless and absurd. The due apportionment of the truth to the time is already provided for. That same modification of man's nature which produces fitness for higher social forms, itself generates the belief that those forms are right (p. 382), and by doing this brings them into existence. And as opinion, being the product of character (pp. 24, 141), must necessarily be in harmony with character, institutions which are in harmony with opinion must be in harmony with character also.

**7.** THE CANDID READER MAY NOW SEE HIS WAY OUT OF THE dilemma in which he feels placed, between a conviction, on the one hand, that the perfect law is the only safe guide, and a consciousness, on the other, that the perfect law cannot be fulfilled by imperfect men. Let him but duly realize the fact that opinion is the agency through which character adapts external arrangements to itself; that *his* opinion rightly forms part of this agency—is a unit of force, constituting, with other such units, the general power which works out social changes —and he will then perceive that he may properly give full utterance to his *innermost conviction*, leaving it to produce what effect it may. It is not for nothing that he has in him these sympathies with some principles and repugnance to others. He, with all his capacities and desires and beliefs, is not an accident, but a product of the time. Influences that have acted upon preceding generations; influences that have been brought to bear upon him; the education that disciplined his childhood, together with the circumstances in which he has since lived, have conspired to make him what he is. And the result thus wrought out in him has a purpose. He must remember that while he is a child of the past, he is a parent of the future. The moral sentiment developed in him was intended to be instrumental in producing further progress; and to gag it, or to conceal the thoughts it generates, is to balk creative design. He, like every other man, may properly consider himself as an agent through whom nature works; and when nature gives birth in him to a certain belief, she thereby authorizes him to profess and to act out that belief. For—

> nature is made better by no mean,
> But nature makes that mean: over that art
> Which you say adds to nature, is an art
> That nature makes.

Not as adventitious, therefore, will the wise man regard the faith that is in him—not as something which may be slighted and made subordinate to calculations of policy; but as the supreme authority to which all his actions should bend. The highest truth conceivable by him he will fearlessly utter and will endeavor to get embodied in fact his purest idealisms; knowing that, let what may come of it, he is thus playing his appointed part in the world—knowing that, if he can get done the thing he aims at—well; if not—well also, though not so well.

**8.** AND THUS, IN TEACHING A UNIFORM UNQUESTIONING OBEDI-ence, does an entirely abstract philosophy become one with all true religion. Fidelity to conscience—this is the essential precept inculcated by both. No hesitation, no paltering about probable results, but an implicit submission to what is believed to be the law laid down for us. We are not to pay lip homage to principles which our conduct willfully transgresses. We are not to follow the example of those who, taking "*Domine dirige nos*" for their motto, yet disregard the directions given and prefer to direct themselves. We are not to be guilty of that practical atheism which, seeing no guidance for human affairs but its own limited foresight, endeavors itself to play the god and decide what will be good for mankind and what bad. But, on the contrary, we are to search out with a genuine humility the rules ordained for us—are to do unfalteringly, without speculating as to consequences, whatsoever these require; and we are to do this in the belief that then, when there is perfect sincerity, when each man is true to himself, when everyone strives to realize what he thinks the highest rectitude—then must all things prosper.